T0100089

SAP® Analytics Cloud Performance Optimization Guide

Erik Bertram, Carl Dannenhauer, Melanie Holzapfel,
Sandra Loop, Stephanie Range

SAP® Analytics Cloud Performance Optimization Guide

Editor Rachel Gibson
Acquisitions Editor Hareem Shafi
Copyeditor Elisabeth Herschbach
Cover Design Graham Geary
Photo Credit iStockphoto: 853780090/© deepblue4you
Layout Design Vera Brauner
Production Graham Geary
Typesetting SatzPro, Germany
Printed and bound in Canada, on paper from sustainable sources

ISBN 978-1-4932-2396-1

1st edition 2023

Library of Congress Cataloging-in-Publication Control Number: 2023024491

Contents at a Glance

Dear Reader,

If it wasn't clear from my job as an editor, I prefer to stay behind the scenes rather than take center stage.

While I was in school, I joined the technical theater program. We were responsible for building and painting sets, assembling costumes and props, manning the lights and sound, and managing all of those elements together—plus the actors—during live performances. I took a number of different jobs throughout the years, from swapping telephones and chairs into dinner scenes and even pulling open windows and hooking students up to wires in a production of *Peter Pan*.

Our morale was best when all the separate components of the play came together seamlessly: the sound was crisp and clear (and no one's microphone spontaneously turned off), the costumes looked great, the actors spoke their lines well, and the set stayed sturdy (our biggest fear was an actor accidently tipping over a wall panel mid-sentence). If even one element was thrown off, we could feel its effect throughout the rest of the performance.

In a similar way, fine-tuning your SAP Analytics Cloud performance takes coordination from many different aspects. Whether you're optimizing backend settings, writing efficient scripts, or streamlining load times, the authors of this book have the tips, tricks, and standards you need to follow. Their "golden rules" and industry-tested advice will help you ensure that SAP Analytics Cloud runs as smoothly and effortlessly as a Broadway show.

What did you think about *SAP Analytics Cloud Performance Optimization Guide*? Your comments and suggestions are the most useful tools to help us make our books the best they can be. Please feel free to contact me and share any praise or criticism you may have.

Thank you for purchasing a book from SAP PRESS!

Rachel Gibson
Editor, SAP PRESS

rachelg@rheinwerk-publishing.com
www.sap-press.com
Rheinwerk Publishing · Boston, MA

Contents

Preface

Our team has been involved in creating dashboards with SAP Analytics Cloud for many years now. Back in the days when we took our first steps with SAP Analytics Cloud, we could advance our skillset in such a way as to also offer consulting to people inside and outside of SAP. We started with internal customers and have now become a point of contact when it comes to building dashboards for external customers as well. We often observe that companies fail to leverage the opportunity to build great-looking and efficient dashboards. Thus, companies waste a lot of time and money within their businesses, although tiny changes could make a huge impact.

When we design dashboards, we are concerned about performance from the beginning because we know that a slow dashboard causes enough friction for users to not want to use the dashboard at all or for a very long time. Not surprisingly, designing an efficient dashboard involves understanding the performance of the technical aspects of such an application, including charts, controls, and data modeling capabilities. Is a dashboard more efficient when you use one chart rather than another? Can we gain more time out of the application when we rebuild our data model or do data manipulations early on? And which role does our backend play when the dashboard is loading? Questions like these shall be addressed throughout this book.

Furthermore, designing a dashboard also involves understanding your users' needs. If the user doesn't need those three extra charts, then don't add them. If they only need those extra charts in particular circumstances, such as upon seeing a poor score elsewhere, then move them to another page where they can "drill in" to see the extra detail. Using your knowledge of the performance of the dashboard components and the users' needs, you can make the best decisions to create an efficient dashboard. In the following, we would like to guide you through this (sometimes complicated) process and support you as best as we can in optimizing your dashboard experience. Have fun reading!

Target Audience

This book is for those who are interested in designing dashboards with SAP Analytics Cloud or analytics designer and are concerned about the performance of the dashboards that they create. We assume you have some knowledge of these SAP tools, meaning we won't explain to you again what an SAP HANA backend is or what SAP Business Warehouse (SAP BW) means. However, we will show you step by step how to technically implement performance improvements in the front end. Therefore, the book is written for both users with a strong technical background and for users who are new to SAP Analytics Cloud.

In Chapter 1, we will also present an overview of different personas that are involved when building a dashboard or optimizing its performance. Those users might all find useful information in this book.

How to Read this Book

You may want to fully understand performance before you start building your dashboard, in which case you may want to read all the chapters one after the other, although perhaps you don't need to read the chapter about analytics designer if you are not using that tool. Or you may already have performance issues and you want to jump into the relevant details quickly. In this case, we encourage you to use the table of contents to navigate to the areas that are of most interest to you.

In all other cases, we recommend reading the introduction to Chapter 1 and Chapter 2 because they provide a basic understanding of what performance is and what determines performance in a cloud application. Afterwards, feel free to check out the different chapters individually, since they don't build on each other, but rather consider different aspects of SAP Analytics Cloud.

Finally, we recommend also reading through the very last chapters, Chapter 8, Chapter 9, and Chapter 10, since they look at how to build simple efficient dashboards that users can work with in an efficient way. They might also provide guidance on your first steps if you are not an expert in the field and help you set up a first dashboard quickly and easily.

What You Can Expect from This Book

Whether you are new to SAP Analytics Cloud or are already a skilled app designer or developer does not really matter because all groups might find different aspects that they might not have known before on how to optimize the dashboard performance. All these tips and tricks are also closely aligned with our in-house development organization, which means that you get hands-on information directly from the right source. Thus, what you can expect is a book that provides technical insights into performance optimizations while guiding you through building the correct dashboard step by step.

To provide a better overview of the possible ways to optimize dashboard performance, we have created ten golden rules of dashboard performance optimizations, which we introduce in Chapter 2. These rules provide a rough guide through the book, while we also summarize the most important aspects in a dedicated table. A performance equation will also be introduced in Chapter 2, highlighting the most relevant sources where time typically gets lost when users create a dashboard.

Talking about what you can expect from such a book means also talking about those things that you *cannot* expect from it. First, we'd like to point out a few limitations of the text. Although we did our best to try to bridge the gap between the frontend and backend parts, we note that this book was primarily written to optimize the SAP Analytics Cloud frontend. You will also find useful information about several backend aspects in the following text. But given the fact that we cannot control or dictate the backend companies will use, we needed to limit our backend considerations to a few examples, like the well-known SAP BW or SAP HANA backends. Hence, we recommend also looking out for more specific literature on the topic of backend optimizations, depending on which backend you are using.

Second, we also tried to measure performance before and after some of the implementations. Nevertheless, we remind you that performance measurements are usually quite biased toward different variables like the network traffic, server load, and other potential fluctuations that can cause performance numbers to vary a lot. Hence, you should not take measurement numbers as a scientific result that can be published in a journal but understand them rather as a relative source of information about the potential impact of a specific change and draw your own conclusions. In the end, performance will always be dependent on the different settings of the end user.

Third, this book is written primarily on the topic of performance optimizations. It is less about how to build beautiful dashboards that put data and information into the focus of the dashboard designer, although we of course respect the most important rules here. For this purpose, we'd like to refer you to our first book about how to design brilliant and great-looking dashboards with SAP Analytics Cloud. Taking both books together, you get a great resource on how to build dashboards that your users will love (book number one, more information below) and that are efficient (this book).

Further Reading

If you are also interested in how to design great dashboards, arrange information properly, choose the right charts or colors, or use the correct tables, you may want to look at our first book: *Designing Dashboards with SAP Analytics Cloud* (SAP PRESS, 2021, *www.sap-press.com/5235*).

How This Book Is Organized

The book starts with Chapter 1 and Chapter 2 providing an overview of performance considerations and common performance issues and introduces our SAP Analytics Cloud Performance Equation. The performance equation sums the performance contributions of the various components of the dashboard solution and use. Each component in this equation corresponds to a separate chapter in Chapter 3 through Chapter 7.

Chapter 8 through Chapter 10 pull the performance contributions discussed in the earlier chapters into full dashboard design scenarios. Here is a short summary for each chapter:

- **Chapter 1** discusses performance and its relationship to the user experience, including a discussion of why the design phase is important, who manages performance, and why you should validate your design trade-off choices with your end users. It also discusses why performance matters and how the performance may affect the usage and adoption of your dashboard. It discusses common performance problems and describes software architecture to help you understand how architecture impacts performance.
- **Chapter 2** discusses measuring, testing, and monitoring performance. It describes various performance testing types, what the general process is for testing, what metrics are used to measure performance, and how to measure performance using Chrome DevTools. It introduces the SAP Analytics Cloud performance equation as well as our ten golden rules on how to build efficient dashboards.
- **Chapter 3** is the first of five chapters that shows performance behaviors of the components in the performance equation. The focus of this chapter is on the elements available in the SAP Analytics Cloud story builder.
- **Chapter 4** focuses on the elements that are only available in analytics designer. Elements that are available in both the story builder and in analytics designer are described in Chapter 3.
- **Chapter 5** focuses on the modeler. It discusses how general modeling settings can affect the overall performance of the story. It also reviews different model types and their relative impact on the performance of the dashboard, such as models using acquired data or live connections.
- **Chapter 6** focuses on the backend and tenant settings, including specific data connection settings for SAP BW live connections and SAP HANA live connections. It also discusses data preparation steps such as filter settings, calculations, and data blending, which happen before data is fed into the SAP Analytics Cloud model. It discusses system configuration settings that a tenant administrator can set and personal settings for each story and for queries.
- **Chapter 7** focuses on what the end user of a dashboard can do to improve its performance. Most optimizations involve the environment of the user, like the browser, network performance, and choices, computer resources, and other limiting factors.
- **Chapter 8** is the first of three chapters that take the optimizations discussed in Chapter 3 to Chapter 7 and combines them into practical examples. This chapter shows how to build an efficient dashboard based on data acquired from an Excel spreadsheet.
- **Chapter 9** shows how to build an efficient dashboard based on a live data connection to a backend source.

- **Chapter 10** shows how to build an efficient dashboard using our SAP analytics designer with self-scripted solutions.

Performance Measurements

Throughout the book, we made several performance measurements with SAP Analytics Cloud to benchmark dashboards and features against each other. Thereby, we always measured five times and took the simple average over all numbers to ensure a proper time value. The values quoted in the tables are a result of this operation.

Acknowledgments

This book would not have been possible without tremendous support from various people, who either consulted and encouraged us, provided textual or graphical support, or gave us important advice on how to fine-tune the performance of a dashboard.

First, we would like to say a big "Thank you!" our colleague Viola Stiebritz, who supported us in creating many of the beautiful illustrations that you can find throughout this book. Her passion in bringing ideas to life via illustrations is mind-blowing, and clearly this book would not look as it is without her support.

We would also like to thank Nina Hollender for helping to shape this book. Her experience in helping to structure our earlier SAP PRESS book, *Designing Dashboards with SAP Analytics Cloud*, was immensely helpful.

We also want to thank Tunir Kapil for helpful and insightful discussions around the topic of optimizing SAP Analytics Cloud performance.

Finally, we'd like to thank our publisher SAP PRESS for providing us with the great opportunity to write a book on this interesting topic. We'd like to acknowledge the support from Hareem Shafi, who helped us define and shape the content of this book. Rachel Gibson was always a tremendous help in consulting with us throughout the writing process and for providing important annotations on the manuscript itself.

And of course, all the authors finally would like to thank their families and friends for being lenient with us when we were busy writing. Now that this book project is done, our time management will surely become better. We promise!

Conclusion

We hope that you'll find lots of useful information and tips that will help you create efficient dashboards with SAP Analytics Cloud that your users will enjoy. However, please note that development will continue to evolve after we have published this book. Thus, it can be that some parts of the application made a big step toward even better performance and that various parts of this book might become more relevant than others in the future. Nevertheless, we expect all baseline discussions to remain similar, even if SAP Analytics Cloud evolves further in the future.

A last word on the book as a whole: No text comes without mistakes. We tried our best to minimize the errors by reading and correcting the text multiple times. Nevertheless, we cannot guarantee that all errors have been eliminated. Therefore, we would appreciate it if you send us an email if you encounter any mistakes or if we forget important concepts that are also worth mentioning.

And now, let's start our journey by looking into the very first performance concepts and getting more insights into performance theory.

Chapter 1
Introduction

In this chapter, we introduce basic performance concepts and discuss their relation to the user experience. Afterwards, we deal with SAP Analytics Cloud and highlight potential performance bottlenecks and how they can impact the business of your company.

We welcome you to an exciting journey ahead about the optimization of the dashboard performance in a cloud environment! This chapter is nothing more than an introduction to the topic of performance with SAP Analytics Cloud. We are pretty sure that you have many questions. How can I optimize my dashboard performance? Which buttons can I push to make my SAP Analytics Cloud solution run faster? Which trade-off choices do I need to make, and where do I need to compromise? We will answer many of these questions (but maybe not all) in the following, sticking to the very basic concepts without going into too many technical details; these will follow in later chapters.

This chapter is structured as follows. We will first discuss the topic of performance and its relation to the user experience in general. We start by elaborating on the fact that spending more time during the design phase is a must and that changes are hard to implement once a dashboard has already been released. We continue with a discussion of the different personas and who manages (and influences) performance topics. Afterwards, we provide a few insights into some user research techniques that can be used to evaluate your dashboard designs.

In the next part of this chapter, we will focus on the performance of SAP Analytics Cloud itself. We start discussing why performance matters and talk about some well-known performance flaws that many customers experienced in the past with the tool, separately addressing the frontend and backend. Afterwards, we will provide a few more details on the software architecture of SAP Analytics Cloud. Many technical implementations can be done only if one generally understands how the tool is operating and which technical components it includes. We end this chapter with a more general discussion of the difference between the old on-premise and the new cloud world and how they are related, since this comes with several limitations regarding performance management.

Clearly, this chapter provides many basic concepts about performance management and its relation to SAP Analytics Cloud. Therefore, we recommend reading it first before jumping into other chapters later. Let's start with a discussion of performance and its relation to the user experience (UX).

1.1 Performance and Its Relation to User Experience

Performance is directly connected to the user experience of a product. If the performance is bad, users won't consume an application or a dashboard. Therefore, we need to discuss various aspects of performance and how performance relates to the user experience. We start with a discussion of why the design phase is important. Afterwards, we describe who manages performance, followed by guidelines on how to validate dashboards regarding performance.

1.1.1 Why the Design Phase Is Important

In this section, we want to convince you that the design phase plays an important role in the dashboard creation process and that it is inevitable to think about performance aspects before you start building your dashboard. But before we start, let's take a first look at a very important question: What is performance?

This question seems easy at first view, but if you start thinking about it, things can quickly get complicated. Firstly, and obviously, performance has something to do with time. Looking into the area of physics, it is defined as the work that is done within a specific time frame, also called power. In computer science, one could define it as the number of operations (or computations) performed within the same time frame, and that is probably the most descriptive definition people can think of when they talk about performance.

Having said this, the question comes up of which time we are referring to. In physics, there is only one timeline, and there is no doubt about the uniqueness of an absolute time coordinate (at least in our naïve understanding of Newtonian physics). However, in computer science (or better to say, when talking about user experience design) something we could call *perceived time* might exist, which clearly has a psychological aspect to it. This comes from the fact that we are all humans, and sitting in front of a personal computer while waiting for a piece of software to finish loading is something that sometimes can take a very long time (the reader might know what we are talking about).

That means that perceived time typically differs from time measured on a clock. Or as the famous physicist Albert Einstein once said, "When a man sits together with a girl for an hour, it seems like a minute. But let him sit on a hot oven for a minute, and it might feel longer than any hour. That's relativity." Similar concepts apply to performance management, which has to do with managing the user experience of a product.

Further Reading

We recommend reading the following resources on the topic of performance in UX design and how it relates to psychology:

- Denys Mishunov, "Why Perceived Performance Matters, Part 1: The Perception Of Time," available at *http://s-prs.co/v566943*
- Bojan Pavic, Chris Anstey, and Jeremy Wagner, "Why does speed matter?," available at *https://web.dev/why-speed-matters/*

For that reason, it is relevant to talk about the user experience of your dashboard. Whether you are a dashboard designer, modeler, or just a consumer, performance raises clear expectations from everybody. Imagine you previously used a similar dashboarding solution that was significantly faster. Here, it doesn't really matter what kind of solution it was. But simply the fact that you used to be able to do your work faster is a good reason for you to think that a new system should at least not get worse. If your new dashboard is slower, perhaps it is because you switched to a new cloud vendor, which takes just a bit more time to load an application, whereas before things were done manually in your company. Because the application takes them more time now, people in your company might feel in the end that the whole cloud process got slower with a new workflow.

What they don't see perhaps is that, *overall*, they might save a lot of time with the new cloud processes. This is a typical scenario that happens day by day in many companies. Thus, you need to manage expectations from employees and users toward the products and processes if you want them to stay with your dashboard solution.

Many people claim that they cannot really change the way an application runs and that performance topics are out of their control. This is clearly wrong; the opposite is the case. The performance of a dashboard is something that heavily depends on many choices that the dashboard builder has made before. In this book, we will show several examples of how good and bad dashboards differ, and what kind of choices you need to make to move the needle. We want to be very clear. Performance *can* be influenced. It can be influenced proactively by you, not only by loading indicators. This is the most important thing you should keep in mind.

Thus, taking a deep breath first and thinking about the design phase before the proper implementation starts is crucial. The reason is that, once a dashboard has already been set up, it becomes harder and harder to modify it later while it is in productive use. Of course, smaller things can always be adjusted, but it might become even more difficult to change larger parts. That means don't jump into the dashboard creation process right away. Instead, first list the requirements needed to serve your user. Then, create a plan as to how to best provide these services and mark which trade-offs you potentially would have to make to realize your dashboard, keeping performance at the forefront of your mind.

Hence, a detailed plan is required in the design phase on how to scale a dashboard later such that it stays efficient even when the number of users assigned to it has doubled, for example. There are some great techniques involving user research that one can leverage as well to gain some useful insights into how users use a dashboard or might plan to use it in the future. We will talk about those briefly in the following sections.

1.1.2 Who Manages Performance?

It is crucial to think about the different roles that appear in the process of designing and building a new dashboard. Different people will likely contribute to and influence the appearance as well as the performance of your dashboard, so it is worth spending some time thinking about the stakeholders who will be involved in all of this.

Figure 1.1 highlights the relations between different personas in a company. An initial caveat is that this overview might not be complete since other personas (or, better, user types) might exist in your company. Or you might find it difficult to relate all personas to people in your company. It may simply be the case that some roles don't exist (yet). In any case, you should not worry too much about this.

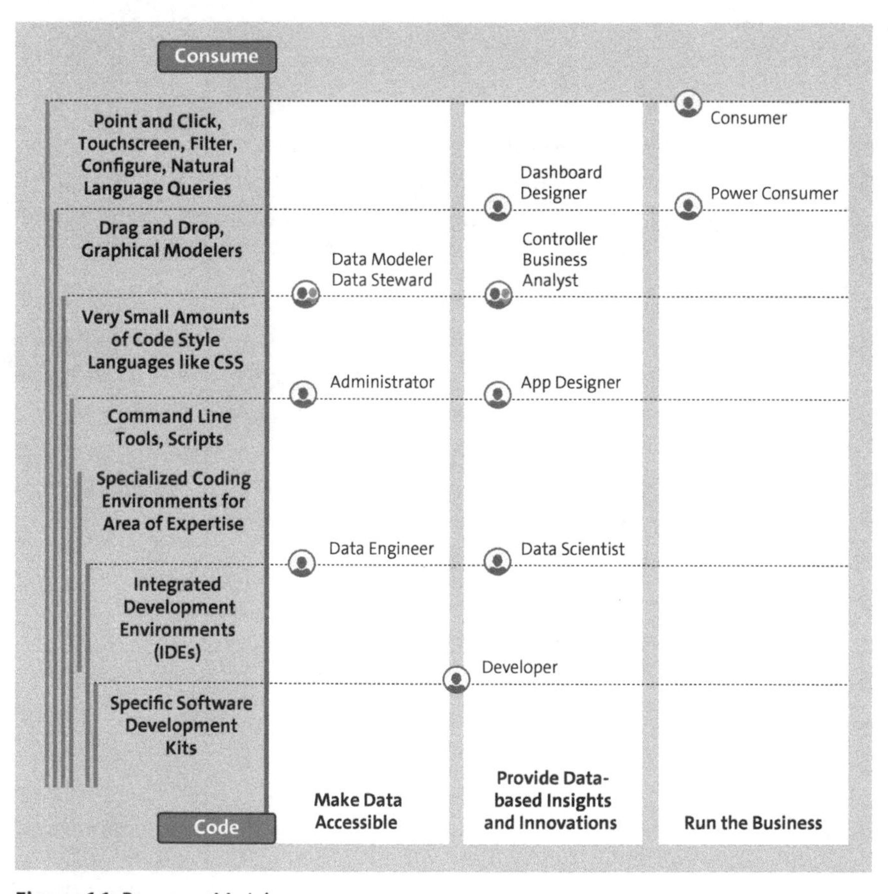

Figure 1.1 Persona Matrix

In the following list, we provide a few examples of personas that (in our opinion) are clearly key influencers when building a dashboard and therefore also influence dashboard performance (be it either consumers or developers):

- **Consumer/power consumer**
  The consumer (or power consumer) probably has the lowest impact on the performance of a dashboard; this person is just viewing and playing around with it. It is one user out of many who got a license for viewing purposes only and who was told to perform a few smaller analyses. However, this does not mean that the consumer could not affect the performance itself. In Chapter 7, we will show that there are many viewer choices that can be made that surely affect performance, e.g., when the internet bandwidth is low, or the personal computer is too old for browsers to run heavy calculations in the frontend, resulting in a high CPU load.
- **Dashboard designer**
  The dashboard designer has a bigger impact on dashboard performance. This person is responsible for ensuring that the user experience is great, that charts and tables are placed in the right position on the screen to quickly convey the message, that images are used adequately to ensure users adopt the dashboard, and that people can identify with the corporate identity. Thus, as we will show in Chapter 8 through Chapter 10, the experience of a dashboard can significantly impact the way it runs and how it is finally used.
- **Data modeler**
  The data modeler plays a crucial role when it comes to optimizing dashboard performance. This person is responsible for creating proper data structures either in a native SAP Analytics Cloud model or in a remote database. Clearly, the way a model has been set up in the backend is the basis for a good performance. If you are using redundant columns or unnecessary calculations, for example, it might result in poor performance or slow down the dashboard significantly. Thus, the data modeler needs to take care that data structures are smoothly integrated into the dashboard. In Chapter 5, we will provide more insights into how a data modeler can positively impact dashboard performance.
- **Administrator**
  The administrator's task is to set up the system and provide the infrastructure needed for a good cloud environment. And although one might think that nothing could go wrong at this stage, this is clearly not the case. Instead, the administrator can also negatively (and positively, of course) impact dashboard performance through the tenant and backend settings they specify. In Chapter 6, we will give some best practice tips on how to select the correct tenant and backend settings and how the administrator can positively contribute to a smooth working dashboard.
- **Controller/business analyst**
  A person whose role should not be underestimated is the controller and/or business analyst. Why? Because they most likely make the decisions on what content

(numbers, charts, tables, etc.) should be displayed on the dashboard. Depending on what data will be shown, performance can be heavily influenced. Hence, these people should think carefully about what material is exposed to consumers and whether all that data is really needed. Putting too much data on one dashboard page can crash every application performance. In Chapter 8 through Chapter 10, we discuss different scenarios in which the decision on what kind of data should be exposed becomes evident.

- **App designer**
  The biggest responsibility probably lies on the shoulders of the app designer. The app designer is a person who builds dashboard applications and takes on some coding tasks. It is clearly the app designer who can significantly influence the performance of a dashboard by optimizing stories and their individual pages. The app designer also needs to work together with both the dashboard designer and the data modeler to interconnect the frontend part with the backend data via the interface. In Chapter 3 and Chapter 4 of this book, we give many instructions for this persona and how dashboards can be optimized.
- **Data engineer**
  The data engineer is a person who makes data available. In contrast to the modeler, the data engineer can connect and join different data models together and create a data infrastructure suitable for use by different parts of the application. Data engineers have multiple touchpoints with other personas, like app designers, administrators, or modelers. Mostly in Chapter 8 through Chapter 10 we describe different scenarios of how you can bring data together in one story and where the data engineer can provide value.
- **Developer**
  Developers live more on the coding side of the house. SAP Analytics Cloud comes with a variety of coding possibilities, but most of them are mainly decided by the app designer (e.g., when using the application designer tool). That means that pure in-depth application development might not really be needed. However, having a developer on board a performance project is always beneficial since they can often better understand the code lines of the tool and hence make suggestions on how different performance scenarios could be approached. Development topics can be found across many chapters of this book, most notably in Chapter 3 to Chapter 7.

In the following, we look at how we can validate our dashboards regarding their performance.

1.1.3 Validating Dashboards for Performance

Just building a dashboard and hoping that it is efficient on its own is a wishful dream that will not come true in many cases. Instead, getting the best performance out of an application requires some work from your side before the dashboard can be rolled out to a larger audience. The following tips show what you need to keep in mind during your validation phase.

Don't Forget to Validate Your Designs

In the past, we have seen many people designing dashboards without even knowing the tool in use. This can be a big mistake. As described before, different personas might have different roles when it comes to the creation of an efficient dashboard. Thus, we strongly recommend that these different personas sit together and create a plan for building a great dashboard. There might be one person who takes on all the design work, and another one who takes care of the modeling aspects, while a third person would do the proper app building. Letting these people work individually in silos without listening to each other will not lead to a great result.

Furthermore, you should ensure that the dashboard designs created by the dashboard designer are built in such a way that they allow the application builder to implement them in an efficient way. Sometimes a design can be great, but when it turns out to be too complicated to be realized in a way that improves the dashboard performance, it does not really make sense to continue the journey.

Conduct Interviews with Your Users

We always recommend planning corresponding validation sessions with multiple users before a dashboard can go live. These kinds of validation sessions help you find out what the end users think about the current dashboard solution, and if there are things that still should be improved. There are many possible ways of interacting with users. One great way that we use regularly internally and when working with customers is to conduct interviews. Interviews can help to sharpen our view on things that might still not work properly. In this case, you have still got time to fix problems before the dashboard is released to a wider audience.

How to conduct such an interview? First, you should identify the right business users so as to get the most information out of this exercise. Ask them if they would be willing to spend a few minutes of their time with you to help identify some problems with your current dashboard. The interview itself can be done either in person, via telephone, or via an internet meeting tool. Typically, we prepare an interview questionnaire guide that helps guide the discussion. However, please note that most of the interview should be dedicated to listening to the users, not talking on your own too much.

During the interview, you should stay open-minded and not criticize anybody because of their opinion; ultimately, you want to learn something from other people. Additionally, you might want to ask the users for their permission to record the session so that you can easily listen to everything again afterwards; that way you don't need to take notes the whole time, making the process less stressful. After gathering all the information from the users, it is time to condense the qualitative information from your interviews and draw conclusions from them to further optimize your dashboard.

Sample Interview Questions

Below, we provide a few sample questions that might inspire you and that you can pick freely for your own interviews in the future:

- General questions regarding the user's work:
  - Can you please briefly explain your current job role? As which persona would you classify yourself? (Remark: Here you can also show the persona matrix above to the people and ask them to pick one or two entries that match their role best.)
  - Why do you want to use this dashboard? Which tasks do you want to perform?
  - Can you please describe a typical workflow that you intend to follow with this dashboard?
- Questions regarding the user's pains:
  - What are your biggest problems in general in your work that you'd like this dashboard to solve?
  - What are the main problems you encountered with this dashboard?
  - What could be done to either fix your problems or the problems that you have with this dashboard?
- Questions regarding the dashboard and its performance (only when they have already used it):
  - How did you perceive the performance of the dashboard?
  - What are your expectations regarding the performance?
  - What loading time would still be acceptable for you?
- Questions regarding the information that is displayed on the dashboard:
  - Which charts, tables, or key performance indicators (KPIs) need to be displayed for you on this page?
  - What information could be removed to save computation time?
  - Would it be possible to move certain information to other pages or stories?

Run an A/B Test

An A/B test can be of great help when you want to find out what your users are willing to accept in terms of performance. A/B tests are known as a common user research tool that can be applied in many situations.

In general, A/B refers to the fact that you have two ways to decide: either for A or for B. For example, you could use an A/B test to find out what performance compromises your users are willing to accept. Here, A could be a dashboard that is performing much better than B but that shows less data on it (for example, when you dropped certain charts). You can visualize the A/B test also as a tree (or decision) diagram.

What you could do now is to show both solutions A and B to your users and ask them for feedback. Maybe some of them would like to see better performance on their screen, while the other group cannot live without the missing data. You can then go deeper and refine your A/B tests until they converge and the users would accept the performance. This way you can easily find out what users are willing to accept or not.

In Figure 1.2, we give an example of what an A/B test could look like. With an A/B test, you can easily check what changes your users are willing to compromise on. For example, they can either vote for option A (the faster dashboard with less data on it) or option B (the slower dashboard with more data displayed on it).

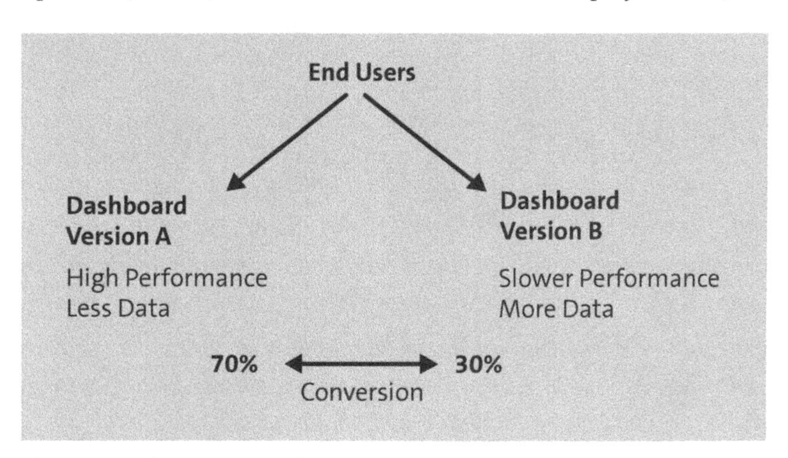

Figure 1.2 A/B Test Example

Validate Performance by Measuring It

How can we define a successful dashboard? And how can we measure success? Well, there is not only one definition of success, but we could think about various metrics that might indicate whether your dashboard is successful or not. And let's be clear here: If the performance of your dashboard is bad, then you will most likely not see users adopting it. Things are clearly interconnected. If you want to find out whether your dashboard is successful or not, you might look at the following KPIs:

- **Consumption rate and traffic**
  How much traffic does a dashboard produce? How often are users using it?
- **Mean usage times**
  How long are users staying with your dashboard on average before losing attention?
- **Adoption rate**
  How many users are using the dashboard per month? How many users are onboarded every month?

- **Interaction numbers**
  How often do users interact with the dashboard? How often do they click on a specific link?
- **Usage tracking**
  How are users using your dashboard? What is the end-to-end path they take for work?
- **KPIs related to business goals**
  Can you measure other business-related KPIs (e.g., the net promoter score)?

More detailed information on this specific topic can be found in our previous book, *Designing Dashboards with SAP Analytics Cloud* (SAP PRESS, 2021, *www.sap-press.com/5235*).

Furthermore, you should continuously measure the performance of your dashboard over time and ensure that the performance does not get worse. This can be done, for example, by measuring how long the dashboard needs to fully show all relevant information to the users. If you are applying incremental updates and changes to it, you also might want to measure the before and after states by using a performance tracker tool (as it is meanwhile available in most browsers, e.g., in Google Chrome; see our discussion in Chapter 2). In Chapter 3 of this book, we will also describe how the SAP Analytics Cloud onboard performance tracking tool works and how it can be used to measure the dashboard performance.

We also recommend regularly performing benchmark tests. Such tests can help to identify weaknesses and where space for improvements exists. In Chapter 2, we will go into further details on how such benchmark tests can be conducted.

1.2 SAP Analytics Cloud Performance

This book is about building efficient dashboards with SAP Analytics Cloud. To master this task, we first need to take a closer look at the application itself and understand all its characteristics. We start with a discussion of why performance matters, followed by some common performance issues that often show up in SAP Analytics Cloud. We then briefly talk about the overall software architecture. This section ends with a discussion of the major differences between the on-premise and the cloud software world.

1.2.1 Why Performance Matters

Nobody likes slow applications, that is for sure. In this sense, performance has become one of the key drivers of why people abandon (cloud) applications or switch to competitor solutions. Performance is simply everywhere. When you start your computer, you expect that your machine will be up and running quickly. When you open a website, load an application, or even play a video game, you expect the software to move fast. We clearly see that performance is important and matters.

If we focus on the cloud business solely, applications were moved to a browser recently. However, for many years now we have observed that the total average web page sizes on the internet have continuously increased. Thus, there is an even stronger need to take performance perceptions seriously. According to various articles, the average web page size in 2017 was approximately 3.5 MB, with roughly 1.8 MB being images, 800 KB being videos, and the rest scripts, fonts, CSS, HTML code, and others (see Figure 1.3).

Further Reading

More information on average web page sizes can be found from the following resources:

- Tammy Everts, "The average web page is 3MB. How much should we care?," available at *http://s-prs.co/v566944*
- Jay Kang, "Webpage Size – Why is it important? And how do you optimize it?," available at *http://s-prs.co/v566945*

Comparing this to the total average number of only 1.6 MB in 2014 we observe that web page sizes have dramatically increased within just three years. Taking these numbers seriously would result in an average web page size in the year 2023 of roughly 7.3 MB in total (assuming linear growth), which is a significant amount of data to be downloaded and processed by the browser every time a new page is downloaded. Thus, it is no wonder that developers continuously need to optimize their code to compete with the ever-increasing growth of multimedia material on the web.

In a cloud product for businesses, things might get even worse because it is typically necessary to download large packages of JavaScript code for both the applications and specific user interface (UI) frameworks, together with visualizations or onboarding videos. Thus, we can say that for business applications there is perhaps an even stronger need to get performance problems under control.

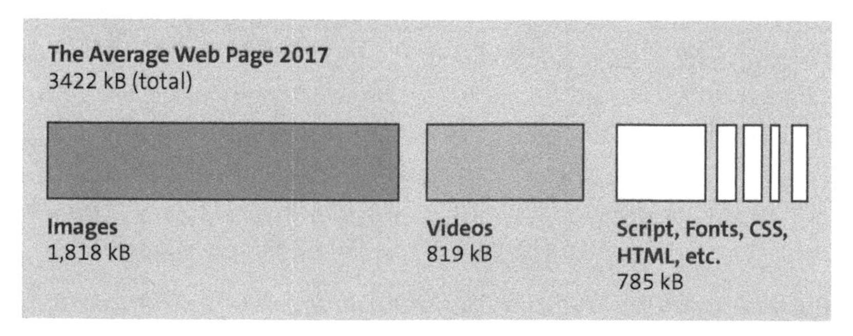

Figure 1.3 Average Web Page Size

Having stated these preliminary points, we now come to the important question of why performance matters at all. Why should IT administrators, developers, or dashboard builders take care of performance? There are many reasons to do so. Let's talk about a few important ones.

- **Poor performance can negatively impact your business goals and numbers.**

  Hence, it wastes time and money.

  When time gets lost, things can quickly get expensive. When users need to wait for a dashboard to load day by day, they are losing a lot of time—time they need to work instead of wasting by looking at the screen of their personal computer. Ultimately, this can have direct and indirect consequences. For example, businesses might lose revenue, affecting sales and customer satisfaction in a negative way. Thus, every optimization that can be done to improve the performance of, for example, a finance or sales dashboard should be rolled out quickly.

- **Poor performance can decrease your dashboard adoption.**

  Hence, users won't use it (efficiently).

  Imagine a poorly performing dashboard that takes a long time to load all relevant data into the browser. Why would any employees use such a solution? Instead, what happens very frequently is that users start building work-arounds when they feel that a dashboard takes them more time than they are saving. The result is that nobody uses the dashboard, and its adoption starts declining. This also costs money, depending on the number of licenses that the company has purchased. Thus, a dashboard designer should do everything to ensure a great adoption of the dashboard so that it can become a great success. Another clear risk is that the dashboard is not used efficiently enough to provide a great output. In any case, poor performance causes problems on the business side.

- **Poor performance can negatively impact communication between users.**

  Hence, users won't share and communicate it.

  Above we already discussed the connection between dashboard performance and user experience. Bad performance values can easily result in a terrible user experience, with the effect that users tend to avoid the dashboard. Connected to this is the idea that a dashboard itself should also serve communication purposes and improve the alignment between different stakeholders. Having built a great and outperforming dashboard allows one to improve the communication not only between different users but also between different departments of a company because they can more easily exchange information and data via the onboard communication streams (as it is the case when you are using SAP Analytics Cloud, for example).

Thus, we see that performance matters. Typically, we don't improve performance just for performance's sake, but because there are strong business reasons behind it. Therefore, we will go into more detail about what kind of performance issues we typically encounter before we provide a high-level overview of the software architecture of SAP Analytics Cloud.

1.2.2 Common Performance Issues

If you are using SAP Analytics Cloud, there are a bunch of well-known performance issues (or traps) that story builders tend to run into, often without even knowing that several aspects could cause issues on the viewer side. It is the responsibility of the dashboard designer and application builder to ensure that none of these traps exist in a dashboard.

In this section, we review some of the most common performance problems that we have observed in the past when talking to customers. Of course, this list is again far from being complete, but we hope to give at least some overview of where things can go terribly wrong. (The reader might also look afterwards at the next section of this chapter to understand the architecture model of the tool.) We will separate the SAP Analytics Cloud environment into the backend and frontend part to give you a better idea of where time can get lost. Here come a few typical performance killers:

- **Frontend**
  - *Loading too much data into the dashboard at once*

    Imagine you created a story with only one or a few pages, and you are wondering why it takes so much time to load data into your dashboard. This is because SAP Analytics Cloud is a cloud tool. There is a browser with a calculation engine that needs to process all the information first. All of this takes time. Try to leverage the lazy loading capabilities of the tool and split up your content into multiple pages within your story. That ensures that the content is split in pieces and will be loaded step by step, instead of loading everything at the same time. To get more information on this topic, you can consult Chapter 3 of this book.
  - *Displaying too much information to the viewer on one page*

    This is a similar problem to what was described above. If the data load is too heavy, the tool (or better, your browser) will struggle to process all the information on a specific page. Try to set filters whenever possible. After all, the question is what kind of information you want to show to your users. Why would you need to show all the information at once? This is typically not useful because the dashboard viewer might be overwhelmed by the amount of information. By setting filters (e.g., filtering out a specific product, region, or country), you can ensure that only the most important data pieces are loaded into the frontend. Chapter 3 will provide more information on how to best display your content on a dashboard.
  - *Too heavy load on the OLAP engine*

    Everything that you build into your dashboard needs to be processed. SAP Analytics Cloud comes with a very strong online analytics processing (OLAP) engine, but this does not guarantee that things will move fast. If you put a heavy load on the engine, the performance can get worse, such as when you apply overly expensive formulas in the frontend. Instead, it is better to move such computations into the backend where they can be performed more quickly (e.g., when you are using an SAP HANA database from SAP). Try to leverage the full backend power, not the much slower JavaScript frontend engine. Chapter 3 and Chapter 6 have more information on this topic.

- *Story overload with unnecessary material*

  Unnecessary material includes big images and company logos or charts without any meaning or functionality. Ask yourself what a dashboard viewer really wants to see. Any redundant information can distract from the proper data message that you want to convey with a dashboard. If you want to make your dashboard look good and style it in a way that it gets adopted, we recommend that you also read our previous SAP PRESS book, *Designing Dashboards with SAP Analytics Cloud*. Images can easily be compressed. Use the smaller SVG file format instead of heavy JPEG images. And check that charts with similar information exist only once. In Chapter 3, we go into further details on this topic.

- *Too many self-scripted applications*

  SAP Analytics Cloud comes with a huge number of onboard applications and possibilities to design a dashboard and get the most out of your data. SAP Analytics Cloud also includes a powerful Analytics Application Designer tool as well as lots of opportunities to write your own R scripts. These are all great possibilities, but keep in mind that every additional piece of code that you are inserting on your own takes the OLAP engine time to evaluate. First ask yourself if there are already similar onboard functionalities within the tool that you could leverage before you reinvent the wheel. Typically, such functionalities are already coded in a maximally efficient way, and there is no need to rewrite existing code on your own. Chapter 4 has more information on self-scripted applications.

- *Too many queries sent to the backend*

  Assume you build a story that contains multiple widgets, including charts and tables. That means that SAP Analytics Cloud needs to prioritize which elements are loaded first. This is done for you automatically, probably without letting you know about it. Therefore, every chart or table needs to fire an event that triggers a request to the backend to fetch some data from the database. But the point here is that there is a natural limitation in some browsers, which restricts the maximum number of queries the frontend can send off at the same time. (Within Google Chrome, the recommended browser for using SAP Analytics Cloud, the maximum number is six queries.) This means that only six concurrent queries can be fired, and the user needs to wait until some of these queries are done before the next queries are put in the queue. That again speaks to the fact that a story builder should split up the content into multiple pages instead of letting a dashboard fire too many queries in parallel. In Chapter 3 of this book, we discuss further details of this topic.

- *Bad network bandwidth, slow personal computers*

  Maybe this point seems weird to some readers, but we have observed in the past that users complain about their bad dashboard performance while fully ignoring their own personal computer. Running a heavy browser dashboard needs CPU power, and if you are busy executing a Windows update in parallel with some heavy graphics computations, the performance will suffer. Ensure that your local machine has enough CPU power and memory available to do all computations as defined. Therefore, your browser plays a crucial role. You should wisely choose your browser; SAP recommends Google Chrome to properly run SAP Analytics Cloud. Similar arguments are held for your network bandwidth. If you let a dashboard fire a ton of queries in parallel to the backend while downloading a few gigs of data and sharing your desktop in Microsoft Teams, the performance can naturally get slow. Ensure that you have enough local bandwidth for all your tasks. In Chapter 7 of this book, we go into the details on how viewer choices can affect dashboard performance.

- **Backend**

  - *Incorrect or inappropriate model structure*

    As a dashboard designer you also need to define how the model of your story is set up. In principle, there are a lot of possibilities for how to model your data. You can model data in a native SAP Analytics Cloud model or leverage the live data connections to an SAP HANA view or to an SAP Business Warehouse (SAP BW) backend. Many things can go terribly wrong because one should not underestimate the way the model structure has been set up. Are you using redundant or too large dimensions or even too many measures? That can significantly slow down computations. Instead, try to leverage your backend capabilities directly, where the CPU power is potentially higher. Sometimes it might even make sense to question whether your database is the correct one at all. Maybe you can gain better performance by migrating your data to another data source that is better optimized for the specific tasks you are looking for. Chapter 5 and Chapter 6 provide further information on this important topic.

  - *Slow database backends do not speed up the dashboard performance*

    You might also want to check that the execution power of the backend itself is high enough that it can deal with the number of queries and the load it receives from users at the same time. We recommend using an SAP HANA database from SAP to better scale your business, since SAP Analytics Cloud is optimized for proper communication with this database. But even if you are using another data source, such as an SAP BW system, you should take care of the backend performance. The response time of the server typically makes up a significant fraction of the total loading time. Check your backend configuration settings. In Chapter 2,

Chapter 3, and Chapter 6, we provide further information on this topic and demonstrate how to measure performance with standard tools such as the onboard SAP Analytics Cloud performance analysis tool or the well-known Google Chrome debugger.

- *Too large data packages pushed to the browser*

  This point seems self-evident, but let's talk through it clearly. Don't try to push your whole backend database into the user's browser at once. It might feel natural when coming from an on-premise world to have all information available at the same time for analysis purposes, but in a cloud world this is often not very straightforward because of the limitations that one encounters due to bandwidth and browser capabilities. Instead, try to preselect and slice data packages. This will decrease the load and save bandwidth. At this stage, we point out that both front-end and backend need to play together correctly to ensure smooth execution. Ensure that both have the correct settings so that your dashboard can run in an efficient way. In Chapter 6, we will go into details on this topic.

- *Incorrect tenant settings can slow down the system*

  There are a few SAP Analytics Cloud tenant settings that the IT administrator can adjust to optimize system performance. We won't go into further details here, but Chapter 6 will provide some more information on this topic.

Further Reading

We recommend reading a few great resources on the web provided by SAP that deal with the topic of optimizing performance in SAP Analytics Cloud. The article "SAP Analytics Cloud Performance Best Practices for BI, Planning and Application Designer" contains a collection of many resources that can be considered when optimizing dashboard performance and can be found at the following URL: *https://community.sap.com/topics/cloud-analytics/best-practices-troubleshooting.*

1.2.3 Understanding the Software Architecture

In this book, we want to understand how the dashboard performance of a tool like SAP Analytics Cloud can be optimized to get the best user experience out of it. To do so, we first need to understand the high-level software architecture of SAP Analytics Cloud and how the different components work together. We do this because we need to gain a basic understanding of where computation time can quickly get lost and how this can be fixed. Therefore, let's first look at Figure 1.4, which provides a rough overview of the software architecture of SAP Analytics Cloud. The SAP Analytics Cloud client itself is embedded in a JavaScript engine that runs in the browser. Requests are put via HTTP in both directions for acquired data and live connections. We will discuss all listed components separately:

- **Frontend**

  On the frontend side, we observe that all interactive components, e.g., the chart engine, the request generator, and the UI itself, are embedded into the SAP Analytics Cloud client, which is written in JavaScript. The JavaScript engine executes all JavaScript code, thereby running in a browser of the user's choice. Looking at where performance could get lost, we can already identify multiple touchpoints. That means that all these components require time to execute code and to load widgets, images, data, etc. into a dashboard. Ways time can get lost include:

  - Rendering too many widgets, charts, geo maps, etc. all at once
  - Parallel requests to the backend (some might even be redundant)
  - Leveraging an overly heavy user interface (which is currently based on SAPUI5)

  The communication between the frontend and its backend is mediated via the HTTP protocol for both acquired data and live connections. Thus, all kinds of data need to go over this stream, which limits the size of data packages that get transferred. The frontend sends all requests to the backend, thereby waiting for a response.

  In Chapter 3 to Chapter 5, we discuss how you can best optimize your frontend dashboard and minimize the time needed to load all relevant information.

- **Backend**

  On the backend side, the situation is a bit more complicated because it clearly depends on where the data is stored. In principle, there are two possibilities.

  Let's first discuss the case in which an SAP Analytics Cloud tenant has been set up before. This is the case when the application builder uses a model with acquired data (e.g., when someone uploads an Excel file with data into the data wrangler and then saves it on the server). The data itself and the model metadata are stored in an SAP HANA database (with technical subcomponents called Contentlib and EPM Models). This is the standard way of storing data in SAP Analytics Cloud and probably also the fastest.

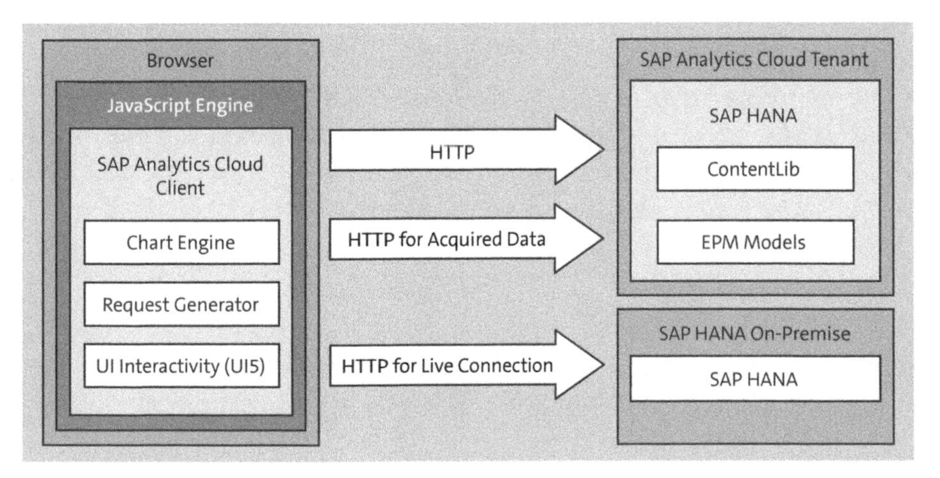

Figure 1.4 Software Architecture of SAP Analytics Cloud

In the second case, the user could decide on a live data connection to another existing data source of his or her choice. Meanwhile, there are several possible data sources the frontend can connect to, including SAP Business Warehouse (SAP BW), SAP HANA, SAP SuccessFactors, Qualtrics, and SAP S/4HANA backend.

As an example, let's look at the SAP HANA on-premise system. Imagine that a company purchased an SAP HANA backend a few years ago and now wants to leverage the analytics capabilities of SAP Analytics Cloud. In this case, the data resides in an SAP HANA database and needs to be loaded into a frontend dashboard. To do so, the frontend needs to establish a live data connection to this SAP HANA database. Within the SAP HANA server, there is a CalcView engine running that can efficiently be used for direct backend calculations. The multi-dimensional services (MDS) engine is used to process multi-dimensional queries and to transform and aggregate the data.

One major advantage of having such an SAP HANA system in the backend is that it can significantly speed up heavy calculations compared to a simple browser engine. That is why it is generally recommended to move such CPU-demanding calculations from the frontend into the backend, where there is more computational power.

In any case, whether you are using data residing in an SAP Analytics Cloud tenant or within an SAP HANA database, the data needs to be processed first and then the response will be sent to the frontend. This creates a waiting time in which your dashboard should ideally tell the user that it is currently busy and waiting for a response from the server. Otherwise, a user might quickly get lost, depending on the total load of the system (a discussion of loading times will follow in Chapter 2).

Furthermore, in Chapter 6 we briefly describe how the administrator can optimize the tenant or backend settings to speed up the loading process and to increase performance.

1.2.4 On-premise versus Cloud: General Limitations

There are several differentiators between an on-premise and a cloud ERP system. Let us first start by discussing the following key drivers: costs, deployment, control, security, flexibility, scalability, and compliance. As you will see in the following sections, each of these might have an impact on a company's decision on the direction in which the IT system landscape will move. And of course, each also contributes to the level of performance measured by an end user.

On-premise Setup

Let us start with a company that still works with an older on-premise setup. What does that mean? It means that the company acquired local servers some time ago that they run and maintain on their own, typically in local server stations by their own IT administrators. Such a setup surely comes with a lot of challenges:

- **Costs**
  Let's start by discussing the costs. As we can see in Figure 1.5, a large fraction of the total cost of ownership (TCO) is generated by activities that are not directly related to the software license, such as the IT personnel, maintenance, training, or hardware costs. Typically, only roughly 9 percent of TCO goes to the software licenses, in contrast to a cloud software setup.
- **Deployment**
  Talking about deployment, the company itself remains responsible for setting up the corresponding software and services, while leveraging their own infrastructure. On one hand, this has the advantage that maintenance can be done fast. On the other hand, deployments might take a lot of time and contribute to TCO as well.
- **Control**
  Similar arguments hold for having full control of the in-house hardware architecture. Server crashes and shutdowns can ultimately be controlled by the company itself; nobody relies on other IT personnel.
- **Security**
  Concerning security aspects, companies tend to believe that the hardware and software security of their infrastructure might be better than anywhere else, but this surely depends on how the company manages it to get common security problems (hacking or denial of service attacks) under control.

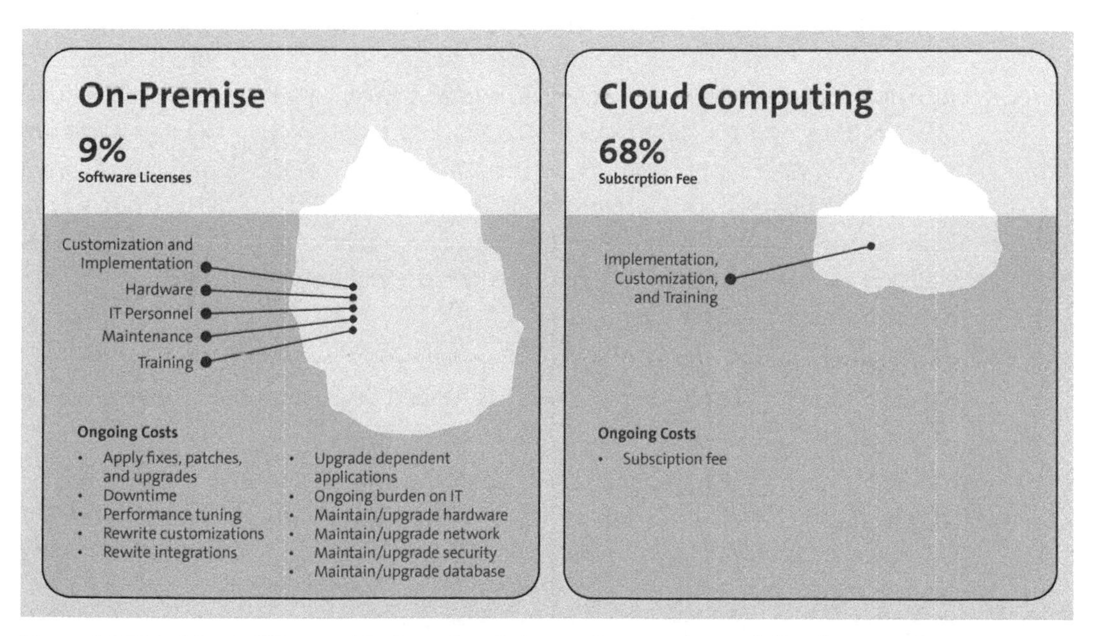

Figure 1.5 Total Cost of Ownership Overview Between On-premise and Cloud Computing Software

- **Flexibility**
  In terms of flexibility, a local on-premise setup is clearly lacking a flexible structure since hardware mostly remains in the place where it used to be installed.
- **Scalability**
  Talking about flexibility, a local on-premise setup has several limitations, which are dictated by the space available to buy new hardware machines. This is a serious point for many fast-growing companies.
- **Compliance**
  One of the big disadvantages of an on-premise setup is that companies need to check their system compliance on their own. One needs to keep government regulations in mind as well as regulations from the economy.

Cloud Setup

Moving to a cloud setup has the big advantage that local hardware machines are no longer necessary. Instead, every company can rent remote hardware space on a provider machine and use it for their own purposes. The provider typically hosts several data centers where computers are joined to networks. Access to these data centers can be granted via a web browser (such as Google Chrome or Safari). The key drivers we discussed in the previous section now read as follows:

- **Costs**
  Again, an important driver is the TCO. The TCO between on-premise and cloud computing software is a great example of how different on-premise and cloud products are. Typically, the ongoing costs for on-premise products are significantly larger than for cloud products. As shown in Figure 1.5, roughly 68 percent of all costs go into the (recurring) subscription fees, in contrast to only 9 percent for the software licenses. However, the devil is in the details. The reason is that the 9 percent on-premise TCO is only the tip of the iceberg. While such a setup comes along with a long list of maintenance activities, these are completely lacking in the cloud world. Only costs for training might play into the game, which *can* make the cloud financially quite attractive. Most of the cloud TCO is controlled by the number of licenses that a company has purchased.
- **Deployment**
  No deployment of hardware or software is needed because all server machines are hosted by the external provider and not by the company.
- **Control**
  This is more difficult. Since hardware is hosted by an external provider, one might think that control could play a major role. However, the question is what a company really wants to control. What is typically shared with users are certificates and other regulatory documents, while server downtimes are no longer under the control of the company. Giving up control might seem awkward to people, but the question is whether this is really a problem. The management of the company needs to decide

if they trust another provider to be responsible for hosting most of their own data and hardware infrastructure.

- **Security**
  Sometimes people are afraid of security risks and have strong concerns about the cloud because of this. However, things have changed, and providers have started to invest heavily in the security aspects of their software systems. Of course, nobody can guarantee in the end that every system is 100 percent safe, whether in an on-premise or in a cloud world. However, the risk of data manipulation or corruption has become significantly smaller over the past years in the cloud world, and this will surely improve further in the future. For example, multiple parallel hardware systems ensure the stability (and availability) of servers and protect the whole system from malfunctions. Privacy will be guaranteed.
- **Flexibility**
  As you can imagine, flexibility is very high in the cloud. There are no hardware issues that companies need to deal with, no migration issues, no system maintenance, and no implementation aspects. People can work on the remote systems from anywhere and anytime. Furthermore, if licenses are not needed anymore, they can be returned, or if more licenses are needed, they can be purchased within just a few hours.
- **Scalability**
  Like flexibility, scalability is a key argument for moving to the cloud. Companies can easily rent more space or purchase further licenses. This allows for quick scalability of the business.
- **Compliance**
  Similarly on the compliance side, a company no longer needs to take care of compliance issues on their own. This problem is mostly solved by the external provider. However, one should always check if all compliance regulations and industry standards are met.

Implications for Performance

What does all this mean when we talk about performance in this book? First, we need to keep in mind the different constraints discussed above, which all have (indirect) performance implications. Let us discuss just a few examples:

- **The data might not be living close by**
  Since in an on-premise world data lives locally on server machines, data access may have been faster in the past. However, this is no longer the case today. Due to better and faster internet connections and cable technologies on the market, the impact of the data connection has become more and more irrelevant. That is one of many reasons in favor of the cloud world. However, all the data that a user wants to analyze still needs to be transferred via an internet connection, which naturally limits the size of data packages. If you decide to create a dashboard that needs to download

hundreds of megabytes of data to your browser, this will take time. So, we need to create awareness that things can get really slow if a dashboard is not correctly built. This is one important topic of this book.

- **The data is processed not only on the provider's side, but also on the end user's side**
  Assume that you have created a nice dashboard with SAP Analytics Cloud, and you want to implement some downstream calculations to display specific KPIs on the screen. Such calculations are typically done in the browser of the end user directly, not necessarily on the server side of your provider. This means that your dashboard is directly limited by the hardware of the end user. If they use an old notebook with low computation power, things can finally get slow. Ultimately, performance also depends on the way the dashboard is created and the amount of data that is continually requested by the user from the server.
- **End user settings can have a big impact**
  Given the restrictions mentioned above, specific settings on the side of the end user can affect cloud performance. Wrong system settings, slow web browsers, a heavy VPN connection running in parallel, screen sharing, or other viewer choices can significantly affect and lower the dashboard performance. Getting such different limiting factors under control is one of the many topics of this book. Users need to be made aware that they can control cloud performance to a significant degree on their own, which requires understanding some technical details.

This list is surely not complete. One could list many more factors that limit the performance of a cloud dashboard. However, the most important thing to say is that one should keep in mind that even small changes can have big performance impacts, which add up and cost time and money—time that could be easily saved by applying the right settings beforehand.

1.3 Summary

In this chapter, we have talked about various topics that are important for understanding the subsequent chapters of this book but that required little or no technical knowledge.

We started with a general overview of performance and its relation to user experience, where we first discussed why the design phase is of high importance and why you should carefully think about it before you consider building a dashboard. This is primarily because it gets harder to make notable changes to your dashboard solution once it has already been rolled out to the users. We continued with a discussion on the question of who manages performance. Many people can be involved here, and they all have different roles and tasks. We reviewed a bunch of them and discussed how they can properly contribute to the success of a dashboard by optimizing its performance.

We then talked about several user research techniques that allow you to gain insights into how users perceive an inefficient dashboard. Validation sessions are important for getting the opinion of dashboard consumers, which should then be channeled back into the application design process. That allows you to get the most value out of a dashboard.

Afterwards, we switched to SAP Analytics Cloud and discussed a few details regarding the performance of the application itself. We started with a short review of why performance matters, stating the uncontroversial fact that nobody really likes slow applications and that bad performance can heavily impact your business goals in a negative way. Since data needs to be downloaded and processed, the ever-increasing amount of data on the internet, in particular the average size of a web page, requires careful treatment of performance.

Subsequently, we talked about common performance flaws that are well-known within SAP Analytics Cloud and that dashboard designers and application builders should keep in mind during their work. We divided those flaws into ones that can only be fixed in the frontend (e.g., when the OLAP engine gets overloaded or when too much data needs to be processed by the browser) and those that can only be fixed in the backend (e.g., when an inappropriate model structure has been chosen or when too large data packages are pushed into the browser).

Afterwards, we gave a high-level overview of the software architecture of SAP Analytics Cloud, discussing the different technical components of the frontend and the backend and how they impact dashboard performance.

Finally, we talked about common misunderstandings between cloud and on-premise solutions, which are mixed up quite often. There are substantial differences in relation to costs, deployment, control, security, flexibility, scalability, and compliance between cloud and on-premise products. It is very important that the reader is aware of these differences. They can also impact the performance of a business dashboard.

In the next chapter, we will learn more about how to measure, test, and monitor the performance of an SAP Analytics Cloud dashboard. To do so, we will first discuss a few basics of performance theory and see how these apply to our dashboards.

Chapter 2

Measuring, Testing, and Monitoring Performance

This chapter is about measuring, testing, and monitoring performance. We will investigate different types of performance tests and tools before we discuss the differences between performance testing and engineering. A typical performance testing process is presented, including a discussion of important metrics that can be measured. Afterwards, we present a practical example of how to measure performance with Google Chrome. Finally, we present a performance equation and ten golden rules of efficient dashboards.

In this chapter, we go into the details of measuring, testing, and monitoring the performance of an SAP Analytics Cloud dashboard. We will learn a lot of basic performance concepts that are commonly used in computer science. Whenever possible, we also provide references to other scientific resources that might help you to improve your understanding of performance optimizations.

This chapter is structured as follows. We start with a very fundamental discussion of different types of performance tests. We think that it is important to understand these types, because they provide an idea of what a dashboard builder must look at when building a dashboard. The types differ by the number of virtual users that access an application over time. We describe the differences between load, spike, stress, breakpoint, endurance, scalability, and volume tests. Furthermore, we recommend a bunch of great performance test tools on the market that can help you run performance tests in a reliable way.

Afterwards, we discuss differences between performance testing and performance engineering. Performance testing refers to the process of evaluating the performance of an application *after coding*, while performance engineering means that one must take care of code optimizations *before coding* to ensure that every application can run smoothly. We then review different areas of performance engineering and how one can contribute to the success of a dashboard.

In the next section, we then highlight the performance testing process. Every performance test comes with a specific process that needs careful planning beforehand. We describe how you can leverage this process to make any kind of performance test in your company successful.

Afterwards, we define the right metrics that you want to measure. These include metrics that measure time (like the total loading or document object model (DOM) rendering time) or some system KPIs, for example. However, you could also measure various dashboard-specific KPIs (e.g., the loading time of a singular chart or the number of requests put to the server).

This discussion is closely connected to the next subsection, in which we talk about the concrete performance goals that you need to define beforehand. We provide various examples of what a goal could look like, such as "Ensure that the total loading time does not exceed ten seconds when more than 100 users access the dashboard in parallel."

The proceeding section then talks about how to practically measure performance and different system KPIs, such as network bandwidth, memory consumption, or CPU consumption.

We then describe how to create your own benchmark tests and derive an SAP Analytics Cloud specific performance equation that can help you optimize your SAP Analytics Cloud dashboards in a smart way. Different contributions enter this equation. All of them will be discussed later in the book in individual chapters.

We conclude this chapter with ten golden rules of an efficient SAP Analytics Cloud dashboard that will help you track and check the performance of your own solutions. The chapter ends with a summary.

2.1 Different Types of Performance Tests

Before we analyze various performance scenarios and map them to SAP Analytics Cloud, we first need to gain a basic understanding of different types of performance tests. All these types are standard test types in computer science when it comes to performance testing and monitoring. However, they all serve different purposes, as we will see below.

2.1.1 Performance Test Types

There are various test types, which are summarized in Figure 2.1: load tests, spike tests, stress tests, breakpoint tests, endurance tests, scalability tests, and volume tests. These are the most important ones. Together they form a set of performance test types for properly testing an application or a dashboard. Figure 2.2 shows all the different performance tests, where we plot the number of virtual users against test time.

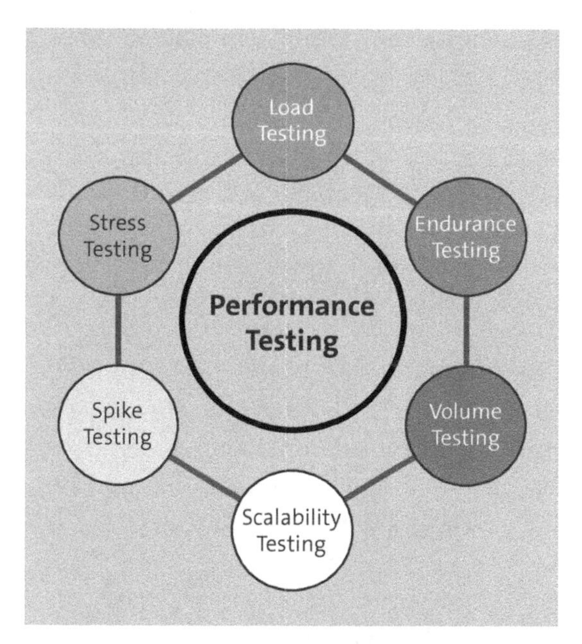

Figure 2.1 Overview of Performance Tests

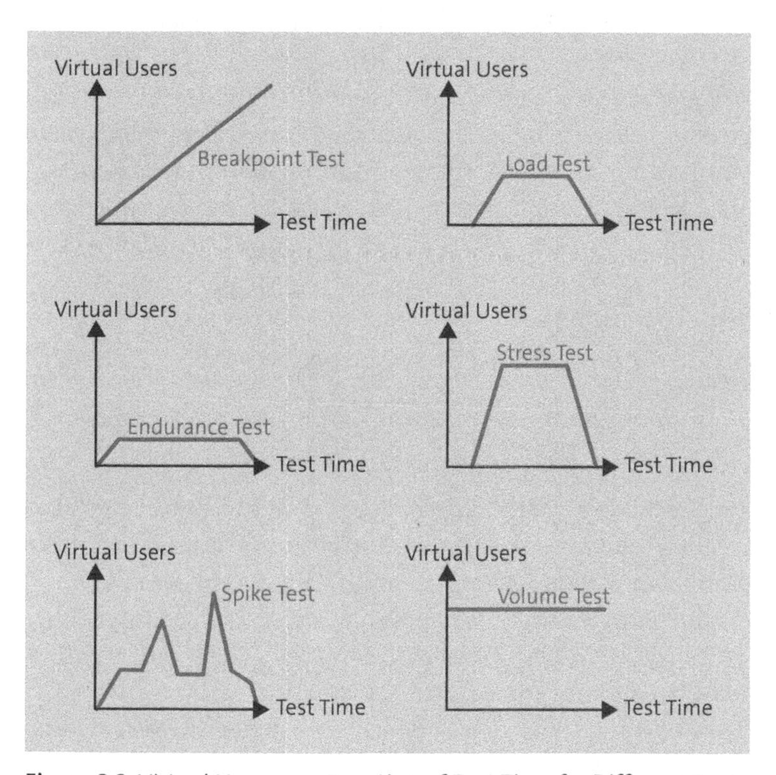

Figure 2.2 Virtual Users as a Function of Test Time for Different Tests

Let's discuss these different types of performance tests individually, relating their pros and cons to the number of virtual users and the time needed to perform the tests:

- **Load tests**
  Let's start with load tests. Such tests are perhaps the most common performance tests one can think about. They measure how an application reacts against a sudden increase of load, such as when multiple users open the application at the same time. Such a load test can be easily simulated. You just grab a bunch of users and let them open your dashboard at the same time. You will then already get a good feeling for whether scalability can be guaranteed or not. However, this clearly depends on the peak user numbers that you foresee for your company. It might be that your solution can manage ten people easily but struggles with a few hundred. In such a case, scalability is not guaranteed any longer. It will become important for you to get a feeling for this by doing such an exercise. Furthermore, you will learn how the response time reacts in such a situation and if data consistency and integrity is still guaranteed.
- **Spike tests**
  The spike test clearly differs from the load test in that there can be multiple singular events with very extensive loads over time. For example, during a marketing campaign, a celebration party, or some media hype around a product, a high number of users may access the web platform at the same time, thereby creating prominent access signatures called spikes (or peaks). If you are using your dashboard for such an event, you must ensure that all components (frontend and backend) can handle such spike events. This can be a real stress test for your dashboard because such a sudden increase (and decrease) of traffic is something that can occur regularly on the web. You could try simulating such spike tests by setting up a separate test environment where a high number of users get the task to perform heavy performance calculations in parallel. You might then monitor the system performance (e.g., by using an Apache web server) and check how the system reacts against the sudden increase in load.
- **Stress tests**
  This test is very similar to the load tests but comes with an even higher number of users that run the application in parallel. The idea of this test is to bring an application to the upper limit of what it can still lift, and therefore, sometimes, it will crash. Identifying the level of stability is important because then you get a feeling for the absolute maximum number of users that an application can still handle. Furthermore, you will also realize quickly where the weak points are, which components are likely to fail first, and which might be more stable. This can help you to focus on bottlenecks. A stress test is a great test to ensure that the robustness of a web application can be guaranteed over time.
- **Breakpoint tests**
  Breakpoint tests are like stress tests but with the only difference that finding the

breakpoint really means that you want to find out the point where the application can crash practically. Thus, you will need to incrementally increase the load on the system. At some point, the system will stop responding, which is a good sign for you that you might have identified the breakpoint. However, keep in mind that your system is offline then, which speaks for the fact that you should never perform a breakpoint test within your live environment. It might take some time to set it up again afterwards.

- **Endurance tests**
  Endurance tests exist to ensure that a certain load can be managed as well over a longer period. Endurance tests check if the application can stand the load for a time longer than the spike tests probed. Therefore, it basically falls into the category of load tests, but with the additional property that the load will last for a longer time. You can perform an endurance test by letting various users access the dashboard continuously, for example over a whole day, and then monitor the stability of the system. Endurance tests are crucial to ensure that your system does not suddenly stop working and that stability is guaranteed over the long run.
- **Scalability tests**
  The scalability tests are different in that they do not focus on the application or dashboard itself, but check how typical system parameters like CPU usage, memory, network usage, RAM, and others react on an increasing performance load. The idea is to find out what it would cost a company to scale up their infrastructure to handle an increasing user load. Such a test can help the IT administrator to find out what it really needs from the system side to manage high loads. Often the result is that new or better computer machines with higher CPU power would be required to adequately scale the business.
- **Volume tests**
  Volume tests are like scalability tests. The idea of a volume test is to focus on increasing the amount of data packages, not just increasing the number of users. With such an exercise we can learn a lot about how the database reacts, since this is the central component that is needed to deal with large volumes of data. Volume tests are important if you already know that your business requires huge data packages to be processed and transferred via the internet. They can also be easily simulated by increasing the data load coming from and going back to the server, thereby carefully monitoring the performance of the backend (which can be, e.g., either an SAP HANA database or an SAP Business Warehouse [SAP BW] backend). Volume tests are also great for assessing the general state of your company's infrastructure.

What do all these test types mean for you as an application builder or system administrator? First, it is important to know that these test types exist so that you are aware of when performance problems could occur, especially when you are using a web-based business application like SAP Analytics Cloud. Second, we recommend going one step further and regularly simulating whether your dashboard still passes those kinds of tests.

Thus, performance management should become some sort of quality management for you and your company soon. However, we also strongly recommend not performing those tests in your live environment. Instead, set up a parallel testing environment and use a proper web server monitoring tool (such as Apache or any other tool of your choice; see also the next chapter for further information) for monitoring the system activities during your tests.

2.1.2 Performance Test Layers

We also want to highlight that all these different performance tests can be used to test different scenarios. This does not necessarily mean that you would need to perform all of them. For example, in many cases you might already know that spikes are unlikely to occur. In such a situation, then, it is less important to focus on spike tests, but maybe other tests would be more meaningful.

Even more important is that you start developing a holistic performance test strategy for your business and continuously reevaluate it along the way. Furthermore, we remark that it is crucial to divide the different application layers into different technical components and, if possible, to test them end-to-end together and separately. The most important layers are:

- **Web server (frontend)**
  This is the technical layer where data is presented to the consumers. In the case of SAP Analytics Cloud, this is the OLAP engine that processes all JavaScript code, engages with end users, and supports them in completing their tasks.
- **Application server (middleware)**
  This layer is a middleware layer that operates between frontend and backend. Typically, it supports communication between the two, takes events from the frontend, and converts them into a query that can be sent to the backend. In SAP Analytics Cloud, the middleware layer is called Firefly.
- **Database (backend)**
  The database is responsible for storing the data and for ensuring that incoming queries are processed quickly and efficiently. It takes the signal from the application server and starts various computations in the background. Once it is done, it provides a response to the user again.

Typically, if you perform an end-to-end test, all different kinds of layers are automatically incorporated into the test routines. This has advantages and disadvantages.

The biggest advantage is that you can easily observe how these different layers play together. This is essentially what defines the user experience: When using a tool like

SAP Analytics Cloud, all components will automatically operate together, supporting end users in fulfilling their tasks.

The biggest disadvantage is that you might not immediately be able to tell where the performance could get lost. If your dashboard is built in a way that is too slow and the OLAP engine takes too much time, then you know where to fix the problem: in the front end. However, it could also be that the database in the backend suffers from some issues. In this case, optimizing your dashboard in the frontend won't help you out. That is why we always recommend splitting the experiences up into the different layers and analyzing and optimizing them separately.

Further Reading

There are a few great articles on the web on the topic of performance tests that we can recommend to you for further reading:

- Software Testing Class, "What Is Performance Testing?," available at *www.softwaretestingclass.com/what-is-performance-testing*
- Thomas Hamilton, "Performance Testing Tutorial," available at *www.guru99.com/performance-testing.html*

2.1.3 Performance Test Tools

There are a bunch of great performance test tools that one can use to simulate some of the above test types. However, the problem is that customer end users typically do not have access to the cloud tenant of the application. Therefore, these tools are less of a practical use for SAP Analytics Cloud users directly and better suited for cloud applications where you have full control over the web server handling. Nevertheless, we would like to provide an overview of the general availabilities on the market for completeness' sake (listed without any specific order):

- **Apache JMeter**
  Apache JMeter is an open-source tool written in Java that was designed to simulate load scenarios and perform web application performance tests. You can use it to perform different load tests via various protocols or servers (HTTP, HTTPS, POP3, IMAP, FTP, etc.), where you can also record and debug your test scenarios. It works on both static and dynamic resources.
- **HP LoadRunner**
  The LoadRunner tool is sold by Hewlett Packard and is one of the most used products on the market. It can simulate a huge number of users in parallel to gaining more insights into application loads. It can also record its activities and comes with a virtual user generator. However, it is non-free software and comes with different enterprise versions.

- **WebLOAD**
  WebLOAD is a performance testing tool specifically written for web applications. It can be used by enterprises with a heavy user load. It allows you to perform load and stress tests with your application and can be applied to both cloud and on-premises machines. It can help to clearly analyze and identify performance leaks and comes with a huge number of built-in functions for integration with Jenkins, Selenium, and others. It is non-free software.
- **HeadSpin**
  HeadSpin is also non-free software but comes with a bunch of functionalities to optimize performance across an entire user journey. It can leverage various AI capabilities to conduct root cause analyses and make recommendations on how the user can improve the application performance. It can also run scalability tests and provides valuable information about metrics like wait and response time and average load time.
- **LoadView**
  LoadView is a cloud-based performance analysis tool that, in contrast to most other performance test tools, uses a real browser environment for its testing purposes. That makes it a powerful tool because it can produce extremely accurate data, while simulating tool usage by multiple end users. It is cloud-based and easy to deploy. However, it is non-free software.

Where to Find These Tools

You can find the above listed performance test tools on the following websites:

- Apache JMeter, *https://jmeter.apache.org/* (one of the very few open-source tools available)
- HP LoadRunner, *www.microfocus.com/en-us/products/loadrunner-enterprise/overview*
- WebLOAD, *www.radview.com/load-testing/*
- HeadSpin, *www.headspin.io/*
- LoadView, *www.loadview-testing.com/*

A comprehensive list of further performance testing tools can be found at the following URL: *http://s-prs.co/v566931*.

2.2 Performance Testing versus Performance Engineering

In this section, we will briefly describe the main differences between the areas of performance testing and performance engineering. Both should be considered by companies who want to optimize their application performance. They are of course not the same, as one might think on first view (although they can overlap). In the previous section, we already went into the details of different types of performance tests. Let's summarize the key ideas here again.

2.2.1 Performance Testing

The idea of performance testing is to simulate different numbers of end users and check how an application is responding to their behavior. With such an approach, we can check for performance, stability, reliability, and scalability of an application and a system. Ultimately, we want to generate a report that we could hand over to the developers and IT system administrators, showing where the bottlenecks are and how they could be fixed. Typically, what is being measured are the server response times, code and browser performance, and other metrics. Later in this chapter we will go deeper into the details on which metrics are important to measure in performance tests.

As described above, different performance tests like load tests, spike tests, stress tests, breakpoint tests, endurance tests, scalability tests, and volume tests exist.

A last comment needs to be made about who is responsible for performing such tests. Typically, a quality assurance (QA) engineer should decide on which tests are the best to be executed. QA colleagues are trained in a way that they can recognize performance flaws and patterns and help developers fix them.

2.2.2 Performance Engineering

In contrast to performance testing, performance engineering refers to the discipline of optimizing the application code so that it operates efficiently. There are various things that can be influenced by performance engineers (or, better, by the software developers, since every developer should ideally also be a performance engineer):

- **Software architecture**
  The software architecture plays a crucial role in any software application. If the architecture is bad, developers can write the best code they want, but it won't help fixing the most pressing performance problems. Creating a solid and stable software architecture requires a lot of knowledge. Typically, senior developers are responsible for creating architecture models (like the high-level SAP Analytics Cloud software architecture shown in the previous chapter) and for evaluating them against feasibility and performance. The architecture can be understood as the architecture of a house: If the basement is not stable, how could the house ever be?
- **UX design**
  The UX design is the central touchpoint between the system and the end users. A bad UX Design can lead to missing adoption, dropping revenues, and frustrations on the customer side. Hence, creating a great user experience is something that should be done by trained UX designers, and not only by developers. Bad UX designs can

influence performance a lot. For example, whether the user has to perform redundant clicks, wait for a reaction of the system without any feedback, or generally struggle with the use of the UI, these are all cases of bad performance. Performance is not always connected only to the code lines but can also manifest itself in the form of the interaction design.

- **Code quality**
  The code itself plays of course a central role when optimizing performance. Bad code quality (for example, when you are dealing with old legacy code) can heavily slow down the performance of an application. Writing efficient code means that you should deal with the theory of algorithms and how such codes should be optimized. For example, it clearly matters whether a sorting algorithm performs like $O(n^2)$, like the Bubblesort algorithm, or $O(n*log(n))$, like the Quicksort algorithm (both given in Landau notation, where the first means that the algorithm has a quadratic and the latter "only" a logarithmic dependence). We don't want to go into too many details of these computer science topics, but we see that there are different ways of solving a problem, some of them faster and more scalable than others.
- **End-to-end process**
  Overall, a business end user cares most about the end-to-end process. He neither sees anything from the code, nor will he have a clue about how the software architecture was designed. Ultimately, it is of uttermost importance that architecture, UX designs, and code quality can work together to create a holistic and seamless end-to-end experience.

Good software developers have established and cultivated a culture within their development framework that allows people to focus on quality, which also includes performance optimizations. Performance is nothing that can be done as a side project. Instead, it requires a lot of knowledge and focus to create web applications that are efficient. Thus, performance engineering should be a crucial part of the overall development process.

It also means that performance testers and performance engineers need to work closely together. If a performance tester measures a performance flaw, then he should get in contact with the engineer and inform him about the problems that occurred. The engineer should then take the reports and try to fix the problems identified by the quality assurance colleagues. Usually, the performance testers are not as deeply involved in the code as the developers. Hence, only the engineer can really identify why and where performance is getting lost because of his deep code knowledge.

Thus, like performance engineering, performance testing also should be integrated into the company's software development processes. Both are crucial quality steps that require the full support of management. In this book, we will less focus on the engineering part but rather explain how a good dashboard can be built by using onboard features of SAP Analytics Cloud.

2.3 Performance Testing Process

In the following, we discuss a typical performance testing process as it has been commonly known in computer science for many years. Performance testing is sometimes a very individual thing. That means that not all steps discussed below might be required by your company. Instead, we want to provide an overview of the most common steps that one should keep in mind when it comes to executing the testing process itself.

Further Reading

If you are interested in finding out more about this process, we refer you to the following article from Thomas Hamilton, who describes the process in more detail: *www.guru99.com/performance-testing.html*.

This process can also be applied to your own test strategies regarding the optimization of dashboards within SAP Analytics Cloud. Figure 2.3 gives an overview of the performance testing cycle together with all the individual steps, which are described below:

❶ **Identify test environment**
To begin with, you should gather some information about your test environment. That involves knowing all the details about the available hardware and software as well as the network connection that you are using. Document your test tools and think about your test strategy. Who are the personas involved and in which phases? Where will the performance tests be done? We recommend that you switch to another system before executing the tests because there is a risk that the system might crash. Ultimately, we want to set up a successful environment that allows your performance tests to be executed and that you are ready to scale.

❷ **Determine performance criteria**
This is an important step where you should involve the people who are participating in the performance tests. You should define the performance acceptance criteria, which means that you need to think about several metrics and their specific values that a performance test must fulfill. Such metrics will also be discussed later in this chapter, but typical examples for such metrics could be the server response times or the time that it takes to fulfill some specific tasks. Furthermore, besides the metrics themselves you should also define your goals that you want the application to achieve. Here, you should be as precise as possible. For example, you could say: "The loading time for the homepage to be fully loaded and displayed to the user should be less than three seconds." You can then benchmark your application against these goals that you have defined (see also Sections Section 2.4 and Section 2.5 about metrics and goals).

❸ **Plan and design**
In this stage, you define your proper test scenarios. These are the scenarios that you

are going to test during a later stage. For example, you could think about planning and designing a load test, which takes hundreds of users accessing the same page at the same time. Or you could plan for a stress or endurance test, which means that you need to define a proper test strategy as well. Try to cover as many test scenarios as possible for your business. Define which measures shall be taken when and by whom.

❹ **Configure test environment**
At this stage, you should ensure that all relevant test tools are ready for use. Identify bottlenecks in your test environment and ensure that they can be overcome. Also prepare the test environment, including all tools and resources. That means setting up the system in a way that it is ready for the different performance tests defined in the previous step. For example, if your system is not available because of a bad internet connection, it does not make sense to move on with the next steps. You might also want to check for important properties of your machine, e.g., ensure that the CPU is free of load and that no other applications are executed in parallel that might disturb your measurement. The same holds true for (virtual) memory.

❺ **Implement test design**
Now, you basically combine your work from steps 3 and 4 and implement your test design into your system environment. With this, you finally get ready for the test execution in the next step. Last checks can still be done before the tests start.

❻ **Run tests**
It is now time to execute your performance tests and gather real measurement data from your system. You should also not forget to monitor and record all your activities for later analyses. The numbers from the metrics defined in step 2 are especially crucial to measure. During the tests, you might also want to monitor a bunch of other system KPIs (CPU or memory, for example) beside those metrics that you have defined. This information will help you later to identify major performance flaws. Ultimately, you want to get an idea of where there is space for improvements and how performance flaws could be fixed by a performance engineer. If one of your tests fails, stop it immediately and run it again so as not to waste time and computational resources (more on the details of how to measure will be discussed in Section 2.6).

❼ **Analyze, fine-tune, and retest**
After having completed your performance tests, you need to consolidate and analyze the data that you gathered during your measurement. These results should also be discussed with the developers who work on the code. You will quickly get an idea of where performance flaws occurred and get initial proposals on how these could be fixed. Furthermore, you can also think about repeating some of the tests if you think that more data would be helpful. Then you can just rerun some of your tests and measure your metrics again. Your developers can then start to fix some of the

issues that came up during the tests. Or maybe you already decided to increase the test load and run tests incrementally one after the other.

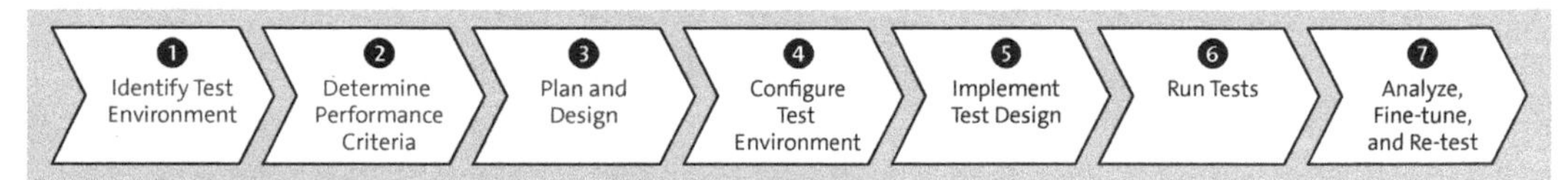

Figure 2.3 Different Steps of a Performance Testing Process

Most importantly, the whole process should be understood as a real cycle in which things should not be seen in an isolated manner, but as an interconnected web that requires continuous adjustment. After having completed the cycle once, you may think about starting it from the beginning again and reiterating the whole process. In this way you can really guarantee the quality of your dashboard or application. We recommend going through this process regularly so that performance problems can be identified at an early stage.

Tips for Your Performance Tests

Here we list a few tips that might be interesting for you to know when you follow the above performance testing process:

- **Try to automate your performance tests**
  Typically, performance tests are manually executed. That means tests need to be set up again and again by hand, and there seems to be less space for automation. However, you can still try to set up und run some of the basic reoccurring tests automatically by configuring scripts that take over most of the test tasks. This will help you to get things done quickly so that you don't lose time for more important test scenarios. You also might check the above list of test tools that we provided to see which tools provide the possibility to create automated tests.
- **Perform your tests multiple times**
  If you perform a test only once, then it is likely that the time measurement that you captured is off by a significant factor, since it is (by definition) only one data point. However, a good measurement always comes with multiple data points. Therefore, you should perform your tests multiple times in a row, maybe even at different times during the day or week, and then record and measure the relevant KPIs that you have defined before. This way you can reduce the statistical error. You might also want to compute a mean value as well as its standard deviation (or the error on the mean). These values can give you a much better idea of the "true" value of your performance test. Further details on this can be found in every standard textbook about statistics. And very importantly, don't change your test environment in between, because then you cannot compare your values with each other anymore (at least from a statistical point of view, this would not make sense).

- **Create acceptance for your tests**
  If you want your performance tests to be successful and developers to take your measurements seriously, you should involve all different kinds of stakeholders from the beginning. A good overview of who should be involved in the optimization of the dashboard performance was given in Chapter 1. That prevents you from investing a lot of time in going through the process chain shown above and then realizing that your measurements are not taken seriously by people. You should create trust and transparency. Every measurement is also (sometimes) a (bad) mirror of the coding truth. But when all stakeholders understand that those measurements do not exist to criticize people's work, they can be a real game changer in many cases.

2.4 Defining the Metrics to Measure

We already talked about a standard process that defined how to perform a performance test. During this process we emphasized the importance of so-called performance acceptance criteria, which define when a test will be successful and when it will fail. Together with these criteria comes the challenge of defining the right metrics that you want to measure.

Tons of metrics could be used. All of them provide some insights into different areas of your application or dashboard. That means that the challenge is to identify the right metrics for your situation and how a measurement could be set up to gain insights into the performance level.

In the following sections, we provide an overview of typical performance testing metrics that can be used to infer some important information about your application. Again, this list is far from being complete. Instead, we want to give an idea of what can be measured and how.

2.4.1 Metrics that Measure Time

We start with those metrics that measure the time it takes to complete some specific tasks. We will start with time measurements in the frontend and then move on to time measurements that can be derived in the backend. Together, they sum up the total loading time for a dashboard. We also try to quantify all qualitative descriptions at the end:

- **DOM rendering time**
  The document object model (DOM) rendering time measures how long a browser needs to properly render the dashboard page. The DOM is a programming interface represented by a hierarchical tree structure that every browser can read and understand. It consists of knots that represent an object on a web page. For example, take

a specific element on a HTML page—let's say, a headline with some text. This headline is embedded in a larger network of specifications that allow browsers to interpret the HTML code and display the web page in the correct way. Figure 2.4 shows an example of a typical DOM that is processed every day by countless browsers all over the world. Measuring the DOM rendering time gives you a good indicator of how heavy the load on the browser is after it receives the response from the backend. Please note that we also include the proper download time here. The download time is the time that the system needs to fully download all multimedia material that will be displayed on the dashboard, e.g., images or videos. Since images also significantly contribute to the rendering time, it makes sense to treat the download time as a part or sub time of the total DOM rendering time.

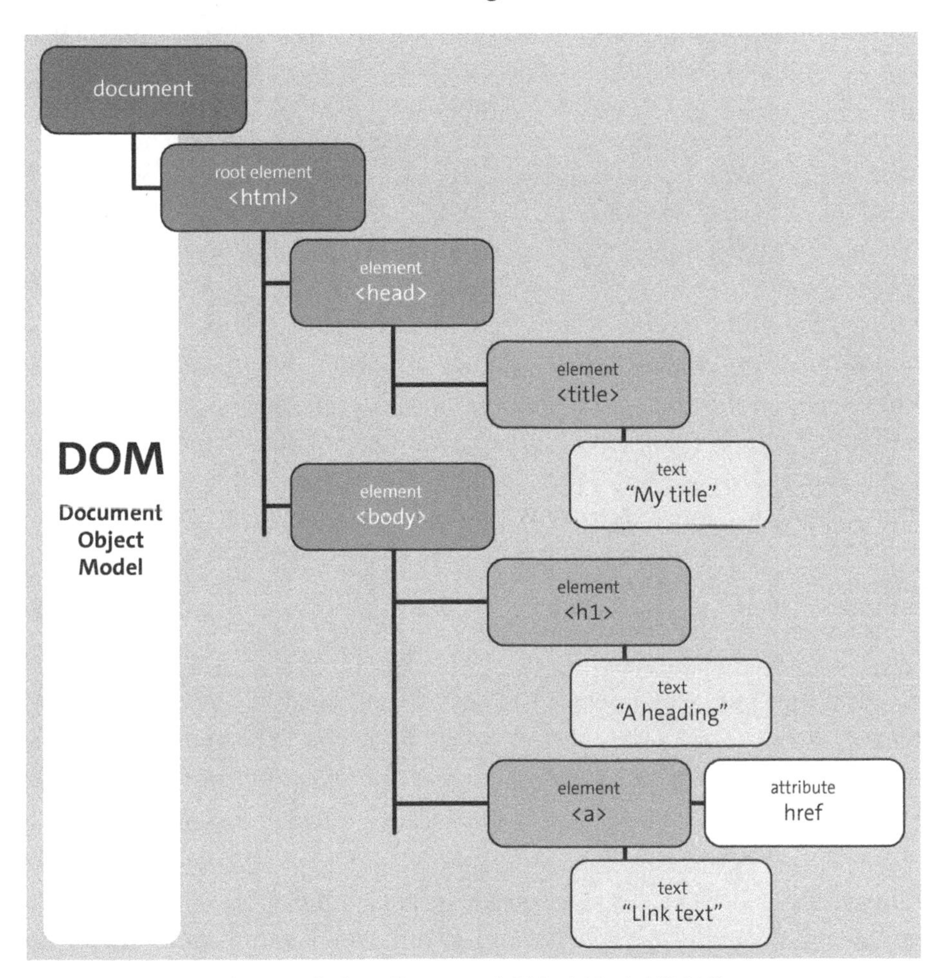

Figure 2.4 A Typical Example for a Document Object Model (DOM)

- **Throughput time**
  The throughput is the time that it takes a backend to receive different requests from the frontend. It measures how fast queries walk through the frontend code, going

via the connecting line until they finally reach the destination where they can be processed (sometimes this is also called the request time). Clearly, the throughput depends on various parameters, like, e.g., the network bandwidth and network quality. The time differences between the point in time when a query has been fired and the point in time when it finally reaches the backend gives an estimate for the throughput time. Typically, these times are rather small, but this clearly depends on the network connection. In general, it is quite hard to estimate the throughput time.

- **Database execution time**
  The database execution time is the time that the database needs to process a set of queries. The database can be anything, an S4/SAP HANA or SAP BW database, or another source that serves as a connectivity endpoint. Since the database plays a crucial role when building a dashboard in SAP Analytics Cloud, we emphasize that separately testing the database for its performance makes sense. This is not a difficult task. Just run your dashboard or simulate the queries that are given to the backend and then check how long it takes the database to respond with an output. You sometimes may be surprised how long the database execution time is compared to the time that is needed to display data on a dashboard, but typically the database should work much faster since it is supported by the whole computational power of a local machine.
- **Answer time**
  The answer time is the time that is measured from the point in time when the database has finished with its computations until the final response has been sent back to the frontend. Thus, the answer time may be interpreted as the "mirror" of the throughput time. The ingoing time that it takes until a signal reaches the backend is the throughput time, the outgoing (response) signal is the answer time. Similar to the throughput time, the answer time is supposed to be quite small and depends on the network bandwidth and quality.
- **Response time**
  The response time is the full time that it takes from the point when a user sends off a request in the browser and waits until the backend signal reaches the frontend again. The response is not really a brand-new contribution, but can rather be calculated as the following sum over various (previous) time contributions:

  Reponse time = Throughput time + Database execution time + Answer time

  We also note that the database execution time is often larger than the throughput and answer times (if we assume a reliable and stable internet connection that can deliver the signals fast and efficient). That is why the response time often provides a great approximation for the database execution time itself, particularly when the request from the frontend is more involved. In these cases, we can claim very roughly:

  Database execution time > Throughput time + Answer time

- **Total loading time**
  This is perhaps the most intuitive metric that one can think of and that we will measure throughout the following chapters. The total loading time is the time the system needs to fully download and process the content that is visible to the viewer. This clearly marks an important KPI for a dashboard since it's the time when users sit and wait in front of their computers for a dashboard to show up. The total loading time has different contributions (all of which we will discuss in the following). For example, it consists of the server response time, plus the time it takes to download all the content (scripts, images, videos, etc.) and process or display it in the browser. The loading time can be measured with a standard performance analysis tool as it is provided with many browsers (e.g., the performance tool in Google Chrome, which will be discussed in Section 2.6). You may also try to measure the total loading time by scaling up the number of users that work in parallel on your dashboard (and perform a stress or spike test). This gives you a good indicator of whether your dashboard still works properly even in busy times. Again, we can provide a formula for the total loading time, which is the sum over all time contributions defined above:

  Total loading time = Σ all time contributions = DOM rendering time + Response time

  = DOM rendering time + Throughput time + Database execution time + Answer time

A typical question that might come up is how the different time-specific KPIs compare with each other. In general, this is difficult to specify because it depends on the setup of, say, the database or the network. However, what you could do is to think about rough order estimates and compare those against each other.

In that case, the throughput and answer times are those that might require the smallest amount of time, followed by the database execution time and the DOM rendering time. Since the database execution time depends on the specific request put by the user, you cannot really claim that the database is always faster than the browser, even though it runs on-premises.

There might be database-intense queries that take the database a long time to perform certain calculations, while the DOM rendering time might be faster. The other way around is of course also possible.

At this point, we would like to refer to Section 2.8, where we talk about our performance equation of SAP Analytics Cloud. This is strongly connected to the discussion above. Later, we will further break down the different performance contributions to the tool and discuss contributions individually, providing hands-on optimization tips and tricks.

2.4.2 Metrics that Measure System Key Performance Indicators

The following metrics measure KPIs that are related to the machine(s) where code is executed. This can be either the end user computer where a browser is running that eats up CPU power or the local (remote) machine where a database is running, (although it can be that you might not get access to the remote machine as an administrator). The metrics below can be measured in both scenarios:

- **Processor, RAM, and memory usage**
  This metric measures how much CPU a requests needs to be executed and how much memory (both physical and virtual memory) is being blocked. In particular, if you perform a stress test where thousands of virtual users want to access a dashboard in parallel, the CPU load will increase dramatically. You should check that the corresponding machine can handle such stress tests. On the end user's side, you may also want to measure the CPU load that a dashboard produces within a browser to see whether your own local machine might limit the dashboard usage or not. The same arguments apply to memory and RAM consumption.
- **Network bandwidth**
  Network bandwidth measures how much data can flow over the internet per unit of time. It is typically measured in number of bits per second (download rate). Bandwidth is a metric that is very individual. That means that the network bandwidth strongly depends on the location where the user or provider is located. In general, to ensure a good dashboard performance, one should check that sufficient bandwidth is available. Nevertheless, a dashboard should always be designed in a minimal way such that it also allows scaling for people who have a lower internet bandwidth. This means that one should generally limit the number of images and videos displayed on the screen. Measuring the bandwidth is not difficult and will be explained in Section 2.6.
- **Amount of cached data**
  Especially in cloud dashboards it is important to leverage existing caching possibilities to an extensive amount. Caching data can be done both on the system and on the browser side, which is because the amount of cached data is also a good metric for the end user's computer and thus for the dashboard (see discussion below). Caching data means that the data does not change over the lifecycle of a dashboard and will be constantly reused. Several databases automatically have built-in caching possibilities; the same holds true for nearly all browsers. SAP Analytics Cloud comes with onboard functionalities to cache data automatically. You could try to measure the cached data and put it in relation to the total amount of data requested by the user. The smaller the amount of data that needs to be refreshed, the better the user experience will be.

2.4.3 Metrics that Measure Dashboard-specific Key Performance Indicators

There are a few KPIs that measure dashboard-specific properties in SAP Analytics Cloud. These can be either the number of requests that a dashboard sends to the backend, the individual loading time per chart, the number of acquired versus remote data models, or simply the number of dashboard widgets, such as charts, images, tables, filters, and others. Let's discuss some of these dashboard-specific KPIs in the following:

- **Number of requests**
  The number of requests typically goes hand in hand with the loading time described above. If you are building a dashboard with SAP Analytics Cloud, every chart that you insert into the user interface will send off one query to the backend to retrieve some information. The more charts you display on a single page, the more queries are fired, leading to a bad performance if the individual data packages are large. Thus, you should carefully measure the number of queries that are fired by a dashboard and try to reduce them if possible. Please also keep in mind that some browsers can process only a maximum query number at the same time, which naturally limits the performance of your dashboard.
- **Number of acquired versus remote data models**
  If you own a dashboard that connects to a variety of data sources, it matters which data sources you are connecting to. For example, if you could bring your data into an acquired data model that lives within SAP Analytics Cloud itself, the data connection can be significantly faster than if your dashboard needs to connect to a remote data source that lives somewhere else. Hence, the number of acquired versus remote data models provides another measure of how to speed up a dashboard. If you can manage to migrate data from a remote on-premises system to an internal SAP Analytics Cloud model, the performance can significantly increase. You might want to check this with every model that you are using within your dashboard.
- **Number of charts, calculations, images, and others**
  The number of widgets, such as charts, images, tables, filters, as well as the number of calculations performed by the browser, provides another interesting measure for quantifying dashboard performance. The more widgets with different data sources a dashboard contain, the longer it will take to load all the data into the browser. That means that it should be a goal of any dashboard optimization to reduce the number of total widgets that need to be executed in parallel. This can be done, for example, by leveraging the lazy loading capabilities within SAP Analytics Cloud, by splitting up larger pages into smaller subpages, or by combining widgets together to minimize the number of total queries (see above) sent to the backend.
- **Loading time per chart**
  You might wonder how long different chart types could take to load before they display the relevant information to the user. On one hand, this depends on the data size that needs to be retrieved from the backend, and on the other hand you can control the view by setting the right filters from the beginning to select only a subset of the total data. The chart loading time is a quite individual measure and depends on factors such as the network bandwidth, the total number of charts that are loaded in parallel, or the specific filter settings. Measuring the individual loading time per

chart can nevertheless help you to identify the biggest performance killers in your dashboard.

- **Time to interactive**
  The time to interactive is the time that the browser takes to release the user interface to the end user. It is connected to the DOM rendering time but can sometimes slightly differ from it. SAP Analytics Cloud comes with a bunch of performance features that might block the user from continuing to work until some widgets have finished loading. In such cases, it can be that the DOM is already fully rendered, but some JavaScript programs are still waiting for the final signal to release a specific UI element. Then, the users cannot continue their work until the time to interactive has passed.
- **Error rate**
  The error rate measures the percentage of how many requests fail compared to the total number of requests transferred to the backend. Such errors can occur quite often for any reason, and usually it is hard to prevent errors from happening and impossible to predict them. That is why it is important to constantly monitor the error rate and react if anomalies pop up.

In the next section, we discuss what kind of performance goals allow you to connect the above metrics to more concrete performance measures. In Section 2.6, we then present more details on how to practically measure the performance of a dashboard in SAP Analytics Cloud and how the above metrics could be derived using different measurement tools.

2.5 Setting Performance Goals

In the previous section, we defined a bunch of metrics (metrics that measure time, metrics that measure system KPIs, and metrics that measure dashboard-specific KPIs) that allow you to measure the performance of your dashboard. In this section, we will discuss how to set reasonable performance goals—quantitative measures that you would like to achieve with your dashboard. Not all measures will make sense. For example, a goal like "I want to reduce the loading time from 20 seconds to 0 seconds" might not be an appropriate performance goal, since it is quite unlikely that you will be able to achieve it. Your browser takes time to load and display data to the user, and the database needs time to perform certain calculations and to fetch the right data. Hence, we should carefully think about setting the right performance goals.

Let's take the metrics from the previous section and give a few examples to see how we could define reasonable performance goals, knowing that these are in no way the only possible goals you might think of to test your dashboard. We will combine the metrics from our discussion above with the discussion from Section 2.1 about the different performance test types.

Further Reading

A great review of further performance metrics can be found in the following article by Thomas Hamilton: *www.guru99.com/performance-testing.html*.

2.5.1 Performance Goals for Different Test Types

We start with a discussion of different performance goals for the various test types given in Section 2.1. We won't cover all of them here again, but this list should give you a solid overview of what kind of goals would make sense. All times and user numbers given below are artificially chosen to make it clear how to define a meaningful goal. It is likely that those numbers will vary for your specific business situation.

Let's investigate a few examples:

- **Bring total loading time below five seconds when 100 users enter the dashboard**
  As we can see, this is a standard example for a *load test*. We restrict the total loading time of our dashboard to a maximum of five seconds and carefully monitor what happens with the total loading time when more and more users access the dashboard. Afterwards, we could also increase the number of virtual users from 100 to 1,000 (one more order of magnitude) and observe what happens. Are we still able to keep the total loading time below the desired value? Or do we observe an exponential drop in the total loading time? Feel free to arbitrarily adjust your parameters in this case and play around with the numbers.
- **Check that the response time stays below three seconds when one user loads the dashboard**
  This is just another example of an easy *load test*, but this time we only ensure that some basic performance functionalities are guaranteed. A similar test could also be done for any of the different architectural components with SAP Analytics Cloud, as provided in Chapter 1. As discussed previously, a major contribution in the response time is the database execution time, when we assume that the throughput and answer times are small compared to the time the database takes to process a request. That is why we can often safely take the response time as an approximate measure for the database execution time (see our discussion in Section 2.1). Verifying that the response time stays below a critical value of three seconds (just as an example) ensures that the user observes that the dashboard continues to load and that it is now just a matter of time until all content is downloaded from the server. We will mainly focus on this test type in the book.
- **Check the maximum number of users that the dashboard can handle before it crashes**
  This is a nice example of a *breakpoint test*, as was described in Section 2.1. We slowly increase the number of virtual users and observe what happens to the performance

of the application. At some point you may observe that the dashboard becomes slower, which is a good sign that you will soon reach the desired breakpoint (or at least the point where loading the application gets so slow that it does not make sense anymore to wait for it). You might also want to define a threshold where you would say that waiting for the dashboard to load is not acceptable anymore (e.g., when the loading time exceeds ten or twenty seconds).

- **Check that the total loading time stays below five seconds when the response size exceeds 100 MB**
  This is an example for a *volume test*. Imagine you have created a dashboard with big data models in the background, and some users set their filters in a way that the database needs to do some calculations and sends back larger data slices (that could be larger than 100MB, for example). In such a case you don't want the total loading time to exceed a specific threshold value, let's assume five seconds for the moment. Of course, you could also try to increase the response sizes and see how the system reacts to this. In this case you will get a feeling for how big the response can be that your dashboard can still be run in a nice and user-friendly way.
- **Ensure that CPU load does not exceed 30% when a dashboard is loaded for the first time**
  Once you open your SAP Analytics Cloud dashboard you will observe that the CPU load of your local computer will increase. Depending on the number and type of widgets you may observe a higher or lower increase of CPU power needed to render the dashboard. In this case, you could define a threshold for your CPU that should not be exceeded, for example 30%. This is a *scalability test* that helps you to find out how much computational load you can put on the user's machine. Naturally, SAP Analytics Cloud comes with a standard computational load when you open an application that is not adjustable. However, this basic load needs to be added on top of the dashboard load that you generate by adding widgets to the screen.

2.5.2 Performance Goals for Different Metrics

In the following list, we provide a few more examples for performance goals for metrics that we defined in Section 2.4. Again, we won't cover all of them, but instead will give a solid overview of how to set a meaningful metric goal. Again, like above, all numbers given are arbitrarily chosen and do not match any system status because those numbers are likely to vary from business to business.

Here are a few examples:

- **Ensure that the loading time per chart lies below two seconds**
  Keeping the loading time of a chart as low as possible sometimes requires a few tricks that need to be applied. Use the filter capabilities within the tool to restrict yourself to a specific data slice, instead of loading tons of data into the dashboard. Furthermore, there are a few chart types that we can recommend because they load

faster than others; more details will be given later in the corresponding chapter about how to build efficient SAP Analytics Cloud stories (Chapter 3).

- **Verify that the total amount of data that gets downloaded does not exceed 200 MB**
  Every time the user switches to another story page, for example, there is an amount of new data that needs to be downloaded from the server. Although we recommend using as much caching as possible and that you let the dashboard change as little as possible, we won't come around to the fact that some data might require an update or that completely new data needs to be displayed. In that case, you might ensure that no more than, for example, 200 MB of data are transferred from the backend to the frontend after every action triggered by the user. Try to let any views change as little as possible. Don't download tons of new images all the time. This will save you time that would be wasted otherwise.
- **Check that the DOM rendering time is below three seconds**
  As discussed above, the DOM rendering time is the time that the browser needs to properly display content on the screen to the user. Meanwhile, SAP Analytics Cloud interacts with the user to provide some information on the loading status, and unless a dashboard has not fully been loaded, it won't release the user interface. Ensuring that the DOM rendering time lies below a threshold of, e.g., three seconds is important to keep users on track with their tasks. Furthermore, the DOM rendering time gives a good overview of the heaviness of the implemented calculations that are performed in the frontend. That's why it is always a good idea to check if certain calculations should not be done in the backend or at the model level directly.
- **Verify that the loading time of remote models is at maximum 20 percent above the value for acquired models**
  With this condition we can ensure that the loading time for remote models is significantly lower than the time that it would take a comparable acquired model to load the same data into your SAP Analytics Cloud dashboard. Usually, SAP Analytics Cloud operates faster when using data coming from built-in models in the cloud. That is why you might check if things can be sped up when moving from a backend model to an SAP Analytics Cloud native model that directly lives in the cloud system. However, this makes sense only if the gain in performance is at least 20 percent. Otherwise, you might just waste your time in moving data from A to B without any larger effect.

2.6 Measuring Performance and System Key Performance Indicators

In the previous sections, we defined a bunch of metrics and discussed different performance goals. Now we come to the critical point of how to measure and track the performance of a web application such as an SAP Analytics Cloud dashboard.

There are many different tools on the market that can be used to gain insights into different performance metrics. In the following, we will introduce a few well-known and common web tools that are free for use and can be easily installed on any computer.

Since SAP recommends running SAP Analytics Cloud in Google Chrome, we will primarily focus on this browser. However, SAP Analytics Cloud can also be executed in other web browsers, such as Microsoft Edge, for example. The general principles that we are going to highlight below hold for any browser.

For the experiments covered in this section, we are using a dashboard created within SAP Analytics Cloud that contains ten charts, one table, various filters, and a few self-scripted UI elements. However, the details of the dashboard itself do not really matter here since we are only interested in how the recording tools work in general. Thus, all experiments can be easily extended to other dashboards as well.

2.6.1 Measuring Performance Using Chrome DevTools

The Google Chrome browser comes by default with a great performance measurement tool, which can be found in the Chrome DevTools window. First, you need to install the standard Google Chrome browser on your computer (which can be easily found on the web at *www.google.com/intl/en/chrome/*).

Afterwards, you have different possibilities for opening Chrome DevTools. First, open Google Chrome and navigate to the page (or SAP Analytics Cloud dashboard) where you want to do some initial performance measurements. Next, you can take two routes:

- In the property's menu, click on **More Tools** and then select **Developer Tools**.
- On the target web page, press `Ctrl` + `Shift` + `I`.

In both cases, the Chrome DevTools window will open, which looks like the one in Figure 2.5. Let's briefly talk about the different tabs that are visible. When the window opens for the first time, we see the HTML inspection tab (called **Elements**) that allows you to analyze the whole DOM structure of your page. At the very bottom, a console shows up for inserting some code directly into the environment (for example, JavaScript code). We won't go into the developer details here, nor will we show how standard HTML pages are set up. If you are interested in gaining more information about this, we refer you to standard textbooks about HTML and JavaScript coding.

Next, we click on the **Performance** tab at the top. This is now the proper environment where we can capture our first performance snapshot. To record and then analyze the performance of a dashboard, we need to load the full page first, creating a recording of the total page load.

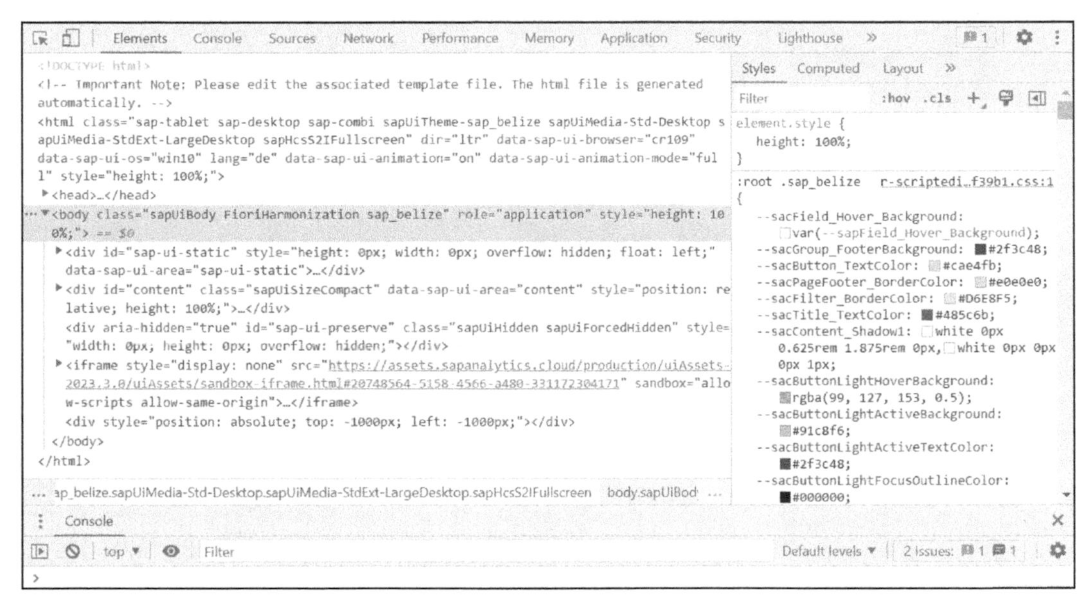

Figure 2.5 Chrome DevTools after Installing the Google Chrome Browser

> **A Note on Browser Caching**
>
> Once you reload a web page, your web browser checks the browser's cache first to see if there is data that can be used to load the page quickly. These caching mechanisms, however, disturb your proper performance measurements. Thus, we always recommend that you first empty your cache before you start new measurements. To do so, open Chrome, and on the top right side click **More (...)**, select **More tools**, and clear your browsing data. That way you can clear your cache and start a proper measurement.

You should now do the following steps:

1. Click on the recording icon (the black circle on the top left corner of the window) or press `Ctrl` + `E`. The UI will now tell you that it is capturing a profile of the web page.
2. Immediately after this, reload or load your SAP Analytics Cloud dashboard. While loading, the performance tool listens to the network traffic and tracks all relevant KPIs and measures in parallel.
3. When you think that the dashboard has fully been loaded, go back to the performance tracking tool and click on **Stop** (it's the same button that in the meantime turned red).
4. Finally, Google Chrome automatically creates a detailed performance report for us, which might look like the one shown in Figure 2.6.

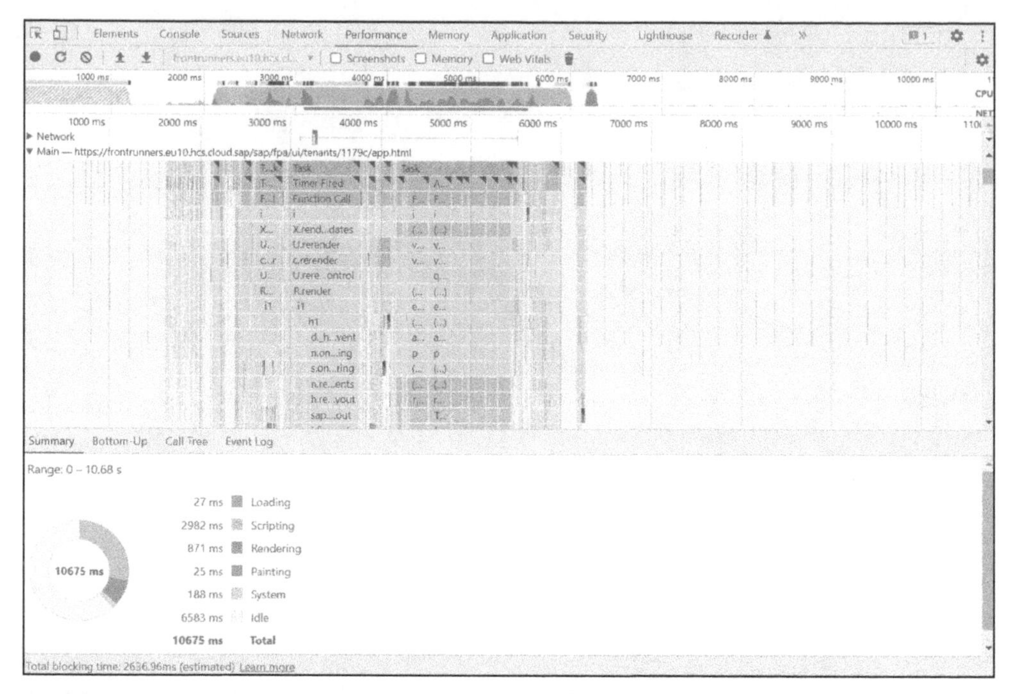

Figure 2.6 Full Performance Report within Chrome DevTools

Let's investigate the results shown in Figure 2.6 in more detail. On first view, this seems to be a very colorful and crowded diagram, but it is quite easy to interpret. What you can see are a CPU breakdown over time, the network traffic, a CPU flame chart, and a CPU summary report.

Let's first look at the chart at the bottom of Figure 2.6, which provides a summary of the CPU activities. In our case, the total recording time was around 10.7 seconds, where 3.0 seconds were occupied by running scripts, and 0.9 seconds went into the DOM rendering of the dashboard elements. These are the biggest time buckets. The idle time of roughly 6.6 seconds means that this was pure waiting time for the performance tool where nothing happened. This could be, for example, the time in between pressing the record button and then clicking the reload button within the browser, and the same at the end, when the page was fully loaded, but the recording did not stop yet. All other pieces (painting, loading, and the system time) are rather negligible compared to the other categories.

Important Note

We note that these numbers strongly depend on the individual computation power from the user and can hardly be compared to other absolute numbers that people might have recorded. A slower computer might lead to slightly larger time values, while a better machine could perform these computations and load the dashboard much faster. In our case, we were using a Lenovo ThinkPad X1, 6. Generation, Intel Core i7, 512GB-SSD, 16GB, 3.0 GHz.

If you really want to compare numbers, you should capture the performance trace before and after the optimizations on the same machine. The relative difference then gives you a good indicator of how much better the performance has become (for example, you could then claim that the rendering time decreased by roughly 20 percent).

A similar but connected view on the CPU activities that happened over time are given at the very top of the Chrome DevTools window. Here, you can see how the different times (loading, scripting, rendering, etc.) are distributed over the whole capturing process and where peak loads occurred.

The CPU flame chart in the middle of the screen is a bit more involved. It basically shows a very detailed breakdown of which scripts were executed at which time and how long it took your computer to finish the computations for them. Feel free to play around with the flame chart as well.

The only information that we have about the response time (and thus also the time that the backend took to send an answer) is shown in the network traffic lane. The network traffic lane provides a numbering on how long the total performance recording took (these are the number descriptions given at the top of the lane). Small task bars with the label **GetResponse** indicate that, during this time, the frontend was waiting for an answer from the backend. In our example, when we sum all network traffic contributions, it took approximately one second until the backend provided the necessary information.

Unveiling the CPU Flame Chart

A few more sentences about the CPU flame chart. The flame chart basically gives a nice and structured view of the hierarchy of scripts that were executed during the recording time. This hierarchy can be arbitrarily complex, as you can see in Figure 2.6. You can also drill down to lower-hierarchy script levels if you want to find out which code lines caused which performance contributions. Everything is measured at any time. If you click on one of the small bars, you can even jump to the corresponding script lines of the JavaScript code. Everything is possible here. This is typically how software developers work when they analyze the performance of a web page, which means they drill down very deep into the software code to find the performance bottlenecks in this way.

Further Reading on Chrome DevTools

If you want to read more about Chrome DevTools, we recommend reading the following online resources about how to best use and leverage the performance tool:

- Chrome Developers, "Chrome DevTools," available at *https://developer.chrome.com/docs/devtools/*
- DebugBear, "Profile Site Speed With The DevTools Performance Tab," available at *www.debugbear.com/blog/devtools-performance*
- Jordan Irabor, "How to Use Chrome Dev Tools to Find Performance Bottlenecks," available at *http://s-prs.co/v566932*

2.6.2 Measuring Network Traffic Using Chrome DevTools

Another tool that can be easily used to record network traffic is the corresponding "Network" tool within Chrome DevTools widget. To create a network recording, just follow the same steps a described above when using the performance tool:

1. Click on the recording icon, or press Ctrl + E. The tool will now start to create a network recording.
2. Now reload or load your SAP Analytics Cloud dashboard again. While loading, the network tool listens to the network traffic and tracks all relevant KPIs.
3. When you think the web page has finished loading, press the stop recording icon.

The result could look like the one shown in Figure 2.7. What you can see here is a full list of items that were downloaded from the server. This can be either JavaScript or CSS files, images, fonts, or media files. You can filter for each of them by just clicking on the corresponding buttons in the third row of the window to see what files have been downloaded and when.

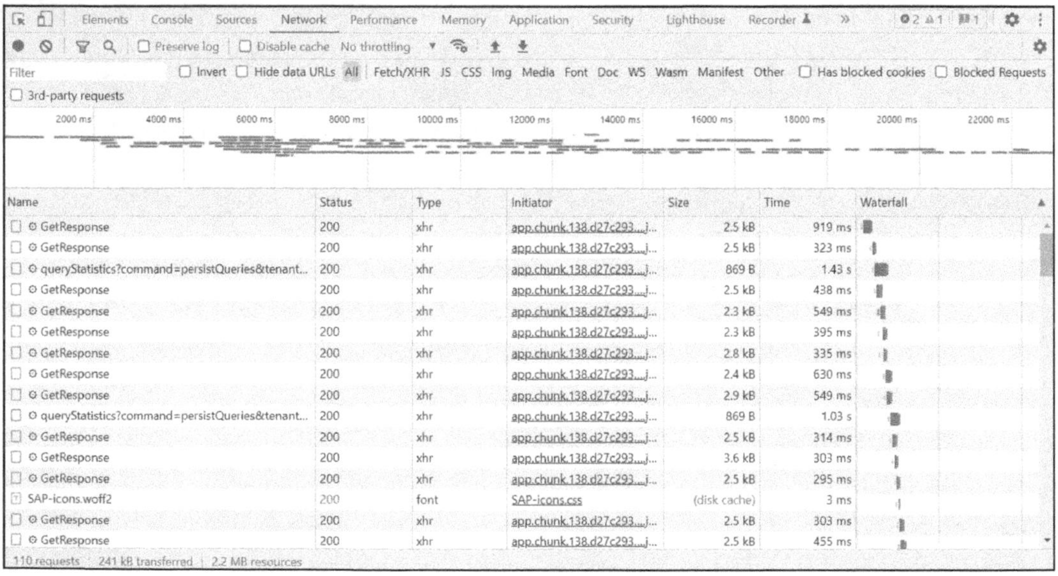

Figure 2.7 Network Report within Chrome DevTools

Below, you can see a full history of the network traffic and how it is composed: either waiting time for servers, download time, or other sources. You can go into further details of this timeline by selecting the corresponding range with your mouse. The tool will then filter only in this time frame. This provides a nice and easy way to check all content that has been downloaded from the server.

2.6.3 Measuring Memory Consumption Using Chrome DevTools

In this section, we want to discuss how the memory consumption of a dashboard can be analyzed. To do this, we again follow the same instructions given above and click on **Memory** in the Chrome DevTools window. To create a memory heap snapshot, we do the following:

1. Click on the recording icon. The tool will now start to create a memory heap snapshot.
2. Again, reload or load your SAP Analytics Cloud dashboard. While loading, the tool listens to the network traffic and tracks all content that got downloaded.
3. When you think the dashboard has fully loaded, press the stop recording icon.

The result could look like the one shown in Figure 2.8. We observe a list that we sorted by the size of the retrieved data. You can now start analyzing the different memory contributions of the web page. For example, we see that the biggest amount of data that was downloaded from the server is the compiled code with 26 percent of shallow and 29 percent of retained size of all downloaded data.

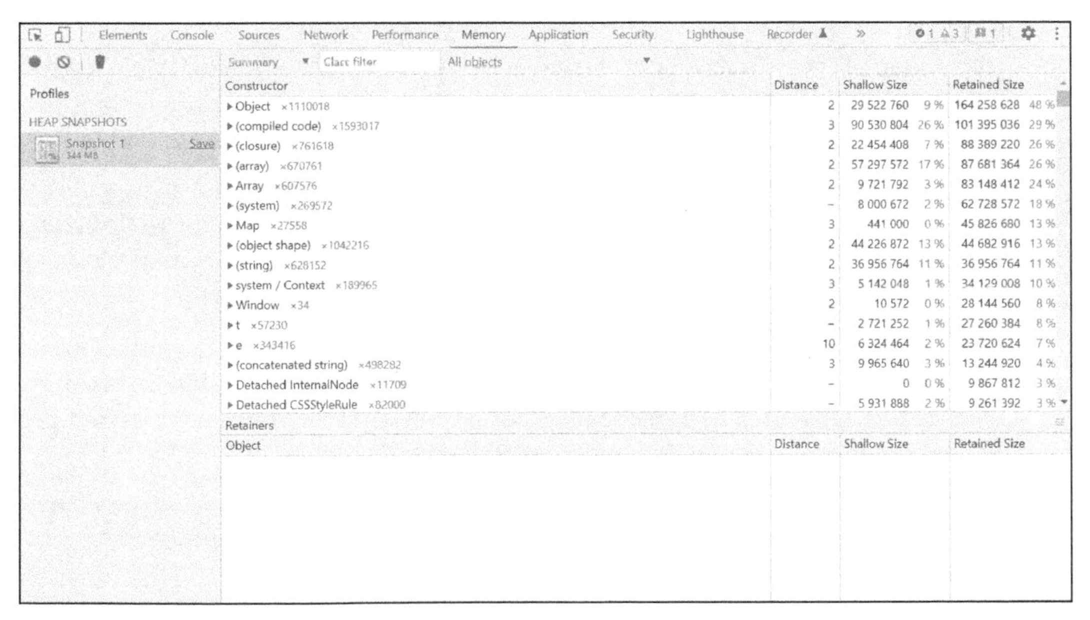

Constructor	Distance	Shallow Size		Retained Size	
▸ Object ×1110018	2	29 522 760	9 %	164 258 628	48 %
▸ (compiled code) ×1593017	3	90 530 804	26 %	101 395 036	29 %
▸ (closure) ×761618	2	22 454 408	7 %	88 389 220	26 %
▸ (array) ×670761	2	57 297 572	17 %	87 681 364	26 %
▸ Array ×607576	2	9 721 792	3 %	83 148 412	24 %
▸ (system) ×269572	–	8 000 672	2 %	62 728 572	18 %
▸ Map ×27558	3	441 000	0 %	45 826 680	13 %
▸ (object shape) ×1042216	2	44 226 872	13 %	44 682 916	13 %
▸ (string) ×628152	2	36 956 764	11 %	36 956 764	11 %
▸ system / Context ×189965	3	5 142 048	1 %	34 129 008	10 %
▸ Window ×34	2	10 572	0 %	28 144 560	8 %
▸ t ×57230	–	2 721 252	1 %	27 260 384	8 %
▸ e ×343416	10	6 324 464	2 %	23 720 624	7 %
▸ (concatenated string) ×498282	3	9 965 640	3 %	13 244 920	4 %
▸ Detached InternalNode ×11709	–	0	0 %	9 867 812	3 %
▸ Detached CSSStyleRule ×82000	–	5 931 888	2 %	9 261 392	3 %

Figure 2.8 Memory Heap Snapshot within Chrome DevTools

Shallow versus Retained Size

You might wonder what the difference is between the shallow and the retained size of an object. This can be easily understood: The shallow size is the size of an object that is allocated to store only the object itself. This distinguishes it from the retained size, since objects could also have references to other objects accessible from this one, and the retained size would also count the size of the referenced objects.

You now can also drill down into the different object classes and gain further information on the biggest memory contributions from this dashboard. However, note that the list of sub objects downloaded can be very large, since SAP Analytics Cloud is a highly complex application that requires a lot of objects to be downloaded into the browser.

This concludes our discussion of the most important performance measurement features in Chrome DevTools. These are mostly tools that are frequently used by experienced developers. We recommend regularly involving software engineers to help track those metrics.

2.6.4 Measuring CPU Consumption

There are other important metrics that one should have under control when talking about optimizing the dashboard performance. First and foremost, CPU consumption is another important metric that should not be underestimated. In the following, we will show how to measure the CPU consumption of your dashboard by utilizing standard onboard tools of your operating system.

If you want to measure the CPU load under Microsoft Windows, you first need to open the task manager. To do this, you can either press `Ctrl` + `Alt` + `Delete` or right-click on the Windows button at the bottom left corner and select **Task Manager**.

Next, the task manager window will open, which looks like the one shown in Figure 2.9. To measure the CPU load, you again refresh your SAP Analytics Cloud dashboard and track the CPU loading status in the task manager. The screenshot shown in Figure 2.9 was captured at a time when the dashboard had finished loading.

You can also see how the CPU load evolved over time to determine the peak load, for example. Furthermore, the tool also allows you to analyze the history of RAM and other interesting properties. Feel free to play around with it while loading your dashboard solutions.

If you are not using a Windows machine but rather a Mac, you will get a slightly different window, which, however, shows the same measures and plots as Windows. To open the activity monitor on a Mac, open the Spotlight search and type "Activity monitoring." The tool that you will get will look like the one shown in Figure 2.10. By clicking on the tabs on the top right side of the window, you can go deeper into system properties like RAM, energy, and so on.

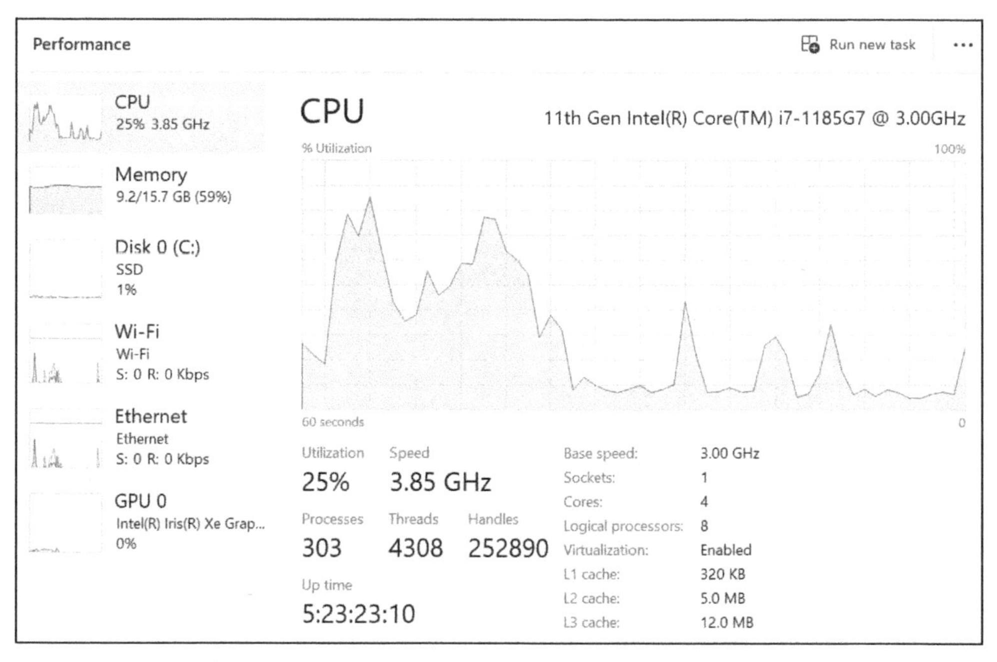

Figure 2.9 Screenshot Created While Loading a Dashboard within SAP Analytics Cloud

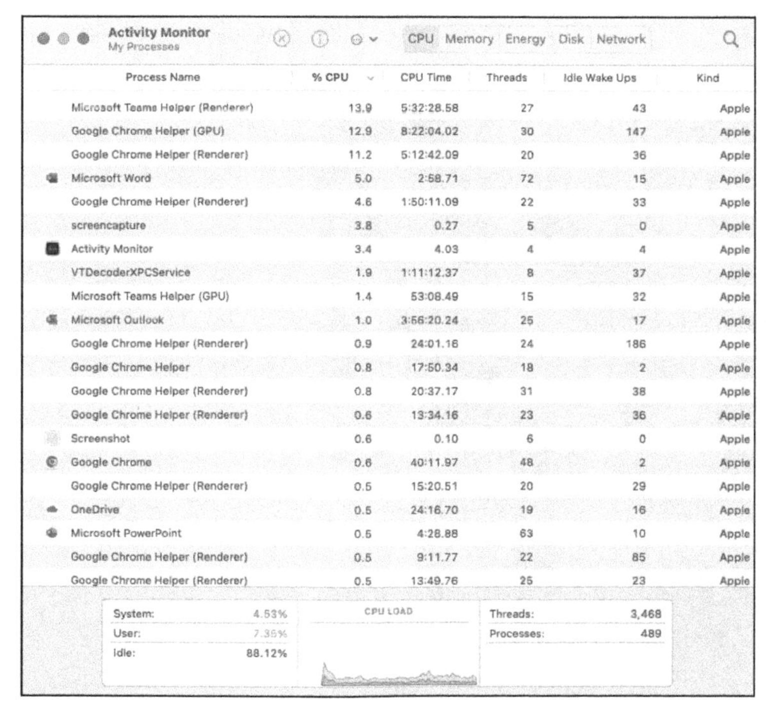

Figure 2.10 Activity Monitoring Tool on a Mac

Other CPU Monitoring Tools

There are a bunch of other great CPU monitoring tools that you can use to check for your CPU activities. Unfortunately, not all of them are free, but you may find your favorite one under them:

- HWMonitor (for Windows), *www.cpuid.com/softwares/hwmonitor.html*
- GeekBench (for Winows, Mac, and Linux), *www.geekbench.com/*
- CoreTemp (Windows only, for measuring CPU temperatures), *www.alcpu.com/CoreTemp/*
- OpManager, *www.manageengine.com/de/network-monitoring/cpu-monitoring.html*

2.6.5 Measuring Network Bandwidth

We also talked about measuring the network bandwidth, which is an important measure to ensure a maximally performing dashboard. If the network bandwidth is too low, loading a dashboard can take a very long time since the amount of data that needs to be downloaded can sometimes easily exceed 100 MB. That is why you should at least know how good (or bad) your internet connection is.

There are several ways to measure the network bandwidth, but the most straightforward one is probably by using an online measurement tool. There are thousands of such tools; we present just one example of a tool that is quite commonly used.

To use it, open a browser and navigate to *www.speedtest.net*. You will see a screen that looks like the one shown in Figure 2.11.

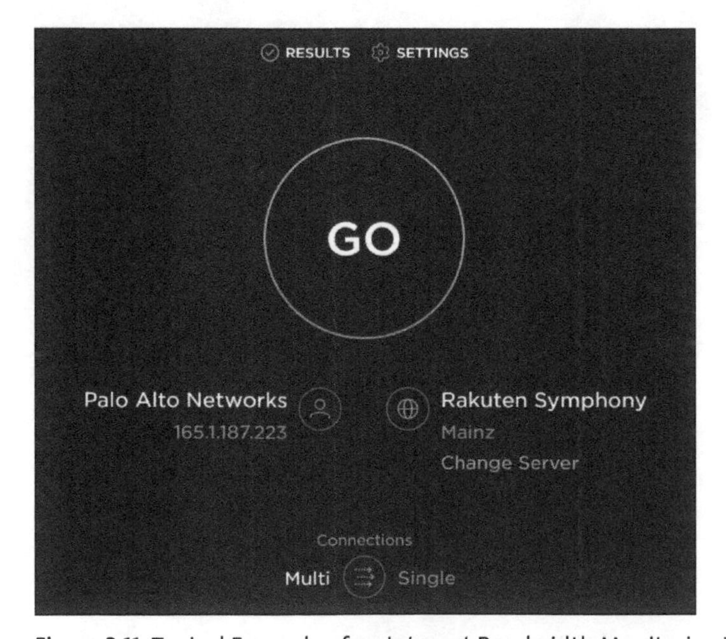

Figure 2.11 Typical Example of an Internet Bandwidth Monitoring Tool

Before you start a measurement, you should ensure that no other bandwidth-demanding processes are running either on your machine or in your local internet. Those processes can significantly influence and disturb your measurements. Thus, before moving on, just close all network-demanding tools in your local network.

Network Demanding Tools

In today's times, one can hardly believe how many tools on a computer try to connect to the internet on a regular basis. You should identify those before your measurement starts and close all of them (or at least limit the number of programs that can disturb your measurement). A good indicator for the network traffic on your local machine is the Windows task manager, or correspondingly Mac's activity monitoring tool (refer back to Figure 2.9.) There you can see which apps require the most network traffic. Just click on the **Network** tab and look for those tools that eat up a lot of traffic.

However, there might be other sources in your local network as well that limit the amount of traffic. In the following, we give a few common examples. Look out for those devices, apps, or processes that can heavily influence your bandwidth measurements:

- Windows or Mac auto system updates (which silently download new software in the background)
- Mobile phones connected to the internet via Wi-Fi (and download new software in the background)
- Printers, scanners, game consoles, and other devises that can go online
- Generally, all Internet of Things (IoT) devices (e.g., robot vacuum cleaners, cars, controllers, etc.)

Having done all the preparation work, we can now start the bandwidth measurement by clicking the **Go** button. The measurement might take a few seconds until the browser is connected to the right server stations available in your neighborhood. The resulting report might look like the one shown in Figure 2.12.

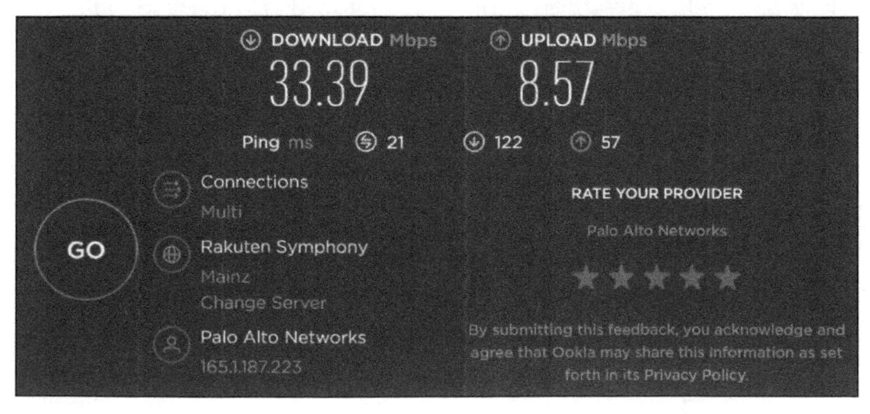

Figure 2.12 The Results of Our Speed Test

In our case, we measured a total download rate of 33.39 Mbps and a total upload rate of 8.57 Mbps (we agree that the numbers the authors measured here are not very convincing compared to today's available speed options).

Required Download Rates for SAP Analytics Cloud

You might wonder which download (and upload) rates you should come up with to properly run an SAP Analytics Cloud dashboard. Well, this is not easy to answer because it generally depends on how much data you need to load into the browser.

In Section 2.6.2 and Section 2.6.3, we described a way to measure the network traffic and memory consumption of your SAP Analytics Cloud dashboard. These numbers can give you a rough estimate of the amount of data the application consumes. When loading only the basic components in SAP Analytics Cloud, you can expect a total memory load of approximately 150 MB that the application needs to download from the servers to your browser (at least that was the consumption at the end of 2022).

This means that everything you build into your dashboard and all the data you want to fetch from your database is on top of that. This can easily result in a total download size of >200 MB when a user opens the dashboard for the first time.

Given a download rate of roughly 33 Mbps (as measured above), this will result in a pure download time of > 4 seconds for the basic SAP Analytics Cloud components (the processing time afterwards is further added) and even higher when opening a dashboard containing more data.

However, the authors hope that no readers have such a bad download rate, which means that things should speed up significantly because the total loading time won't get hung up by the pure download time of system components.

2.6.6 Measuring Dashboard Performance Using Onboard Analysis Tools

There are further possibilities to leverage onboard functionalities within SAP Analytics Cloud that allow you to analyze and track the performance of a dashboard. These onboard analysis tools will be described in more detail together with the tool itself in the corresponding chapters:

- **Performance analysis tool for stories**
  This tool will be described in Chapter 3 when we talk about optimizing the performance within the story building process.
- **Performance analysis tool for the application designer**
  This tool will be described in Chapter 4 when we talk about optimizing the performance within the application designer.

2.7 Creating Benchmark Tests

In this section, we take all the ingredients that we have learned so far in this chapter and bring them together in a so-called benchmark test. A benchmark test is nothing else than a standard development process for software deliveries that relies on several assumptions.

For example, we could say that the expectation of a bicycle racer to complete a course (e.g., the Tour de France) must lie below a certain time value. A benchmark test helps to assess the performance (or productivity) of an application; it's a quality tool that should be applied during every software development process. We assume that every benchmark test is repeatable (i.e., it can be run every time) and quantifiable (i.e., we can choose specific numeric measures as a benchmark).

2.7.1 Prerequisites of a Benchmark Test

Why do we perform benchmark tests? Ultimately, we want to get an idea of how well or badly an application is performing. For example, we could benchmark an SAP Analytics Cloud dashboard against another one and compare different metrics against each other. This way we can ensure that we get the most out of our performance optimizations. However, we first need to guarantee a few simple things, as listed in the following:

- **Test types were identified (Section 2.1)**
  The test types were identified based on knowledge about the performance bottleneck issues.
- **Performance changes are finished (Section 2.2)**
  The test can start only once all performance changes are finished and applied to the system.
- **Performance testing process was set up (Section 2.3)**
  The performance testing process was understood and can be applied.
- **Metrics have been defined (Section 2.4)**
  The metrics that will be tested have been defined.
- **Goals have been defined (Section 2.5)**
  The goals against which we will measure have been clearly defined and are specific, measurable, achievable, relevant, and time-bound (SMART).
- **Test tools for measuring were prepared (Section 2.6)**
  The test tools that will be used to measure various KPIs are ready to use and prepared.

Next, we will go through the different steps of a benchmark test and learn how all the things from our previous sections finally come together.

2.7.2 Phases of a Benchmark Test

The phases of a benchmark test are illustrated in Figure 2.13. They can be divided into four phases: planning, analysis, integration, and action.

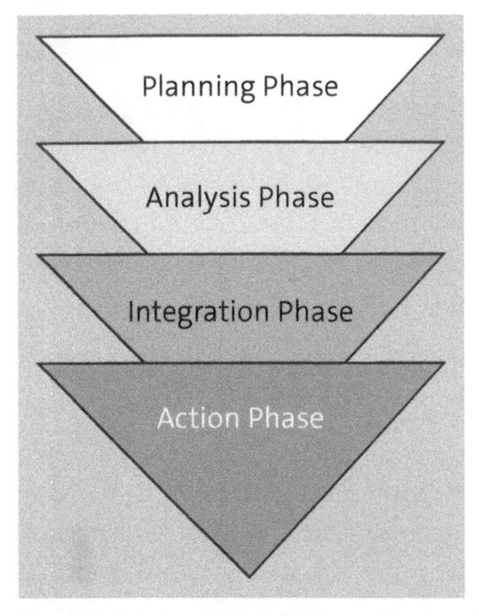

Figure 2.13 The Typical Phases of a Performance Benchmark Test

Let's discuss these phases individually:

- **Planning phase**
  In the planning phase, we identify standards and set requirements for the later stages. That means we define what to benchmark and when. Our metrics and goals were defined and test tools were prepared. This is a crucial phase that deserves a lot of attention because if things go wrong later, this might be related to insufficient preparation during this first phase. All actionable stakeholders should be involved early on to clarify responsibilities.

  Example: An SAP Analytics Cloud dashboard will be benchmarked. We define all stakeholders involved in the process and set clear expectations on what to achieve and by when and by whom. The test process is discussed.

- **Analysis phase**
  In the analysis phase, we run our tests and check for errors that might come up to improve quality. Data is collected that can be analyzed. A root cause analysis will be run to identify performance bottleneck problems. This is the execution phase in which we use our test framework together with our performance testing process.

  Example: We run several performance tests and measure them against our goals to identify bottlenecks in our SAP Analytics Cloud dashboard.

- **Integration phase**
  In the integration phase, we collect all information gathered in the analysis phase and share it with our stakeholders. Possible actions will be defined. The integration phase marks the consolidation phase between the analysis and the action phase. We are trying to get approval for follow-up activities to improve the quality of our dashboard.

  Example: We decided on an action plan to further observe our dashboard performance on a weekly basis to ensure that our goals are kept in the future.

- **Action phase**
  In the action phase, we start implementing all changes discussed in the integration phase. It needs to be ensured that changes have the right effect on the dashboard performance, for example. Actions need to be monitored; documentation should be created based on our findings. The progress of our efforts will be continuously checked.

  Example: We realign the chart and model structure of our SAP Analytics Cloud dashboard that has been identified as the largest performance bottleneck. Developers will set up an acquired model and feed the data into it. Afterwards, we will start the benchmark test again and measure against potentially new goals.

Going through these individual benchmark phases allows you and your company to improve on your dashboard quality to create a successful SAP Analytics Cloud dashboard. On first view, these steps seem to be a bit bureaucratic, but we assure you that things will pay off later when such a structured approach has been followed.

2.8 SAP Analytics Cloud Performance Equation

During this chapter, we have learned that optimizing performance requires some in-depth technical knowledge. Things can get complicated very quickly, and thus we rely on the help of many different stakeholders so that we can succeed.

Getting performance issues under control also means understanding many different technical layers of an application, from the frontend to the backend. Typically, there isn't only one performance bottleneck in an application. Instead, we must try to understand the whole system holistically. That means that we cannot simply optimize our SAP Analytics Cloud story alone and expect that from now on the whole performance will be great; nor can we expect this from considering only the backend part.

What needs to be done is that we must analyze all technical components of a dashboard individually. This is what this whole book is all about. Analyzing many kinds of contributions means that we need to discuss all components separately, and we will do this in the remaining part of the book.

Thus, we can ask whether we can (at least conceptionally) write down an SAP Analytics Cloud performance equation that relates the total loading time (which we identified as our key performance measure) to the sub times spent for going through the different technical layers. This is what we want to do in the following.

Throughout this and the previous chapter, we have already learned where time can get lost, in both the frontend and the backend. Conceptionally, we already discussed a similar time equation in Section 2.4, when we defined our metrics that measure different times. In this section, we will build on this, but break our previous equation down to the SAP Analytics Cloud case.

The SAP Analytics Cloud Performance Equation

The SAP Analytics Cloud performance equation is basically a sum over all time contributions that add up to the total loading time of a dashboard application:

Δ Performance optimization= Σ all individual optimization contributions

= Optimizations within the story (Chapter 3)

+ Optimizations within Analytics Designer (Chapter 4)

+ Optimizations within the data models (Chapter 5)

+ Optimizations within the backend and the tenant (Chapter 6)

+ Optimizations on the viewer side (Chapter 7)

As we can see, the total performance optimization consists of a sum of individual optimization contributions throughout the whole end-to-end loading process. We also provided the corresponding chapter numbers next to the different contributions so that you can see where the relevant content is discussed in the book.

In total, we can identify five areas where performance optimizations could be applied:

- **Optimizations within the story**
  This is probably the most important and biggest source where performance optimizations could become effective. Within a story you have many possibilities to optimize your dashboard directly. This could be either the story design, together with the use of calculations, filters, and Linked Analysis, or if you just want to optimize the mobile experience of your dashboard. Chapter 3 takes a broad view on how to optimize your SAP Analytics Cloud stories.
- **Optimizations within the analytics designer**
  Analytics designer can be used to build application widgets and use scripting possibilities with JavaScript to enhance a dashboard with more customized widgets. There are a few general settings that you should keep in mind when building your own widgets. Furthermore, we also show how to optimize the application structure and increase the performance for scripts. Chapter 4 takes you through this exciting journey within the analytics designer.

- **Optimizations within data models**
  Another very important source of bad performance is the data model. You should carefully think about which models you use, their data structures, and where they live. Chapter 5 takes up these ideas and walks you through different scenarios on how to build a proper and high-performing data model structure. We briefly discuss the optimizations of remote models and data sources, although we also recommend reading the corresponding literature on these topics separately.
- **Optimizations within the backend and the tenant**
  Backend and tenant settings often can (when incorrectly set) significantly slow down the performance of a dashboard. We will give you a few insights into what settings you can influence and what the impact will be. For example, when you are an administrator, you might think about optimizing the backend data storage connection or simply choose the correct system configuration settings. Chapter 6 will guide you through this content.
- **Optimizations on the viewer side**
  This clearly is one of the most underestimated categories when it comes to optimizing the dashboard performance. We have already discussed the impact of things like bad network bandwidth and old computers with low CPU power on the performance. As you can imagine, there are more sources on how the viewer can positively contribute to a great dashboard performance. Chapter 7 is dedicated only to the viewer choices and what impact they can have on performance.

Further Reading on Performance Optimization

This book is dedicated to optimizing the performance of SAP Analytics Cloud dashboards. However, there might be other reasons why a dashboard can become terribly slow, such as when the data source in the backend is not correctly set up. Due to several constraints, we cannot discuss all possible backends and their model optimizations in this book. Nevertheless, you might also want to consult other sources on how to optimize, for example, the model performance, be it a simple SAP HANA view, an SAP BW backend, or something else. SAP PRESS offers a great number of books that go into details on this topic and that discuss performance optimizations from different angles. You can find specific recommendations in Appendix A.

2.9 Ten Golden Rules for Efficient SAP Analytics Cloud Dashboards

As a summary of this book, we have created a comprehensive list of ten golden rules that every dashboard builder can apply to check if a dashboard operates at maximum performance. The rules can be understood as a chain of subsequent actions and proposals, ranging from the backend through the modeler to the frontend. Here are our key rules, also illustrated in Figure 2.14:

❶ **Tenant and backend: Optimize settings in the background.**
This rule asks you to think about performance optimization in the backend and the tenant itself, including data connection–specific settings for, e.g., SAP BW live connections and SAP HANA live connections. Finally, the system configuration settings cover different settings as a tenant administrator, personal settings for each story as well as for queries. You might also need further literature depending on your SAP backend system. References to other books are provided in the corresponding chapters.

❷ **Data manipulation: Do aggregations and calculations early.**
This rule is about the data itself. Very often, complicated calculations are performed to aggregate data up to the top-level node. However, such aggregations, especially when done during runtime, can eat up a lot of computer resources. Therefore, it is important to think about how such reoccurring computations could be outsourced and performed beforehand. It also includes other data manipulation tasks, such as blending of different models, where you might want to bring data from various data sources together before you start building the dashboard.

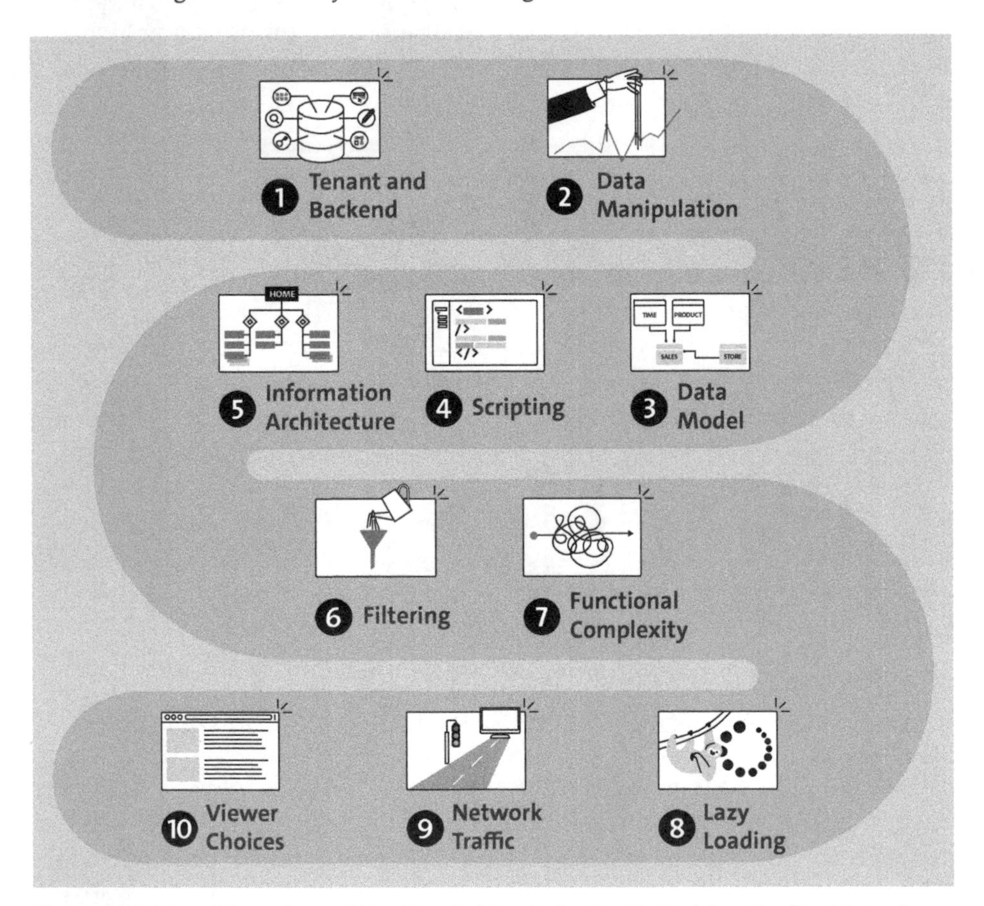

Figure 2.14 Visual Overview of Our Ten Golden Rules for Optimizing the Dashboard Performance

❸ **Data model: Pick the appropriate model type and settings.**
Finally, it is time to build the correct data model. An incorrect and bad data model can crash the best dashboard performance. This rule should be reviewed together with the previous rule about getting the right data into the model by performing aggregations and calculations early. Remove redundant and unnecessary dimensions and think about using an analytical instead of a planning model. If planning models are needed, you should optimize them in the most efficient way.

❹ **Scripting: Write your own code in an efficient manner.**
Generally, we advise leveraging as many of the onboard features SAP Analytics Cloud provides as possible. However, there might be special situations in which you cannot get around own scripts that can be written in different languages, such as JavaScript or R. In these situations, you need to be aware that scripts might generally slow down your dashboard performance and hold users up from completing their tasks. It all depends on your scripts. While short and easy script might even improve the dashboard performance, heavy calculations can significantly slow down the loading time. Think about optimizing your scripts if they are really needed.

❺ **Information architecture: Reduce the number of charts, pages, and images.**
Generally, this is one of the most obvious rules to follow in this book, and it seems almost stupid to talk about it. But we have seen so many examples of bad dashboards in the past that neglect these simple steps that we think this deserves its own rule. The overall information architecture plays a crucial role. What information do you really need to see? Are all charts relevant to be seen at once? Do you need so many pages in just one story? Splitting up content into different sections, like when splitting up a story into substories can help to improve the performance. And every widget that you display on the dashboard needs to be loaded, be it a chart, or an image. Images in particular can require long loading times when they are too big. Think about the most critical information first and then decide whether and how to incorporate it into your dashboard.

❻ **Filtering: Limit the information shown on the dashboard.**
Very often, too much information is displayed on the dashboard at once. However, this can create problems regarding the performance because all the data needs to be loaded in parallel. The important question that you should ask is whether all this data needs to be visible directly on the first view to the dashboard viewer or whether it is enough to first load the dashboard structure itself and then give the user the chance to pick the most relevant information for himself by applying a story or page filter. By using the filtering techniques in SAP Analytics Cloud, you can easily restrict any view to the most relevant information. Try to use filters as much as you can.

❼ **Functional complexity: Keep the dashboard as simple as possible.**
The functional complexity of a dashboard is related to the information architecture as well but goes deeper into its functional components. When a dashboard is not correctly set up, complexity can create long loading times. For example, applying

too many styling rules in a table can cause the OLAP engine of SAP Analytics Cloud to perform unnecessary computations. Also avoid any redundant resizing of widgets and reduce the number of data-related widgets that are linked together. Keep the dashboard as simple as possible.

❽ **Lazy loading: Only load information when needed.**
Another important method that many dashboard creators are not fully aware of is the capabilities of lazy loading content in the background. When a dashboard pops up on the screen, this does not mean that it has already finished loading. Instead, you might want to use the focus time of the user to continue bringing in more data into the dashboard in the background. SAP Analytics Cloud already handles a lot of this automatically, but you can contribute to it by, e.g., using progressive chart rendering or by delaying loading of your charts. Generally, the basic rule is to load information only when it is really needed.

❾ **Network traffic: Limit query numbers to the backend.**
You should not underestimate this important role and the heavy influence of bad network traffic on the dashboard performance. This includes, e.g., controlling the number of refreshments to bring in new data to the dashboard. Furthermore, you should know that every chart or widget in your dashboard sends off an own query to the backend to request a dataset. This means that the number of backend requests scales with the number of total widgets that you implement on the screen. Try to use query batching to bundle queries together and reduce the overall number of queries put to the backend. You might also think about pausing any refresh of data during runtime. Try to limit the overall query numbers to the backend and your performance will increase.

❿ **Viewer choices: Optimize the end-user environment.**
Finally, we'd also like to underpin the big impact of viewer choices on dashboard performance. There are multiple actions you can take to improve this. Most of them involve the environment of the user, like browser or network choices, computer resources, and limiting other applications on your computer that can affect the performance. Another time-consuming process arises when users present to others via screen sharing. You might want to consider preloading your dashboard for some presentation purposes or use special presentation viewer tools in SAP Analytics Cloud (e.g., the digital boardroom or explorer view) to get the most out of your presentation.

In Table 2.1, we present our ten golden rules together with important key concepts and references to the corresponding chapters in this book.

Ten Golden Rules	Concepts	Reference
❶ Tenant and backend	▪ SAP BW parallel queries, memory limits ▪ Further SAP BW/SAP HANA settings	▪ Chapter 5, Section 5.3.2 ▪ Chapter 6, Section 6.2 ▪ Chapter 6, Section 6.3.2 ▪ Chapter 6, Section 6.3.4 ▪ Chapter 6, Section 6.3.5
❷ Data manipulation	▪ Do calculations in the backend ▪ Perform aggregations early ▪ Restricted measures ▪ Import data as xls rather than blending ▪ Reduce the number of metadata loading into your widget	▪ Chapter 3, Section 3.3.2 ▪ Chapter 5, Section 5.1.2 ▪ Chapter 5, Section 5.1.4 ▪ Chapter 6, Section 6.1.1 ▪ Chapter 6, Section 6.1.4 ▪ Chapter 6, Section 6.1.5 ▪ Chapter 6, Section 6.2.6 ▪ Chapter 6, Section 6.3.5
❸ Data model	▪ Build high-performing data model ▪ Remove unnecessary dimensions ▪ Use on-premises data instead of live-data connections ▪ Use analytical instead of planning model ▪ Optimize planning model ▪ Avoid too much blending	▪ Chapter 5, Section 5.1 ▪ Chapter 5, Section 5.2.1 ▪ Chapter 5, Section 5.4 ▪ Chapter 6, Section 6.1.2
❹ Scripting	▪ Use built-in functionalities instead of complicated scripts ▪ Use scripting API calls in the most efficient manner ▪ Optimize advanced formulas ▪ Avoid installing an initialization script	▪ Chapter 3, Section 3.6.4 ▪ Chapter 4, Section 4.3.3 ▪ Chapter 4, Section 4.4.1 ▪ Chapter 4, Section 4.5
❺ Information architecture	▪ Optimize your story design and structure ▪ Use optimized design experience ▪ Avoid fancy charts or heavy images ▪ Reduce number of pages ▪ Reduce number of charts per page ▪ Increase information density ▪ Optimize responsive design ▪ Split up content to distribute loading time ▪ Optimize your design for mobile devices	▪ Chapter 3, Section 3.2.1 ▪ Chapter 3, Section 3.2.4 ▪ Chapter 3, Section 3.4.3 ▪ Chapter 4, Section 4.2.3 ▪ Chapter 4, Section 4.3.5 ▪ Chapter 4, Section 4.4

Table 2.1 Our Ten Golden Rules for Efficient SAP Analytics Cloud Dashboards

Ten Golden Rules	Concepts	Reference
❻ Filtering	▪ Enable unrestricted drilling ▪ Leverage drilling capabilities ▪ Use collapsed filters ▪ Deactivate cascading effect ▪ Show unbooked data ▪ Filter instead of hidden data ▪ Use story and page filters instead of widget filters ▪ Use TopN ranking	▪ Chapter 3, Section 3.2.2 ▪ Chapter 3, Section 3.2.3 ▪ Chapter 3, Section 3.3.1 ▪ Chapter 5, Section 5.4.2
❼ Functional complexity	▪ Use appropriate styling rules for tables ▪ Reduce number of data-related widgets that are linked ▪ Avoid redundant resizing of widgets ▪ Don't overcomplicate things	▪ Chapter 3, Section 3.2.3 ▪ Chapter 3, Section 3.3.1 ▪ Chapter 4, Section 4.2.2 ▪ Chapter 4, Section 4.4.2
❽ Lazy loading	▪ Load invisible widgets in the back-ground ▪ User progressive chart rendering ▪ Delay loading ▪ Optimized view mode	▪ Chapter 3, Section 3.1.5 ▪ Chapter 4, Section 4.3.2 ▪ Chapter 6, Section 6.3.2
❾ Network traffic	▪ Control number of refreshes ▪ User query batching and merge queries ▪ Increase the number of SAP BW parallel queries ▪ Reduce number of queries to the back-end ▪ Pause the refresh of data at runtime ▪ Optimized view mode	▪ Chapter 3, Section 3.1.5 ▪ Chapter 4, Section 4.3.4 ▪ Chapter 6, Section 6.3.3 ▪ Chapter 6, Section 6.3.4
❿ Viewer choices	▪ Ensure high enough bandwidth ▪ Avoid other network-heavy operations ▪ Use the explorer view ▪ Use Chrome ▪ Check impact of VPN and computer resources ▪ Consider impact of screen sharing ▪ Preload the dashboard	▪ Chapter 3, Section 3.5 ▪ Chapter 7, Section 7.1 ▪ Chapter 7, Section 7.2

Table 2.1 Our Ten Golden Rules for Efficient SAP Analytics Cloud Dashboards (Cont.)

2.10 Summary

In this chapter, we have learned a lot about how to measure, test, and monitor the performance of an application, particularly of an SAP Analytics Cloud dashboard. The basics gathered in this chapter will allow us in the subsequent chapters to apply various tips and tricks to optimize the dashboard performance. Therefore, we have learned a few fundamental concepts.

Before measuring performance, one must think about an appropriate test type. There are plenty of them, and not all need to be applied in parallel. Instead, think about the scenario that you want to test and then decide on the right performance test type, including load, spike, stress, breakpoint, endurance, scalability, and volume tests. We also learned about a few performances test tools that can help you guide your way through the performance jungle.

Furthermore, we learned about the differences between performance testing and performance engineering. While performance testing provides a framework for executing performance tests after the implementation, performance engineering refers to the process of optimizing the code performance early on.

Afterwards, we learned what a typical performance testing process looks like, and which steps you need to follow (from identifying the test environment and planning and designing the test to running and evaluating the test results).

This led us to the question of which metrics might be the right ones to look at when analyzing dashboard performance. Such metrics can quantify different loading times (e.g., the total loading time, the DOM rendering time, or the request time), system KPIs (e.g., the CPU load, memory consumption, or network bandwidth), or dashboard-specific KPIs (e.g., the total number of requests sent to the backend or the time to interactive).

Defining the metrics then led us to the definition of concrete performance goals. Performance goals need to be quantifiable. For example, you could specify that "the amount of total data that gets downloaded will not exceed 200 MB." The more concrete your goal is, the better you can handle your measurements.

We then discussed how to measure performance in practice and described the usage of some standard developer tools that are frequently used to analyze web performance. We examined Chrome DevTools in detail and explained how to leverage its functionalities.

Afterwards, we discussed how benchmark tests work. Benchmark tests basically provide a framework for going through the whole end-to-end testing process. We connected the different steps of the test phases to our previous sections.

Then, we derived an SAP Analytics Cloud performance equation, which provides a formula consisting out of different time contributions that add up to the total performance of an SAP Analytics Cloud dashboard. The reader can take this equation as a practical example of how to improve your own dashboard performance. It is based on all chapters of this book, where the different contributions will be split up and discussed separately.

Finally, we derived ten golden rules for building efficient SAP Analytics Cloud dashboard. Those rules can be used and applied to every dashboard to ensure that it is highly efficient and is of reasonable quality.

In the next chapter, we will discuss a major time contribution within the SAP Analytics Cloud performance equation: the story building part. As we will see, there are plenty of possibilities to optimize the loading time within a story.

Chapter 3
Optimizing Performance in the Story Builder

In this chapter, we look at the different phases of the dashboard building process using the SAP Analytics Cloud story builder and discuss how to use charts, tables, images, and calculations in a meaningful way and focus on possible performance. Furthermore, we present the performance analysis tool, a built-in feature in SAP Analytics Cloud that allows us to properly measure the performance of our stories on a very detailed level.

Now that we are familiar with the concept of performance in the context of dashboards and the common measurement methods, let's move on to the actual dashboard building process.

In SAP Analytics Cloud, we have the option of creating either a *story* or an *application* for this:

- **Story**
  A story is created within the main central development environment. The dashboard designer can access a wide range of functions and setting options, both design-specific and related to model connections, and does not need any scripting experience. The disadvantage of a story are the restrictions imposed by the fixed layout, consisting of a page navigation bar above and the main content area below, and the predefined widgets, whose functionality cannot be modified by scripting.
- **Analytical application**
  An *analytical application* is a file created in the analytics designer for SAP Analytics Cloud. This is an extended development environment that allows the designer an immensely higher degree of freedom and flexibility and makes it possible to meet complex design and functionality requirements. The dashboard creation itself turns out to be less beginner-friendly and requires a higher technical understanding, since in addition to the creation process in the story builder, scripting can be used to influence graphic elements such as filters and buttons.

The latter will be covered later in detail in Chapter 4. In this chapter, we will focus only on stories and explore the different ways of creating high-performance dashboards within the SAP Analytics Cloud story builder.

To do this, we will focus on the steps of the building process, individual graphical elements such as layout, different chart types, use of filters and calculations, and the dos and don'ts of performance maximization. In line with this, we will also look at how the *explorer view* can be effectively included as a supplement to the actual dashboard and how we can get the most out of the otherwise rather performance-impairing *planning scenarios*. Finally, to give us some guidance in this jungle of best practice tips, we will look at the *performance analysis tool*, which we can use to localize performance weak points more precisely and thus narrow down the optimization measures suitable for our dashboard.

For some of the best practice tips listed in this book, time measurements were performed using examples, as described in Chapter 2, to show the resulting improvement in load times.

Important Note

Testing in this chapter was done using the Chrome DevTools and using the following computer: Lenovo ThinkPad X1 Yoga Gen 5; i7-10610U CPU @ 1.80GHz 2.30 GHz; 16GB RAM.

3.1 General Settings to Improve Performance

In the following sections, we will look at general settings that might improve performance. Starting with the handling of multiple models and so-called query merging, we will then move on to the *optimize story building performance* mode and look at when a re-save might be useful. Afterwards, we will then take a detailed look at the *optimized view mode*, a package of features to improve usability and performance. Finally, we will show the various performance warning notifications provided by the system as additional user guidelines and take a brief look at the *progressive chart rendering* feature.

3.1.1 Using Multiple Models in a Story

Although we will go into detail about data models in Chapter 5, a few points must be mentioned here as well. One thing that might seem obvious but is nevertheless often overlooked is removing unused models from a story. It happens quickly: A dashboard is created and suddenly an error is noticed in the data model, which is then completely recreated and added to the story. The old model often remains unused in the story. From a performance point of view, this is unnecessary ballast for our story, so when saving, the user is informed about the unused models with the suggestion to remove them from the story, as shown in Figure 3.1.

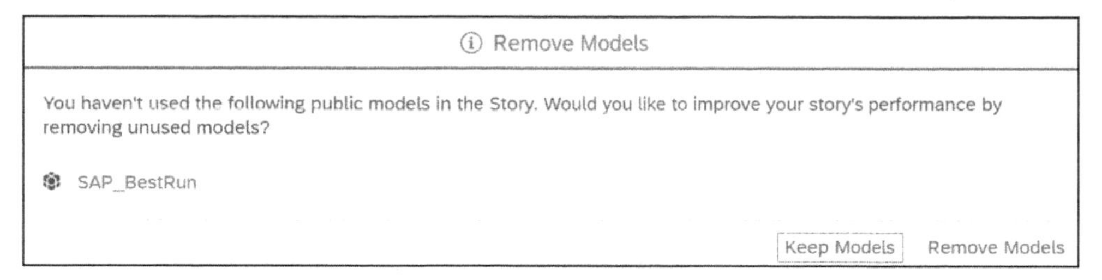

Figure 3.1 Remove Unused Models from the Story

If a story uses more than one model, these are often linked via a common dimension. To ensure performance, the number of linked models should be kept as low as possible, and the linking should not be done by using a calculated dimension.

3.1.2 Query Merging

For each data-related object within a story, SAP Analytics Cloud executes a backend request. The number of queries executed in parallel can be manually increased by batching queries together to reduce the number of browser requests. This can be applied for stories that use an SAP HANA or SAP Business Warehouse (SAP BW) system as a data source, provided your data source provider allows this. For further information, see Chapter 5 and Chapter 6.

To enable *query batching and merging*, as shown in Figure 3.2, follow these steps:

1. In your story, click on the **Settings** wrench tool.
2. Select **Query Settings**.
   - When using an *SAP HANA* database:
     - Toggle on **Enable Query Batching**.
     - Set a **Min** and **Max** number of queries per batch.
   - When using an *SAP BW* database:
     - Toggle on **Enable Query Merge**.

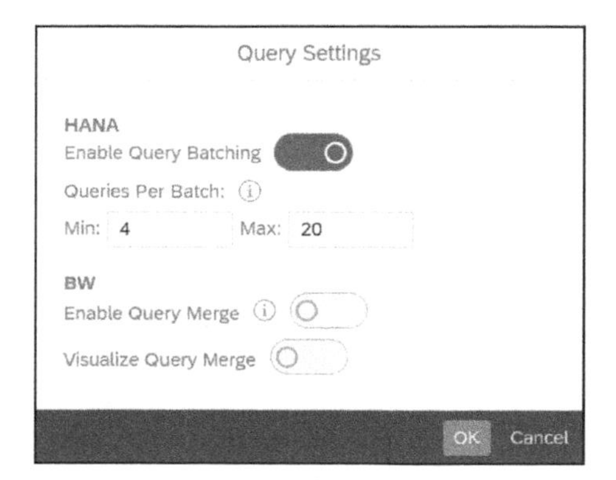

Figure 3.2 Speed Up Rendering Times with Query Batching

3.1.3 Optimize Story Building Performance

Performance impairments can occur not only when loading a finished dashboard, but also in the middle of the building process. If you activate the **Optimizing Story Building Performance** function in the model presets, an automatic data update during story design is prevented.

To turn off the automated data update during story design, follow these steps, as shown in Figure 3.3:

❶ Open the corresponding model and click the wrench tool to enter the modeler's settings menu.

❷ Select the tab **Data and Performance**.

❸ Toggle on the switch under **Optimize Story Building Performance**.

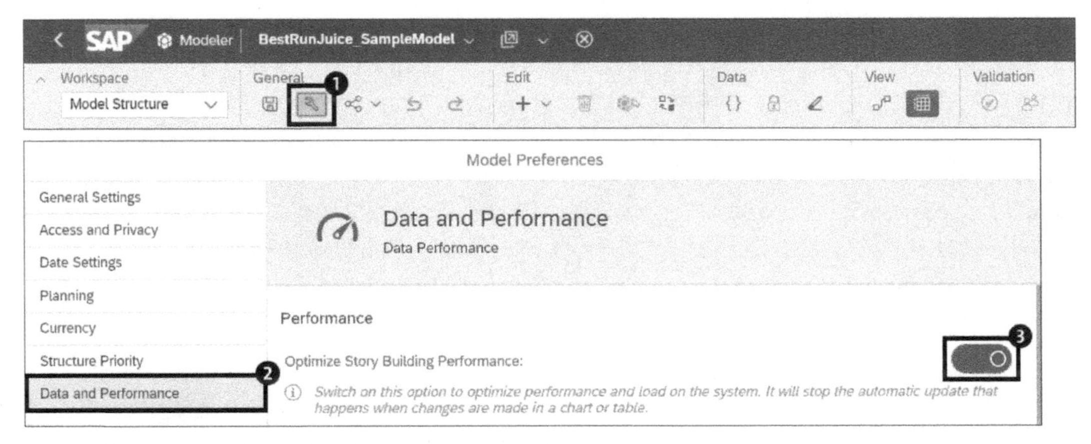

Figure 3.3 Activate the Optimize Story Building Performance Mode in the Story Preferences

Whenever required, the data update can be triggered manually within the story builder in the builder panel of the respective chart during the building process, as shown in Figure 3.4.

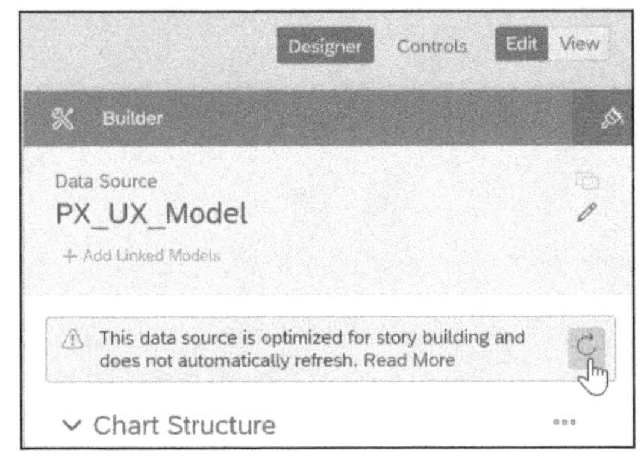

Figure 3.4 Refresh Button in the Charts Settings to Update the Data in Optimized Story Building Mode

3.1.4 Re-save the Story

The SAP Analytics Cloud product management team is continuously working on improvements within the tool. Updates are therefore applied on a regular basis. To benefit from these improvements, it is recommended that you open and re-save the story after each update release and thus transfer technical updates to your own stories or analytical applications.

3.1.5 Optimized View Mode

With the Q3 2021 release of SAP Analytics Cloud, *optimized view mode* has been introduced. This mode can be activated individually for each story and, in addition to features for simplified handling in view mode, also offers improvements in the performance area, which we will look at in more detail in the following sections.

> **Note**
>
> It should be noted here that optimized view mode does not correct any performance weaknesses resulting from problems in the backend or network, such as slow-running backend queries (server-side) or a sluggish network. Instead, optimized view mode addresses dashboards with client-side performance issues only.

Enable Optimized View Mode

Enable optimized view mode via pop-up with these steps:

1. Open the relevant story.
2. Enter the **Edit** mode.
3. In the pop-up that opens next, click on **Yes, Enable Feature**, as shown in Figure 3.5. Click the **Learn More** link for further information about optimized view mode.

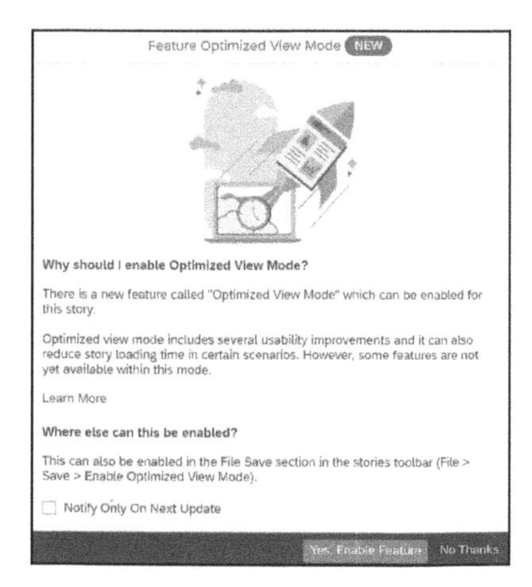

Figure 3.5 Enable Optimized View Mode

Enable optimized view mode in the **Save** menu with these steps:

1. Open the relevant story.
2. Enter the **Edit** mode.
3. At the top menu bar in the **File** section, enter the **Save** dropdown menu and select **Enable Optimized View Mode**.

Active Viewport Rendering

With the optimized view mode, the user now has the option of activating *active viewport rendering*. Only those objects that are in the visible screen area are rendered. This has a positive effect on performance, especially for large dashboards with many data-dependent widgets that can be viewed only with a lot of scrolling. Any content outside of the viewport will not be rendered until the user actively brings it into the visible area by scrolling.

To enable active viewpoint rendering, follow these steps:

1. Open the relevant story.
2. Switch to **Edit** mode.
3. Under the dropdown menu of the **Refresh** button, click on **Enable Viewport Loading**, as shown in Figure 3.6.

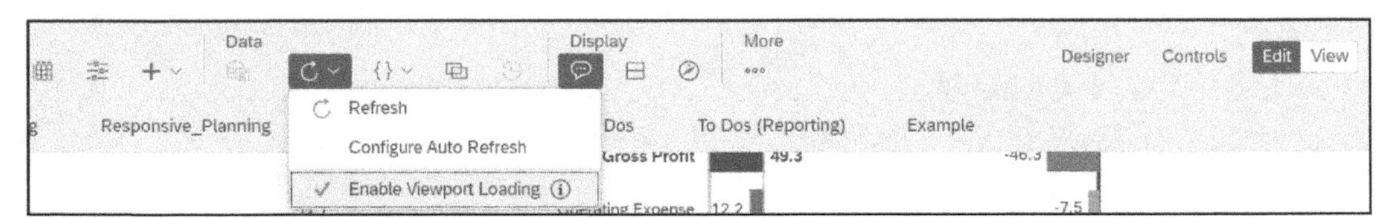

Figure 3.6 Faster Loading Story Pages with Enable Viewport Loading

Improved Rendering on Story Open for the First Page in a Dashboard

In the optimized view mode, the rendering of the first page when opening a story has been accelerated. This is done using *persisted query information*, which is created after a story is saved in optimized view mode. Whereas, outside of the optimized view mode, the first few seconds of opening a story are used to create all available queries, persisted query information is used to deal with widget rendering and server processing in parallel. With this, data-related queries can be sent to the backend earlier, which allows a faster rendering of the first page.

Ghost Loading Indicator

When opening a story in optimized view mode, an animated ghost widget is displayed instead of the loading icon, which provides the user with information about the expected widget type even before the actual chart is available. Even if this additional function does not really speed up the actual loading process, it is still comforting advance information to bridge the rendering time.

Model Information Downloaded on Demand

A main approach to improving client-side performance in optimized view mode is to no longer load all available data information from the model per se when opening the story, but to load data only on demand and then only the information that is actively requested by performing an action.

This has an effect, for example, when switching to another story page, expanding a filter, and filtering by data point selection.

The optimized view mode also accelerates the loading of complex hierarchies since information of lower-hierarchy levels is loaded only by consciously expanding the corresponding parent node. In addition, those hierarchy members for which no data is available due to filter settings are hidden by default. Besides improving rendering time, this also leads to a better overview of the available members.

Limitations to Performance Improvements

The optimized view mode does not cover all features in SAP Analytics Cloud. Some of those even might have to be removed or changed before the story file can be converted into the optimized view mode. In Table 3.1, we show a list of features and in-built tools that underline the limitations of using the optimized view mode. Keep in mind that these limitations are likely to change over time as work is continuously done to improve both the functionality of individual SAP Analytics Cloud features and their compatibility. You can check the current list of restrictions on the SAP Analytics Cloud Help Portal at the following URL: *http://s-prs.co/v566901*.

Unsupported Features	Comments/Recommendation
Grid pages	No possibility of converting/saving file to optimized view mode.
Sections on story pages (only available for Canvas pages)	No possibility of converting/saving file to optimized view mode. Each section must start on a new page. In the **Styling** panel, select **Show all instances on pages**. Then select **Start section on new page**.
Non-optimized presentation table	No possibility of converting/saving file to optimized view mode. Enable **Optimized Presentation** in table's **Builder** panel.

Table 3.1 List of Unsupported Features in Optimized View Mode, Status as of Q1 2023

Unsupported Features	Comments/Recommendation
Widgets (charts, tables, etc.) using local range filters with unrestricted drilling off	Object gets permanently lost when converting to optimized view mode. Enable **Unrestricted Drilling** in the **Edit Filter** panel.
Time series charts (with timestamp dimension)	Not applicable in optimized view mode.
Tables basing on linked models	Not applicable in optimized view mode.
Predictive forecast in tables	Not applicable in optimized view mode.
Geo map based on location dimension with area enrichment	Not applicable in optimized view mode.
Partial range story filter	No possibility of converting/saving file to optimized view mode. Set the selection of the range filter back to default.
Partial range page filter	Object gets permanently lost when converting to optimized view mode. Set the selection of the range filter back to default.
Display full range slider	With optimized view mode, automatically converted to open-ended filter.
Geographical distance input control	Not applicable in optimized view mode.
Smart discovery widgets	Not applicable in optimized view mode.
Legacy value driver tree	Object gets permanently lost when converting to optimized view mode. Legacy value driver tree is deprecated and therefore no longer supported. In the **Builder** panel, transform to **New Value Driver Tree** objects.
Controls panel	Not applicable in optimized view mode.
Explorer	Not available as the entry points are disabled.
Input task	No possibility of converting/saving file to optimized view mode.

Table 3.1 List of Unsupported Features in Optimized View Mode, Status as of Q1 2023 (Cont.)

Unsupported Applications	Comments/Recommendation
Digital boardroom	Optimized view mode not yet available.
SAP Datasphere	Optimized view mode not yet available.
Search to Insight (Global Search)	Optimized view mode not yet available.
Unsupported Model Types	**Comments/Recommendation**
Live Universe	–
Unauthorized Data Models	–
Live SAP HANA Models with option **Load Parent-Child Hierarchies Independent of Metadata** enabled	–

Table 3.1 List of Unsupported Features in Optimized View Mode, Status as of Q1 2023 (Cont.)

Further Reading

You can find more information on performance improvement limitations from the following resources:

- Tunir Kapil, "Experience Performance and Usability Improvements with SAP Analytics Cloud Stories," available at *http://s-prs.co/v566902*
- Tunir Kapil, "The New Rendering Experience – Active Viewport Rendering," available at *http://s-prs.co/v566903*
- SAP Analytics Cloud Help Portal, "Optimized Story Experience Restrictions," available at *http://s-prs.co/v566904*
- SAP Analytics Cloud Help Portal, "Optimized Story Experience Improvements," available at *http://s-prs.co/v566905*

3.1.6 Performance Warning Notification

In addition to the best practices recommended in this book, there are performance improvement tips that appear automatically in the dashboard creation process, i.e., only in edit mode, and thus draw the user's attention to performance traps during the design process. For the following situations, a notification will show up:

- Too many pages are added to a story
- Too many widgets are added to a page
- Designer is told to collapse filters
- Designer is told to enable optimized mode

3.1.7 Progressive Chart Rendering

Another setting that we would like to mention at least briefly at this point, even though it will be presented in detail later in Chapter 6, is the so-called progressive chart rendering feature. Activating this setting shortens the waiting time while a story is opened or refreshed. A version of a chart is retained for one hour and then displayed as a kind of temporary placeholder for the duration of the data refresh process. If the user tries to interact with this chart during this time, he will be informed by a loading icon that this chart is still in the update process. This feature can be particularly helpful if there have been no drastic changes in the story, such as data changes, but only minor ones, such as changes in the design, within the last hour.

Note

You will need an admin role to access the system configuration settings.

3.2 Optimizing the Story Design

Now that we know the most important settings within the story builder that might help us pave the way to a high-performance dashboard, we come to the actual building process.

The foundation for the final performance of a story is usually laid by the design concept. The use case and the target group already determine the amount of required data as well as the scope of visualizations. Performance optimization therefore begins before the actual design process.

It is usually the complex and multi-layered dashboards, those that shine with an unusual design and a high number of graphic elements, where the rendering time suffers. These are usually accompanied by a high number of backend queries that must be executed with every dashboard update and slow down performance.

Especially when an attempt is made to respond to special design requirements when building a dashboard, it is not uncommon to experience a performance impairing construction method. The strengths and in-built functions of a tool are often not used effectively since the focus is more on the detail and the attempt is made to stay as close to the design concept as possible. The result is a dashboard that, although it meets the requirements of the designer in terms of both design and content, is unsuitable for frequent use due to the long rendering times.

For a satisfactory performance, there is usually no way around compromises. The be-all and end-all for an efficient design is, on the one hand, to know the main purpose of the dashboard, i.e., the essential core requirements, and, on the other hand, to be very clear about the strengths and weaknesses of the tool to be used. Only then will it be possible to find the right compromise between design and performance.

In this section, we will go through the basics of story design and show possible performance traps. We will refer to layout-related things like pages and widget count and work our way from there to the individual widget types like charts and tables.

3.2.1 Story Structure

In the following sections, we will look at concept-related aspects. Starting with a description of the page styles *responsive* and *canvas*, we will then learn how the number of pages and charts per page influence the story rendering times.

Canvas versus Responsive

If you want to start creating a dashboard, the first thing you will be asked is whether you want to use a **Canvas** or **Responsive** style page for the story, as shown in Figure 3.7.

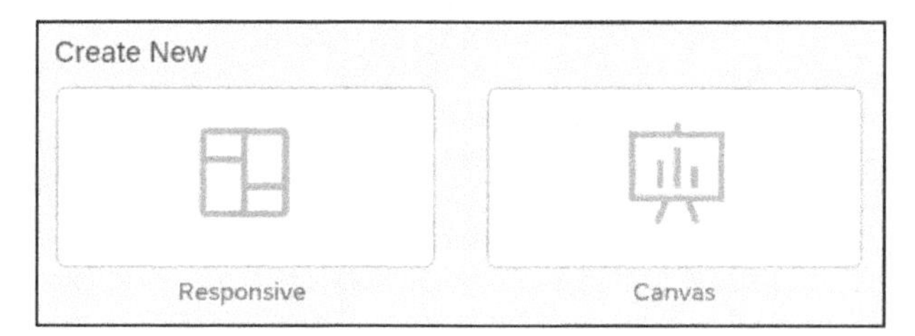

Figure 3.7 Responsive and Canvas Style

Leaving performance aside for the moment, both styles have their undeniable advantages:

- **Canvas pages**
  - Pixel-precise control over page size, widget position, and widget size
  - Possibility to overlap story elements
  - Bring overlapping objects to front/back
  - Group objects, which is especially useful while editing or moving multiple objects at once
- **Responsive pages**
  - Content automatically rearranges itself according to the window size → scroll bars are avoided
  - Adapts to different screen sizes → can be rendered on mobile devices
  - For small screens, some elements, such as labels, are automatically omitted to maximize the chart area
  - Can be used more effectively, with interactions, such as filtering and sorting, in the *digital boardroom*
  - Responsive story pages can be viewed via the SAP Analytics Cloud mobile app for iOS

For understandable reasons, a designer's heart often beats a little more for the canvas style, since he has complete control over what the user ultimately sees, regardless of the screen resolution. However, from a performance point of view, it is recommended to design your story pages in responsive style, as they load faster.

Performance Tip

Prefer responsive pages to canvas as they load faster.

Number of Pages

The more complex a use case is in terms of the parameters to be analyzed and the more diverse the target group and thus the dashboard requirements are, the more likely it is that our dashboard consists of more than one page.

Dividing the dashboard content across multiple pages gives us the ability to:

- Group an issue thematically to address a specific audience with each page
- View data-rich issues from different perspectives and levels of detail. For example, the first page can serve as an overview page, which contains the most interesting information for the user and shows only a high-level summary of a data situation, while additional pages approach the topic by going more into the details and the context of the topic

However, in terms of performance, you should avoid using a large number of pages, as this will likely decrease your story's performance. Of course, one way to reduce the number of pages would be to regroup the widgets and divide them into fewer pages. However, this inevitably leads to a higher number of widgets per page, which, as we will explain in the following chapter, also has a negative impact on performance. Therefore, instead of working with one story, we recommend working with several and splitting the content into separate stories according to the use case or subtopic. A pane with hyperlinks can be used to navigate from one story to the next.

Number of Charts

As will be explained in more detail in Chapter 7, it is generally recommended to use Google Chrome as your default browser, both for performance reasons and to always take advantage of the latest updates. Nevertheless, as with other browsers, there is a maximum number of parallel connections per host that are possible. If you use Google Chrome, these are six queries that can be started simultaneously.

When transferred to our dashboard, this means that six widget calls can take place simultaneously. This inevitably leads to the conclusion that a high number of widgets will inevitably have a negative impact on performance. One recommendation for saving runtime is therefore to reduce the number of data-related widgets to 12 or less.

Note

With the same number of widgets, the performance can vary greatly if several different data models are used for these widgets instead of a common one.

However, this is only a rough rule of thumb that does not consider the different rendering times from widget type to widget type. If you want to be more precise, calculate the so-called weight per page. Here, *process-heavy widgets*, i.e., widgets with a significantly greater impact on performance, are given greater importance. For this purpose, a unit weight is assigned to each widget type, as shown in Table 3.2.

Widget	Unit Weight
Table	0.6
Chart	0.3
Geo map	1
Filters, expanded	0.4
Filters, non-expanded	0.2
Section on page	0.5
Value driver tree	1
R widget (with at least one data frame)	1.2
Text box with dynamic text	0.2
Dynamic image	0.3
Commenting widget	0.1
Text box	0.1
Iframe/ web page	0.1
RSS feed	0.1
Image/shape/clock	0.1

Table 3.2 Unit Weight per Widget

To determine the total weight of a story page, the weight units of all widgets used per page must be added up. The lower this value, the less the performance of the story is negatively affected. To achieve the best possible performance, the maximum weight per story page should be five units or less.

Example

Let's assume we have a story page containing the widgets shown in Table 3.3.

Widget	#	Unit Weight
Text boxes	5	$5 \cdot 0.1 = 0.5$
Shapes	4	$4 \cdot 0.1 = 0.4$
Charts	8	$8 \cdot 0.3 = 2.4$
Tables	3	$3 \cdot 0.6 = 1.8$
Grand Total		**5.1**

Table 3.3 Typical Page Setup for a Common Story

With this setup, we get a total page weight of 5.1 and are thus slightly above the specified maximum limit. Since we may already notice negative effects on our performance, it would be advisable to reduce the number of widgets.

When it comes to reducing the number of widgets, a good first approach is to take a close look at the individual charts along with their information input and ask yourself for each individual chart whether and why it is really needed here.

Experience has shown that information that could easily be presented in a single chart or table is often spread across several individual widgets. In addition to a shorter loading time, using as few charts per page as possible also leads to a tidier overall impression, which allows the user to get to the information they are looking for in less time.

This can be achieved by choosing chart types that can display a higher number of dimensions and measures, such as line charts, combinations of stacked bars and line charts, and bubble charts.

Another way to reduce the widget density per page is to group the widgets thematically and spread them over two pages or more. However, since the number of pages also has an impact on our performance, this option should be approached with caution and in compliance with the best practices mentioned in this context.

Performance Tips

- For performance maximization, either use twelve widgets or less per story page or aim for a maximum weight per story page of five units or less.
- Prefer a few charts with high information density to many charts with little content.
- Prefer charts that can display multiple dimensions.

To illustrate the influence of the number of charts on the performance with measured figures, we will look at three different dashboards below. For these, we came up with a dataset consisting of two dimensions, two measures, and a total of 10,144 rows, which was copied into an SAP Analytics Cloud model.

Figure 3.8 shows a dashboard with one page that includes twelve scatter plots, each consisting of 400 to 500 data points, a text box, and a shape that was used as the background for the header. Fully loading this story in view mode via the corresponding link takes an average of 12.4 seconds.

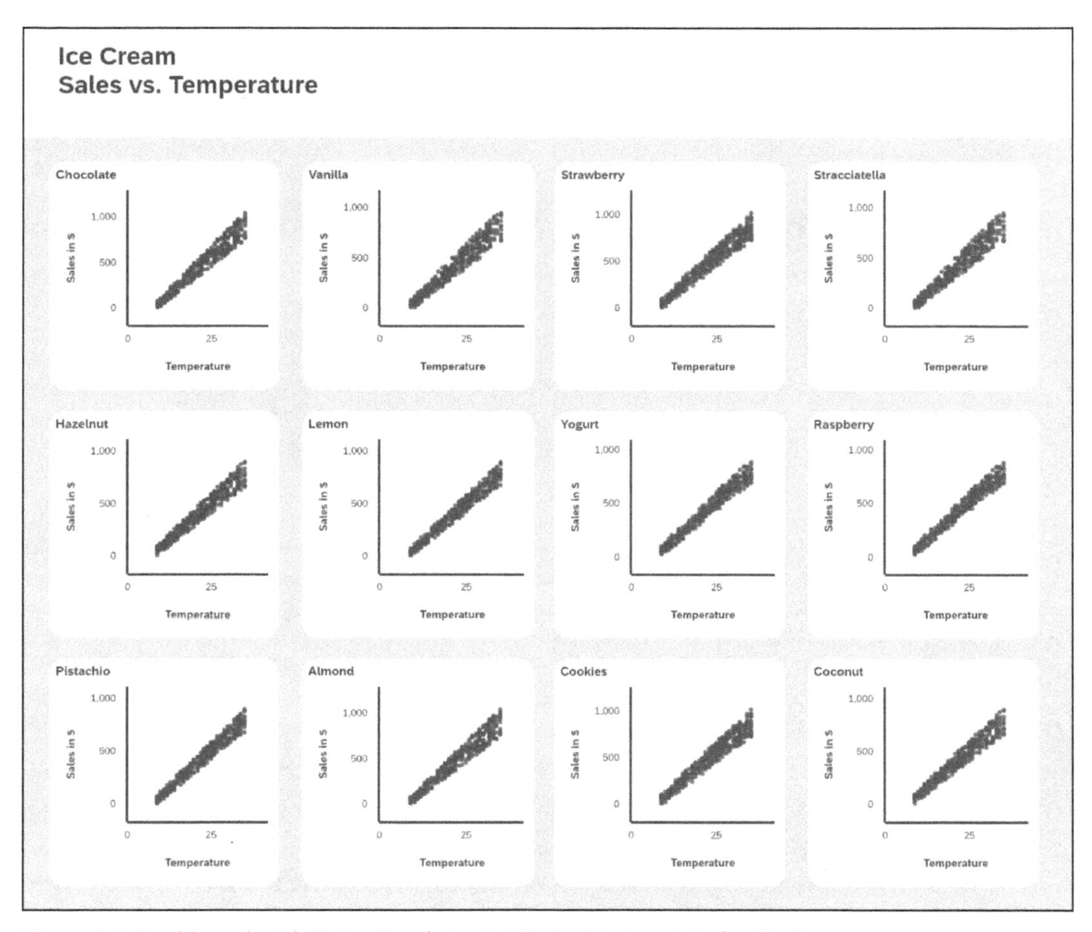

Figure 3.8 Dashboard with 12 Scatterplots at 400–500 Datapoints for Testing

To now give a counterexample, we removed all but one of the scatterplots from the previous dashboard in Figure 3.9. This reduced our dashboard by eleven charts and 4,656 data points, which now achieves a load time of just 9.0 seconds, as shown in Table 3.4.

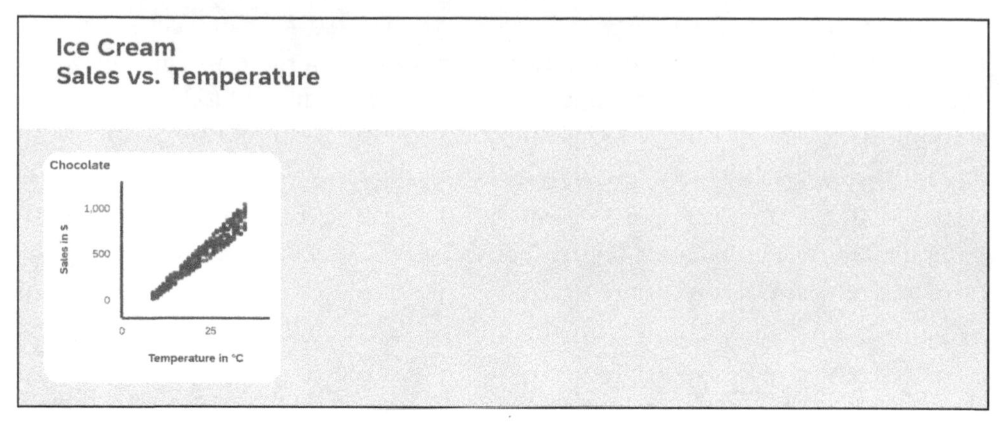

Figure 3.9 Dashboard with Only One Scatterplot after Removing Most of the Content

Number of charts / Datapoints	Measured Time
12 scatterplots / 5,072 datapoints (Figure 3.8)	12.4s
1 scatterplot / 416 datapoints (Figure 3.9)	9.0s

Table 3.4 Time Measurement Results When Reducing the Number of Data-Related Widgets

However, this step also removed about 90 percent of the relevant information from our dashboard.

This example only shows how far we can theoretically minimize the loading time by reducing the number of charts used and should by no means be understood as a recommendation to remove most of the content from the dashboard. This is not goal oriented.

Next, let's try a compromise instead, again based on the same testing setup. Our first dashboard, Figure 3.8, was twelve scatterplots based on the same measures (sales and temperature) and the same dimension (ice cream type). Only the filter for the dimension "ice cream type" was set differently. Instead of representing this by twelve individual charts, we now use a trellis chart in the third example, with the "ice cream type" as the dimension to be subdivided. Thus, we still show the same number of data points, but by using one widget only. With this, we have still achieved a much shorter loading time than in the first setup, Figure 3.8, and are only 0.8 seconds over the time of the last example, Figure 3.9, without having to give up any information.

Table 3.5 shows the time measurement results, while Figure 3.10 shows an additional example of a trellis chart version to give an option of reducing the number of widgets without limiting the content.

Number of charts / Datapoints	Measured Time
12 scatterplots / 5,072 datapoints (Figure 3.8)	12.4s
1 scatterplot / 416 datapoints (Figure 3.9)	9.0s
1 trellis chart / 5,072 datapoints (Figure 3.10)	9.8s

Table 3.5 Time Measurement Results

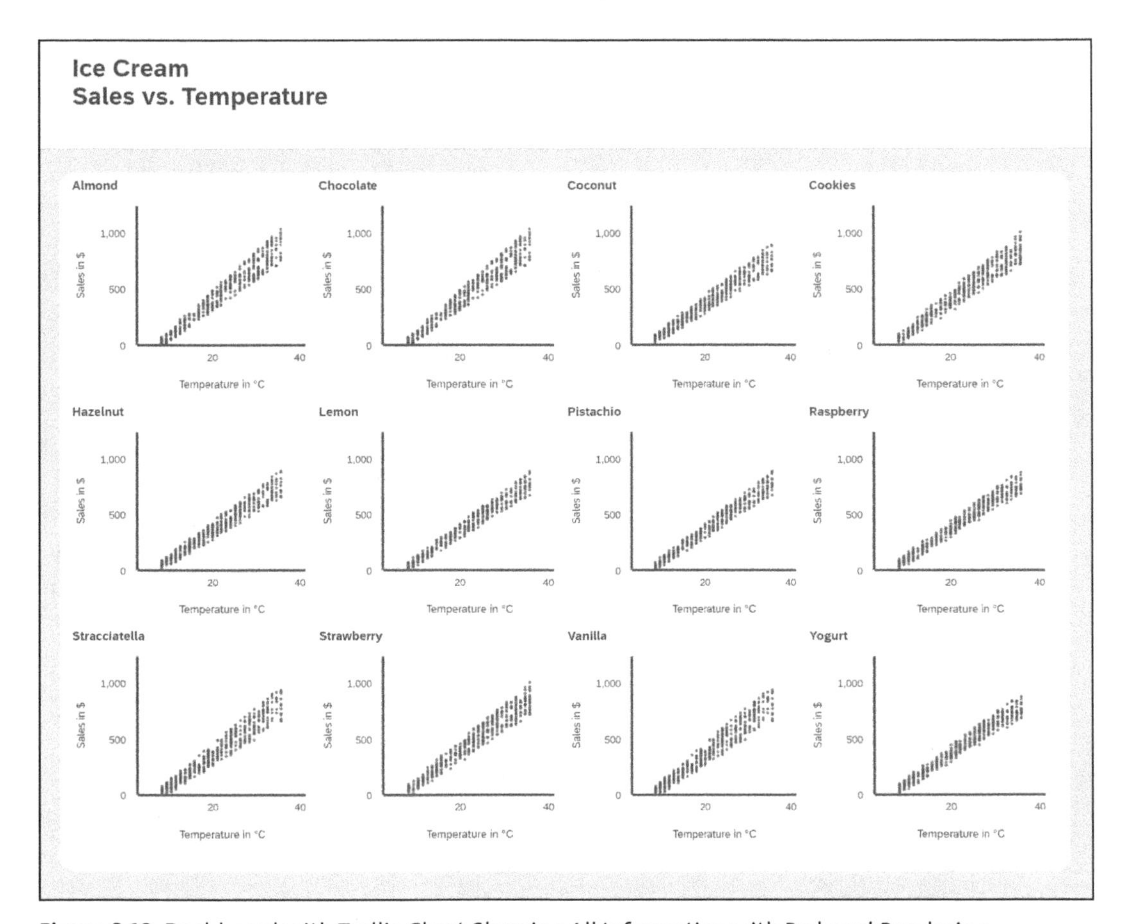

Figure 3.10 Dashboard with Trellis Chart Showing All Information with Reduced Rendering Time

3.2.2 Charts

After looking at process-heavy widgets and weight units in the previous chapter and how the performance impact varies from widget type to widget type, this section will focus solely on the charts. We will look at chart specific settings and preferences that can help reduce individual chart rendering time in the following sections.

Most of the recommendations refer to all chart types equally, only for geo maps there are some additional aspects that need to be considered and that we will also talk about in this chapter. Charts created with R programming are not covered here.

Reducing the Number of Data Points

The key factor that determines the performance strength for a data-dependent widget, regardless of whether it is a chart or table, is the amount of data it must display.

Therefore, the most effective step in optimizing a chart's performance is to keep the number of data points displayed as small as possible. A general recommendation is to limit this to 500 points or fewer per chart. However, keep in mind that the number of charts is also a determining factor for the performance. In the previous chapter, we showed by means of an example that it can sometimes make more sense for performance to increase the number of data points, i.e., the information density, of a widget if this is done with the purpose of reducing the number of data-dependent widgets in general, as we saw with the example shown in Table 3.5. Therefore, try to limit the number of widgets first and then focus on the data points.

All the best practice tips in this section focus on constraining the data size of a chart using different methods, which we will look at below:

- **Data aggregations**
  The most important rule in advance: In general, do not load any information into your story that you do not need to build your dashboard. This affects both additional measures and each additional dimension along which further subdivisions take place that are not shown in the dashboard itself. Especially the latter leads only to an unnecessary duplication of our data. It is not uncommon for the thought "Maybe I'll need this later" to tempt us to include such additional information in the model just in case. The fact is, however, that each additional row of data affects our loading times.

  If possible, reduce your data volume in the backend. Use aggregated data if, for example, your plan is to show the information only at the quarterly level or you don't need it for each individual product at all, but only for each product group.
- **Filtering**
  This is probably the most common method for restricting data within a chart. You can use filters to reduce your data to the essentials afterwards. However, it should not be used as a replacement for the aggregations just mentioned, but rather as a supplement to them. In SAP Analytics Cloud we have the choice between different types of filters, which we will take a closer look at in Section 3.3.1.
- **Drilling-out**
  When we work with hierarchical dimensions in SAP Analytics Cloud, we can choose the hierarchy level at which our data is displayed in the initial view. The end user then has the possibility to drill further into or out of the hierarchies and thus change the level of detail of the information.

From a performance point of view, it is recommended to initially display the data at a high hierarchy level when opening the story. This keeps the amount of data that must be loaded directly at the beginning low, and the end user can request additional information, if necessary, by zooming into the corresponding dimension. We will go into more detail about hierarchies later in Section 3.3.1.

- **Manual set of Top N**
  Especially for *high cardinality dimensions*, i.e., dimensions with 100 or more members, it often makes sense to output only a Top N subset instead of all members to keep the number of data points displayed low. For the sake of performance, the auto Top N variant should not be used here since all data must first be read from the backend to determine the Top N from it.

  If you create a Top N ranking manually instead, the data in the backend is first sorted and then only the data that falls into this ranking is loaded.

Further Reading

If only the Top N or Bottom N are to be permanently displayed for a dimension, set this up in the backend if the selected source system allows this. Information on how this can be done, e.g., for an SAP BW system, can be found here: *http://s-prs.co/v566906.*

Geo Maps

Geo maps are a popular way to visually assign data to a location. Provided the user has basic geographic knowledge, he doesn't have to work his way through a series of written country names and match numbers, but subconsciously uses his geographic mapping ability. It also gives your dashboard that certain decorative something in terms of design and interaction.

However, it is precisely this fanciness that can make a geo map a performance slowdown. In Table 3.2 of Section 3.2.1, geo maps are assigned a weight unit value of *1*, which is more than three times higher than that of an ordinary chart (*0.3*).

To keep the performance impact of geo maps as low as possible, follow these tips:

1. **Reduce the number of displayed data points.**
   By default, location clustering is executed in the bubble style of a geo map if more than 5,000 points are displayed. This can be further optimized by manually enabling location clustering and selecting 1,000 as the maximum number of displayed points. You can limit the number of displayed data points, as shown in Figure 3.11, by following these steps:

   ❶ Select the relevant geo map chart.

   ❷ Enter the **Designer/Builder** panel.

❸ Scroll down to the **Cluster Properties** section and change the number of **Maximum Display Points** to 1,000.

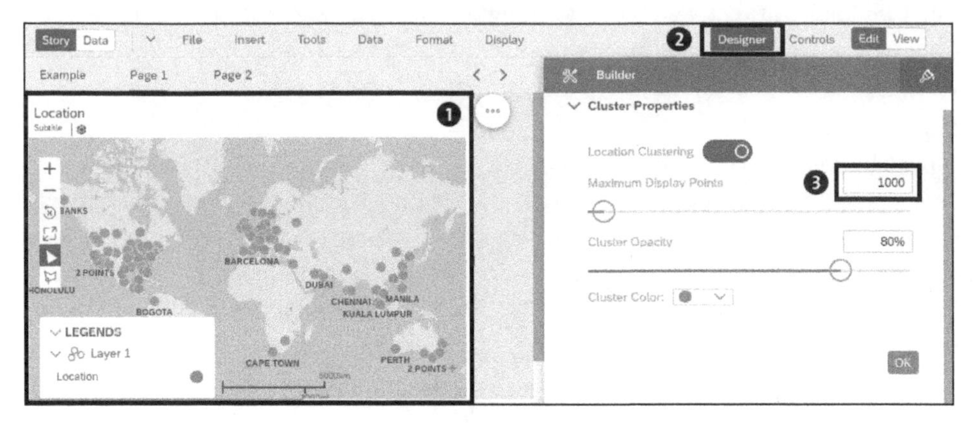

Figure 3.11 Use Location Clustering and Reduce the Number of Displayed Data Points

2. **Use the choropleth layer for many locations.**
   Another way to aggregate a large amount of data points is to use the choropleth layer. With a choropleth map, a set of predefined geographical areas is visualized by setting the color in relation to a given measure. This is recommended whenever thousands of locations need to be represented. It aggregates the location data into areas that can be drilled into to obtain information at a detailed level. Thus, by default, fewer data points are requested from the backend and more information is output only when manually triggered.

   When creating a geo map, the bubble layer is selected by default. You can manually replace it with the choropleth layer using these steps:
   - Select the relevant geo map chart.
   - Enter the **Designer/Builder** panel.
   - Under **Layer Type,** select **Choropleth/Drill Layer**, as shown in Figure 3.12.
   - Under **Style,** select **Choropleth.**

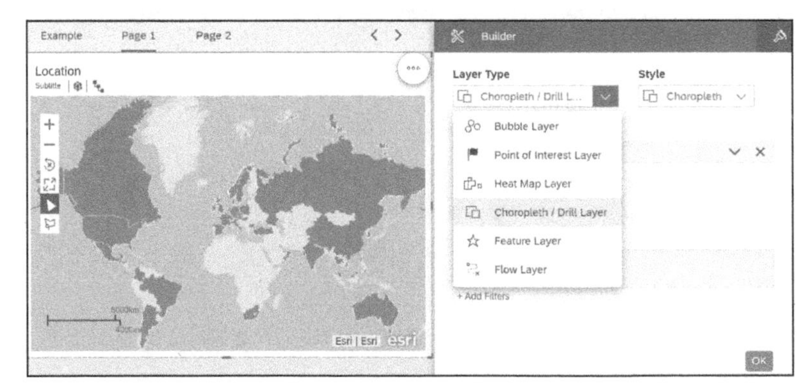

Figure 3.12 Aggregation of Location Points into Areas with Choropleth Style

3. **Choose the shown map section wisely.**
   Select the section and orientation of the map in a way that does not require the user to zoom or pan back and forth, if possible, as each of these movements executes a backend request.

3.2.3 Tables

After going through the various performance traps and performance booster tips related to charts, we now come to tables. Tables are a simple way to display many dimensions and key figures together. In addition to the general figures, we also get insight into the hierarchy structure of the dimensions used and can expand and collapse them as desired and display subtotals and totals at each hierarchy level accordingly. This further condenses the density of information.

In Section 3.2.1, we learned that tables belong to the process-heavy widgets and have a weight unit twice as high as conventional charts. However, it should not be ignored that tables can hold and display a considerable amount of information. Often, several charts can be replaced by a single table, which in turn has a positive effect on the overall weight unit.

But since tables are less eye-catching and allow for less visual comparison compared to charts, they should be used as selectively and sparingly as possible in a dashboard. Reducing the number of tables per page to the bare minimum will also help keep the number of backend requests low.

Of course, we cannot do without tables entirely. Especially for planning scenarios, which are a feature of SAP Analytics Cloud and are designed for financial business planning (Section 3.6), we rely on tables. Therefore, in the following sections, we will provide an overview of the various performance traps around tables and learn how these can be avoided.

Top N

What applied to charts in the previous chapter also applies to tables: the fewer data points that are displayed, the more positively this affects our performance. Therefore, with tables too, the main effort should be to reduce the information shown to the most necessary.

It is therefore advisable to use the *Top N* function for dimensions with a high number of members. With this feature, we can limit the number of dimension members shown to the Top N most. In addition to reducing the amount of data, this also improves the readability of a table and prevents endless scrolling.

Enable the Top N functionality for tables using these steps, shown in Figure 3.13:

1. In **Edit** mode, right-click on the data area of the relevant table.
2. Select **Create Top N**.

3. In the Top N settings window, set **Type**, N **Value**, **Related Dimensions**, and the **Version**.

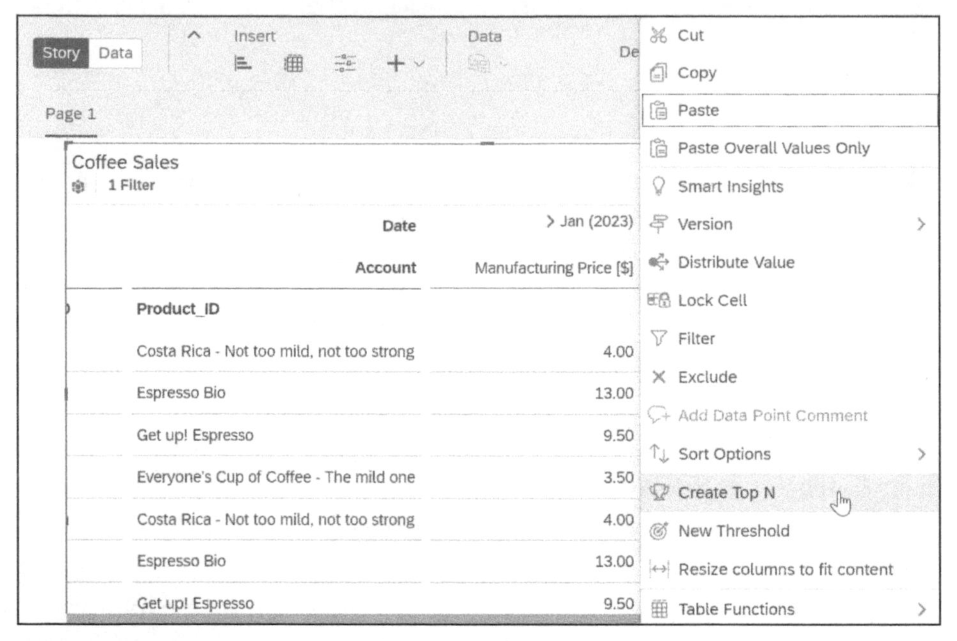

Figure 3.13 Top N Feature to Reduce Table Content

Filter versus Hide Function in Tables

If you're working with larger tables, do not try to reduce the number of rows or columns by using the function **Hide row/Hide column**. Hiding rows and columns does not represent a real reduction in the amount of data that must be consumed. Use a filter instead to limit the table to the necessary columns and rows needed for the information to be transferred.

Optimized Table Presentation

Optimized table presentation is a package added to SAP Analytics Cloud that is intended to improve the user experience when working with tables. These are features that focus less on the actual rendering time of the widgets and more on making the handling of tables smoother for the end user, thus creating a more efficient feeling, which is why we don't want to leave this setting unmentioned here. The following features are included in this set:

- Smooth scrolling
- Faster loading of in-cell charts
- Simplified responsive logic of columns
- An always visible table title
- Consistent row height

For about two years, the optimized table presentation setting has been activated by default in all newly added tables. For tables created before that, however, it must be enabled manually. To do so, follow these steps:

1. Select the relevant table.
2. Enter the **Designer/Builder** panel.
3. In the section **Table Structure**, enable the check box **Optimized Presentation**, as shown in Figure 3.14.

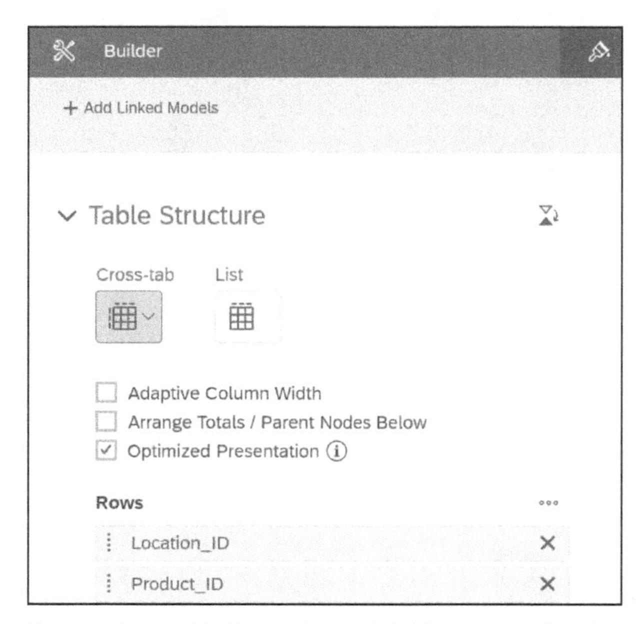

Figure 3.14 Enable the Optimized Table Presentation Package

Styling Techniques in Tables

In the previous sections, we witnessed how performance can fall victim to a specific design idea. And especially with tables, which appear to be more textual than charts and don't exactly give a dashboard an innovative touch at first glance, attempts are often made to get that certain something out of the appearance through formatting and thus achieve a certain clarity. And, yes, here too caution is advised regarding performance, as excessive formatting can severely affect it.

But before completely dispensing with formatting, you can first test whether the observed performance weaknesses are due to unfortunate formatting. The best way to do this is to measure the performance of a table once with styling and once completely without styling and compare these results. The measurement can be done either with the widget-specific *performance analysis tool*, which we will discuss in Section 3.7, or with ChromeDevTools, which measures the load time of the entire story page, including the table.

To remove all applied formatting styles, *templates* can be used. Selecting a template opens a window that informs the user that, with this selection, all previously applied formatting will be removed, and the table will be completely reset in terms of styling—exactly what we are looking for.

If the measured load times for the table without formatting are significantly lower, this is a clear indication that the previously applied formatting has caused performance weaknesses and should be revised accordingly.

There are three ways to style a table—*templates, ad-hoc styling,* and *styling rules*—which we will discuss in detail in the following regarding their performance losses:

- **Templates**
  The above-mentioned styling templates are a quick first possibility to give a table a uniform and clean formatting with a favorable load time. You can apply a template to format your table effectively and quickly using these steps:
  - Select the relevant table.
  - Enter the **Designer/Styling** panel.
  - In the **Table Properties** section within the **Template** dropdown, select a template, as shown in Figure 3.15.

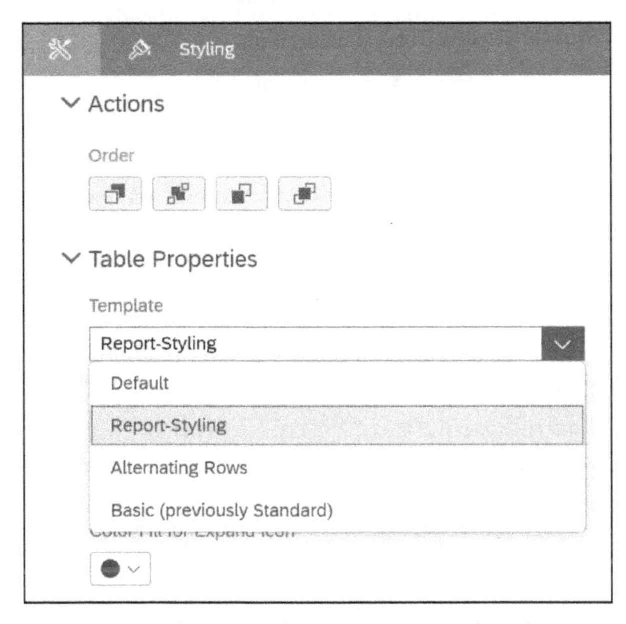

Figure 3.15 Styling Templates for a Fast and Performance Cheap Table Formatting

- **Ad-hoc styling**
  Another way to format a table is to use so-called *ad-hoc styling*. Ad-hoc styling is a very flexible styling technique in which an arbitrary number of cells or an arbitrarily large table section is selected and then directly formatted together in the **Styling**

panel. In terms of loading time savings, however, care should be taken here with the exact procedure, as the way the formatting is done across several cells determines the number of backend requests executed and thus the loading time of the table.

If a specific table region, such as the header or a specific dimension, is selected and formatting is applied to this area, SAP Analytics Cloud saves the entire context, i.e., **Header** or the selected dimension, for this formatting. The entire selected area is thus defined by one styling rule, as shown in Figure 3.16.

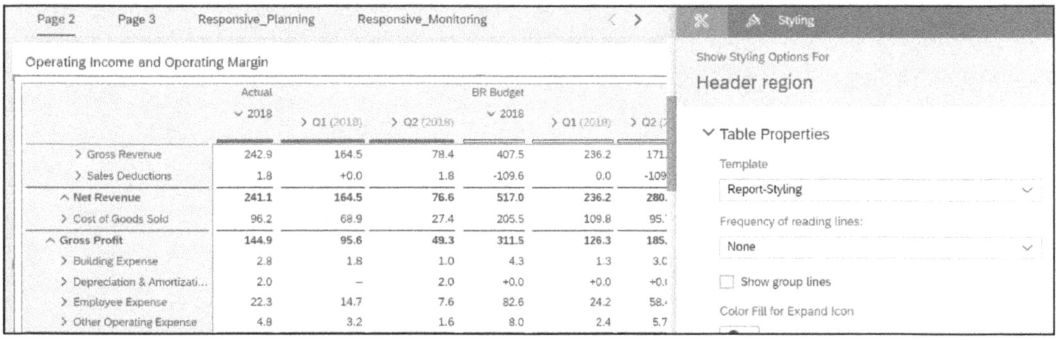

Figure 3.16 Use of Ad-hoc Styling for Predefined Table Areas

The situation is different when many individual cells are selected within the table. Each of these selected cells is treated as a separate area, for which a separate styling rule applies, regardless of whether the applied formatting is the same. This has a negative effect on our performance, as shown in Figure 3.17.

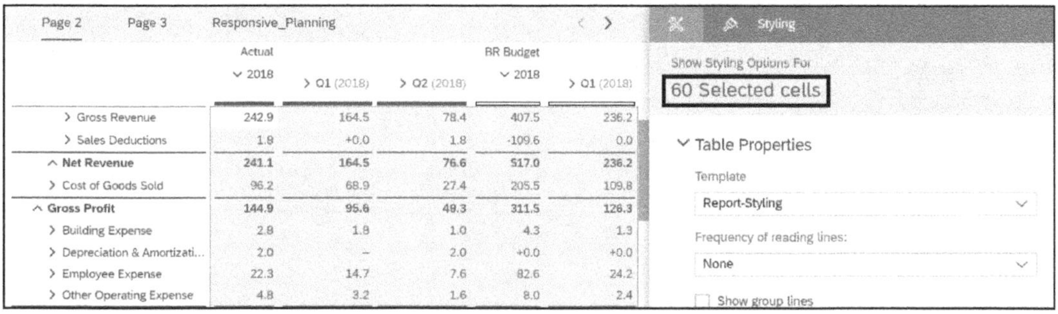

Figure 3.17 Avoid Selection of Multiple Individual Cells

Tip

If possible, use ad-hoc styles only in combination with large table areas, e.g., the header area or single dimensions, and refrain from styling many single cells via ad-hoc styling because a styling definition is created for each cell.

- **Styling rules**
  Up to now, we have established that, for effective table styling, as few styling definitions as possible should be created so as to minimize the impact on performance. Styling rules make it possible to set up complex and large-scale formatting and to store them in only one rule. A styling rule results in a styling definition that must be stored and executed in the system. Styling rules are thus an effective supplement to ad-hoc styling.

  To add a styling rule to your table, follow these steps, as shown in Figure 3.18:
  - Select the relevant table.
  - Enter the **Designer/Styling** panel.
  - In the section **Styling Rules,** click on the **+** button ❶.
  - In the **Styling Rule Panel**, enter a **Name** ❷.
  - Select the **Content** for the styling rule (in this case, we've selected **Header** ❸).
  - Under the **Style** dropdown, select **+Add New Style** ❹.
  - In the next panel, adjust the formatting and click on **Apply, as shown in** Figure 3.19.

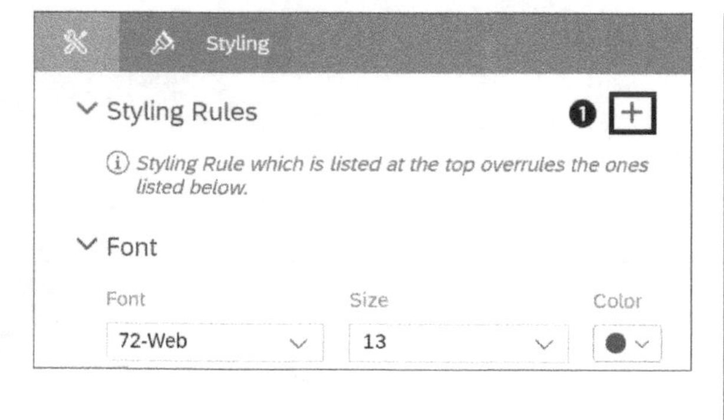

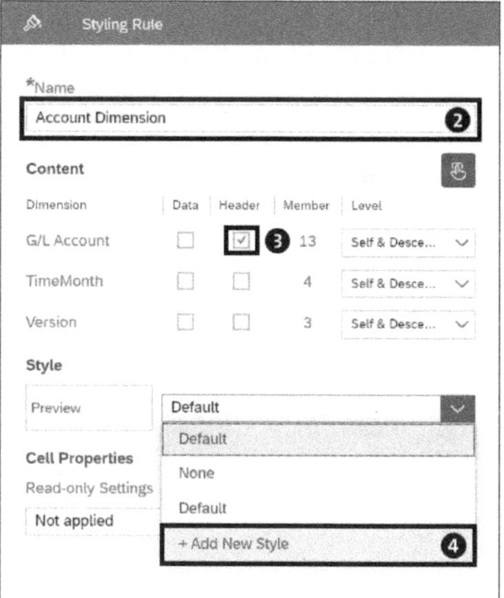

Figure 3.18 Styling Rules with a Defined Table Content as Powerful Formatting Tool

To illustrate this, we have chosen a simple example, in which we colored the first column of our table. In the corresponding styling rule, only the **Header** of the Dimension **G/L Account** was selected as context, as shown in Figure 3.18. This means that the styling rule applies only to the members, i.e., the labels, of this dimension, but not to the associated data itself, as shown in Figure 3.19. By defining a context, the applied styling remains even if the story builder filters the table or changes the drill.

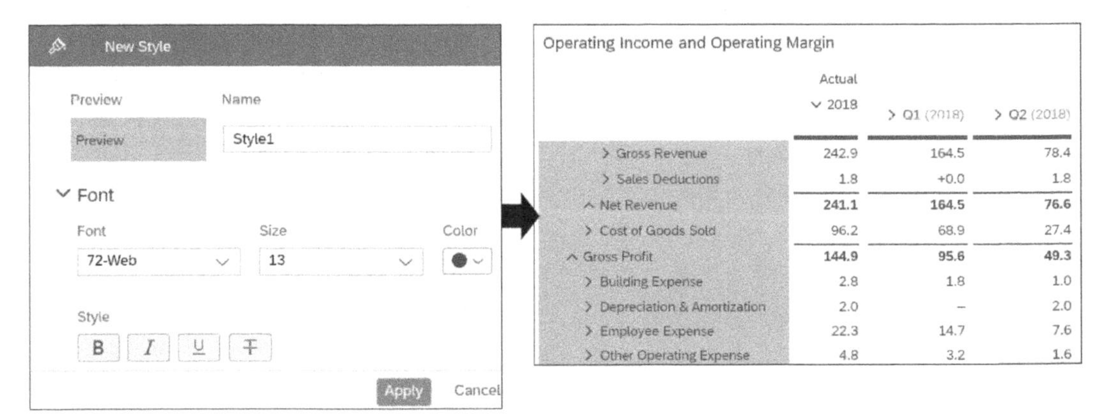

Figure 3.19 Color Definition of First Column by Using a Styling Rule

Warning

Even though styling rules are generally considered performance-friendly, it is advisable to do without them in the case of tables based on extremely large datasets. The stored logic that must be retrieved and checked each time when loading and updating, such as by filtering, can lengthen the rendering time of the table.

Performance Tip

We have now learned about three ways to format tables. In terms of performance improvements, we can summarize as follows:

Use styling rules whenever possible. They are a powerful tool that allows many formatting specifications to be stored within one styling rule and are therefore very cheap from a performance point of view. Ad-hoc styling should be used only in combination with a defined table range and not on multiple selected cells.

Further Reading

You can find more information on boosting the performance of SAP Analytics Cloud tables with proper styling techniques at the following URL: *http://s-prs.co/v566907/*.

3.2.4 Images

Images are a nice way to give a dashboard that extra something in terms of design or to add a visual explanation. However, in order not to negatively influence the loading time of a story, only images with a maximum size of 1Mb should be used, if possible. If you want to guarantee a high image quality at the same time, compressed web images or SVG images are recommended. The latter brings high quality even with a small image size. If this image format is not supported for whatever reason, PNG images are still preferable to JPG format.

Tip

Small icon-like images can be replaced with icon fonts such as SAP Fiori styles and fonts. To use them, icon fonts must first be added to the system. This can be done under **System • Administration • Default Appearance**. If you then scroll down to the **Fonts** section, you can add the link to access the corresponding icon fonts.

Further Reading

You can find more information about optimizing story design from the following resources:

- Janet Nguyen, "Best Practices for Performance," available at *http://s-prs.co/v566908*
- Nina Kunc, "SAP Analytics Cloud Performance Issues and Best Practices," available at *http://s-prs.co/v566909*
- Bernhard Sauerteig, "SAP Analytics Cloud – Performance dos and don'ts," available at *http://s-prs.co/v566910*
- SAP Analytics Cloud Help Portal, "Best Practices for Performance Optimization in Your Story Design," available at *http://s-prs.co/v566911*

3.3 Optimizing Filters, Calculations, and Linked Analysis

In the following sections, we will deep-dive into aspects related to filtering and drilling, such as the various filter types, hierarchy-level settings, and linked analysis. Afterwards, we will then learn how calculations and restricted measures can be used judiciously to keep the performance high.

3.3.1 Filtering and Drilling

Filtering and showing data in an aggregated state are both easy and highly recommended methods to reduce the number of shown data points in a chart and thus save performance. They visually lighten up the content of a dashboard and give the end user the opportunity to interact with and thus have a say in the content displayed.

Performance Tip

When opening the story, i.e., for the initial view port, let your dashboard initially display the data only in a highly aggregated state. The user can drill down to get the information at a more detailed level, if needed.

Story, Page, and Chart Filters

When using filters in SAP Analytics Cloud, you have the choice between chart filters, page filters, and story filters. The difference between these filters lies less in their function and setting options and more in their control area, which is derived from their name.

While the chart filters, according to the name, are anchored in the chart or table itself and thus control only this one element, page filters initially refer to all widgets of the corresponding page by default. The exact selection of widgets for which the filter is to take effect can be specifically adjusted in the filter menu under **Linked Analysis**. Story filters, on the other hand, address all widgets of all pages equally, which is why they are displayed in an extra bar above the page navigation.

To set up a story filter, follow the steps shown in Figure 3.20:

❶ Select the three-dots menu under **More**.

❷ Enable **Story Filter/Prompt**.

❸ Click on the filter icon and choose the requested dimension/measure.

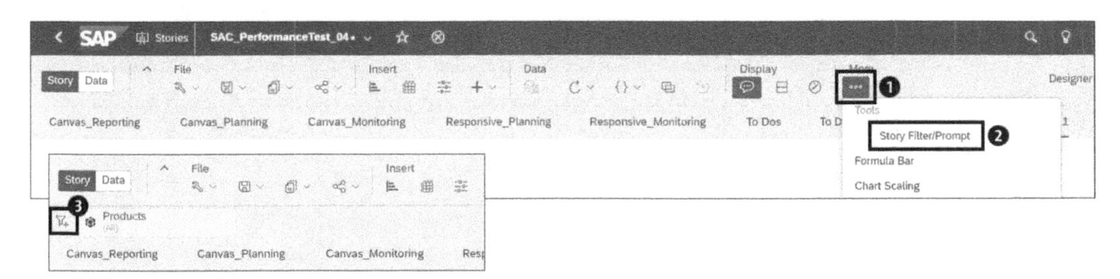

Figure 3.20 Story Filters to Address Multiple Widgets with Same Filter Settings

In the context of performance improvement, it is recommended to do without individual chart filters and instead to address as many elements as possible with a common filter, such as a story filter.

> **Exception**
>
> The situation is different for stories that feed their information from multiple linked models. Even if the same filter is required for all widgets, the filter should be set up on widget level. A story filter would have the opposite effect here and negatively affect performance.

Limiting Members and Hierarchy Levels in Filters

When you create a filter, you automatically enter the **Input Control Edit** menu. In the left area of the window, the user has the option to select the dimension members that are to be available for selection in the filter and reduce them to the most necessary, as shown in Figure 3.21.

The same applies to the hierarchy levels. In the lower right half of our **Input Control Edit** menu, you can specify a maximum number of levels to be displayed in the input control. This function should be used especially when working with dimensions with many hierarchy levels to make it easier for the user to navigate within the filter.

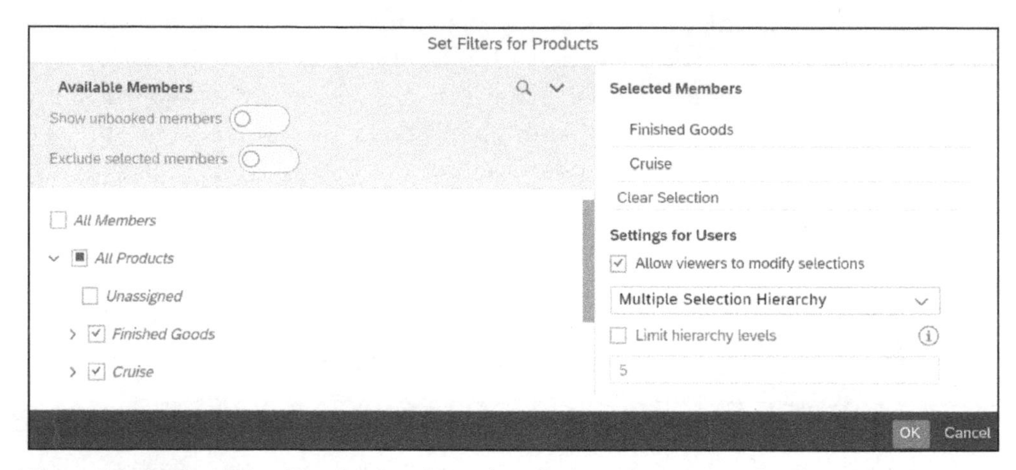

Figure 3.21 Define Filter Members and Number of Hierarchy Levels to be Shown in Input Controls

Expanding and Collapsing Filters

When displaying a filter, you have the option to choose between an *expanded* and *collapsed* filter. From a performance point of view, a collapsed filter is preferred, as shown in Figure 3.22 ❶.

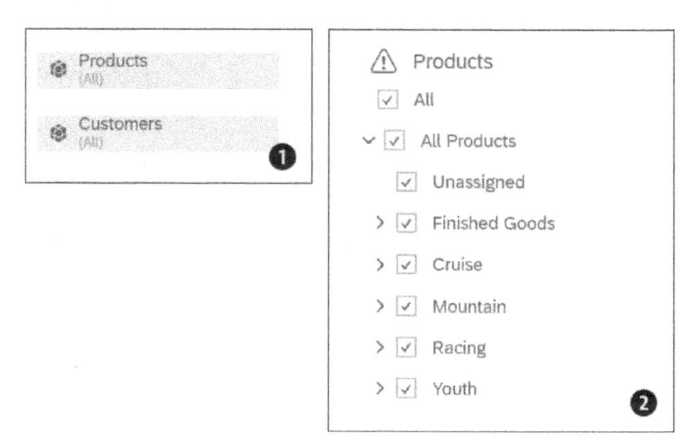

Figure 3.22 Avoid Expanded Page Filters and Prefer Collapsed Filters

An expanded filter has the advantage that all or many members are visible at first sight, and the filter selection is therefore faster ❷. However, it reloads regularly and therefore, for hierarchy dimensions or so-called *high cardinality dimension*, i.e., a dimension with 100 members or more, in an expanded state it can negatively affect your story's performance.

Unrestricted Drilling

For charts where a date range filter is applied, you can enhance the performance by enabling unrestricted drilling. With this, the user can drill to any hierarchy level of the corresponding dimension, regardless of the set filter.

To enable unrestricted drilling, as shown in Figure 3.23, follow these steps:

1. Select the chart with the date range filter applied.
2. Enter the **Builder** tab in the **Designer** Panel.
3. Scroll down to the **Filters** section and click on the time filter.
4. Scroll down to **Settings for User.**
5. Enable check box **Unrestricted Drilling.**

Figure 3.23 Unrestricted Drilling for Data Range Filters to Stop Hierarchy Updates

Cascading Effect

If multiple filters are used on a page, the *cascading effect* is activated by default. Through this effect, a set story or page filter influences the selection of available members of a related filter. This leads to a clear display of the filter members, but also increases the query volume. For performance purposes, the cascading effect should therefore be deactivated.

Deactivate the cascading effect by following these steps:

1. Select the relevant filter.
2. Enter the **Action Menu** button of the selected filter, as shown in Figure 3.24.
3. Disable the **Cascading Effect.**

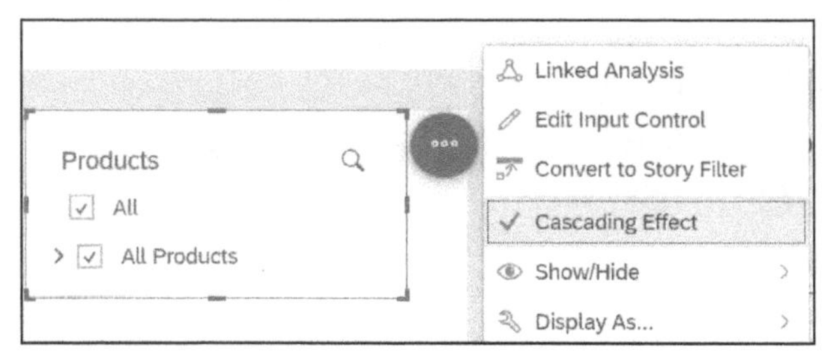

Figure 3.24 Deactivate the Cascading Effect

Linked Analysis

Depending on the use case, it might make sense to create a dependency between different visualizations, so that filter settings made in one chart automatically influence other visualizations. For example, by clicking on a bar of a bar chart or column chart, the entire page can be filtered according to the selection, provided that these charts use the same data model or different linked models.

However, you should proceed with caution and keep the number of linked charts as small as possible. With each new selection or filter change, those charts must be updated, which in turn triggers new queries.

3.3.2 Calculations and Restricted Measures

In SAP Analytics Cloud, we can create calculations, which can be added to the existing dataset as an additional measure and included in the dashboard accordingly. This can be done either in the modeler as part of the backend or in the story builder during the dashboard building process.

However, such calculations, which are created in the story, lead to performance losses since they do not use the backend but are processed in the browser's JavaScript engine instead. Therefore, in terms of performance improvement, it is advisable to either do without additional calculations or to set them up already in the model.

When it comes to aggregations, however, you should avoid setting up exception aggregations in the model for the sake of performance, as shown in Figure 3.25.

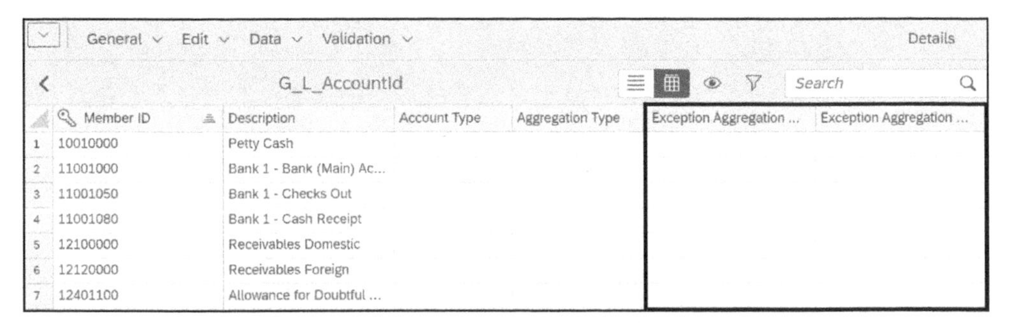

Figure 3.25 For the Sake of Performance, avoid Exception Aggregations

Instead, it is recommended to use restricted measures or calculations in the story itself, as they are processed faster. To set up a restricted measure, as shown in Figure 3.26, follow these steps:

1. Select a chart and enter the **Designer/Builder** panel.
2. In the **Measures** section, click on **+ Add Measure**.
3. Select **+Create Calculation...**
4. In the next window under **Type**, choose **Restricted Measure**.
5. Enter a measure **Name**.
6. Fill out the fields **Measure, Dimensions, Values, or Input Control**.
7. Click on **OK**.

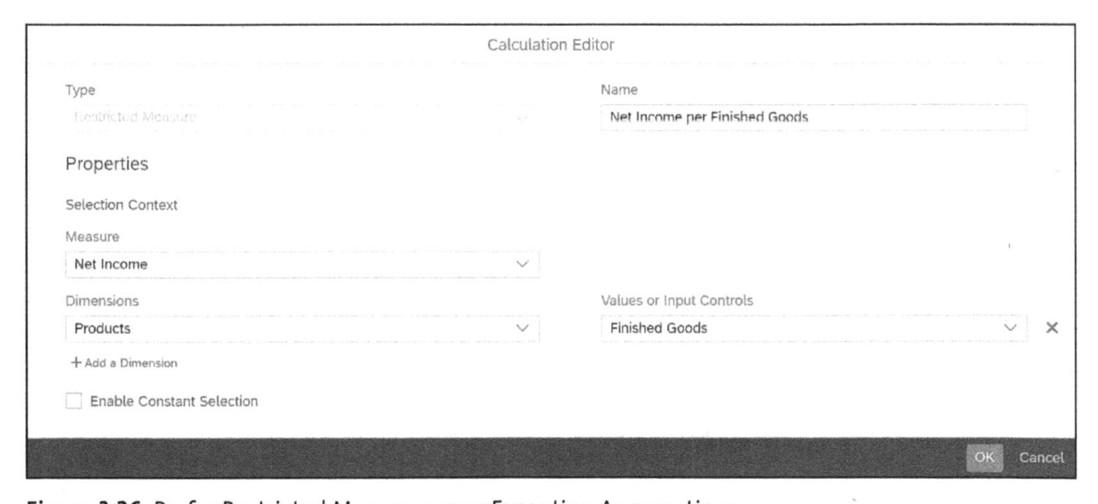

Figure 3.26 Prefer Restricted Measures over Exception Aggregations

Further Reading

You can find more information about optimizing filters, calculations, and linked analysis from the following resources:

- Janet Nguyen, "Best Practices for Performance," available at *http://s-prs.co/v566908*
- Nina Kunc, "SAP Analytics Cloud Performance Issues and Best Practices," available at *http://s-prs.co/v566909*
- Bernhard Sauerteig, "SAP Analytics Cloud – Performance dos and don'ts," available at *http://s-prs.co/v566910*
- SAP Analytics Cloud Help Portal, "Best Practices for Performance Optimization in Your Story Design," available at *http://s-prs.co/v566911*
- Janet Nguyen, "Enhance your Analysis with Restricted Measures," available at *http://s-prs.co/v566912*

3.4 Optimizing Mobile Device Performance

In the previous sections, we looked at the general best practices that we can use in the story builder to achieve the lowest possible load time when creating a standard dashboard. Now, let's look at dashboards designed specifically for mobile devices and the specifics of improving performance.

3.4.1 Device and App Settings

When viewing SAP Analytics Cloud Stories on a mobile phone, it is generally recommended to use the *mobile app for iOS*. This app is designed to render even so-called heavy widgets in terms of rendering time, such as geo maps, time series charts, tables, etc. in a device environment with only 2 GB RAM.

Make sure you use the latest iOS device and update your app to *release v2.106.0* or higher to ensure maximum performance. Also, for the app to run smoothly, you should always have at least 2 GB of free memory on your device. Like the desktop version, the SAP Analytics Cloud mobile app makes use of cache memory the first time a story is opened. This means that the story is rendered faster when it is reopened.

Constantly refreshing the data on the mobile device can be very annoying. Especially if the data situation does not change anymore or changes only in large intervals after setting up the model once, it is not necessary to request the data from the backend every time the story is reopened. Instead, disable the automatic refresh option in the device settings. This will display a snapshot of the previous session when the story is reopened until a data update is explicitly triggered.

To deactivate an automatic refresh in the mobile app, follow these steps:

1. Enter your user profile.
2. Select **Settings**.
3. Disable **Automatically Refresh**, as shown in Figure 3.27.

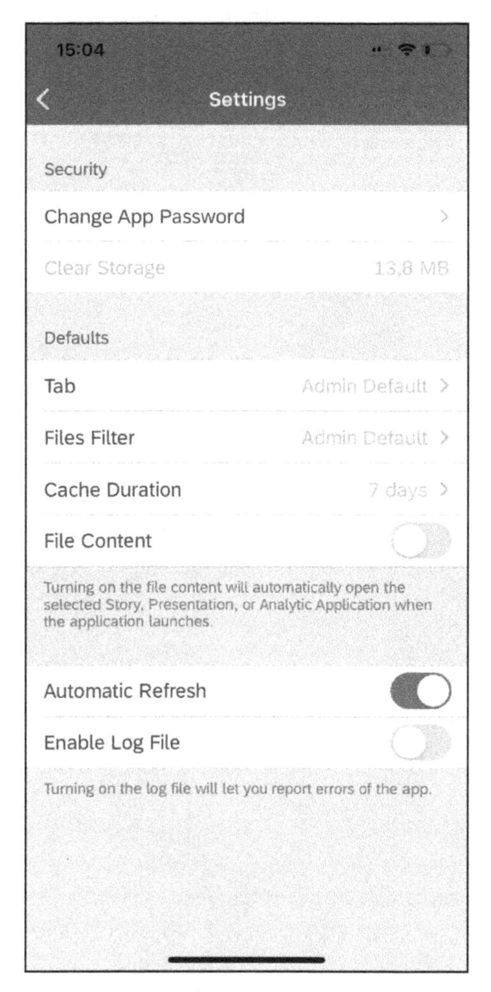

Figure 3.27 Disable Automatic Refresh for Mobile Devices

3.4.2 Optimized iOS and View Time Optimization

In Section 3.1.5, we looked at the usability and performance improvements of the optimized view mode of the SAP Analytics Cloud desktop version. In this section, we will now move on to the story optimizations for mobile devices.

In general, if a story was created with the *optimized design experience mode*, no optimized settings must be made in the mobile app. This applies to both the iOS and Android versions. For stories to which this does not apply, there are two settings that can help improve performance:

- **Optimized iOS**
  When this mode is enabled, content loads faster on iOS devices by using the embedded browser. Since this is an iOS-specific setting, it does not apply to stories viewed through the Android app.

- **View Time Optimization**
  This setting is available for both iOS and Android devices and provides features that improve dashboard performance and usability for some scenarios.

To enable both modes, follow these steps:

1. Open the relevant story.
2. Enter the **Edit** mode.
3. In the Settings menu (wrench tool icon), select **Story Details**.
4. Under **Optimized iOS**, select **Enable for iOS App**.
5. Under **View Time Optimization**, select **Enable Optimized Mode**.

Note

Before view time optimization mode can be applied for your iOS stories, the optimized iOS mode must be enabled first.

3.4.3 Rethink the Design on Mobile Devices

Now that we have dealt with the general settings, let's move on to the special features of the dashboard design for mobile devices.

Today, it is impossible to imagine our everyday working life without mobile devices, which are now firmly integrated into our work processes, whether it is to check the appointments of the day on the way to work, to write a short email, or to quickly investigate some document for gathering some last information in preparation for the next meeting. Number-based analyses or dashboards, as we will discuss in this book, also fall into this latter category and are increasingly accessed using smartphones.

Mobile devices and desktop devices are used in completely different ways when it comes to dashboards, and the requirements we place on a dashboard differ depending on the device we use to access it. While we would use the desktop application of SAP Analytics Cloud to obtain detail-specific information that is distributed over several pages and in different drilldown levels or to compare dimensions across several charts, we use the mobile app primarily to gain a quick overview. The focus here is mostly on high-level summaries and the current key performance indicators.

Since this is often done on the go, e.g., on the way from one meeting to the next, one of the main requirements is that it should be fast. This applies to the design of our story as well as the general performance. There should be no need to spend a lot of time filtering or scrolling through countless widgets to find the required information, and of course the story should not have to load for minutes before you get to see anything at all, which brings us back to performance.

Users who retrieve information on the go with their smartphone while keeping an eye on their surroundings or possibly having to join in on conversations are usually less willing to be patient and wait a long time for it. This should, therefore, be considered when creating dashboards that will also be accessed with mobile devices, and the design should be adapted to these needs accordingly to create high-performance stories even on devices with small screen sizes and low memory. In the following list, we will look at best practice tips that have proven their worth:

- **Use responsive pages for mobile devices**
  Responsive pages are the only page type supported by the mobile app that is in line with our ten golden rules (see Chapter 2, Section 2.9) and the recommendation of Section 3.2.1 to prefer them over canvas pages for a better-performing dashboard. By using a responsive style page, the content will automatically rearrange, adapting to the screen resolution and hiding elements such as legends or labels if necessary to make room for the main chart area.
- **Reduce the story content**
  When it comes to the information content of dashboards for mobile devices, less is more! Too many design elements make it difficult to find the one relevant piece of information, and the smaller the resolution, the fewer widgets there are in the visible screen. This means that we must scroll endlessly through the entire content, and quickly lose track of the available information. We are forced to navigate back and forth between the individual widgets again and again. As mentioned above, especially for users of mobile devices, who are not always in an environment that promotes concentration, the information must be available in such a way that it can be consumed in an effortless and, above all, time-saving manner.

  For our dashboard, this means keeping the design minimalistic and limiting the information to what is necessary. In Section 3.2.1, we also learned that by keeping the number of data-related widgets per page as low as possible, we automatically improve the rendering time of our story. Thus, from a performance point of view, there is reason enough to reprioritize and either reduce or restructure the story content if necessary.

  A first approach should be to reduce non-data-related elements, such as shapes and images, to the bare minimum. These do not contain any information of value to the user but serve solely for design and layout. Purely decorative elements should be used only sparingly and should not dominate the visible screen area to not distract from the actual content and thus make the transfer of information more difficult. On small devices, there is not much space for decorative details or pure placeholders next to charts and tables anyway.

  One possibility is to rely on summaries instead of detailed views and display only high-level information. By using highly aggregated data, we also reduce the number of data points shown, following the best practices from Section 3.2.2 and Section

3.2.3. If necessary, then we can also keep the information on lower data hierarchy levels in our story but keep the hierarchy collapsing until the user actively drills in and, with this request, the information is loaded from the backend. With this, we make sure that only the really needed information is loaded.

Further Reading

If you want to read more about performance improvements for SAP Analytics Cloud Stories on mobile devices, we recommend the following online resources:

- Jacob Stark, "Canvas vs Responsive Layouts in SAP Analytics Cloud," available at *http://s-prs.co/v566913*
- SAP Help Portal, "Preparing Stories for Mobile," available at *http://s-prs.co/v566914*
- Insight Software, "Designing for Mobile," available at *http://s-prs.co/v566915*

3.5 Using the Explorer View to Improve Performance

With the explorer view, you enter an area outside of the dashboard where you can take a closer look at the data yourself. In doing so, you can subdivide and compare the available dimensions and measures as desired. Thus, the explorer view is an interactive supplement to the dashboard, which enables the viewer to obtain additional information beyond what is shown.

For the designer, this means that by leaving the possibilities for their own detailed analysis to the viewer and thus virtually outsourcing them, they do not necessarily have to accommodate all the parameters available in the dataset in visualizations in the actual dashboard and do not have to provide a chart with comparisons and dependencies at each hierarchy level. This plays into the designer's hands, so to speak, in terms of performance.

3.5.1 Accessing the Explorer View

Before the user can access these functions, the explorer view must first be activated to allow further data exploration. One option to do so is on a per visualization level, by entering the chart settings using these steps, as shown in Figure 3.28:

1. In **Edit** mode, select the relevant chart.
2. Enter the **Builder** tab in the **Designer** panel.
3. Scroll down to the **Properties.**
4. Activate **Enable Explorer.**

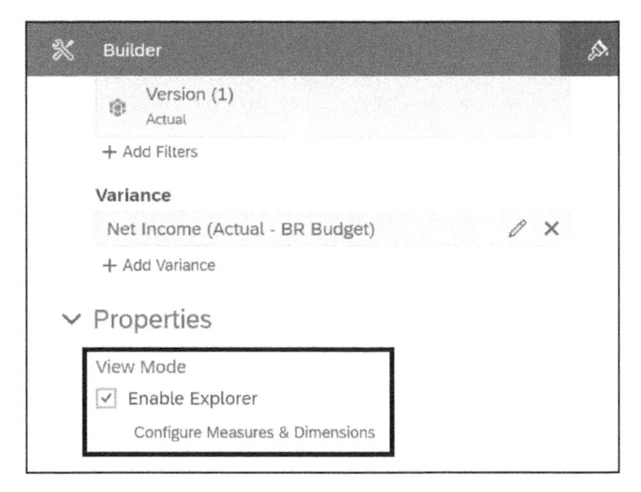

Figure 3.28 Enabling of the Explorer View on a Per-Widget Basis

In addition, SAP Analytics Cloud also offers the possibility of applying this setting to all charts and tables in one go. To do this, make sure that you have not already enabled explorer view for a chart or table and then simply select the explorer view mode icon in the story menu (see Figure 3.29 ❶). Afterwards, you will get prompted by a pop-up message to **Enable Explorer View for all Charts and Tables** in your story ❷.

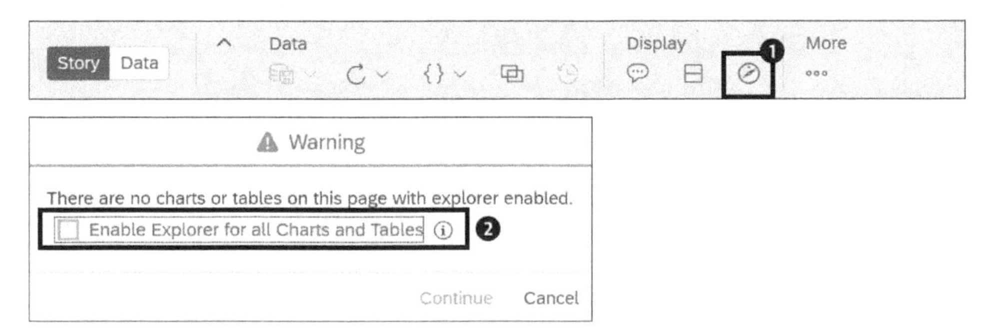

Figure 3.29 Enabling of the Explorer View for All Charts and Tables in One Go

After one of the two options has been executed, you can launch the explorer mode directly from the view mode of the story by either clicking the **Explorer View** link displayed above the relevant chart or by clicking the explorer view mode icon in the top menu bar of the story.

3.5.2 Deactivate Auto-Synchronization

Once in the explorer view, you can then scroll through all the measures and dimensions displayed there and select those you plan to examine in more detail. These are then displayed in the visualization output in the lower half of the window.

To ensure a smooth interaction with the explorer view during that selection process, it is recommended that you disable the automatic synchronization by deselecting the **Synchronize Visualization Automatically** button, as shown in Figure 3.30 ❶. This way, you can make your selection of dimensions and measures first without the chart refreshing and regenerating in the time in between. After the selection has been made, the visualization can be updated manually by simply pressing the **Refresh** icon ❷.

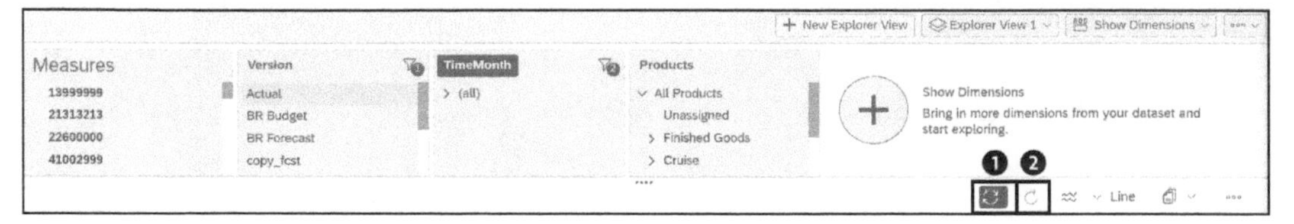

Figure 3.30 Disable the Synchronize Visualization Automatically Button

3.5.3 Show Only Required Dimensions and Measures

In explorer view, all measures and dimensions of a model are listed in the selection window by default. When working with large datasets, however, it is recommended to narrow it down and make a preselection, which makes it easier for the user to find the relevant measure or dimension and reduces scrolling. This setting can be done in the builder panel of the respective chart for which the explorer view was enabled.

Restrict the dimension available for selection in the explorer view using these steps:

1. In **Edit** mode, select the relevant chart.
2. Enter the **Builder** tab in the **Designer** panel.
3. Scroll down to **Properties.**
4. Select **Configure Measures & Dimensions**, as shown earlier in Figure 3.28.
5. In the next window, work through the tabs to the left to select/deselect all the necessary dimensions, as shown in Figure 3.31.

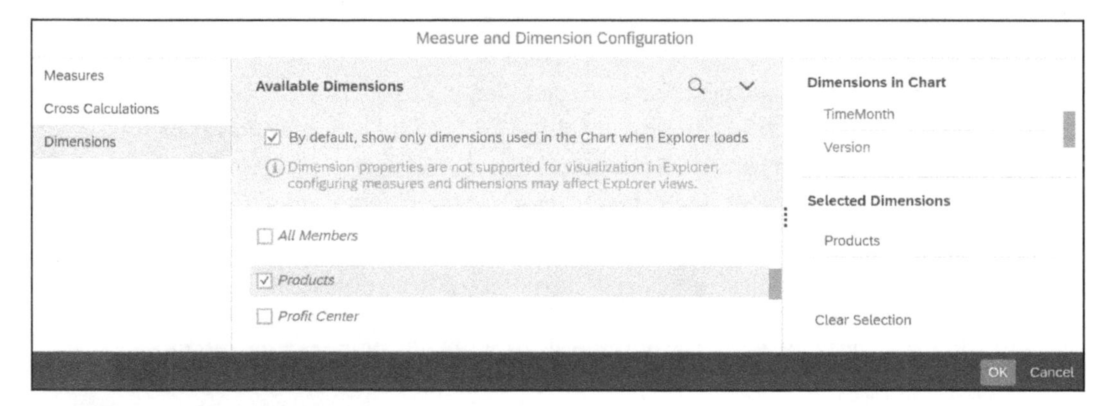

Figure 3.31 Restrict the Dimensions and Measures in the Measures and Dimensions Configuration Panel

Note

Dimensions that are being used in a visualization cannot be deselected in the measures and dimensions configuration menu. They will automatically show up in the explorer view.

Further Reading

If you want to read more about how to use the explorer view for further data explorations, visit the following resources:

- Fabian Aubert, "How to answer business questions by using the Explorer view in SAC?," available at *http://s-prs.co/v566916*
- Fabian Aubert, "New data exploration experience in SAP Analytics Cloud," available at *http://s-prs.co/v566917*
- Ikram El Khadji, "Release 2021.1 – SAP Analytics Cloud Story Exploration," available at *http://s-prs.co/v566918*

3.6 Planning Scenarios: Optimizing Settings and Advanced Formulas

In addition to the classic applications aimed at analyzing current and historical data, such as visualizations and reporting, SAP Analytics Cloud also offers a range of features developed specifically for planning scenarios, such as financial and operational planning.

A major component of planning scenarios is forecasting and modeling for future time periods based on current and historical data.

In Chapter 5, we will learn that, from a performance point of view, analytic models are faster than planning models and therefore the former are to be preferred. However, the use case may make it impossible to do without a planning model, so in the following sections we will look at how we can still get the best performance out of visualizations based on planning scenarios.

3.6.1 Version Management

When working with planning models, users can create different versions and organize them. While it is often standard practice when working with historical data to use only one actual version and update it with regular data imports, multiple versions are often created for predictive scenarios. A common approach, which is mainly characterized by pioneers in semantic notations in the business domain such as the International Business Communication Standard (IBCS), is to store different types of plans, such as forecast, budget, and strategic plans, as different versions. The different versions are created in a separate dimension "version" in the model.

Besides the "public" versions, which can be viewed by all users with the appropriate user roles and permissions, there are also private versions, which can be used only by the user who created them, until he decides to share them and thus convert them into a "public" version.

And exactly here we enter an area that must be approached with care from a performance point of view. For scenarios in which users create their own large private versions based on and in addition to the existing public versions, planning features can cause errors and require re-execution later. Therefore, to not affect performance negatively when working with a mix of public and private versions, try to keep the following tips in mind:

- **Delete private versions**
  As a user with delete permission, you can remove unused private versions or revert them to public versions on your model. For private versions of your model created by other users, you could try to delete all private versions, as further described in Chapter 5.
- **Use filters before copying data to private versions**
  When creating a private version, the data that is copied can be restricted. You should generally copy only what is needed and thus keep the amount of data as small as possible.
- **Limit the data of the public version that you include in the edit mode**
  Avoid putting all data of a public version per se into edit mode and instead limit it to the data required for the corresponding use case. If the planning area is enabled and defined in the modeler, you can also specify that only the recommended planning area can be put into edit mode. We will discuss this in more detail in Chapter 5.

3.6.2 Data Entry

For tables based on a planning model, the user can manually add values or overwrite data by typing in the table cells. When doing so, the tips outlined in the following sections can help to prevent a negative impact on performance.

Limit the Number of Updated Leaf Cells

Do not try to change too many table cells at once, but rather divide them into several stages and deal with them one after another. Otherwise, the system will automatically check pairwise dependency in the background to identify restrictions. The number of these checks thus grows quadratically with the number of modified cells. Therefore, the update process is faster when proceeding in several individual steps instead. For tables with multiple dimensions, split the number of cells to be overwritten with new data into different sets of members for each dimension.

Note

In order not to overstrain the performance endlessly, limits are stored in the system. If the runtime exceeds a certain value, the data input is blocked and an error message is displayed. Such a limit also exists for the number of cells to be changed, since data entries at the highest hierarchy level automatically also affect the lower levels and thus quickly lead to a massively increasing number of update processes.

These dependency checks are not executed and can be avoided if, in our relevant table area, the following points are true:

- The visible cells do not include:
  - Formulas
  - Lookups
  - Dynamic time navigations
  - Calculated dimensions
- All visible dimensions are restricted to leaves.

For the latter, to restrict visible dimensions to leaves, follow these steps:

1. In **Edit** mode, select the relevant table.
2. Enter the **Builder** tab in the **Design** panel.
3. In the **Rows** section, enter the **action menu icon** of the relevant dimension.
4. Select **Hierarchy...**
5. In the next window, toggle on **Show only leaves in widget**, as shown in Figure 3.32.

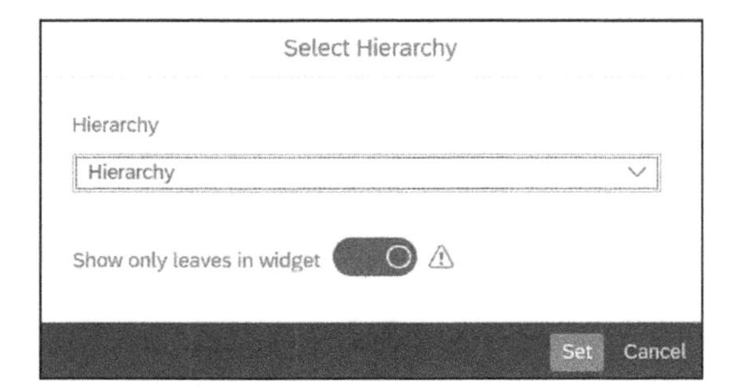

Figure 3.32 Activation of Flat Presentation Style of Hierarchical Dimensions

For models where the **Unassigned (#)** element is missing for many dimensions, splitting the data into the individual leaf members for all dimensions can result in performance degradation. In this case, the system reacts either with a warning or with the recommendation to filter the data beforehand or to transport it to another target cell.

Warning

Keep in mind that we learned in Section 3.2.3 that showing too many dimension members can lead to a massive increase of shown data and thus extend the processing time of the widget. The choice of leaf presentation mode is therefore a trade-off between widget loading time and data entry process. Try both options and then decide which one is better for the intended use.

Limit the Number of Deleted Cells

Almost everything that was mentioned in the previous section about updating can also be applied to the deletion of many table cells. However, there are two exceptions:

- For the delete process, restricting the dimension members to the leaves does not lead to any performance advantages. This step is therefore not necessary.
- To experience an actual performance boost by deleting cells, the cells selected for this purpose must form a complete rectangle.

All the above tips for improving performance apply to removing many cells. If, on the other hand, only a few cells are deleted from a comparatively large table area, even if they are unbooked, this can lead to significant slowdowns.

Note

For entering values into table cells, the following requirements must be fulfilled:

- The relevant table cell is not locked by a so-called value lock or by data locking
- The user must have permission to overwrite model data

3.6.3 Data Actions, Multi Actions, and Allocations

Planning scenarios usually involve special planning features, such as data actions, multi actions, and allocations:

- **Data actions**
  Data actions can be used to execute a series of operations based on a planning model at the click of a button. This can be copying data from a previous period to the current period within one model or between different models or performing complex calculations based on individual measures. You can choose to create data actions via the graphical environment either by using in-built functions or, for developers, by scripting. The execution of data actions does work on command by pressing the **Data Action Trigger**, a button that stores the data actions, or by scheduling it in the calendar.

Note

To execute data actions, the user must have the required role for **Execution** first. In addition, where data access control is applied on individual dimension members, **Write** access for those dimensions is needed to be able to change any data.

- **Multi actions**
  If a user needs to perform a whole sequence of operations one after the other, such as data actions, predictive analyses, publishing private versions, data locking, or a combination of all, then multi actions are an effective tool to save time. The **Multi Action** tool can be accessed directly from the main menu.

Further Reading

If you want to read more about multi actions, visit the blog post by Charlie Lin, "See how SAP Analytics Cloud Multi Actions change the way that you do planning," available at *http://s-prs.co/v566919*.

- **Allocations**
  Whenever a financial plan is created in a company, the first step is usually to define a budget at the top level. These set figures are then broken down and assigned to the subsequent areas. A common use case for this kind of distribution is indirect costs, such as IT expenses, which usually must be determined according to multiple dimensions like **Region** and **Department**.

  Allocations are one of SAP Analytics Cloud's main planning features and allow you to split up a high-level predefined budget amongst another dimension by weighing it based on a so-called driver value.

These special planning features, which run in the background, can affect performance if used incorrectly. To avoid such features limiting each other, we have collected some recommendations below:

- As always, only use data that you really need. Therefore, before you apply any of these features, narrow down your data by filtering.
- If possible, do not use calculated measures or exception aggregations set up in the model to create data actions.
- If you want to add multiple data actions based on the same model and version to a multi action, it is better to do this in a roundabout way to improve performance. First transfer these data actions to a new data action, and then add it to the multi action.
- When using allocations, try to keep the number of reference members by which the allocations are done low. Additionally, filter the reference dimensions to the required members to avoid unnecessary additional combination of members during the allocation process.

3.6.4 Optimize Advanced Formulas

After having provided a brief overview of data actions in general in the previous chapter, we now want to deal with a special data action type, the advanced formulas. These allow us to design formulas for calculations and transformations, and to store them as scripts. By manually triggering this script using a so-called action trigger button, we apply these calculations to the underlying data and overwrite data within a defined area of the model.

Due to their asynchronous functionality, they differ from the standard formulas, the real-life calculations, which are triggered with every data entry or every new update. On first impulse, the latter may seem like the ideal planning dashboard, where formulas are executed virtually invisibly in the background whenever we make changes to the numbers.

But this quickly leads to an increased number of backend queries and thus to an impairment of the workflow. From a performance point of view, data action's advanced formulas are therefore preferable for all those situations where it is not necessary to have new data inputs immediately result in new executions of the calculations.

Now that we have explained when advanced formulas are to be preferred, let's move on to the actual formula content and the performance aspect. As with almost all scripting languages, when formulating calculations and transformations for data actions, there is usually more than one way to get the desired result, and not all of them are equally favorable in terms of processing time. When creating a script for advanced formulas, there are also points to consider if your goal is to create a powerful planning dashboard. In the following sections, we have listed the most important ones for you.

Estimated Function Scope

In SAP Analytics Cloud, you have the possibility to display the scope for some supported functions after creating your script. This helps you to identify unrestricted dimensions more easily. To do this, you must hover over one of these functions with the mouse. Table 3.6 provides a list with all functions supported for this scope check.

Functions Where the Scope of All Dimensions is Shown
DATA
RESULTLOOKUP
LINK
CARRYFORWARD
DELETE

Table 3.6 Functions Supported for Check of Estimated Function Scope

Functions Where Only the Scope of a SPECIFIED Dimension is Shown
ATTRIBUTE
Date functions (DAY, DAYSINMONTH, DAYSINYEAR, MONTH, DATERATIO, DATEDIFF, YEAR)

Table 3.6 Functions Supported for Check of Estimated Function Scope (Cont.)

When you hover over one of these functions, a pop-up window appears with information about the dimensions used in the respective functions and the number of members included in them, as shown in Figure 3.33. Dimensions for which all members are used are also listed in the **Dimensions Not Restricted** list. This list helps to keep track of all dimensions used in functions and to identify those that might cause high runtimes due to many members. To ensure maximum performance, you should always try to keep the scope as small as possible and restrict the dimensions used as much as possible before using them in functions.

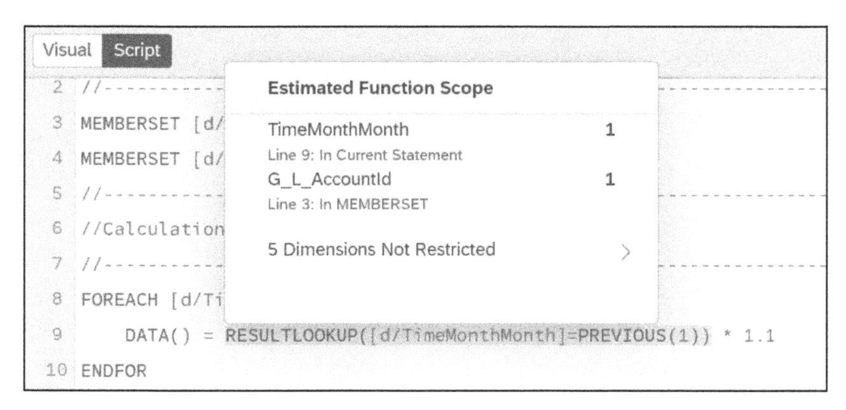

Figure 3.33 Estimated Function Scope as Hover Over Info

FOREACH Functions

Whenever calculations are performed along several members of a dimension and each result represents the initial situation for the calculation based on the next member—i.e., the result increases cumulatively with each further member—FOREACH functions are usually used.

A common application for this is the financial budget planning along the time dimension. Here, for example, a fixed percentage revenue increase per period is assumed and then recalculated for every subsequent period (e.g., 15 percent growth every month). With the FOREACH function, this happens for all periods included using one single script (see Listing 3.1).

Sample Script

```
MEMBERSET [d/AccountID] = "Net_Revenue"
MEMBERSET [d/DateMonth] = "202201" TO "202206"

FOREACH [d/DateMonth]
    DATA() = RESULTLOOKUP([d/DateMonth]=PREVIOUS(1)) * 1.15
ENDFOR
```

Listing 3.1 Example of a Calculation of the Revenue with the Assumption of a Monthly 15 Percent Increase

In the following sections, we will take a further look at what we must pay attention to when using this function, if we don't want to unintentionally fall into one or the other performance trap.

Reduce the Scope

With the example given above, it is not that difficult to imagine that such calculations become more expensive the more members are included in a dimension or, explicitly for this example, the more months for which this calculation must be done consecutively. With every additional member, the calculation will eventually be repeated and will slow down the final performance a little more.

The most effective way to reduce running times for Advanced Formulas is to limit the scope of the calculation. Therefore, when creating a calculation, the first approach should always be to get clarity on the data input that is required for the planned data action and to exclude anything beyond that from the calculation scope. In the following list, we will show you three effective approaches with which this can be achieved:

- **Filtering the scope**
  Let's say, for example, you are only interested in revenue development for the entire last year. In that case, there is no reason to run this calculation over the entire period available in your dataset just for the sake of completeness, even if it goes back an impressive ten years. Instead, you should restrict the date dimension accordingly beforehand. This can be done either with the `MEMBERSET` method function or by including the `FOREACH` function in an IF statement, as shown in Listing 3.2.

Sample Script

```
MEMBERSET [d/AccountID] = "Net_Revenue"
MEMBERSET [d/DateMonth] = "202201" TO "202206"

IF [d/Product] = "GET_UP_ESPRESSO" THEN
    FOREACH [d/DateMonth]
        DATA() = RESULTLOOKUP([d/DateMonth]=PREVIOUS(1)) * 1.15
```

```
    ENDFOR
ENDIF
```

Listing 3.2 Instead of Running Calculations on the Entire Dataset, Filter the Scope Beforehand

- **Reduce the number of dimensions in the** `FOREACH` **scope**
  Another way to effectively reduce the number of calculations performed in the background is to limit the dimensions in the scope of the `FOREACH` function to what is necessary. If more than one dimension is listed in the scope, the calculation must be performed for each existing combination of dimensions members.

Sample Script

```
FOREACH [d/DateMonth] , [d/Region]
    // [STATEMENT…]
```

  This means that, for a scenario where we have two dimensions mentioned in the scope with *n* and *m* dimension members, respectively, there is a total number of $N = m*n$ combinations, and the calculation must be performed for each one of them.

  Therefore, especially with dimensions with a high number of members, care should be taken to include only the most necessary ones in the scope.

- **Run calculations on booked values only**
  The last option, if the use case does allow it, is to restrict the calculation to booked values only with `FOREACH.BOOKED`, as shown in Listing 3.3.

Sample Script

```
MEMBERSET [d/AccountID] = "Net_Revenue"
MEMBERSET [d/DateMonth] = "202201" TO "202212"

FOREACH.BOOKED [d/DateMonth]
    DATA() = RESULTLOOKUP([d/DateMonth]=PREVIOUS(1)) * 1.15
ENDFOR
```

Listing 3.3 Reduce the Scope by Restricting Calculations to Booked Members

Replace FOREACH with DATA()

In Listing 3.3, we showed an example of a cumulative calculation of a month-to-month growth performed along a time dimension by using a `FOREACH` function. There, the expected profit after twelve months was determined using a fixed month-to-month growth rate. In another scenario, we also want to calculate the revenue to be expected after exactly twelve months. But instead of a monthly growth rate, this time we assume a 15 percent growth compared to the same month of the previous year. The crucial difference here is that we do not have to add up our expected profit but can calculate it directly in one step.

In the following, we show two different ways to calculate the revenue, Listing 3.4 and Listing 3.5. Our scope is limited to the entire year 2022, and we assume a year-over-year growth of 15 percent. Both scripts lead to the same result; however, Listing 3.5 does not use the FOREACH method and therefore runs faster.

Sample Script

```
MEMBERSET [d/AccountID] = "Net Revenue"
MEMBERSET [d/DateMonth] = "202201" TO "202212"

FOREACH [d/DateMonth]
    DATA() = RESULTLOOKUP([d/DateMonth] = PREVIOUS(12)) * 1.15
ENDFOR
```

Listing 3.4 Use of Unnecessary FOREACH

Sample Script

```
MEMBERSET [d/AccountID] = "Net Revenue"
MEMBERSET [d/DateMonth] = "202201" TO "202212"

DATA() = RESULTLOOKUP([d/DateMonth] = PREVIOUS(12)) * 1.15
```

Listing 3.5 Sometimes, All You Need Is DATA()

Replace FOREACH with CARRYFORWARD

In the examples above, we have used scenarios in which we assumed a constant percentage growth. Now let's imagine that instead of a regular percentage we add the same absolute value to each calendar period. In this case, we can replace FOREACH with CARRYFORWARD and achieve better performance.

Use BREAK Keyword to Avoid Unnecessary Iterations

In scenarios in which not necessarily all members of a dimension must run through a calculation, and thus their number necessarily determines how often this calculation is to be executed, we can work with so-called BREAK keywords instead. These include a condition in the calculation, e.g., a fixed value. Only if this condition is fulfilled, and/or the given value is reached, does the computation loop stop automatically, as shown in Listing 3.6.

Sample Script

```
MEMBERSET [d/AccountID] = "Travel_Expenses"
MEMBERSET [d/DateMonth] = "202201" TO "202206"

FOREACH [d/DateMonth]
    IF ResultLookup([d/DateMonth]=PREVIOUS(1)) * 1.15 > 1400
        BREAK
    ENDIF
    Data() = ResultLookup([d/DateMonth]=PREVIOUS(1)) * 1.15
ENDFOR
```

Listing 3.6 Use a BREAK Statement to Avoid Unnecessary Computation Loops

IF Statements

Conditional statements, such as IF statements, are a powerful tool for linking actions or calculations to logical checks and are practically indispensable in complex scripts. For particularly complex situations, several of these statements are often built into one another.

However, the scripter must be aware that with each IF statement, an additional query is created with which the validity of the conditions defined in it is checked in the background. Especially with nested IF statements, this check can quickly have a negative impact on performance. Therefore, as intuitive as their use may feel, IF statements should be used with caution.

Therefore, in the following two subsections, we will look at best practices on how to best handle IF statements with performance in mind.

Replace IF Statement with DATA() and RESULTLOOKUP()

If a given condition is resulting in only one single member, there is no need to use an IF statement as a filter statement. Using one here leads only to an unnecessary additional backend request, as shown in Listing 3.7. Instead, include the condition as a filter within DATA() and RESULTLOOKUP(). This way, we reduce the number of executed backend queries to one and thus increase the performance in our script, as shown in Listing 3.8.

Sample Script

```
IF [d/AccountID] = "A" THEN
    DATA() = RESULTLOOKUP([d/Product_ID] = "GET_UP_ESPRESSO") + RESULT-
LOOKUP([d/AccountID] = "B")
ENDIF
```

Listing 3.7 Filter Defined Unnecessarily in an IF Statement

Sample Script

```
DATA([d/AccountID] = "A") = RESULTLOOKUP([d/Product_ID] = "GET_UP_
ESPRESSO" , [d/AccountID] = "A") + RESULTLOOKUP([d/AccountID] = "B")
```

Listing 3.8 Filter Defined with DATA() andRESULTLOOKUP()

Choose the Order of IF Statements Carefully

In complex scripts, several IF statements are often nested within one another. The overview is then quickly lost, and calculations can be repeated unnecessarily. It goes without saying that this has a costly effect on performance.

When using multiple IF statements, carefully consider the order. Calculations that are based on the same conditions should be packed together in one IF statement at the top, if possible.

To illustrate, we first show an example of a performance-impairing script as it should not be written (see Listing 3.9).

In it, we see a calculation repeated in several consecutive IF statements. The same redundant condition [d/LocationID] = "Walldorf" appears in all three repetitions, immediately after the set date condition.

Sample Script

```
IF [d/DateMonth] = "202301" THEN
    IF [d/LocationID] = "Walldorf" THEN
        DATA() = RESULTLOOKUP([d/Product_ID] = "GET_UP_ESPRESSO") + RESULT-
LOOKUP([d/AccountID] = "B")
        DATA([d/FLOW] = "#") = RESULTLOOKUP([d/DateMonth]= PREVIOUS(12)) *
0.5
    ENDIF
ELSEIF
IF [d/DateMonth] = "202302" THEN
    IF [d/LocationID] = "Walldorf" THEN
        DATA() = RESULTLOOKUP([d/Product_ID] = "GET_UP_ESPRESSO") + RESULT-
LOOKUP([d/AccountID] = "B")
        DATA([d/FLOW] = "#") = RESULTLOOKUP([d/DateMonth]= PREVIOUS(12)) *
0.5
    ENDIF
ELSEIF
IF [d/DateMonth] = "202303" THEN
    IF [d/LocationID] = "Walldorf" THEN
        DATA() = RESULTLOOKUP([d/Product_ID] = "GET_UP_ESPRESSO") + RESULT-
LOOKUP([d/AccountID] = "B")
        DATA([d/FLOW] = "#") = RESULTLOOKUP([d/DateMonth]= PREVIOUS(12)) *
```

```
0.5
    ENDIF
ENDIF
```

Listing 3.9 Typical Example of a Performance Expensive Script to Avoid

Now, we try to reduce the number of repeating conditions and calculations to be performed in the background by doing a little restructuring here. To do this, we first filter by location and insert the date-related calculation into a second IF statement (see Listing 3.10).

Sample Script

```
IF [d/LocationID] = "Walldorf" THEN
    DATA() = RESULTLOOKUP([d/Product_ID] = "GET_UP_ESPRESSO") + RESULT-
LOOKUP([d/AccountID] = "B")

    IF [d/ d/DateMonth] = ("202201", "202202", "202203") THEN
        FOREACH[d/DateMonth]
            DATA([d/FLOW] = "#") = RESULTLOOKUP([d/DateMonth] = PREVIOUS
(12)) * 0.5
        ENDFOR
    ENDIF
ENDIF
```

Listing 3.10 Script with Rearranged Order of Filter Statements and Reduced Number of Calculations and Backend Checks

Because we split our calculations and pre-filtered the scope in the first IF statement, the total number of conditions that need to be checked is significantly reduced.

In this customized script, we also see an example of a FOREACH function inside an IF statement.

In principle, it is not impossible to place FOREACH statements outside the IF statement, i.e., in front of it (see Listing 3.11).

Sample Script

```
FOREACH[d/DateMonth]
    IF [d/LocationID] = "Walldorf" THEN
        DATA() = RESULTLOOKUP([d/Product_ID] = "GET_UP_ESPRESSO") + RESULT-
LOOKUP([d/Account] = "Sales")
    ENDIF
ENDFOR
```

Listing 3.11 FOREACH Function Placed Outside the IF Statement

However, this would only cause unnecessary calculations. As we learned above, the key to maximizing the performance of FOREACH functions is to limit its scope and reduce the number of dimension members the calculation must run through. We can achieve this by nesting the FOREACH function inside the IF statement, provided both refer to the same dimensions, and use the defined IF condition to narrow down the scope in advance (see Listing 3.12).

Sample Script

```
IF [d/LocationID] = "Walldorf" THEN
    FOREACH[d/DateMonth]
        DATA() = RESULTLOOKUP([d/Product_ID] = "GET_UP_ESPRESSO") + RESULT-
LOOKUP([d/AccountID] = "Sales")
    ENDFOR
ENDIF
```

Listing 3.12 FOREACH Function Inside the IF Statement to Reduce the Scope

Reduce the Number of RESULTLOOKUP Functions

With RESULTLOOKUP(), we can filter dimension members and thus limit the amount of data. This function can also be integrated into the direct calculation and is therefore one of the most frequently used functions for advanced formulas.

However, its influence on the total runtime of our story should not be underestimated, because for each RESULTLOOKUP() used in the script, a query to the data model is created to load data. To allow fast processing, you should therefore try to include as few RESULT-LOOKUP() functions as possible within a single calculation. Sometimes basic arithmetic rules are sufficient to reduce the number, as the following two examples show, Listing 3.13 and Listing 3.14.

Sample Script

```
RESULTLOOKUP("A")*RESULTLOOKUP("B")+RESULTLOOKUP("A")*RESULT-
LOOKUP("C")+RESULTLOOKUP("A")*RESULTLOOKUP("D")
```

Listing 3.13 Example of Script with Unnecessarily Many RESULTLOOKUP() Functions

Sample Script

```
RESULTLOOKUP("A")*(RESULTLOOKUP("B")+RESULTLOOKUP("C")+RESULTLOOKUP("D"))
```

Listing 3.14 Use of Basic Algorithmic Rules to Reduce the Number of Used RESULT-LOOKUP() Functions

Reduce the Number of DATA Functions

With the DATA() function, we write or overwrite already existing entries in the target scope with given values or with data filtered by RESULTLOOKUP(). As with the RESULTLOOKUP() function, the same applies here: Each DATA() function used in the script creates a query. The goal should be to avoid excessive use of this function.

Whenever the values of a whole group of members should be transferred to another one within the same dimension and with only one move, one possibility would be to do this for each affected dimension member of this group individually and with a separate DATA() function, as shown in Listing 3.15.

Sample Script

```
MEMBERSET [d/G_L_AccountId] = ("A","B","C")

DATA([d/AccountID]= "G") = RESULTLOOKUP([d/AccountID]= "A")
DATA([d/AccountID]= "H") = RESULTLOOKUP([d/AccountID]= "B")
DATA([d/AccountID]= "I") = RESULTLOOKUP([d/AccountID]= "C")
```

Listing 3.15 Use of DATA() to transfer values of a set of members to another one

However, to avoid excessive use of DATA() functions, we can instead create the target members ('G','H' and 'I') as attributes of our source members within our model (see Table 3.7).

ID	Description	Type	Attribute
A	Inventory and supplies	AST	G
B	Vehicle	AST	H
C	Equipment and machinery	AST	I
G	Cashflow01	EXP	
H	Cashflow02	EXP	
I	Cashflow03	EXP	

Table 3.7 Example where Target Dimension Members Are Set as Attributes

This way, we have created a direct link between our source and target members and can refer to them with only one DATA() function, as shown in Listing 3.16.

Sample Code

```
MEMBERSET [d/ G_L_AccountId] = ("A","B","C")

DATA([d/G_L_AccountId] = [d/G_L_AccountId].[p/ATTRIBUTE]) = RESULTLOOKUP()
```

Listing 3.16 Define Attributes to Create a Direct Link between Source and Target Members

Use Default Configuration Settings instead of NULL Comparisons

Often in scripts we check dimension members to see if values exist for them before executing a particular formula. If this is not the case, we react with an alternative action:

- The budget planning for the following year, for example, is usually determined based on the current data. However, this procedure does not work for newly added products for a certain location, since the previous year's value is missing here. So as not to start our financial planning for that product with 0, we would have to fall back on another value here—for example, on another product with comparable conditions or, if available, the same product in other locations.
- However, any '`=NULL`' comparison statement used in the script will cause the script to perform this check for all dimension members first and thus slow down the performance.

We can avoid `NULL` comparisons by using the global configuration function `CONFIG.GENERATE_UNBOOKED_DATA` to specify how to deal with unbooked data, i.e., cells with empty values.

If this is set to `ON`, unbooked cells are treated as 0 values. This allows them to be included in actions where values are copied from one cell to another. If this configuration function is turned off, which is the default setting, unbooked data will be ignored during such transfers and only existing values will be copied.

The best way to avoid NULL comparisons and thus unnecessary data checks in the backend is to keep the default settings of this configuration function, since this already plays into our hands. We can avoid additional NULL checks in the script to exclude unbooked cells from calculations with the following listing:

```
CONFIG.GENERATE_UNBOOKED_DATA = OFF
```

Further Reading

If you want to read more about planning scenarios, for further data exploration, visit the following resources:

- SAP Analytics Cloud Help Portal, "Copying and Pasting Cell Values," available at *http://s-prs.co/v566920*
- SAP Analytics Cloud Help Portal, "Planning," available at *http://s-prs.co/v566921*
- SAP Analytics Cloud Help Portal, "Best Practices for Optimizing Performance During Planning," available at *http://s-prs.co/v566922*
- SAP Analytics Cloud Help Portal, "Performance Considerations," available at *http://s-prs.co/v566923*
- SAP Analytics Cloud Help Portal, "Optimize Advanced Formulas for Better Performance," available at *http://s-prs.co/v566924*
- SAP Analytics Cloud Help Portal, "Understand General Rules for Advanced Formula Calculations for Planning," available at *http://s-prs.co/v566925*
- Damien Fribourg, "SAP Analytics Cloud for Planning: Optimizing Calculations," available at *http://s-prs.co/v566926*

3.7 The Performance Analysis Tool

In the previous sections, we covered the different elements of dashboard creation and discussed in detail where and how we can influence the final performance. With this set of best practice rules, and those described in Chapter 4 and Chapter 5, the dashboard creator theoretically has all the know-how needed to create a strong performance dashboard. Nevertheless, it is not always possible to adhere to all these rules.

One reason for this, which should not be underestimated, is that with the immense variety of setting options to be considered in SAP Analytics Cloud, with which performance can be saved, one or the other of them simply gets lost and is not called up.

Furthermore, when creating a dashboard, it is not uncommon to perform a pure balancing act between the effort to increase performance and the attempt to meet the expectations that are placed on the complexity of the dashboard in terms of design and functionality from the outside. In doing so, it is not uncommon for some best practice tips to inevitably fall victim to compromise in favor of a submitted design draft.

For such reasons, it can be useful to examine the performance of a finished dashboard subsequently for weak points. In Chapter 2, we already got to know Chrome DevTools, a first tool for analyzing performance. Since this is a third-party tool that requires additional expertise to use, SAP introduced another built-in tool with the Q1 2021 release, the performance analysis tool.

This is an analysis application file made available for everyone in the system, which automatically evaluates the performance statistics and saves those in an SAP HANA view. The final output provides a dashboard with detailed information about individual process times divided into backend, network, and frontend. In addition to individual widgets and actions, such as opening a story or entering a page, the data models used are also examined regarding their performance impact.

This enables the user to identify possible causes and assign them to the affected process layer. If performance weaknesses can be clearly assigned to a specific data model, chart, or the total number of widgets, problem solving is significantly simplified. In addition, if the final decision about the appearance and functionality of a dashboard is not in your own hands, you also receive a basis for arguments backed by numbers, which makes it easier to justify a change to a submitted design draft. This makes the performance analysis tool an ideal in-built complement to the preventive measures described in Chapter 3 through Chapter 5.

Restrictions

To access and use the performance analysis tool, an admin role is required.

In the following sections, we will first look at different ways to access the performance analysis tool and go into the general structure and navigation within. Afterwards we will start with looking at the content itself, starting with the charts in the overview section and an introduction to the filter section. We will then move on to the detailed tabular views and the four time series charts, which look at the different processing times, divided into page load times, widget drilldown, runtime distribution, and processing layers. Finally, we will look at how we can use the results provided by the tool to optimize our system accordingly.

3.7.1 Accessing the Performance Analysis Tool

The analysis tool will be available per default in your SAP Analytics Cloud System in the SAP Analytics Cloud content folder of the **System** directory, as shown in Figure 3.34.

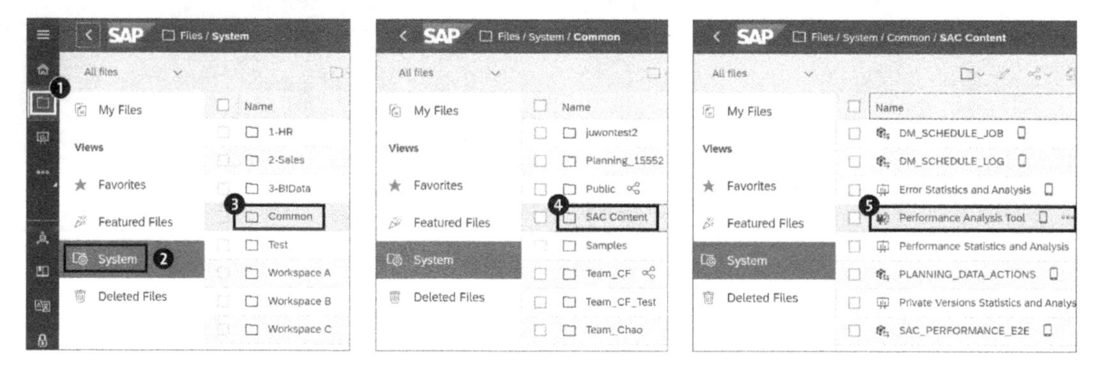

Figure 3.34 Accessing the Performance Analysis Tool via the SAP Analytics Cloud Content Folder

The application file **Performance Analysis Tool** can be accessed via the File menu in the main menu bar and is hidden behind the folder path **Files** ❶ • **System** ❷ • **Common** ❸ • **SAP Analytics Cloud Content** ❹. From there, the tool can be called up directly with a double-click ❺. In this way, you first get to the edit mode of the file.

Once the file has fully loaded, select **Run Analytic Application**, as shown in Figure 3.35.

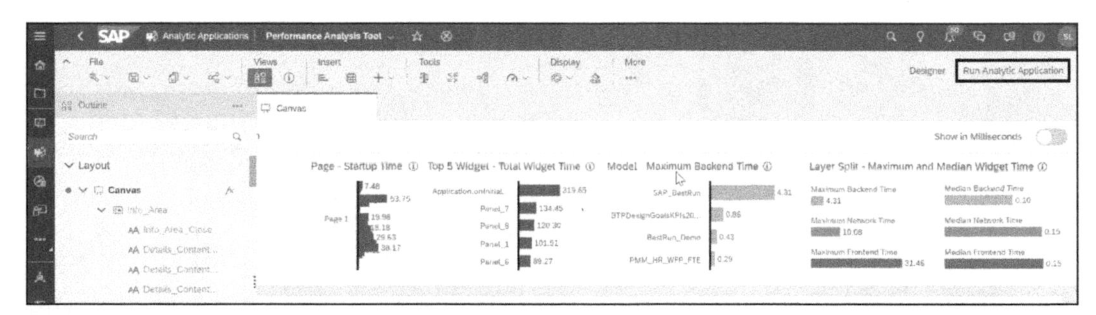

Figure 3.35 Edit View of the Performance Analysis Tool

A new tab will open, showing the entry screen for the tool. Here, the corresponding file to be analyzed must be selected. A date filter shows, per default, the current date but can be adjusted to your needs. To further narrow down the search, the criteria **User** and **Resource** can be set, by clicking on the filter icon (see Figure 3.36). The corresponding file can then be selected from the resulting list.

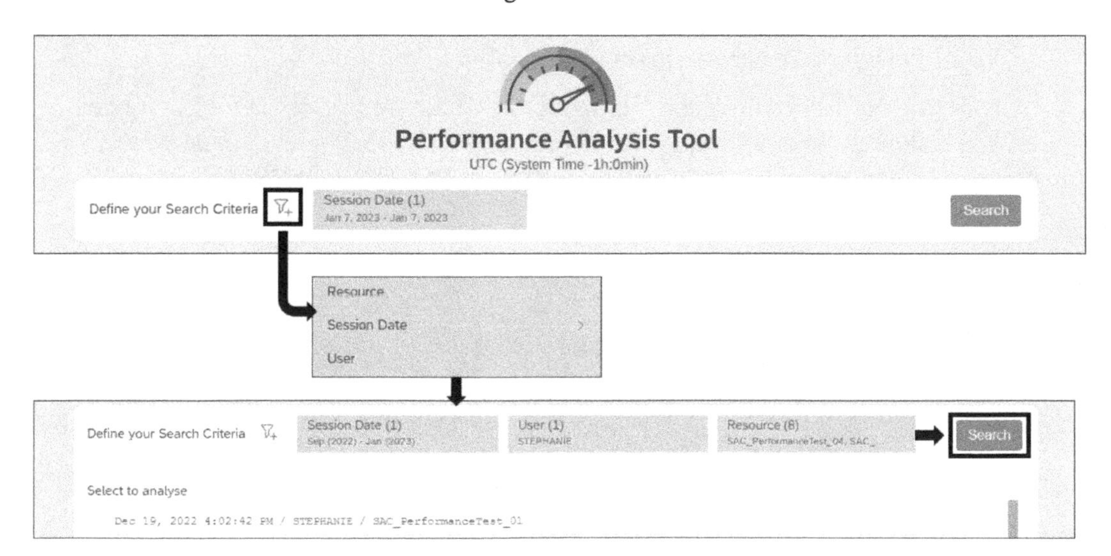

Figure 3.36 Performance Analysis Tool Entry Screen with Filter Panel

Another way to access the tool is via the **System** menu item in the main menu bar on the left, as shown in Figure 3.37. The advantage here is that the edit mode is skipped, and you get to the entry screen directly.

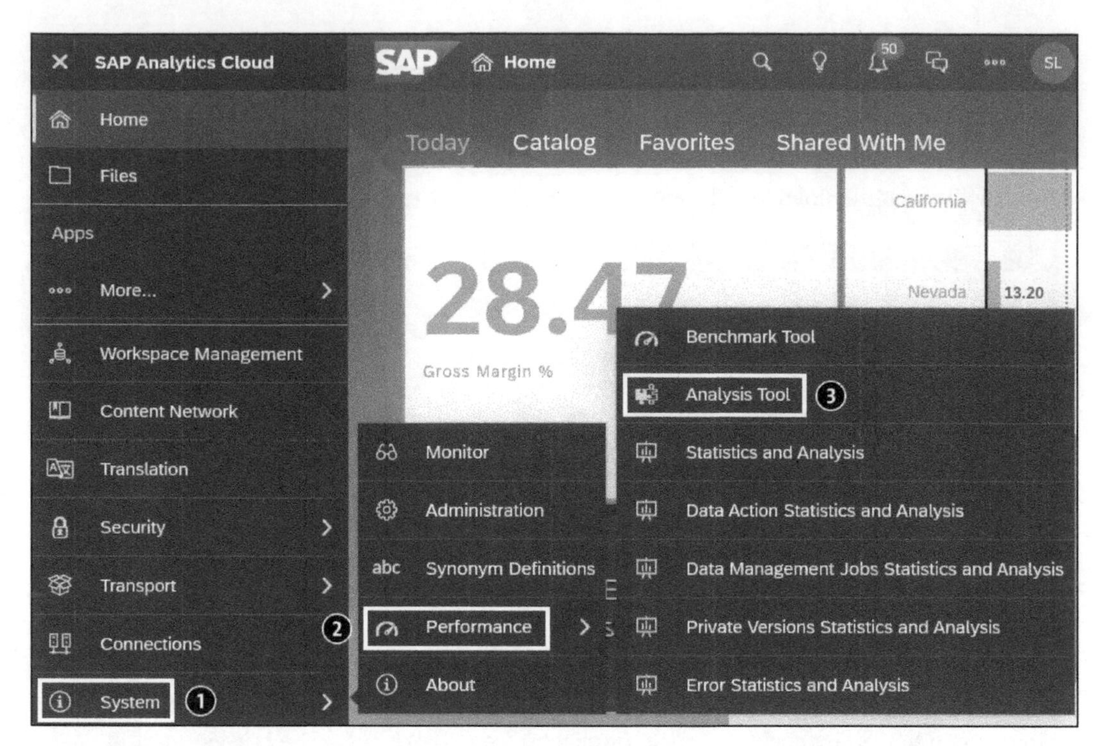

Figure 3.37 Accessing the Performance Analysis Tool Directly from the Main Menu

3.7.2 Using the Performance Analysis Tool

Selecting the desired file takes you to the actual analysis part of the tool. This contains a statistical summary of the various response times for the individual widgets and pages, divided into backend, frontend, and network aspects, which will be described in the following sections in detail.

> **Note**
>
> The performance analysis tool does not just analyze a static file per se, but a session consisting of actions that are made within the file, such as opening the story or entering another story page. Therefore, if there is a desire to analyze the end-to-end times for all pages, it is recommended to open the file to be investigated in another browser tab beforehand and fully load each story page BEFORE selecting it via the entry screen.

General Tool Structure

At the very top of the page in the left corner, as shown in , you can use the button **Back to Search** (Figure 3.38 ❶) to navigate back to the entry screen. This can be used, for example, to replace the selected story/application with another one and run a new analysis. A slider in the upper right corner ❷ allows us to choose between the second and millisecond units since, depending on the use case, one or the other can be of advantage.

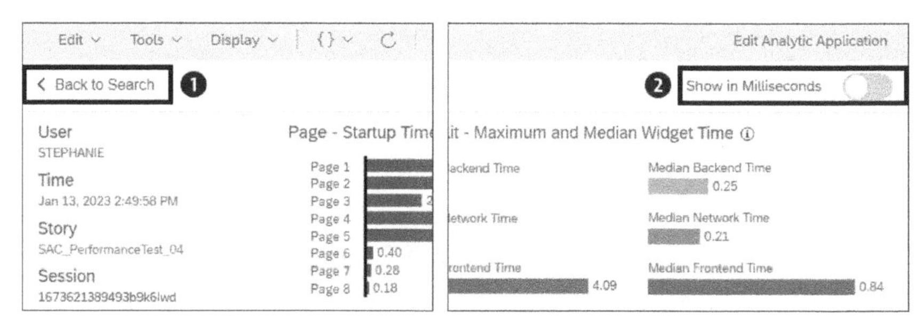

Figure 3.38 Navigate Back to the Entry Screen and Use the Toggle Button to Change the Unit from Seconds to Milliseconds

As an additional help, there is also a separate info icon for each chart, as shown in Figure 3.39. By clicking on it, a window opens with additional explanations about the chart and the displayed parameters.

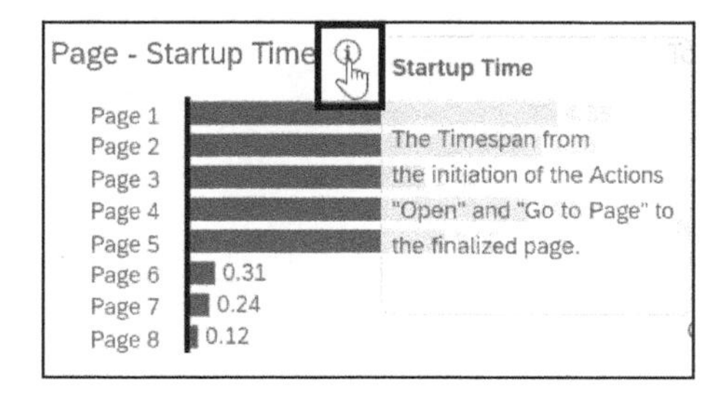

Figure 3.39 Info Icons for Detailed Description of the Corresponding Charts

Overview Section

Below this area follows a short general overview, which is divided into five sections. The first column contains general information about the underlying resource and session, as shown in Figure 3.40.

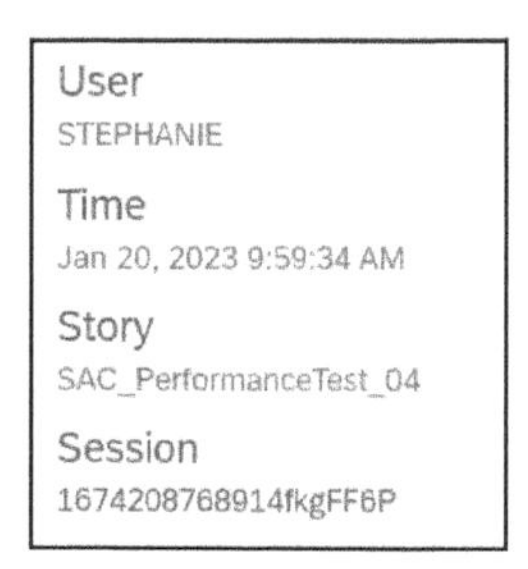

Figure 3.40 Accessing Underlying Source via Deposited Link in Facts Area

In addition to the username and the timestamp, the name of the analyzed story or application and the session ID are specified here. The combination of session ID and resource ID is always unique and enables exact identification of the analysis at any time. In addition, the resource can be opened directly from the tool in another tab via the stored link.

Next to this column, we are given an overview of the startup times for the different pages that have been visited during the analyzed session, as shown in Figure 3.41. These are the timespans measured from the start of an action, such as **Open Story**, in the case of the first page, or **Go to page**, to the time when all elements located on the page have loaded completely. In the story used here, for example, it's noticeable that the last three pages in particular use very little startup time. This was to be expected, since there are no charts or tables on these pages but only two text fields and a shape, which, as we already learned in Section 3.2.1, have a comparatively low impact on performance.

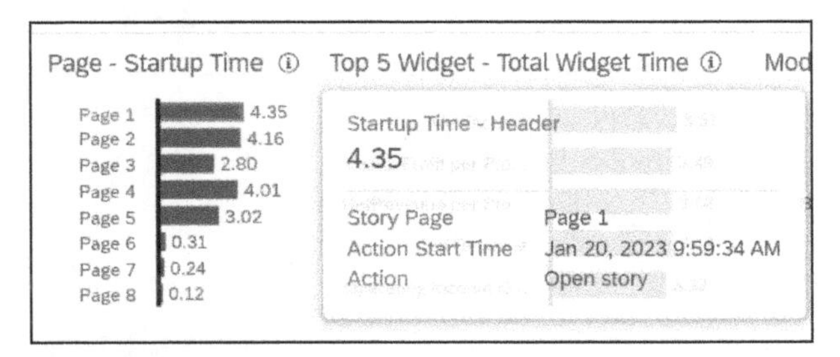

Figure 3.41 Page Startup Times With Information About Action and Action Start Time in Tooltip

> **Note**
>
> This chart can also be used as a filter for the tables and time analysis charts. To do this, simply click on one of the bars and the parameters it contains will appear in the filter panel section below.

The third column lists the top 5 widgets, sorted by their total loading time, as shown in Figure 3.42.

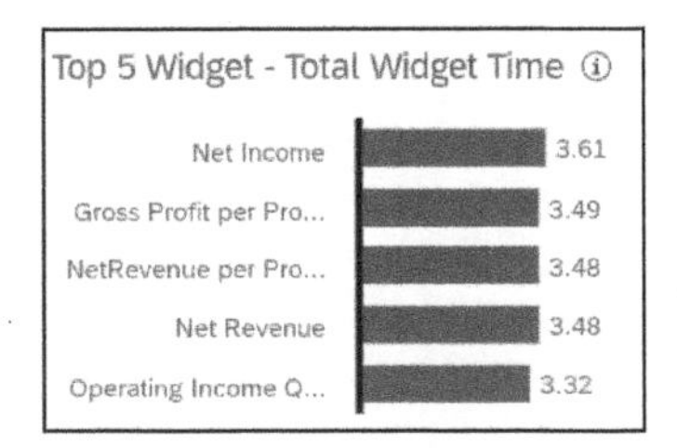

Figure 3.42 Top Five Widgets with the Total Widget Time

Here, the widgets of all accessed pages are considered. For a widget that has been called more than once, for example by re-entering a page, the individual loading time adds up accordingly. A chart that requires a conspicuously large amount of loading time compared to the rest of the story elements, and thus depresses performance, would already be recognizable as such in this short overview.

Note

This chart can also be used as a filter for the tables and time analysis charts. To do this, simply click on one of the bars and the parameters it contains will appear in the filter panel section.

In the next column, shown in Figure 3.43, all models that are actively used with the execution of the story are listed, sorted by their processing time in the backend. Only the maximum operating time for all widgets of a model is given. The model-specific connection is also indicated by hovering over the respective bar.

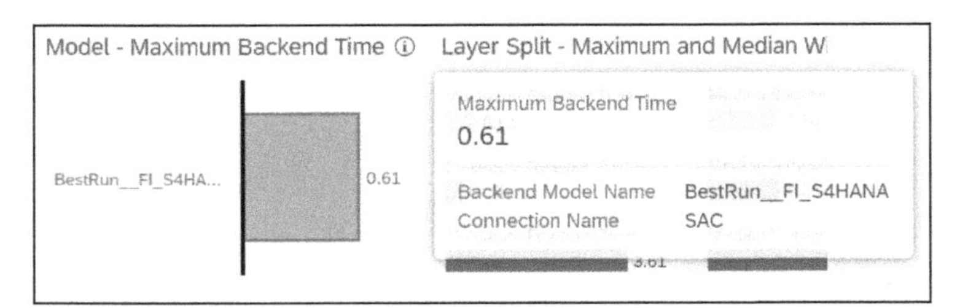

Figure 3.43 Tooltip with Information about the Used Connection

The last column of the **Overview** section, shown in Figure 3.44, shows a breakdown of the processing times of all executed widgets in backend, network, and frontend. Unlike in the previous section, the median widget times are also listed in a second chart, in addition to the maximum widget time.

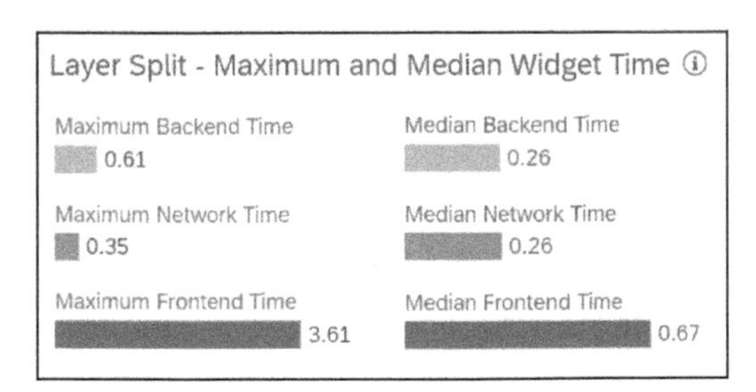

Figure 3.44 Maximum and Medium Widget Times Drilled Down into Process Layers

Filter Area

Below the **Overview** section follows a narrow filter area, as shown in Figure 3.45, which displays all filters that are applied to the tables and time series charts in the following lower area. The filter section is empty by default but fills up with filter buttons as soon as a bar is selected in one of the two left bar charts (**Page Startup Time** and **Top 5 Widget – Total Widget Time**) in the **Overview** section and automatically takes over its parameters as a filter. Clicking on one of these filters brings up the input control edit menu, where the filter parameters can be adjusted, changed, or even completely removed.

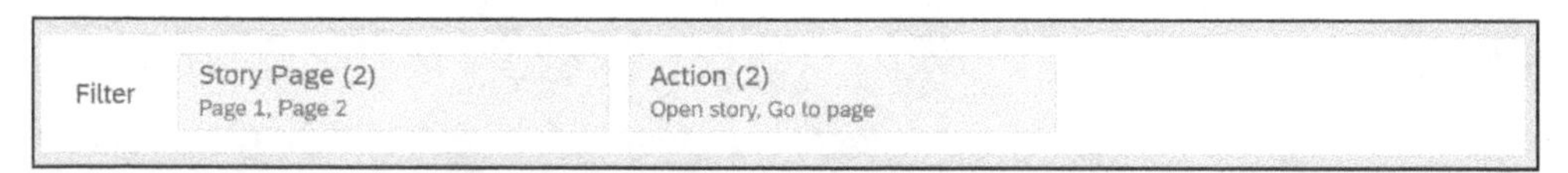

Figure 3.45 Filter Section of the Performance Analysis Tool

Processing Times

This brings us now to the main content of the performance analysis tool, starting with a table area. Via a tab menu bar at the top, you can navigate between three different tables:

- **Page Load Time**
  This table provides the total end-to-end times for each action, divided into three processing layers: the backend, the network, and the frontend, as shown in Figure 3.46. It results from the time span from the initiation of an action, such as **Go to Page**, to the complete loading of a page, including all its widgets. The total end-to-end time is the sum of the partial times **Page Preparation** and **Widget Load Time**. The measure **Page Preparation** describes the time span from the specified action start time to when the first widget starts to load. The **Widget Load Time** is the time from the moment the first widget starts loading until the last widget has finished loading.

Page Load Time | Widget Drilldown | Runtime Distribution

Total End to End Time and Maxima per Processing Layer

Action Start Time	Action	Story Page	Total Time	Page Preparation	Widget Load Time	Number of Widgets	Maximum Backend Time	Maximum Network Time	Maximum Frontend Time
Jan 20, 2023 9:59:34 AM	Open story	Page 1	4.35	0.77	3.58	21	0.26	0.35	3.22
Jan 20, 2023 10:00:19 AM	Go to page	Page 2	4.18	0.20	3.95	18	0.24	0.25	3.48
Jan 20, 2023 10:00:26 AM	Go to page	Page 3	2.80	0.22	2.59	15	–	–	2.56
Jan 20, 2023 10:00:34 AM	Go to page	Page 4	4.01	0.28	3.73	15	0.24	0.17	3.61
Jan 20, 2023 10:00:42 AM	Go to page	Page 5	3.02	0.39	2.64	20	–	–	2.40
Jan 20, 2023 10:00:47 AM	Go to page	Page 6	0.31	0.13	0.19	8	–	–	0.18
Jan 20, 2023 10:00:51 AM	Go to page	Page 7	0.24	0.07	0.17	6	–	–	0.17
Jan 20, 2023 10:00:54 AM	Go to page	Page 8	0.12	0.06	0.06	1	–	–	0.06

Figure 3.46 Page Load Times with the Total End-To-End Times

- **Widget Drilldown**
  The second table provides widget-specific information listed by the respective action and action start time, as shown in Figure 3.47. In addition to the end-to-end loading time of each element, the name and type of the respective widget are also

specified here. Since this list can be extensive depending on the resource being investigated, it is recommended to use the filter described above to narrow it down. In this example, we filtered for page 1 only and therefore received a list of all widgets rendered on this page.

Page Load Time | Widget Drilldown | Runtime Distribution

Per Widget End to End Time ⓘ

Action Start Time	Action	Widget	Widget Type	Measures: Widget Time
Jan 20, 2023 9:59:34 AM	Open story	08c95dbe53464c728328a74b1d699d11	Shape	0.74
		The Gross Profit loss for racing is the top contributor. It was 86.9mUSD below budget.	Text	0.01
		Operating Income Q2, Q1	Chart	3.32
		2f461fa64cb1463fb5853e519e12f2c1	Shape	0.00
		31794309538545789558613525380215	Shape	0.00
		41417956761649439208798178670050	Shape	0.00
		Operating Income	Chart	2.92

Figure 3.47 Widget Drilldown with End-To-End Times

We can receive more information about a widget from our list by clicking on this element. With this, a new filter entry appears in our filter bar, containing the respective widget, and we open a widget detail panel. This panel contains information about the used model along with the processing layer distribution, as well as a list of all executed backend requests, as shown in Figure 3.48.

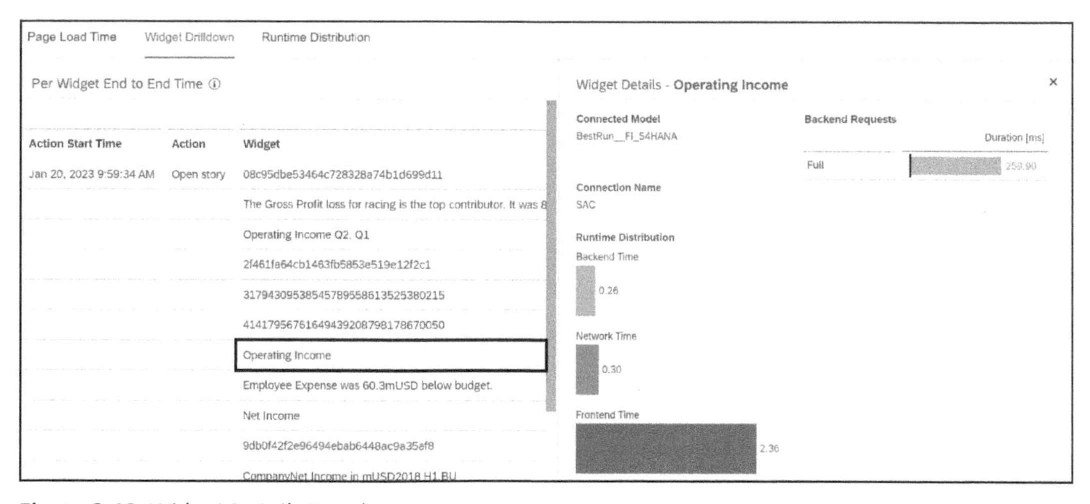

Figure 3.48 Widget Details Panel

- **Runtime Distribution**
  The last table in this section shows the **Runtime Distribution** (see Figure 3.49). It lists the total widget and processing layer times per action start time with respect to the corresponding action and page number. The widget time describes the sum of the

end-to-end times of all individual widgets and consists of the partial sums of all widgets' backend, network, and frontend times.

Page Load Time | Widget Drilldown | Runtime Distribution

Aggregated Widget and Processing Layer Times ⓘ

		Measures	Widget Time	Backend Time	Network Time	Frontend Time
Action Start Time	Action	Story Page				
Jan 20, 2023 9:59:34 AM	Open story	Page 1	29.39	1.27	0.77	27.34
Jan 20, 2023 10:00:19 AM	Go to page	Page 2	23.12	0.75	–	22.47
Jan 20, 2023 10:00:26 AM	Go to page	Page 3	20.12	0.60	–	19.93

Figure 3.49 Runtime Distributions with Aggregated Widget and Processing Layer Time

Time Series Charts

The last section of our performance analysis tool consists of four time series charts. These let us compare the processing times for a single selected user against all SAP Analytics Cloud users. Hereby we can switch from page to widget level by using our filters.

The time series analysis is divided into two parts, each with two charts, as shown in Figure 3.50. While the left side shows the median times per date ❶, the charts on the right focus on the distribution of the runtimes per processing layer ❷. The upper charts on both sides show the times for a single user, whereas the bottom charts stand for the whole SAP Analytics Cloud community ❸.

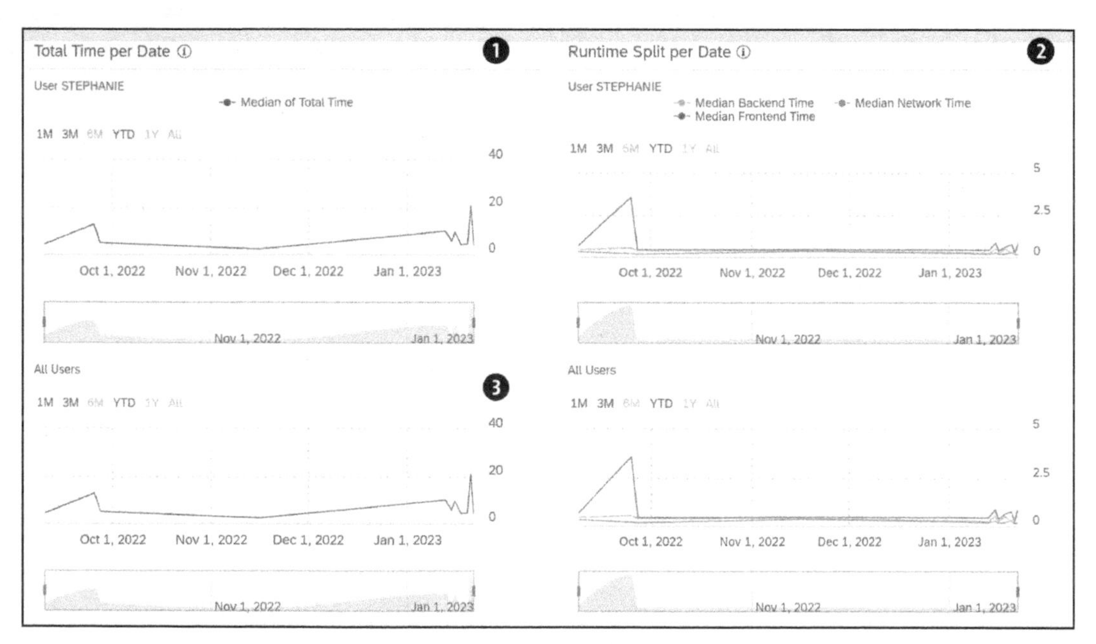

Figure 3.50 Total Times per Date; Runtime Split per Date; and Times for a Single User versus Times of the Whole Community

These comparisons are done both at widget and page level, where our filter comes into play again. The filter mechanism works, as already described for the **Widget Drilldown** section above, by selecting a bar for a respective page or widget in our **Overview** section, as shown in Figure 3.51.

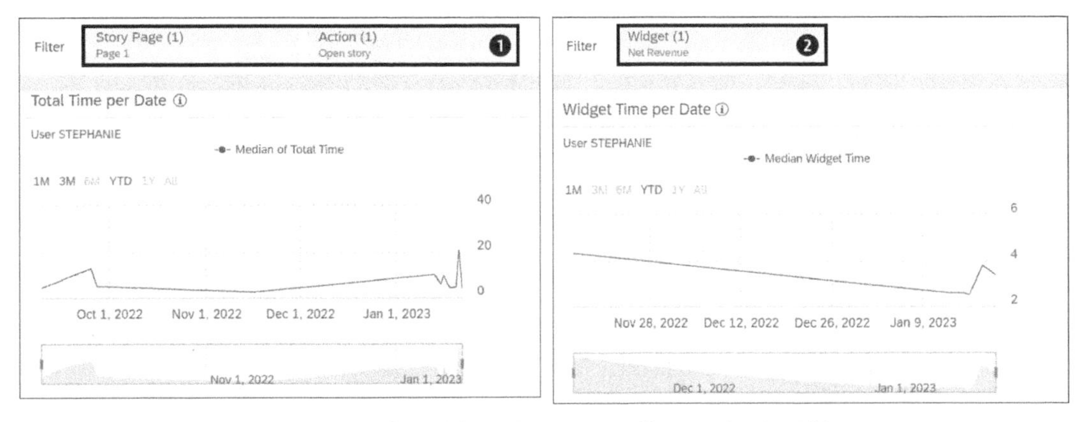

Figure 3.51 Total Time per Date or the Widget Time, Depending on the Set Filters

Depending on the filter state, either the median total time for a specific page and action ❶ or the median widget time ❷ is displayed. The chart title and axis labels will automatically adjust accordingly. This concerns both the charts for the total time per date and those for the runtime distribution on the right side.

3.7.3 Optimizing Your System with the Results

Now that we have identified and localized the main causes of our performance losses within our dashboard using the performance analysis tool, we can use this knowledge to adapt our dashboard using the best practice tips covered in this chapter, as well as those you'll learn in Chapter 4 and Chapter 5.

Depending on the use case, it may not be possible to adopt all the performance improvement measures listed in this book. The more creative and fancy the design presented for a dashboard, the more inevitable it is that a dashboard must be built with canvas instead of responsive style because of its flexibility. Also, a complex use case with a high amount of data usually inevitably leads to an increased number of pages and widgets, even if these should be avoided according to best practice tips.

This is where it now becomes important for the user to prioritize. Knowing exactly where the high launch times are coming from is a first step. And this is exactly what the performance analysis tool is used for. With its results, the user can now pretty much tell whether the performance problem was mainly caused by the backend, network, or frontend. We also see whether a particular chart drives up the total widget end-to-end time for a page or whether it was simply the sum of all widgets.

With this knowledge, the best practice tips in Chapter 3 through Chapter 5 can be called up one after the other, and the dashboard or model can be adapted step-by-step until acceptable performance is achieved. Further useful tips and links for system optimization can also be found on the SAP Help Portal. There, the performance analysis tool and an interactive graphic, the so-called decision tree, shown in Figure 3.52, can be used to call up tips tailored to one's own problem with associated links. The interactive version of this image can be found at the following URL: *http://s-prs.co/v566927*.

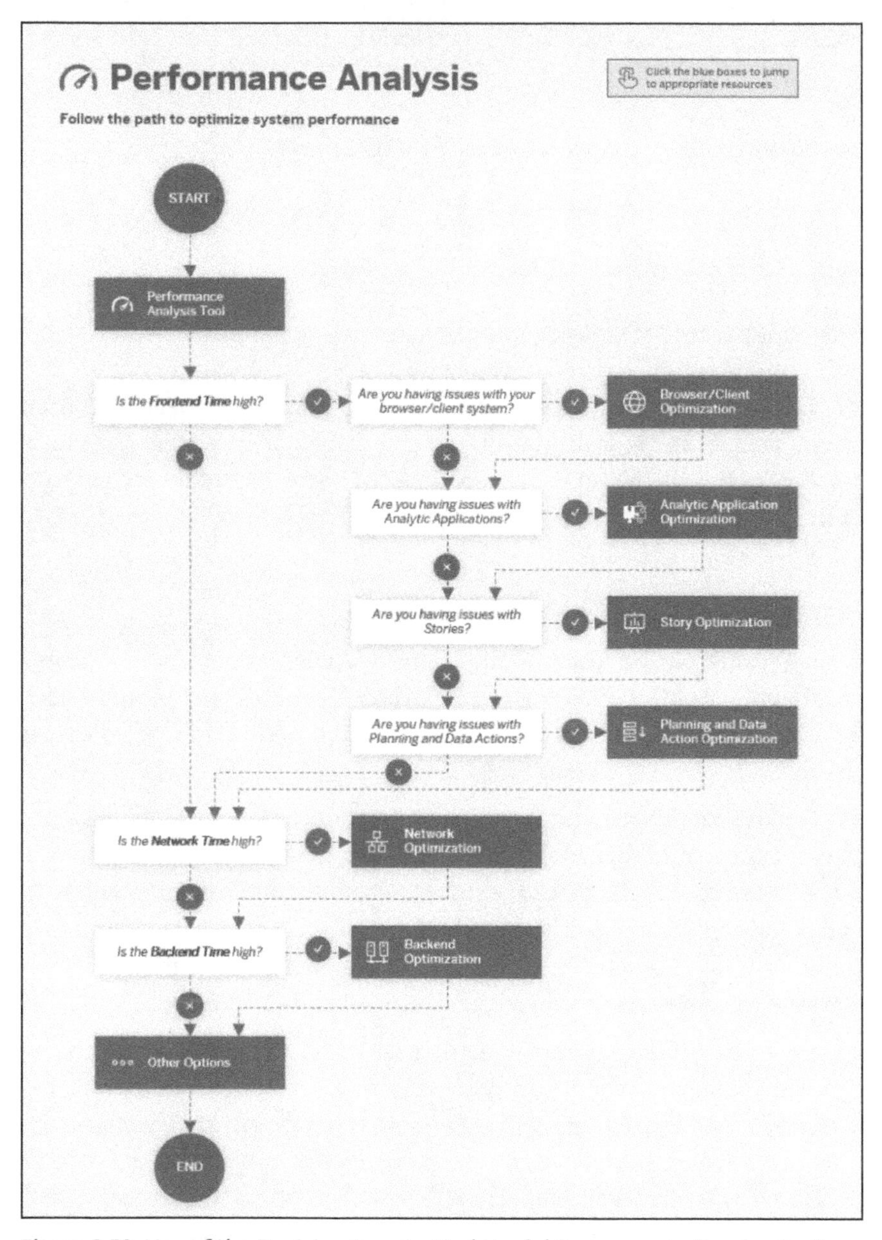

Figure 3.52 Use of the Decision Tree to Find Useful Resources to Resolve Performance Issues

Further Reading

If you want to read more about the SAP Analytics Cloud performance analysis tool, we recommend the following online resources:

- Thomas Fery, "SAP Analytics Cloud Performance Analysis Tool," available at *http://s-prs.co/v566928*
- Giri Raaj Ragupathi, "SAP Analytics Cloud Performance Analysis Techniques," available at *http://s-prs.co/v566929*
- SAP Help Portal documentation, "Optimize System Performance with the Analysis Tool," available at *http://s-prs.co/v566930*

3.8 Best Practices

Now that we have dealt in detail with the individual areas of dashboard design with the SAP Analytics Cloud story builder, we summarize our essential points here once again:

- **General settings: Performance optimization starts before the actual design.**
  - When using multiple models, link as few of them as possible, and if you do, don't use a calculated dimension.
  - Remove models from your story if not needed.
  - If an SAP HANA or SAP BW system is used, enable **Query Batching/Merging**.
  - Stop the automatic refresh of data during the dashboard creation by enabling **Optimizing Story Building Performance** in the model. You can instead refresh your data manually in the story builder.
  - Take advantage of the latest software improvements by re-saving your stories after each update.
  - Enable **Optimized View Mode** to make use of a set of usability and performance optimizations.
  - Enable **Progressive Chart Rendering**.
- **Layout and structure: Consider your design.**
  - Prefer responsive pages over canvas.
  - Limit the number of pages in your story.
  - Limit the number of data-related widgets, especially the process-heavy ones, such as tables and geo maps.
  - For high cardinality dimensions, set Top N manually for charts and tables.
  - For geo maps with a high number of locations, adjust location clustering or use choropleth layer.
  - For tables, instead of hiding columns and rows, use filtering instead.

- Try to design a large table area at once with one styling rule instead of styling multiple cells individually.
- Use images with a maximum size of 1 Mb. Compressed web images and SVG and PNG images are preferable to JPG format.

- **Filtering and calculations: Consider your data.**
  - Choose the filter type wisely: Story filters are to be preferred over individual chart filters, and collapsed input controls should be used instead of expanded ones.
  - Enable **Unrestricted Drilling**.
  - Deactivate **Cascading Effect**.
  - When making use of linked analysis, reduce the number of charts to be linked.
  - Use restricted measures in the story instead of exception aggregations in the model.
  - Instead of showing data in your story down to the smallest level of detail, offer explorer view to allow users to do their own additional data exploration.
- **Mobile devices: Adapt to the screen size.**
  - Enable **Optimize iOS** and **View Time Optimization**.
  - Rethink design: Display only highly aggregated data and eliminate space-consuming elements that serve only as decoration.
- **Planning scenarios: Plan performance orientated.**
  - Restrict the planning table content that can be edited.
  - Where too many private versions created by other users slow down your performance, delete private versions.
  - Avoid changing too many table (leaf) cells at once. When changing records on a higher level, consider the hierarchy structure and the total number of leaf cells that might be affected.
  - Reduce your data before using any planning feature (data actions, allocations, multi actions).
  - Instead of adding multiple data actions based on the same model and version to a multi action in one step, transfer them to a new data action first, and then add it to the multi action.
  - For allocations, limit the number of reference members by which the allocations are done.
  - Regardless of the function used for advanced formulas, always limit the scope as much as possible.
  - When using advance formulas, avoid unnecessary calculations and data checks in the backend by considering the order of statements or the possible replacement of specific functions by others.

Keep in mind that the goal should not necessarily be to cover all those points, but what is possible and appropriate for the particular use case.

As mentioned earlier, performance improvements always go hand in hand with compromises. Therefore, our recommendation is to start with those best practices tips that "don't hurt," i.e., quick fixes that don't change the content itself or the way you use your dashboard and do not require any major restructuring or other changes.

If the load time of your story is still not satisfactory after that, focus on those improvement tips that could lead to a significant improvement as well as seem acceptable in terms of the effort and compromise it requires.

Which of the best practices tips listed here have the most decisive influence on performance, from a purely technical point of view and disregarding subjective priorities, cannot be said in general terms and will always depend heavily on the design and characteristics of your own story.

For example, a dashboard that is based on an extensive data model and uses a separate page for each topic and displays each parameter in a separate widget could especially benefit from those tips that aim to reduce the total number of pages and data-related widgets. While for planning scenarios e.g., the tips around the topic Edit Area and Advanced Formulas become relevant.

Which best practice tips can improve our performance enough to justify a compromise in terms of design will always depend heavily on the build and characteristics of your own story.

3.9 Summary

In this chapter, we have worked through the individual phases of dashboard construction and looked at which elements and construction methods in the SAP Analytics Cloud story builder can influence the final load time of our dashboard.

You now know that performance optimization starts with design planning and the general structure of a story, i.e., the way you organize your presentation of information across pages and widgets, already lays the foundation for this. In the end, it's almost always about keeping the number of backend queries running in parallel as low as possible, as well as the amount of data that needs to be retrieved with each update in the model. We achieve this by using fewer pages and widgets and by limiting our data to the essentials. For the latter, we learned about several methods, such as filtering, drilling, Top N rankings, and aggregations with restricted measures.

In addition to the elements of classic dashboard construction, we also looked at some helpful additions that we can use to make our lives easier. Among other things, we came across the explorer view, which allows us to leave detailed analysis to the user and thus limit our own dashboard to the essentials. And finally, with the performance analysis tool, we also got to know a tool with which we can analyze our story retrospectively and thus clearly identify performance weaknesses, which significantly simplifies the selection of crucial tips and tricks.

In the next chapter, we take dashboard design to the next level with the analytics designer. The new features it contains open a world of new possibilities for us when it comes to creating more complex dashboards, but we will also uncover new performance pitfalls and help you avoid them.

Chapter 4
Analytics Designer Performance

In this chapter, we'll cover in detail how to improve the performance of a dashboard that is built using the analytics designer for SAP Analytics Cloud. This includes general settings, specific optimizations, your analytics application structure, scripting, responsive design, measuring the performance of self-coded features, and much more!

The analytics designer for SAP Analytics Cloud is next to the story builder, which was already covered in Chapter 3, the second capability offered by SAP Analytics Cloud for generating insights and building dashboards of various types. Compared to the story builder, the analytics designer offers additional capabilities, enabling the development of advanced analytics applications based on exciting content. This matches the description used for the analytics designer within SAP Analytics Cloud: "Build applications for data analysis and planning. Benefit from the advanced capabilities of the analytics designer for building highly customized and interactive applications by leveraging the flexibility of JavaScript." Along with the potential for displaying your JavaScript expertise, the analytics designer includes additional built-in widgets, a different way for structuring your analytics applications, and more. While many of the topics covered in Chapter 3 will still be applicable here, the analytics designer understandably comes with its own unique sets of performance tips, tricks, and challenges. These will be the focus of this chapter.

4.1 Avoiding Poor Performance When Creating an Analytics Application

When we think about improving the performance for SAP Analytics Cloud, this typically means creating an improved user experience for the target consumers viewing the dashboard. This is also what this book and this chapter focus on. However, when dashboards built with the analytics designer for SAP Analytics Cloud get very large and complex, performance can start to suffer not just in the view mode but also in the edit mode. As a result, it is worth making a brief excursion to look at a few tips and tricks we use to build dashboards as quickly as possible while enjoying a lag-free dashboard-building experience. This means not only less frustration as an app designer, but also less time wasted and more time freed up to spend on generating valuable insights for the consumer persona.

4.1.1 The Issue of Poor Performance in the Edit Mode

Since you probably already have some experience with building dashboards, we won't have to tell you what a time-consuming and laborious task it can be to create a large and complex dashboard that uses vast amounts of data and contains a substantial number of charts and other widgets—especially with the analytics designer, which offers an increased complexity with scripting and additional widgets. As large sizes can start to make the analytics designer struggle, opening an application in edit mode can take some time, and performing actions in edit mode can involve a noticeable delay, thus making the dashboard creation experience take longer. An example of a larger dashboard that starts to suffer from these problems can be seen in Figure 4.1. Note that because this dashboard has too many charts and no optimizations were implemented, the performance is poor both in edit and view mode.

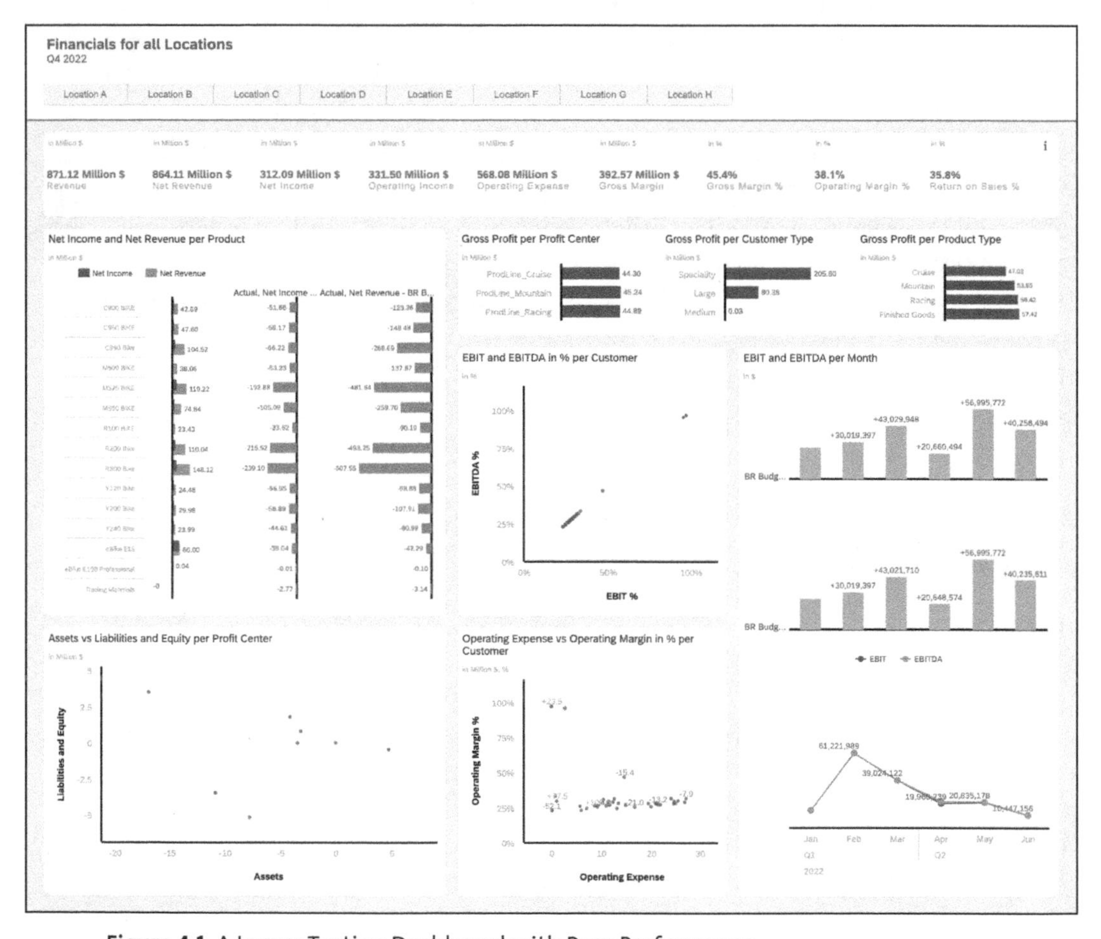

Figure 4.1 A Larger Testing Dashboard with Poor Performance

The dashboard visible in Figure 4.1 shows the first page of a larger dashboard containing 136 charts of different size and variety, seventeen panels and flow layout panels, several other widgets, a popup, and some script object functions for navigating between different location content panels. An SAP Analytics Cloud model is used as data source, containing 185,118 rows of data, several dimensions, and over 200 measures. Fully loading this analytics application by opening the link to the edit mode takes us an average of 43 seconds using the system described below, during which interacting with the application is prevented for the first 33 seconds. Even workflows such as selecting a chart and changing out a measure or going into a script and changing out the names of charts comes with some brief lag. In extremely large dashboards, this can mean that most actions taken come with a noticeable delay, making editing quite nerve-racking. Unfortunately, there is no magic button to avoid these performance issues. Depending on your SAP Analytics Cloud version, there is an option to select the optimized design experience for stories, which will improve performance in edit mode. However, as it can't be used for analytics applications, it is not relevant for this chapter. Instead, the following sections provide a few useful tips that will give you an easier and less frustrating time when working with larger analytics applications in the analytics designer for SAP Analytics Cloud.

Important Note

Performance testing throughout this chapter was done using Chrome DevTools for the Google Chrome browser or the analytics application script performance popup for testing scripting, with an average internet speed of 100 Mbps Download / 40Mbps Upload and using the following computer: MacBook Pro (15-inch, 2017), macOS Ventura Version 13.0.1, Intel HD Graphics 630 1536 MB, 2.9 GHz Quad-Core Intel Core i7, 16 GB RAM.

4.1.2 Split Up Your Dashboard into Smaller Analytics Applications

The tab strip widget and the ability to change the visibility of single widgets and entire panels makes it alluring to build your dashboard as a single large analytics application, such as how the story builder allows for several pages per story. While fine for most dashboards, as we have seen above, a large analytics application can lead to a bad performance in the analytics designer edit mode. So how can we fix this? Well, did you know that you can easily connect different analytics applications together via a simple command? This means that you can split your large dashboard into different applications, thus lowering the number of widgets per application and improving the performance when working on your dashboard. This is a great tip for very large dashboards, as it improves not only the performance when building your dashboard, but crucially also the startup performance when viewing the dashboard. You will see how to use this feature in Section 4.3.5, as this is where we cover this feature in detail to improve the dashboard user's performance.

To see what kind of performance improvements splitting up a dashboard achieves while editing the analytics application, we performed another test. Using the same system and previous dashboard example and splitting it up into eight equal applications, so each only has in it the charts and other widgets visible in Figure 4.1, we can now record an average opening time for the edit mode of just 27 seconds, of which interacting with the application is prevented for 10.5 seconds. To compare this to the previous values, splitting up the analytics application in Figure 4.1 decreases the opening time for the edit mode by 16 seconds, while the time during which interaction with the dashboard is prevented is reduced by 22.5 seconds. So, it is significantly faster. Also, no more lag is noticeable when interacting with the dashboard in edit mode. In this way, working on your dashboard becomes more enjoyable again.

4.1.3 Leverage the Copy and Paste Functionality

We are used to copying and pasting text, images, data, and files in many of our everyday tasks. The same can be done in SAP Analytics Cloud. Many widgets can be copied and pasted within the same analytics application or between different analytics application and stories. Why is this relevant? Well, there are two basic scenarios. If you are building a large dashboard and don't want to split it into different analytics applications, it might be faster for you to build parts of your dashboard in a separate story builder or analytics designer file that is not hampered by its size and thus responds faster and then simply copy and paste the created content into your main dashboard file. There are, however, a couple of things you need to watch out for when leveraging the copy and paste functionality:

- Your two files must be on the same SAP Analytics Cloud tenant.
- The data source used in every chart or table must be available for both files.
- There are limitations to the widgets that can be copied and pasted, as widgets specific to analytics applications, scripting, and popups cannot be moved into the story designer.
- Be aware that, if a calculated measure or dimension is being used, there might be clashes between what has been created in the source location and what exists in the target location.
- Double check that everything was copied over correctly, as global filters won't be connected, and it can sometimes happen that the positioning of some widgets is off.

The second scenario where the copy and paste tip applies is if you are building a dashboard using a repetitive design, like in Figure 4.2. Here you can start by fully building only the first row, then copying and pasting this one down as many times as you need, and then finally changing the chart filters to match the numbers you want to show. This involves much less effort than if you had created every row from scratch.

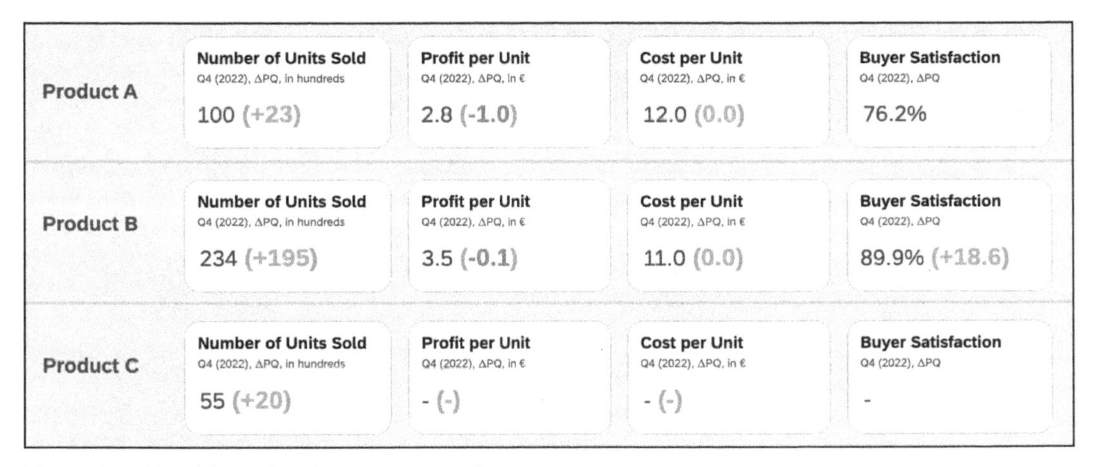

Figure 4.2 A Dashboard with a Repetitive Structure

4.1.4 Test Before Implementing Large Changes

Whether trying out new features, testing how your dashboard is behaving on different screen sizes, restructuring, figuring out how your script behaves, or redesigning parts of your dashboard, testing is always crucial before conducting large-scale changes to your analytics application. It means not having to spend a lot of time implementing a large change fully, only to realize that it is not working or looking as expected. It means quickly being able to figure out what works and what doesn't by testing in a separate analytics application or in only a section of your dashboard. Testing becomes more and more valuable the larger your dashboard gets. Especially for large analytics application files, which might contain bothersome waiting times in the edit mode, testing can be very valuable.

Here are some example scenarios where testing could be valuable:

- When designing your dashboard to be responsive to different screen sizes like phones, tablets, laptops, and monitors, trying out different ways to use panels and flow layout panels to optimally set up a responsive dashboard is done much faster when those panels don't yet contain charts connected to a data source, thus taking up time each time you want to see how things are behaving after a small change.
- Test a change to your dashboard, such as a redesign, on just a portion of it to see how it looks and behaves before rolling out that change to the rest of the dashboard.
- Before adding a new feature to your existing analytics application or redoing large parts of a script, try these changes out in a separate analytics application or on only part of your dashboard. You won't have things perfectly right from the start, and iterating through the changes before you come up with the final solution is more quickly done if you don't have to start a large analytics application each time you want to see if a small script works properly.

4.2 General Rules to Improve Performance

This chapter covers some general rules, settings, and basic tips that can be used in the analytics designer for SAP Analytics Cloud to improve the performance for the dashboard consumer. These basics of what to do and what not to do build the foundation of tips and tricks when it comes to improving your analytics applications performance. This includes lessons from Chapter 3, which remain applicable for the analytics designer, as well as reducing the complexity and size of an analytics application.

4.2.1 Remember Chapter Three

Chapter 3 talked at great length about different ways to improve performance with the story builder for SAP Analytics Cloud. Many of the lessons learned there remain applicable for the analytics designer. Using an analytics application doesn't mean that pictures now load any faster than before or that the number of simultaneously loading charts changes. This is because the analytics designer is based on the architecture of the story builder, adding scripting functionalities in a new container, while still working with the story builder's container for widgets. An overview of this architecture can be seen in Figure 4.3.

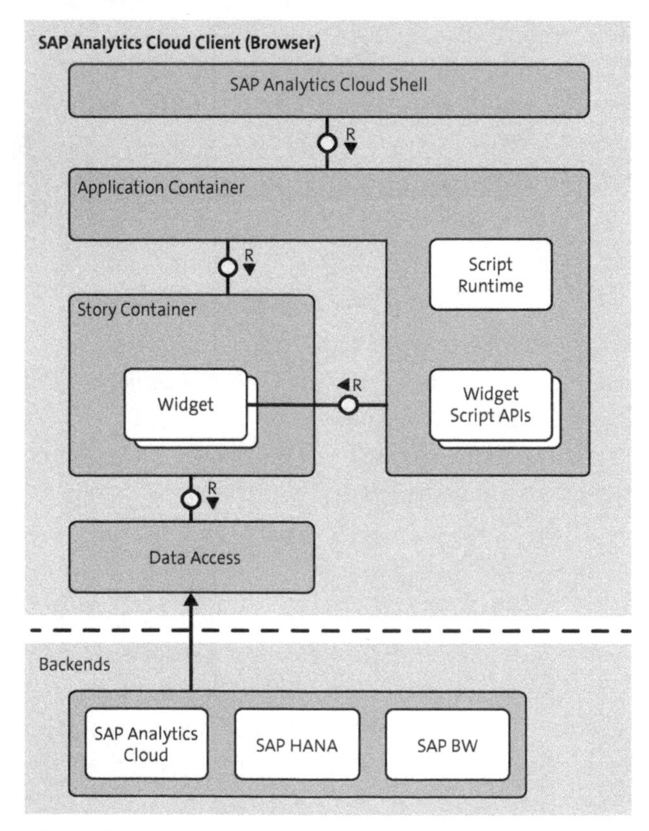

Figure 4.3 Architecture Overview of the Analytics Designer for SAP Analytics Cloud

To give you a rough overview over some of the most important lessons from Chapter 3 that remain applicable for the analytics designer for SAP Analytics Cloud, we have compiled a list of the relevant information in Table 4.1. Some of these topics will also be discussed again in this chapter, focusing on the specific challenges of the analytics designer for SAP Analytics Cloud.

Chapter 3 Lesson	Does it remain applicable?	Notes
Limit the number of widgets, especially process-heavy ones, and optimize the widgets you use	Yes	Limiting the number of widgets remains applicable, but there are additional widgets to consider. This is covered in Section 4.2.3.
Restrict and optimize when using planning scenarios	Yes	
Improve filter and sorting management	Yes	
Rethink your calculation management in the story builder and configure it wisely	Yes	
Page layout	No	As the analytics designer for SAP Analytics Cloud changes how pages are built, tips like using fewer pages and responsive pages over canvas don't remain applicable. How to best structure an analytics application is covered mostly in Section 4.3.
Optimized view mode	Yes	

Table 4.1 Overview of Which Lessons from Chapter 3 Remain Applicable and Which Don't

4.2.2 Don't Reinvent the Wheel or Overcomplicate Things

Most first-time users of the analytics designer for SAP Analytics Cloud who are only familiar with the story builder will be tempted by the wealth of possibilities it offers. New widgets, such as buttons with tooltips, switches, dropdown menus, and panels, and the ability to harness the power of JavaScript allow for more complexity and a more advanced viewing experience. But just because it's possible to create advanced custom dashboards with a high degree of complexity doesn't mean it should always be done, as this comes at the expense of a faster performance. Simply put, when an analytics application increases not only in size but also in complexity, its performance decreases. The more functionality is added, the longer the load times. So, when it comes to developing a high-performance analytics application, simplicity is key, even if it's exciting to add fancy functionalities.

Take, for example, Figure 4.4. Visible there is a feature implemented in the analytics designer for SAP Analytics Cloud by leveraging JavaScript, which allows you to switch between two ways of visualizing the same content. You might have two different dashboard consumers who each prefer their own way of having the data visualized. There is certainly no lack of visualizations to choose from, including bar charts, pie charts, tables, line charts, heat maps, scatterplots, numeric point charts, custom widgets, and so on. The analytics designer makes it possible to implement two options and create a smooth way of switching between them. You can even use JavaScript to check the dashboard consumer's SAP Analytics Cloud user ID to automatically activate the correct visualization for the right consumer. While this sounds like a great thing to have, the increased complexity creates a greater loading time, with the additional chart, other widgets, and JavaScript needing to be loaded and executed.

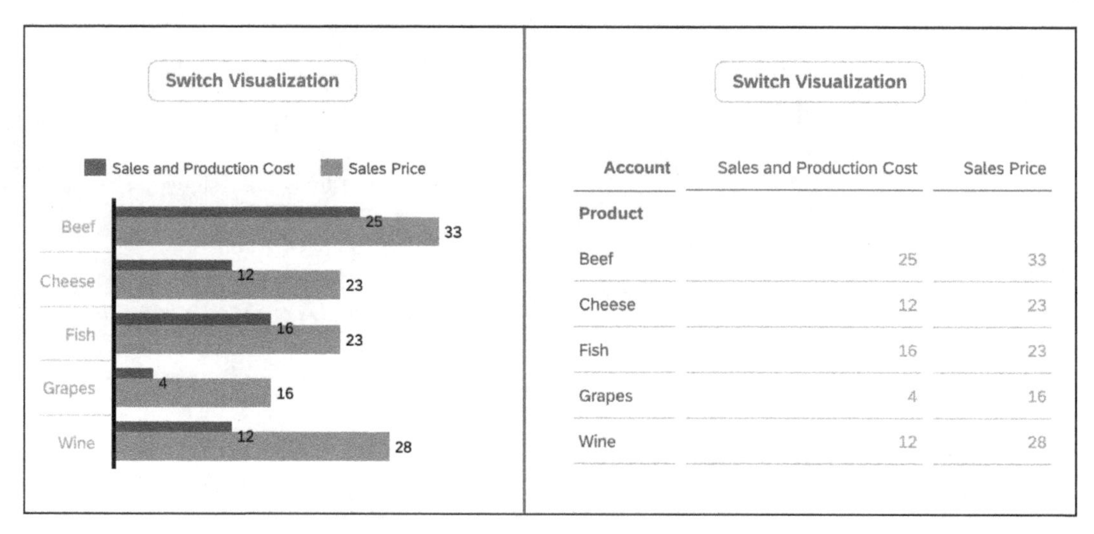

Figure 4.4 Custom-Built Switching between Two Visualizations Feature

So, is it necessary to allow the dashboard user to view the same information in two different ways? Is loading the same information twice and a button and some scripting worth the performance penalty? Knowing a dashboard's target customers and the pros and cons of complex features can help you make reasonable decisions about what to implement and what not to implement. It's useful to keep this rule in mind, because not overcomplicating things is also relevant to many other sections covered later in this chapter, such as optimizing responsive design for different devices and scripting with JavaScript.

4.2.3 Limit the Number of Widgets

This tip should sound familiar if you have read Chapter 3. However, due to its importance, it is worth mentioning it again here. The recommendation for stories and analytics applications for SAP Analytics Cloud is to use a maximum of twelve charts with a low number of data points per chart. Why this is the case is explained in more detail in Chapter 3 and Chapter 7. Sticking to such a low number of charts can be quite difficult and restrictive, and for the analytics designer what constitutes a page is also less clear. Going over this limit will not mean facing immediate performance issues. It shows, however, that you should try to limit the number of elements per page and, as an extension, per analytics application.

Some tips for limiting the number of elements shown on startup and loading invisible widgets in the background, which will help you deal with the performance issues of large dashboards, will be covered in detail later in Section 4.3. However, limiting the number of widgets used in a dashboard wherever possible remains probably the most relevant tip to keep in mind, not just for the story builder but also the analytics designer for SAP Analytics Cloud. In the standard story file, this includes data visualizations like chart, geo maps, and table widgets, as well as other widgets such as texts, images, and shapes. In the analytics designer for SAP Analytics Cloud, there are additional widgets such as buttons, dropdown menus, sliders, switches, and more. While these widgets are not as performance-intensive as charts, they also need to be loaded. Figure 4.5 shows how the loading times of different widgets such as charts, shapes, text, and more can differ.

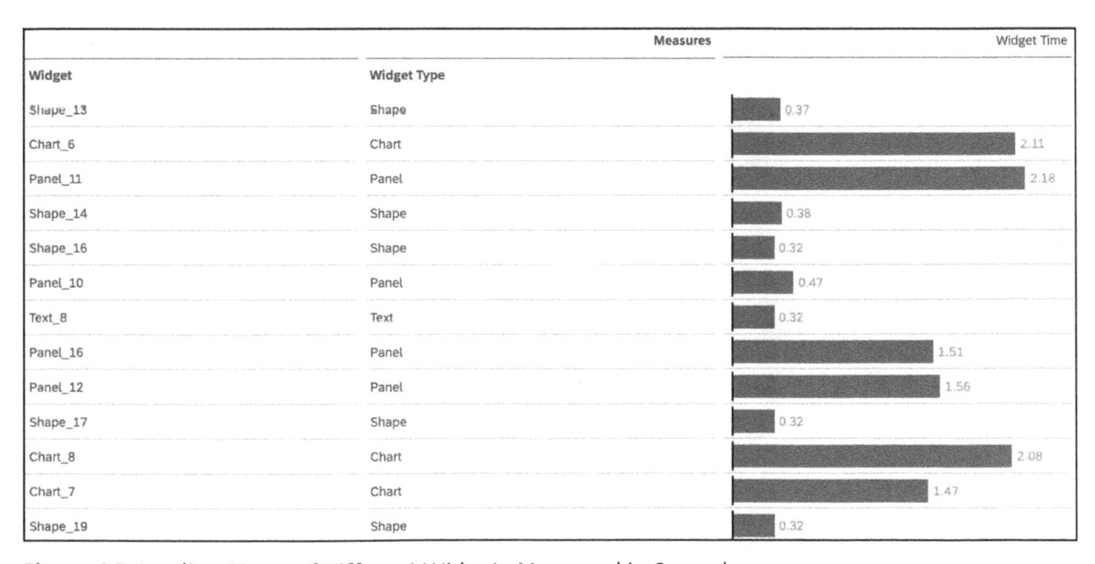

	Measures	Widget Time
Widget	Widget Type	
Shape_13	Shape	0.37
Chart_6	Chart	2.11
Panel_11	Panel	2.18
Shape_14	Shape	0.38
Shape_16	Shape	0.32
Panel_10	Panel	0.47
Text_8	Text	0.32
Panel_16	Panel	1.51
Panel_12	Panel	1.56
Shape_17	Shape	0.32
Chart_8	Chart	2.08
Chart_7	Chart	1.47
Shape_19	Shape	0.32

Figure 4.5 Loading Times of Different Widgets Measured in Seconds

Therefore, it makes sense to reduce the number of elements, especially performance-intensive elements, by removing unnecessary widgets and paying attention to what is added to the dashboard in the first place. While a single widget often won't make a noticeable difference, smaller performance improvements such as leveraging the `setStyle()`,`moveWidget()`, and other methods to reduce duplicate widgets covered later in Section 4.5.3 do add up.

4.3 Optimizing the Application Structure

Especially for larger analytics applications, which are mainly the ones suffering from performance issues, deciding how to structure your dashboard is a sensible first step. It is crucial to minimize the loading time for the end user as much as possible. Things like how content is divided into sections, how an analytics application is laid out, and how it loads can have a big impact on how long and where load times occur. Deciding on these things from the start means starting out with an analytics application that is designed from the ground up to be performing well.

There are two things to keep in mind when embarking on designing your analytics applicating structure. These are the scope and the target user(s):

- **Scope**
  How large will your dashboard become? Your dashboard might start out small, but if you know the scope, you can try to predict if it will grow with time and show more data. With larger dashboards comes more complexity, as performance starts to suffer and splitting up content to distribute loading times becomes more important. Therefore, design appropriately and observe the following tips to be successful.
- **Target user(s)**
  What are your target users and their intended workflows when navigating through your dashboard? Who is your dashboard designed for? An upper-level manager looking for a high-level overview of this quarter's earnings numbers might prioritize the ability to quickly access a summary within the dashboard, while an analyst might want to have a deep dive into the data, prioritizing depth of data over loading time. As you can see, especially if your dashboard must cater to different user groups, making sure everyone is satisfied can become complex. This is why knowing the true priorities of the target user(s) is so important. Use the following tips to, for example, avoid loading times at application start-up by loading invisible widgets in background and by splitting up content. How to validate a dashboard regarding performance with users was already covered in Section 4.1.3.

4.3.1 How Is an Analytics Application Loaded?

By looking at Figure 4.3 in Section 4.2, we have already been able to get an overview of the architecture used by an analytics application. Now we can deepen this understanding by looking at the loading pattern that each analytics application created with the analytics designer for SAP Analytics Cloud follows to load its various components. The order in which widgets and scripts are initialized and executed when a user accesses an analytics application is important to understand when aiming for optimal performance.

Before a dashboard can be loaded, the SAP Analytics Cloud browser client itself must first load. If you are accessing a dashboard through SAP Analytics Cloud, this has obviously already happened. But in many instances, users will not navigate to your analytical application through SAP Analytics Cloud's **Files** viewer or the **Analytic Applications** tab, but rather directly through a hyperlink, in which case the SAP Analytics Cloud browser client is loaded before starting the loading of the analytics application itself. This means loading the SAP Analytics cloud shell, which also involves connecting to the SAP Analytics Cloud servers and authenticating the user (if you've never been logged in, this includes entering username and password). These activities will, of course, take a small amount of loading time, which, however, can't be influenced by the dashboard builder, as it purely revolves around factors such as connection speed and processing power. So, when a user is accessing an analytics application directly through a hyperlink, always expect this small, fixed loading time.

Important Note

Analytics applications can be opened in present and embed mode, in addition to the view and edit mode. Using a link to a dashboard that opens it in embed mode, will mean that you still need to connect to the system and be authenticated but can skip loading the SAP Analytics cloud shell.

After the SAP Analytics cloud shell is loaded, the analytics application can load. Looking at the architecture overview in Figure 4.3 in Section 4.2, this means loading the story and application container, as well as data access. By default, this means initializing the analytics application and all widgets contained in the dashboard, before then executing the `onInitialization` script in runtime and updating any widgets that were affected by it. Figure 4.6 visualizes this process as a lane diagram.

Especially for larger dashboards with data sources where data requests to the backend are more time consuming, the process shown above can be noticed and you will realize that data-related widgets take longer to load than data-unrelated widgets. What could also be noticeable is that before the data is loaded into the widgets, the `onInitialization` script is executed. This is because, while the data to be visualized is being requested, if these requests take quite some time, all the widgets will be initialized after a while and the `onInitialization` script will thus be executed before the data for all the charts is received and visualized in the widgets.

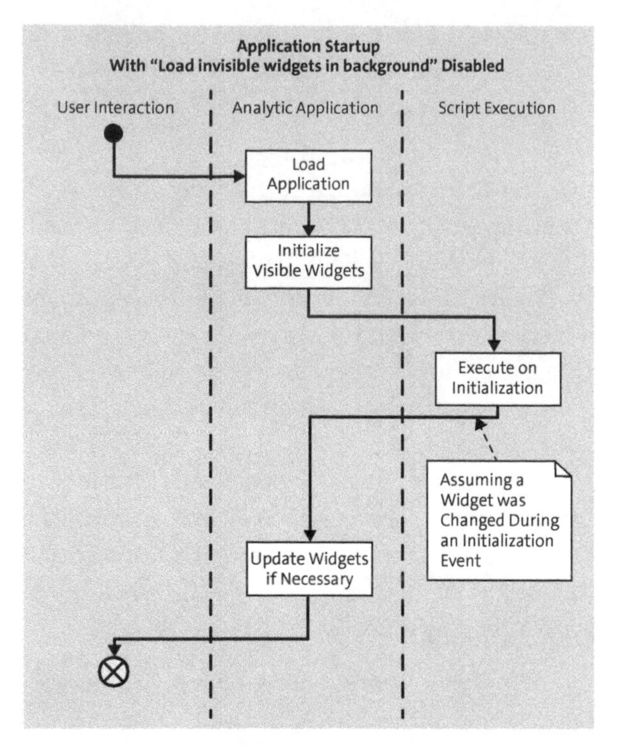

Figure 4.6 Default Mode for Loading an Analytics Application

4.3.2 Leveraging the Load Invisible Widgets in Background Setting

The standard loading behavior of an analytics application, as covered in the section above, means that all widgets are initialized and loaded at application startup. This includes widgets that are not directly visible. As a result, the initial loading time will be quite long, while subsequent navigating through the dashboard will not require any additional loading times. As there are many instances in which having a short initial loading time is more important than having all sections of the dashboard loaded right from the beginning, the analytics designer for SAP Analytics Cloud offers another option for how widgets are loaded. By activating the **Load invisible widgets in background** setting, the perceived loading time can be reduced by making the startup screen load faster, as only visible widgets are initialized at first, and only when this is done are the invisible widgets initialized. This means the user will see and be able to interact with the already loaded part of the analytics application, while the rest of the widgets are being loaded in the background. This setting can be turned on as follows in the analytics designer for SAP Analytics Cloud:

1. In the toolbar, under **File**, select [icon].
2. Select **Analytic Application Settings.**
3. Within the now open dialog window (displayed in Figure 4.7), select **Load invisible widgets in the background**, then press **OK.**

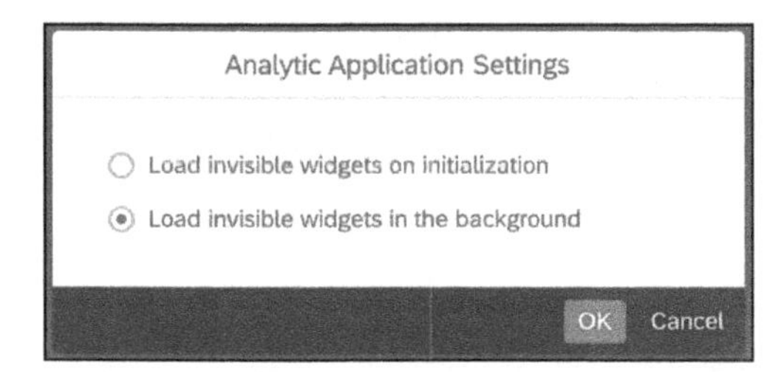

Figure 4.7 Load Invisible Widgets in Background Setting

This setting is sometimes referred to as *lazy loading* or *on-demand loading*. While lazy loading is sometimes defined by having content loaded only when it is needed, with the **Load invisible widgets in background** setting, all the content is still being loaded whether it is needed or not; it is simply prioritizing loading directly needed content before loading not currently needed content in the background. Figure 4.8 shows exactly what an analytics application startup looks like with this setting enabled.

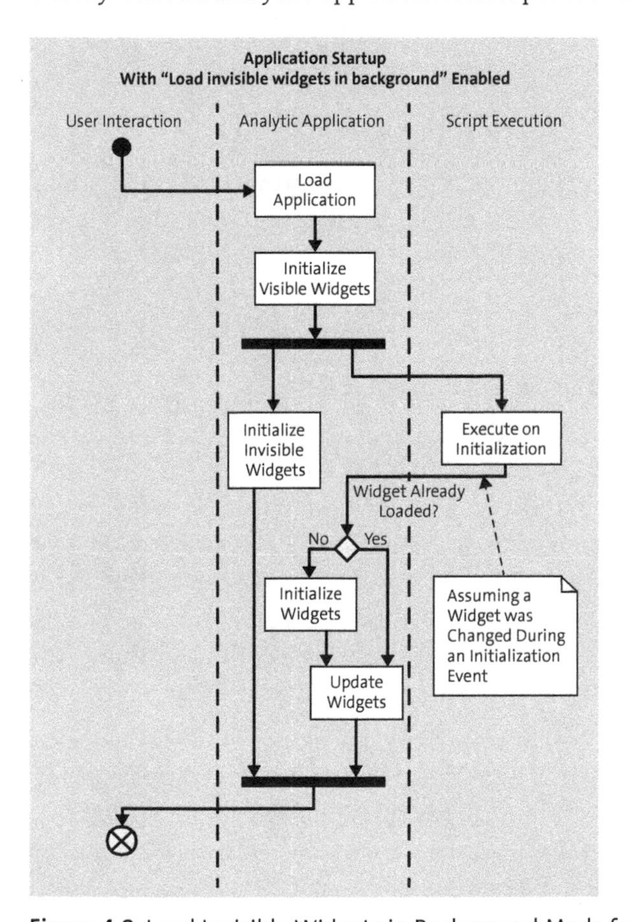

Figure 4.8 Load Invisible Widgets in Background Mode for Loading an Analytics Application

Using the same testing setup and analytics application that was used for the performance test in Section 4.1 (containing 136 charts, several other widgets, popups, and scripts, based on a model containing 185,118 rows of data, several dimensions, and over 200 measures), we carried out a performance test to compare the loading times with the setting being switched on and off. The results of this test can be seen in Table 4.2. There is a clear difference between the two. When the setting is switched on, the time it takes for the dashboard to be interactable (meaning the initially visible page is loaded and can be interacted with) is 4.5 seconds faster. In other words, in our specific test case, about a third of the loading time was saved using this setting. This makes enabling **Load invisible widgets in background** almost always a great tool for improving the perceived performance.

Setting	Time until user can interact with dashboard
Turned off	14 seconds
Turned on	9.5 seconds

Table 4.2 Performance of a Larger Dashboard with "Load Invisible Widgets in Background" Turned On and Off

As this setting has some crossover with another setting, it is worth already mentioning here that to further reduce the number of charts being loaded and to be able to more precisely control this, the refresh of data can be paused, which will be covered in Section 4.3.4.

4.3.3 Avoid Executing a Script in the OnInitialization Event

In the analytics designer for SAP Analytics Cloud, the `onInitialization` event can be used to execute a script on startup of the dashboard in view, embed, or present mode. Using such a script should be avoided. The reasoning for this has to do with the way an analytics application is loaded, which was discussed in Section 4.3.1 and Section 4.3.2. Depending on whether or not the "load invisible widgets in background" setting is enabled, either all or only the visible widgets are initialized before the `onInitialization` event script is triggered. This loading order of initializing widgets first can result in the following issues, depending on what is being done in the `onInitialization` event script:

- By engaging with a widget during the `onInitialization` event, it will be loaded, even if it is not visible and the "load invisible widgets in background" setting is enabled. Hence, limit what is engaged with at startup by avoiding engaging with widgets that don't need to be engaged with. In this way, the performance upside of having the "load invisible widgets in background" setting enabled won't be diminished. When accessing an invisible widget on application startup is unavoidable, make sure that "always initialize on startup" is selected for this widget, which can be done in the

Styling panel under **Actions**, and carefully read the next point, as this way a better performance can be achieved. Avoiding initializing in script what could be initialized at design time will be especially relevant to trying to split up loading times, covered in Section 4.3.5, and to the responsive design topic covered in Section 4.4.

- By modifying the state of a data source or widgets in general during the `onInitialization` event script, a refresh is triggered, which can mean reloading the widget and starting another roundtrip to the backend. Therefore, avoid modifying the state of a data source or widget and, if it is necessary to do this during application startup, use the pause refresh application programming interface (API) covered later in this chapter to avoid loading things more than once.

Loading Indicator Shows If onInitialization Event Script Is Empty

Keep in mind that, currently, when the **Enable loading indicator when necessary** setting is turned on for the analytics application, and the `onInitialization` event script is left empty, then the **Load invisible widgets in background** setting won't work as intended, as a loading indicator will still appear on application startup and will go invisible only once all widgets are loaded, including invisible widgets.

4.3.4 Pause the Refresh of Data to Reduce Loading Times

Another way to avoid loading all widgets right at application startup, which is not the "Load invisible widgets in background" setting, is to pause the refresh of data for individual charts and tables. More precisely, by pausing the refresh of data on a chart, this chart is stopped from being filled with data, which also means no roundtrips to the backend need to be made to get the relevant data. Pausing the refresh of data can thus be great on various occasions, like when a certain part of a dashboard should not be loaded at all until accessed or when global filters should only be applied on currently visible content to reduce loading times. By default, this setting is always switched off for newly created charts and widgets. As can be seen in Figure 4.9, there are three settings to choose from. These settings can be found for all types of charts and tables near the bottom of the **Builder** panel under **Properties**.

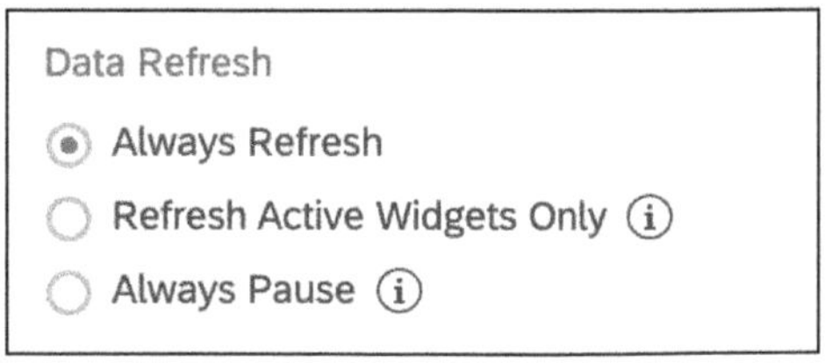

Data Refresh

(●) Always Refresh

( ) Refresh Active Widgets Only (i)

( ) Always Pause (i)

Figure 4.9 Pause Data Refresh Setting

The three settings available and visible in Figure 4.9 do the following:

- **Always Refresh**
  This is the default mode, where the charts data is always loaded and refreshed, either right away or in the background, depending on how the analytics application is setup. When the chart data is being updated, changes to a chart such as applying a filter work normally.
- **Refresh Active Widgets Only**
  This is a somewhat similar mechanism to the "load invisible widgets in background" setting, as only charts that are visible or otherwise active, for example by being accessed via a script, are loaded or changed. However, unlike with the "load invisible widgets in background" setting, inactive and invisible charts don't receive any data updates at all. This makes it a great setting for keeping unused content unloaded, thus supplementing the functionality of the "load invisible widgets in background" setting. Of course, beware of things like scripting, which might activate charts even when invisible.
- **Always Pause**
  This setting means that the refresh of data for the chart or table in question is always paused. It doesn't matter whether or not the chart is visible, whether there are filters being applied, or whether a chart is being changed via a script, the only way of making a chart or table with this setting enabled load data during runtime is if this setting is turned off, which can be done via the pause refresh scripting API.

In summary, pausing data refreshes makes it possible not only to limit the initial loading time, as the number of backend roundtrips and widgets being filled with data is reduced, but also to split up loading times so content is loaded or updated only on an as-needed basis. This topic is further covered in Section 4.5.3, where we will be taking a close look at the pause refresh API. It enables the ability to switch between the three modes mentioned above while in runtime, thus making a great tool for targeted pausing of data refreshing and improving performance.

4.3.5 Split Up Content to Distribute Loading Times and Limit What Is Shown at Startup

The previous sections have covered the important topics of improving the initial loading time by loading invisible widgets in the background, avoiding an `onInitialization` event script that would, for example, access invisible unloaded widgets or reload already initialized widgets and pausing the refresh of data. Especially by pausing the refresh of data, much can be achieved, as it allows the splitting up of loading times, thus also limiting the initial loading time. However, it is limited to reducing the loading time by disabling backend roundtrips for widgets connected to a data source and not by splitting up the loading time of all the content of a dashboard. Hence, we can improve on these tips by limiting what is shown at startup and thus reducing the visible widgets that need to be loaded when initializing and by splitting up the content shown in a dashboard, thus limiting further the number of widgets being loaded.

As covered in the introduction of this section, how to structure the splitting up of content of a dashboard is very much dependent on the scope and target audience. Splitting up content into different applications and panels should be done only where it makes sense. For example, if most users of a dashboard require only a broad overview over some information, with a smaller number of users wanting to dive into specific sections with more detailed information, it might suffice to show only a small overview page at application startup. This limits what is shown at startup, thus optimizing the viewing experience for most target users by reducing the initial loading time. To still cover the needs of all users, the dashboard could also have several more detailed screens for users interested in diving deeper into specific topics.

A good rule of thumb to follow when splitting up content is to show high-level information first and then increase the detail of information as the user dives deeper into the dashboard. In this way, not all the data is loaded right away, but instead loads step by step. This is also a sensible rule from a design perspective.

There are several options for splitting up content in the analytics designer for SAP Analytics Cloud. These are using multiple tabs, using filters, and linking multiple analytics applications. There are different advantages and disadvantages to each of them. What exactly is meant by this, how to set it up, and what the advantages and disadvantages are will be covered in the next sections.

Testing Several Options of Splitting Up Content

To test each option, the dashboard visible in Figure 4.10 was set up once with each option. The figure shows the first of eight identical pages. It is the same dashboard used for performance testing in Section 4.1, which, depending on the option used, is split into eight analytics application files or kept as just one, containing 136 charts of different size and variety, 17 panels and flow layout panels, several other widgets, a popup, and the navigating elements unique to each option. As data source, an SAP Analytics Cloud model is used, containing 185,118 rows of data, several dimensions, and over 200 measures. Keep in mind that you might not get the exact same performance test results with a similarly sized dashboard and data source, as other factors such as your device's processing power and the speed of your internet connection will likely be different. Hence, testing different approaches to splitting up content, which includes mixing the three options discussed below, is often worth it to find the best possible solution for your specific use case.

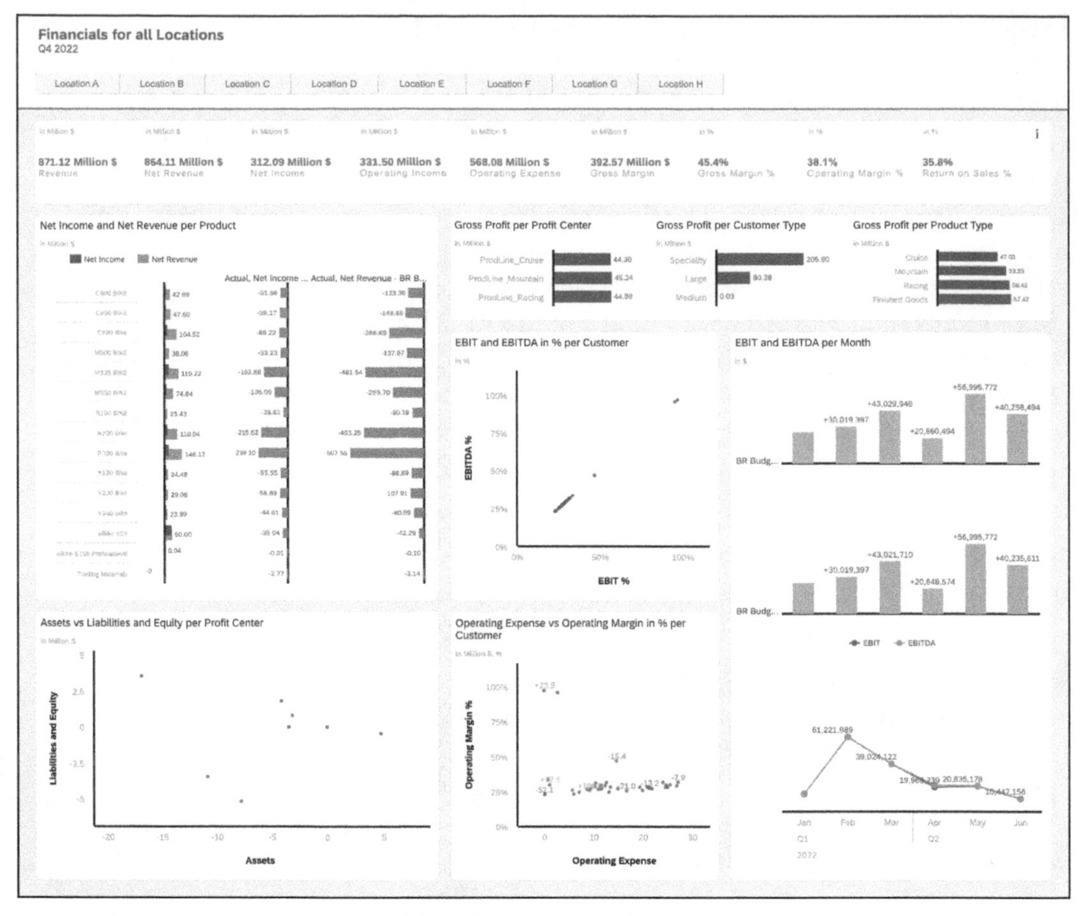

Figure 4.10 A Larger Test Dashboard with Poor Performance

Using Multiple Tabs in the Same Analytics Application

This option calls for building the entire dashboard in one analytics application, just like it would usually be done using the story designer. However, as the analytics designer doesn't have pages, you can use the tab strip widget to merge charts and other widgets into panels, flow layout panels, or tabs, which act as organizational units. In this way, content can be split up into separate sections. However, keep in mind that, for this option, it is important to leverage the tips covered in Section 4.3.2 to Section 4.3.4 to make sure that the default loading mode isn't set to load all widgets, including inactive and invisible widgets, on analytics application startup. This would do the exact opposite of splitting up content to distribute loading times and limit what is shown at startup. Hence, this option can really be summed up as the basic way of creating multiple tabs in an analytics application while keeping the previously mentioned tips in mind to split up and reduce loading times.

When several panels or flow layout panels are used, buttons or other widgets with an `onClick` event are needed to act as navigation elements for the user to switch between panels. The JavaScript should look as follows, setting the visibility of the current panel as false and the visibility of the target widget as true:

```
Current_panel.setVisible(false);
Target_panel.setVisible(true);
```


To avoid initializing still inactive and potentially unloaded widgets, avoid mentioning any panels or other widgets beside the current and target panels. Additional widgets in the script will also be initialized through the script instead of, for example, by being loaded in the background. If you are using the pause refresh API, these navigation buttons are a good place to attach the necessary scripting.

The tab script widget can be added by pressing the [+] icon in the **Insert** toolbar section and then selecting the **Tab Strip** widget. Here, no scripting is needed; simply edit the tabs via the **Builder** panel.

We performed a small performance test by opening the dashboard shown in Figure 4.10 and navigating within it. The results can be seen in Table 4.3. For this test, we used panels as organizational units and buttons to switch between the panels. As the "Load invisible widgets in background" setting is enabled and data refresh is not paused, the load time may vary depending on how quickly users switch to another section, as more or less invisible widgets will have been loaded in the background. For the performance test, we assumed that the user spent at least a minute on page one, which explains the quick switching time.

What is timed?	Measured time
Initial loading time	30 seconds
Switching to another section	2.5 seconds

Table 4.3 Performance Test Results for Using Multiple Panels to Switch between Content

Leveraging Filters to Switch between Content

This method of splitting content is unique in that it can be seen as not actually being a split, but rather a consolidation of content. Instead of having multiple tabs, each filled with charts and other widgets, this method combines all tabs into a single set of widgets. This reduction in the number of charts and other widgets means that fewer widgets need to be loaded overall. For charts and tables to still show the same figures as for multiple tabs, filters are used to switch between the different content. Of course, this means that the content of each section must be identical in structure and share a dimension, such as a location dimension, that can be used to switch between content, just as would be the case with a separate set of widgets for each tab.

To further explain this, when it comes to the first page of the dashboard shown in Figure 4.10, it is not unique but rather the exact same as the other seven tabs. The only exception is that each tab is filtered to another location. This means that, by getting rid of the seven duplicate tabs and using filters to switch between the locations, the number of charts would be reduced from 136 charts split among eight panels to just 17 charts. The number of other widgets is also reduced by a factor of eight.

As we want to keep the same look as visible in Figure 4.10, we attached scripting to the navigation buttons, which changes the filters, instead of giving the user the option to change the filter directly through an input control widget. To change what is selected within a filter/input control through scripting, use the following command:

```
InputControl_
1.getInputControlDataSource().setSelectedMembers("dimensionMember");
```

To change the filter of a chart or table through scripting, use the following command:

```
Chart_1.getDataSource().setDimensionFilter(“dimension”,”dimensionMember”);
```

Leveraging the scripting functionalities can also make sure that some content unique to a location page can still be displayed. If, for example, a unique text needs to be displayed per location, scripting such as the `setStyle()`, `setCssClass()` and `applyText()` methods can be used to change everything about the text widget. Similarly, there could be some unique widgets per location section, which can then be displayed as with the previous option via the `setVisible()` method.

Using the example explained earlier, which is based on the dashboard already shown in Figure 4.10, we conducted a performance test to see the length of the initial loading time as well as the loading time for switching to another tab. The results of this test can be seen in Table 4.4. In these specific circumstances, the initial loading time is nearly twice as quick compared to the previous test case in Table 4.3, while switching to another section takes 1.5 seconds longer. However, since the complexity of the dashboard is not too high, even this is still relatively fast.

What is timed?	Measured time
Initial loading time	15.7 seconds
Switching to another section	4 seconds

Table 4.4 Performance Test Results for Leveraging Filters to Switch between Content

Linking Multiple Analytics Applications

Different from the two previous options, this method requires multiple analytics application files to work. Instead of using the navigation buttons or tab strip to change the visibility of content or switching a global filter, this time we switch the entire file. This means that content is split between as many analytics application files as necessary. As can be seen in Figure 4.11, there are two options for connecting analytics application files: either through the `NavigationUtils.openApplication` command, which can open any analytics application file that is on the same tenant, or via NavigationUtils.OpenUrl, which can open any URL, including the URL of another SAP Analytics Cloud file.


```
function onClick() : void

1 //Option A
2 NavigationUtils.openApplication("application_id",UrlParameter.create("mode", "embed"), false);
3
4 //Option B
5 NavigationUtils.openUrl("application_link", false);
```

Figure 4.11 Opening Another Dashboard through Scripting

With Option B, there are certain restrictions compared to, for example, having one analytics application file with several panels, as data such as information on the selected filters can't be passed to the newly opening file. This, however, is different with Option A, as the ability to attach parameters is provided, thus allowing you to initialize variables via URL parameters to convey information such as selected filters.

Further Reading

How to use the navigation API is covered in more detail in the following resources, including how to implement URL parameters to transport information:

- Visual BI, "SAP Analytics Cloud – Application Design Series 17 Navigation Utility Options," available at *http://s-prs.co/v566933*
- SAP Help Portal, "Use Navigation APIs," available at *http://s-prs.co/v566934*

One thing to keep in mind when leveraging this method, regardless of whether Option A or B is used, is that the transition between two analytics application files will not be as smooth as the transition between two panels, for example. The user will notice a change as a new analytics application file is opened. To limit this and to improve performance, we suggest using the embed mode. For Option A, this can be defined in the URL parameter section, while for Option B this can be defined by creating and using a custom sharing link set to embed mode. To create such a custom link, navigate to the **Share Application** screen and then select **Customize Link**.

The results of the conducted performance test of opening and navigating within the dashboard shown in Figure 4.11 can be seen in Table 4.5. Both the initial loading time and switching to another section take the same amount of time. This is because each time the user switches tabs, the analytics application is newly loaded. This has the disadvantage that pages that have already previously been open have to be loaded anew as they were in another file. It is to be said, however, that it might go faster the second time around, as information was saved in the cache. An advantage of this method is the greatly limited initial loading time, being the fastest compared to the previous two options. Additionally, with very large dashboards, it is easier to work on them in edit mode with multiple files rather than with one large slow file.

What is timed?	Measured time
Initial loading time	13.2 seconds
Switching to another section	13.2 seconds

Table 4.5 Performance Test Results for Linking Multiple Analytics Applications Together

4.4 Optimizing Responsive Design Performance for Mobile and Other Devices

One of the great advantages of building a dashboard using a cloud tool such as SAP Analytics Cloud is the ability to view insights from anywhere. Whether on a laptop from home, a monitor in the office, or a mobile device such as a phone or tablet while on the road, SAP Analytics Cloud users will always be able to access the information they require. Having this easy accessibility can be great and important functionality for the users of a dashboard, but at the same time it creates extra work for the dashboard creators, as dashboards need to be built using a responsive design, or, in other words, a design that automatically adjusts to different screen sizes. Creating such a responsive design takes less additional work when using responsive pages for the story builder for SAP Analytics Cloud than when using the analytics designer for SAP Analytics Cloud. In comparison to responsive pages of the story builder, the analytics designer for SAP Analytics Cloud is less restrictive and offers more functionalities and customizability. However, it also requires more effort to create a dashboard that automatically and dynamically adjusts to different screen sizes.

A design that is not responsive can cause a dashboard to be unusable on specific screen sizes, so making sure the dashboard is perfectly adapted to different screen sizes like phones, tables, and laptops is a crucial step when building a dashboard. We suggest starting to think about responsive design from the very beginning of the dashboard creation process. When the analytics application is still empty, it is easiest to experiment with how to set up panels, flow layout panels, and more. This is because the analytics designer for SAP Analytics Cloud will be quickest to respond without the analytics application being filled with large amounts of content, and it saves time not having to move content around after understanding that the dashboard should be set up somewhat differently. As mentioned in previous chapters, keeping the scope and target users in mind from the beginning will save valuable time. The need for a responsive design will vary for each dashboard. It could be the case that a dashboard would never be used on a small device, eliminating the need to design for tablets and phones. Or it could be the case that a dashboard needs to be usable primarily on mobile devices, but also in the office on a big screen, thus creating the need for a comprehensive look at responsive design. So, there are many use cases for SAP Analytics Cloud dashboards, and determining the scope of the dashboard and the needs of target users early on will allow you to determine the devices for which the responsive design needs to be optimized. This will save time in creating a more efficient responsive design with a more streamlined setup from beginning to end.

The following sections will give you further tips and tricks to make sure that resizing your analytics applications to the correct screen size is as seamless as possible. This can be quite a challenge, especially for large and complex analytics applications, but this is also where the following improvements help the most in building a well-performing analytics application.

Important Note

When building an analytics application meant to be used on a mobile device, don't forget to turn on the mobile support setting. Without it, users won't be able to access the dashboard via the mobile phone app. You can find the setting under **Edit Analytic Application • Analytic Application Details**. Beware, with this setting turned on, certain functionalities won't work, such as geo maps, R, and more.

4.4.1 Leverage Built-in Functionalities Instead of Scripting Everything

In Section 4.3.3, we introduced the tip of leaving the `onInitialization` event script empty in the analytics designer for SAP Analytics Cloud. Completely following this tip when building a responsive design using JavaScript will be impossible, as the earliest instance when loading an analytics application where content can be resized to fit the screen through scripting is in the `onInitialization` event script. This means that, in many cases, already fully loaded widgets will need to be relocated and resized, causing the initial loading time to be longer and the resizing noticeable to the end user. So, while writing a long script makes it possible to program an analytics applications behavior in a very specific way, this will come with noticeable performance downsides. In addition to having an `onInitialization` event script, the `onResize` event will also need to be used for resizing.

One way of avoiding this dilemma completely, that is if the responsive design isn't too unique and complex, is to leverage the flow layout panel, especially with its break points. Widgets contained within the flow layout panel automatically left align. This can be changed to center or right align in the **Styling** panel. Furthermore, break points can determine the screen width at which widgets within the flow layout panel should be hidden, resized to a percentage width, or resized to a pixel height. As these break points are applied right when the flow layout panel is first initialized, the widgets contained in the flow layout panel will themselves be initialized starting with their correct size. This makes using break points significantly faster than doing the same thing via a script. Examples of break points can be seen in Figure 4.12. They are set up via the

Builder panel of any flow layout panel. Make sure that the **Enable the rule in Design Time** setting is switched on.

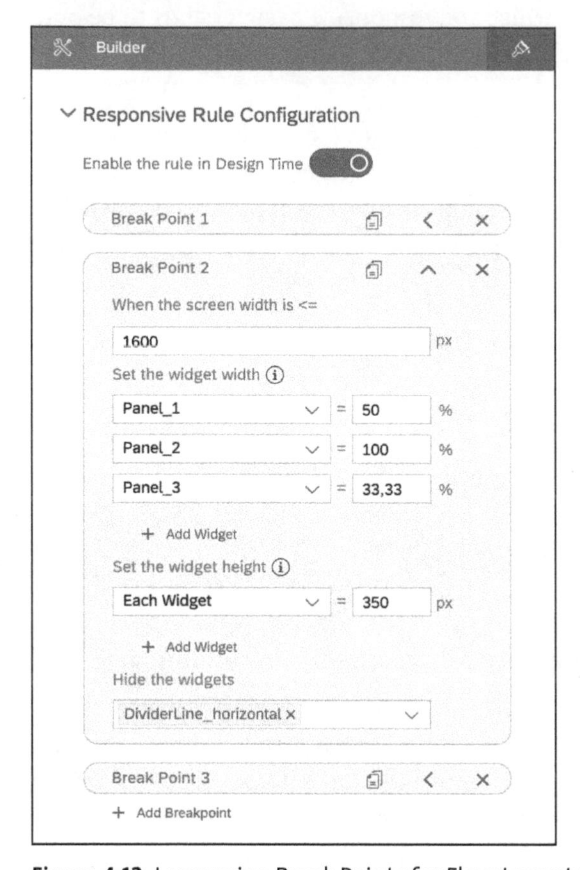

Figure 4.12 Leveraging Break Points for Flow Layout Panels

Note that completely avoiding the use of scripting to create a responsive design might not always be possible. If this is the case, make sure you are following the tips from the upcoming Section 4.4.2.

Note

There are also other examples unrelated to the topic of responsive design for mobile and other devices, in which leveraging built-in functionalities instead of scripting applies. An example of this is displaying the name of the user currently viewing the analytics application somewhere within the dashboard. A text like *"Hey John Doe, welcome to the dashboard!"* can be a nice personal touch. Rather than implementing this via JavaScript using the `Application.getUserInfo()` and `TextWidget.applyText()` commands executed in the `onInitialization` event, it is more efficient to add this information via dynamic text, which can be found in the **More Actions** meatballs menu of a text widget under **Add**, **Dynamic Text**, and then select **Current User**.

4.4.2 Avoid Resizing Unnecessarily

When creating any analytics application designed for multiple devices, most likely at least some content will have to be resized for the dashboard to optimally fit to each screen size. As covered before, this can be achieved through built-in features such as leveraging break points on flow layout panels and through JavaScript by leveraging scripting executed on, for example, the `onInitialization` and `onResize` events. For more complex dashboards, if built-in features can't do the job alone, a mix of the two can be leveraged. For both methods, but especially when scripting, resizing unnecessarily should be avoided. This includes avoiding resizing invisible content, resizing only in intervals, and further limiting the number of individual widgets being changed and will be discussed in the following sections.

Resize Less Often

Instead of trying to improve performance through leveraging built-in features, this tip comes down to simply resizing less to reduce overall loading times. By adapting to a changing screen size less often, performance can be saved. This could, for example, be applicable when users move the browser window around, increasing or decreasing its size or using the zoom functionality to zoom in or out. Although the width that the analytics application uses up changes by a few pixels, this doesn't mean a resizing needs to be triggered.

By defining thresholds to resize and by keeping track of what state the app is in, unnecessary resizing can be avoided, and thus the number of resizes can be reduced to a minimum. An example of this can be seen in Figure 4.13.

```
function onResize() : void

1  if(Application.getInnerWidth().value < 800 && ResizeMode !== "mobile"){
2      // Small Screen
3      Panel_1.getLayout().setLeft(LayoutValue.create(0,LayoutUnit.Pixel));
4      Panel_2.getLayout().setWidth(LayoutValue.create(100,LayoutUnit.Percent));
5      ResizeMode = "mobile";
6  } else if(Application.getInnerWidth().value < 1600 && ResizeMode !== "medium"){
7      // Medium Screen
8      Panel_1.getLayout().setLeft(LayoutValue.create(32,LayoutUnit.Pixel));
9      Panel_2.getLayout().setWidth(LayoutValue.create(100,LayoutUnit.Percent));
10     ResizeMode = "medium";
11 } else if(Application.getInnerWidth().value > 1600 && ResizeMode !== "large"){
12     // Large Screen
13     Panel_1.getLayout().setLeft(LayoutValue.create(32,LayoutUnit.Pixel));
14     Panel_2.getLayout().setWidth(LayoutValue.create(1500,LayoutUnit.Pixel));
15     ResizeMode = "large";
16 }
```

Figure 4.13 Using Scripting to Avoid Unnecessary Resizing

In this example, the alignment of the analytics application is changed, depending on whether the screen is small like a phone, medium like a tablet or small laptop, or large like a monitor. By defining a global variable, in this case called `ResizeMode`, we can avoid unnecessary resizing when, for example, moving the dashboard between differently sized monitors. Also keep in mind that using, for example, a percentage width will mean more frequent resizing as the window size changes, compared to a fixed pixel size.

Avoid Resizing Invisible Content

To further reduce the amount of time being taken up by resizes, mainly applicable for large analytics files containing multiple tabs to be switched between, is to not resize invisible content. For content that is hidden as it is further down the page, this can be tricky and maybe not worth the effort, but for content in another invisible panel like discussed in Section 4.3.5, this can be useful.

To achieve this, ideally at least one global variable is needed to keep track of which tab is currently visible. In this way, when executing a resize in the `onResize` or `onInitialization` events, `if-else` and `switch` statements can be used to ensure that only the appropriate widgets are resized. This will, however, also require that we check what resize mode the analytics application is in when switching between content panels, as the content that we are about to move to might or might not have previously been resized and thus be correctly aligned and sized. This means that, to avoid having to resize for each switching of a tab, more global variables are needed to keep track of the resize mode each panel is in.

If we take the dashboard shown earlier in Figure 4.1 and Figure 4.10, we know it contains 136 charts, several other widgets, a popup, and scripting, while being based on a model containing 185,118 rows of data, several dimensions, and over 200 measures. This results in each tab being made up of two panels, seventeen charts, and a button. Table 4.6 shows the performance test results of comparing two resizing scenarios with this dashboard. One involves changing the size of only one tab from having a width of 100 percent to having a fixed width with a left alignment of 32 px, while the other scenario does the same but for all tabs. It is clear to see that resizing only the currently visible content makes the analysis application faster and saves some time at the moment. However, remember that resizing will still have to occur for the invisible content when it is accessed. So, there may not be any overall time savings, but it might be less annoying for users to wait only a short time several times for a small resize than to wait a long time all at once. For particularly large analytics applications, users may not be accessing all pages, so spreading out the loading times may result in better performance overall.

Is resizing invisible content being avoided?	Measured time
Resizing all content	405 milliseconds
Resizing without invisible content (one tab)	142 milliseconds

Table 4.6 Performance Test Results when Avoiding Unnecessary Resizing of Invisible Content

Limit the Number of Widgets Being Changed

Unlike the previous section, which was about improving performance by resizing only the visible content areas rather than all the content, this section deals more generally with setting up the analytics application so as to resize as few individual widgets as possible when adapting to changing screen sizes. Each widget that is changed has a small impact on performance and, with up to hundreds of widgets, this can add up. Therefore, try to resize as few widgets as possible.

As seen in the previous chapters, the application designer for SAP Analytics Cloud provides the ability to use panels and flow layout panels in addition to other regular widgets to group and structure content. The first thought that comes to mind is to resize a panel with all the content it contains forming a single unit. Unfortunately, each widget must individually adapt in its size; hence, if the goal is for such a unit to always fill the same space on the screen, regardless of whether it is a small or large screen, many individual widgets will have to change. For example, having charts and a text widget contained in a panel could mean having each widget always occupy a certain space in the panel by using a percentage width and by setting the text size to dynamic. One alternative to such a dynamic approach would be having only some widgets dynamically change their size while not doing so for certain others that might not be as noticeable. Another option would be to fix the entire panel in its width and height and change, for example, only the spacing between the panels, so that it still takes up the entire screen but doesn't force large size changes.

If we look at Figure 4.14, for example, instead of resizing each tile to always fit the same percentage width of the screen, the spacing between each tile could be increased or decreased. Or, using the natural left alignment of flow layout panels in combination with some break points, these tiles could be left aligned, filling out a row on larger screens while on smaller screens the tiles could collapse into a second row, so that each product has two or more rows of tiles.

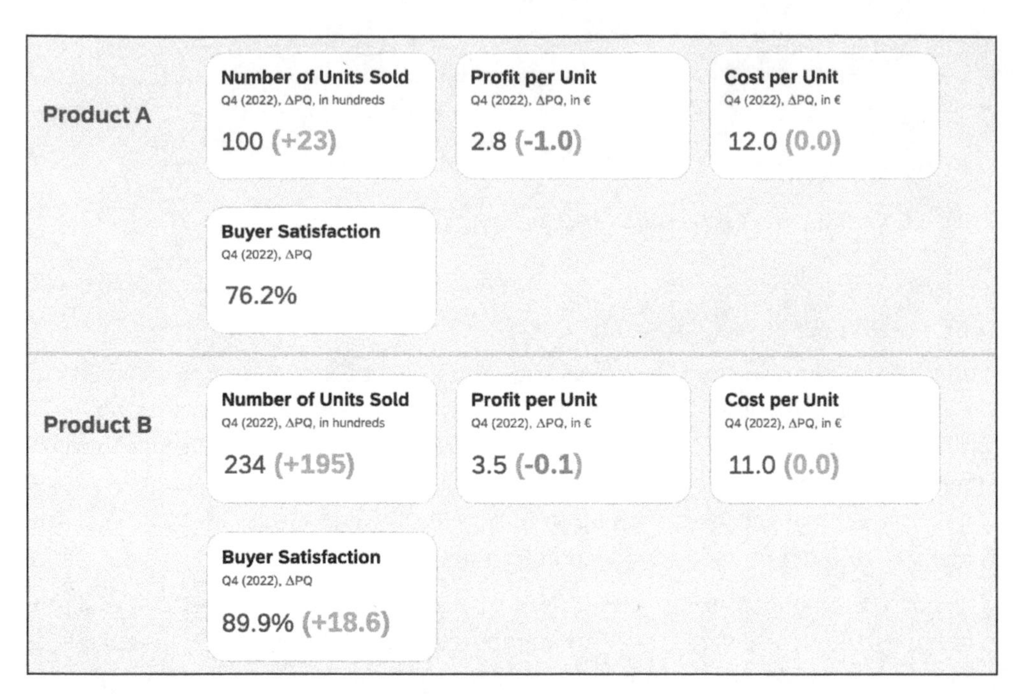

Figure 4.14 A Dashboard with a Repetitive Tiles Structure

4.5 Optimizing Performance for Scripts

One of the great advantages that the analytics designer for SAP Analytics Cloud has to offer compared to the story builder covered in Chapter 3 is the ability to create your own logic using JavaScript. It allows executing program code within your dashboard on different trigger events, like `onInitialization`, `onClick` of a button, `onResize`, and more, which enables the creation of different custom functionalities to enhance your dashboard. However, as mentioned earlier in Section 4.2.2, if you want a well-performing application, do not reinvent the wheel. This means limiting the complexity, leveraging provided features, and writing program code only when necessary. Don't include complex performance-intensive script features just because you can. Rather, leverage the built-in analytics designer functionalities and create quick, non-performance-heavy script where it makes sense. At the same time, how you write your code and what methods and variables you use can make an impact on the performance of a script. As a result, this section will look at optimizing your code by looking at general scripting best practices, where to best apply code, what methods to use and avoid, and more. While some of the general tips and tricks might be self-explanatory to the professional software developer, others won't be.

We have already mentioned some tips related to scripting in earlier sections. We won't be discussing them again here. Instead, below is a short overview:

- Analytics application architecture and loading order, covered in Section 4.3.1 and Section 4.3.2.
- Avoid `onInitialization` scripts and other scripting which initializes widgets unnecessarily, covered mainly in Section 4.3.3.
- Avoid unnecessary resizing of widgets, covered in Section 4.4.2.

4.5.1 Basic Scripting Best Practices

There are always some general rules that, when internalized, result without much thinking in building a better product as these rules become a habit. The same logic can be applied to the basic scripting best practices covered in this section. These include general coding tips any software developer will know that you might find useful when scripting in SAP Analytics Cloud and basic things to keep in mind that are specific to how scripting is done in the analytics designer for SAP Analytics Cloud.

Use Function Arguments and Local Variables Instead of Global Variables

When leveraging JavaScript in the analytics designer for SAP Analytics Cloud, it is possible either to create a global variable, which is permanently saved and always accessible for every piece of code while the analytics application is running, or to use the local variable and function argument, which are saved and usable only within a function. A global variable can be created by pressing the [+] button next to **Script Variables** in the **Scripting** section of the analytics applications outline on the left side of the screen. A function argument can be added by pressing the [+] button in the **Arguments** section when selecting a function, and the local variable can be added in the script as follows `var name = "content";`. When writing a script, use local variables and function arguments whenever the variable is used only in one script and thus a global variable isn't necessary.

Know When to Use If-else or Switch Statements

When writing small conditional statements, `if` and `if-else` statements are most used. However, for larger conditional statements, it often makes sense to leverage the `switch` statement. While it tests only for equality and not also for logical expressions such as < or >=, if you have, for example, ten conditions, the `switch` statement is generally more readable and easier to edit than using `if-else` statements. Crucially, it is also faster than an `if-else` statement when there are numerous conditions, making it a valuable tool for writing efficient code.

More about `if` statements, such as choosing their order carefully, can be found in Chapter 3.

Write More Efficient Loops by Not Repeating Instructions

When writing a loop such as a `for` loop or a `while` loop, don't include instructions inside the loop, which could also be written outside, as they will be repeated multiple times when iterating though the loop, thus resulting in a worse performance. Even if the instruction being repeated seem to be inexpensive, it is always a good best practice rule to follow.

An example of this would be getting a charts data source once in front of the loop and saving it as a variable to be used inside the loop like in Listing 4.1, instead of getting the charts data source inside the loop by doing `Chart.getDataSource().getData(selection [x]);`, which would be repeated multiple times inside the loop.

```
var datasrc = Chart.getDataSource();
for(var x=0; x<selection.length; x++){
    datasrc.getData(selection[x]);
}
```

Listing 4.1 Example of an Efficient Loop

4.5.2 Do's and Don'ts of Scripting

In this section, we'll cover some of the things you should avoid when scripting, as well as some scripting aspects that should be preferred over others.

Try to avoid using the following things in your dashboards custom JavaScript scripting. If you can't avoid them, make sure the potential issues talked about below are limited or don't occur at all:

- Two things that should be avoided were already discussed in previous chapters—these are to avoid unnecessary resizing by using scripting and avoid `onInitialization` scripts and other scripting that initializes widgets unnecessarily.
- When executing an `onResultChanged` event script, be aware that making changes to the chart or other widget that contains the `onResultChanged` script is a dangerous practice that should be avoided, since it could lead to an infinite loop, as the `onResultChanged` event script could keep triggering itself. Infinite loops will most likely slow down the dashboard or even make it unresponsive. Executing further code will also not be possible, as JavaScript is a single-threaded language, meaning it must finish executing one piece of code before moving on to the next.

The following list covers aspects of a dashboard's custom JavaScript scripting that should be preferred over other similar methods:

- **For SAP Business Warehouse (SAP BW) live connections, use `setDimensionFilter()`, as opposed to `setVariableValue()` where applicable**
  When using an SAP BW live connection, use the `setDimensionFilter()` method, as opposed to the `setVariableValue()` method when the variable in question is affecting a dimension, as setting a filter won't result in a roundtrip to the SAP BW

backend server, while using the setVariableValue() method will require such a roundtrip.

- **Instead of getMembers(), use the getResultSet() method**
  Avoid using the getMembers() method when it is possible to instead use the getResultSet() method, as when the getMembers() method is used on a data source (even when limiting the information being collected through parameters), the necessary information is collected from the backend system, while the getResultSet() method is able to use the information already accessible within the widget and thus doesn't require this additional roundtrip to the backend, which saves on performance.
- **Copy filters instead of creating new ones using the copyDimensionFilterFrom() method**
  When applying filters that already exist in the dashboard onto multiple widgets, use the copyDimensionFilterFrom() method instead of the setDimensionFilter()method. In this way, the dimension filter of a data source is copied over, which is faster than creating a new dimension filter for a data source, especially when the setDimensionFilter() method needs to do a roundtrip to the backend, as can be seen in the next tip.
- **When using the setDimensionFilter() method, use it with the MemberInfo object instead of member ID**
  As using the copyDimensionFilterFrom() method instead of the setDimensionFilter()method is possible only in certain scenarios, when using the setDimensionFilter()method it should be done with a MemberInfo object instead of a member ID to improve performance. This is because, when using a member ID for the setDimensionFilter()method, the description fitting to the member ID is gathered from the backend system, while the MemberInfo object itself already contains the description that would be fetched when using the member ID. So, by using a MemberInfo object, when possible, a roundtrip to the backend is spared, thus increasing the speed of the script.

4.5.3 Tools and Settings to Leverage in Your Scripts

Make sure you are leveraging the following in your dashboards custom JavaScript scripting, as the tips discussed below can save on performance for the specific situations in which they are applicable. One example of this, which was already partially covered in Section 4.3.4, is pausing the refresh of data. The corresponding pause refresh API, which was so far not covered, will be discussed at the end of this section. Use the following tips when writing custom scripts:

- **For SAP BW live connections, group multiple backend calls using setVariableValue()**
  When using the setVariableValue() method to make multiple calls to the SAP BW backend server, for example to change the content of multiple charts of the same

data source, the calls can be grouped by writing the commands directly following each other and without being interrupted using any other scripting API methods. In this way, the calls are automatically merged into a single call to the SAP BW backend server, which goes faster than multiple calls.

- **Disable planning on tables, unless it is being used**
  Tables in SAP Analytics Cloud can leverage planning capabilities, which enables, for example, the planning of financial data for future quarters. This requires the correct data source, where planning is enabled in the model and the necessary roles and permissions are given, as well as for planning to be enabled on the table itself. Planning can be enabled or disabled for tables either through the **Builder panel** under **Properties** or via leveraging scripting, more specifically using the `getPlanning().setEnabled()` command on a table. As having the planning feature enabled takes up resources, it is advisable to use scripting to enable or disable planning as it is needed. For example, if a table is not visible on startup, consider enabling planning on this table only when it becomes visible and would be used as such. This is what the code for enabling planning on a table looks like:

  ```
  Table_1.getPlanning().setEnabled(true);
  ```

- **Consider moving widgets using the `moveWidget()` method to reduce duplicate widgets**
  The `moveWidget()` method can be used to move a widget defined in the brackets into the panel or the application the method is applied on. This is a great feature for improving the loading time of a dashboard when your analytics application contains duplicate widgets—for example, a chart that exists multiple times in several panels and could instead exist only once and be moved from one panel to another upon accessing it using the following code:

  ```
  Panel_1.moveWidget(Chart_1);
  ```

- **Use the `setStyle()`, `applyText()`, `setText()`, and `setCssClass()` methods to reduce duplicate widgets**
  To further eliminate unnecessary duplicate widgets, consider using the `setStyle()` method to modify the color, font, and other features of a text widget, the `applyText()` method to modify the text of a text widget, the `setText()` method to modify the text displayed in a button, or the `setCssClass()` method to change the CSS class of a widget. In this way, instead of having multiple widgets with, for example, a green and a red number, different text, or different text icons, you can create only a single widget and still have a change in what is displayed depending on, for example, whether a result shown is good or bad. Keep in mind that for the `setCssClass()` method, you first must create a CSS class in the **Edit CSS** panel and that widgets can already be initialized with a CSS class by entering it into the widget properties, in the **Styling Panel** directly under the widget name.

- **Initialize variables via URL parameters**
  When opening an analytics application via a URL, it is possible to initialize global variables through passing them as URL parameters. This can be useful for performance when using linked variables and variable parameters for filtering, as in this way the global variable will be set before any content is loaded.

Further Reading

More information on this topic and how to apply it can be found in the SAP help documentation at the following URL: *http://s-prs.co/v566935*.

- **Leverage the pause refresh API**
  The pause refresh API enables pausing, unpausing, and more for the data refresh of charts and other widgets. It works to enhance the capabilities provided by selecting one of the three data refresh modes covered in Section 4.3.4 within the **Builder** panel of a widget, as it allows this mode to be changed during runtime. The selectable modes are on, off, and auto. The following methods are part of the pause refresh API:
  - This method returns the data refresh mode of, for example, a chart. This used to be done through the `isRefreshPaused()` method, which is now deprecated and replaced by the `getRefreshPaused()` method. Note that this method is available only for data sources associated with a table or chart. It can be used as follows:

```
var datasource = Chart_1.getDataSource();
datasource.getRefreshPaused();
```

  - The `setRefreshPaused()` method is used to set the data refresh mode of a chart or table widget. It can be used as a Boolean and, as such, set to true and false, corresponding to on and off. Alternatively, there are three pause modes that can be selected from, which are `PauseMode.On`, `PauseMode.Off`, and `PauseMode.Auto`. When this method is executed on a widget, the script will be executed without waiting for the data source–related widgets to be updated before the data refresh is set to false:

```
var datasource = Chart_1.getDataSource();
datasource.setRefreshPaused(boolean|PauseMode);
```

  These methods can be used for things such as pausing the refresh of invisible widgets so only visible widgets are refreshed, enabling pause refresh for invisible planning tables but only after planning was disabled, and more.

4.6 Analytics Application Script Performance Popup Tool

There are numerous options for measuring the overall performance of a dashboard. Chapter 2 covers this topic in detail, including the various types of performance testing, what the testing procedure looks like, and how to conduct performance testing in general. In addition to external tools such as, for example, Chrome DevTools for the Google Chrome browser, SAP Analytics Cloud already provides some built-in features for doing performance testing. We have already seen an example of this, as the performance analysis tool for SAP Analytics Cloud was discussed in Chapter 3. An additional functionality unique to the analytics designer for SAP Analytics Cloud is the analytics application script performance popup tool. It is specific to measuring the performance of built-in custom JavaScript scripting and allowing for quickly viewing the performance of scripting at runtime in the form of a swim lane diagram. How to utilize this tool to maximum effect will be the topic of this section. We'll go over how to activate, access, and navigate this tool and look at two examples, one for measuring specific parts of complex scripting and one for viewing bottlenecks where scripting must wait for widgets to load.

4.6.1 What Is the Script Performance Popup Tool?

As mentioned, the script performance popup is a great tool for measuring the performance of custom JavaScript scripts created in the analytics designer for SAP Analytics Cloud. When active, it measures in milliseconds the time a single action, such as an `onClick` event on a button, takes to run. Time that is spend waiting for widgets to load that are necessary for the script to execute successfully is also recorded and marked in red. As shown in Figure 4.15, all the measured times from scripts being executed in the analytics application are displayed in a swim lane diagram, thus allowing the data to be easily interpreted and analyzed. In the following sections, we'll discuss activating, accessing, and navigating this tool.

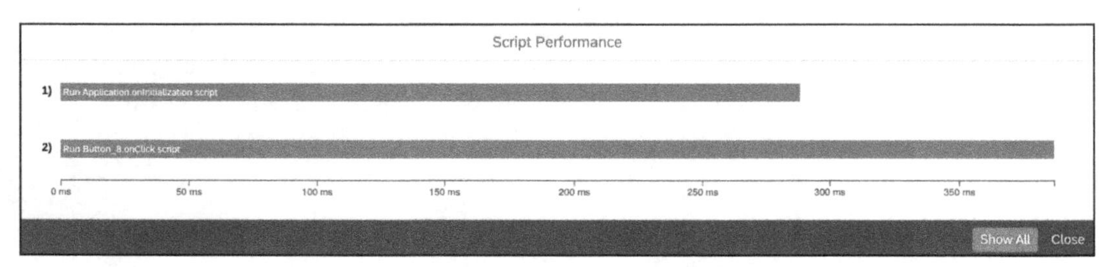

Figure 4.15 Script Execution Time for an OnInitialization and OnClick Event

Activating the Tool

There is one thing to keep in mind when using this tool. The script performance popup tool is not active by default when viewing your dashboard, so activating it must be done first and can be achieved in two different ways. If you are currently editing your dashboard, it will be easiest to open it by navigating through the toolbar. Find the **Performance Optimization** icon under **Tools** and then select **Analyze Script Performance in View Time**, as shown in Figure 4.16. This will open your analytics application in view mode in a new tab with the script performance popup tool active. In addition, you can find the shortcut for opening the script performance popup tool and further information about the tool behind the **Info** icon, as well as general performance advice behind **Look up Best Practices.**

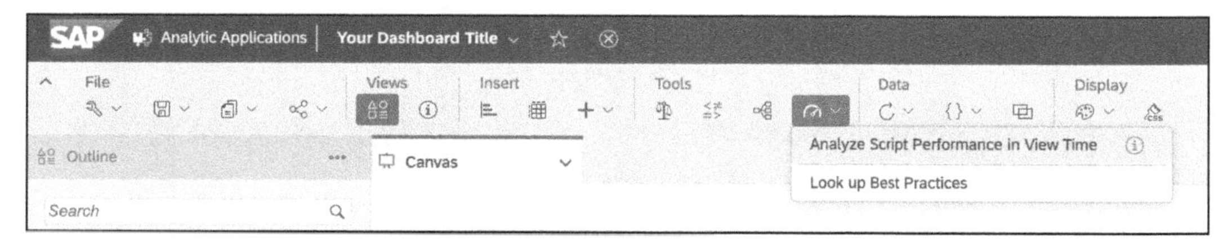

Figure 4.16 Activating the Tool in Edit Mode

The second way of activating this tool is optimal if you are already viewing an analytics application. By inserting the URL parameter `?APP_PERFORMANCE_LOGGING=true` right after `app.html` but before the # character and then reloading the dashboard with the new URL, the script performance popup tool will be activated. This is what the URL should now look like, but with the tenant information, app id, and more being shown as three dots:

```
https://.../app.html?APP_PERFORMANCE_LOGGING=true#/...
```

Accessing and Navigating the Tool

Once the tool is activated and the application is fully loaded, the script performance popup can finally be opened by pressing either the shortcut [Ctrl] + [Shift] + [A] or [Ctrl] + [Shift] + [Z]. You will then be able to see all the script performance measurements already taken so far. If you are using a small screen and there are too many bars being displayed to fit into one view, you can either hide single results by simply clicking on a chosen bar or scroll up or down using your mouse. To show all results once again, simply press **Show All**. To show the exact measurement result in milliseconds and the full event name, simply hover over a chosen bar.

4.6.2 First Example: Measuring Specific Parts of Complex Scripting

Scripting in the analytics designer for SAP Analytics Cloud can easily get more complex than just a few lines of JavaScript written into, for example, the `onClick` event of a button. Splitting up code segments into functions so they can easily be maintained and reused is a common practice. However, when it comes to measuring with the script performance popup tool, regardless of whether there are only a couple of lines changing the visibility of a chart written directly behind a button or whether you are doing something larger with several functions, the script performance popup measures the whole event using only a single bar. This is visible in Figure 4.17. The first bar shows scripting being triggered when clicking a button, which calculates the margin of error for a specific dataset during which a function for calculating the standard deviation is called. If, however, you want to measure individual functions or segments of your code, divide up scripts behind different events. In our example, you can see bars two and three showing the individual time the margin of error and standard deviation calculations take, when they are individually being called behind their own `onClick` event.

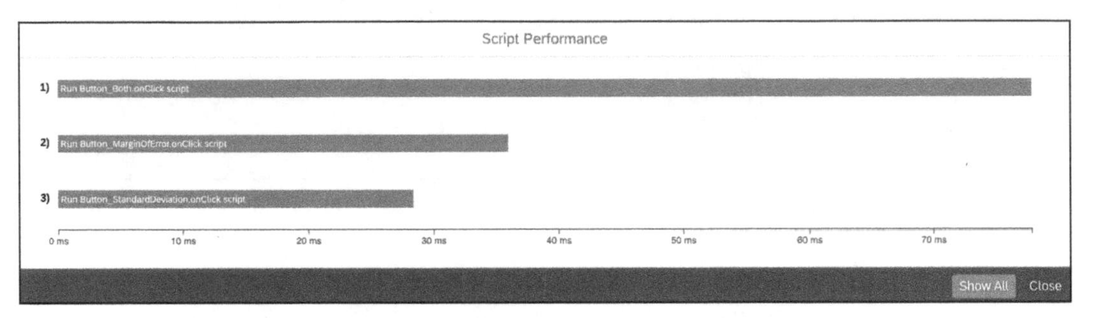

Figure 4.17 Script Execution Time of Three Different OnClick Events

4.6.3 Second Example: Viewing Bottlenecks Where Scripting Must Wait for Widgets to Load

Scripting in the analytics designer for SAP Analytics Cloud is frequently leveraged to change the visibility of widgets. Common examples of this are building a custom navigation panel or having another functionality like a dropdown menu to switch between content. In each case, currently visible content is switched to invisible and vice versa for the requested invisible content. However, if this invisible content is not yet loaded, because, for example, **Load invisible widgets in background** is active and this content was so far never used, the content still must be loaded. As a result, when a script is accessing this currently still unloaded content, before any of the widgets can be changed, the script must wait for all the unloaded widgets to be initialized. To visualize and test this, we set up an analytics application with an `onInitialization` event script that tries to access still unloaded content in the form of Panel_1. As can be seen in Figure 4.18, the first blue bar, which shows the `onInitialization` event script, must wait for Panel_1 to be loaded in the background (as **Load invisible widgets in background** is enabled here and the content isn't directly visible), before the script can finish executing. A simple way to avoid this would be by selecting **Always initialize on startup** for this panel, through which the `onInitialization` event script to access Panel_1 would be triggered only after Panel_1 is already loaded. The second bar shows the `onClick` event of a button. Due to inefficient scripting, the visibility of widgets is changed, although they are not really needed. As the script accesses this content, it must first be loaded. As a result, the second blue bar must wait for Panel_7 and Panel_8 to finish loading, which is indicated by the two red bars, before the script execution can continue. So, the key takeaway is that red always means something influencing the script execution performance in a negative way.

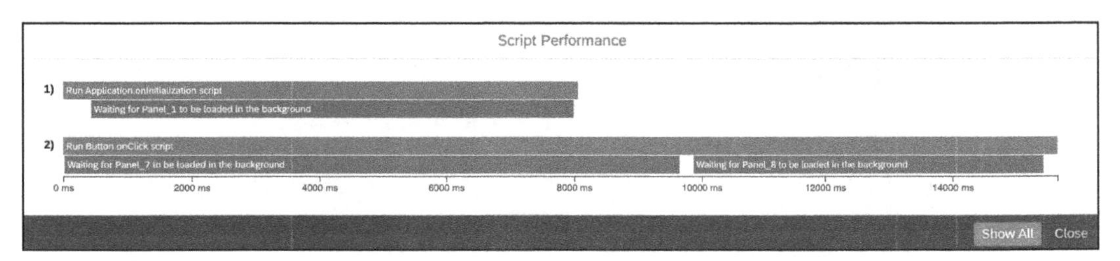

Figure 4.18 Script Execution Time of an OnInitialization and OnClick Event

Further Reading

Learn more about leveraging the script performance popup by reading through a concrete performance improvement case on pages 323–327 of the SAP Analytics Cloud, analytics designer Developer Handbook. In it you can also find further information about improving performance for the analytics designer for SAP Analytics Cloud, as well as a lot of general information about building analytics applications. You can find the handbook at the following URL: *http://s-prs.co/v566936*.

The resources available behind the **Information** icon visible in Figure 4.16 can be found at the following URL: *http://s-prs.co/v566937*.

4.7 Best Practices

When facing performance issues in a dashboard built with SAP Analytics Cloud, consider the entire performance equation. It could be that the dashboard is being viewed with a slow internet connection, that the model is poorly set up, or that there are some issues with the SAP Analytics Cloud tenant. These performance improvement topics unrelated to the story builder or analytics designer will be discussed in the upcoming chapters. If the performance problem is at least partially due to a poorly optimized analytics application, the following tips, discussed in more detail earlier, are the best practices that can help improve performance:

- Keep the dashboard simple, which includes not adding unnecessary scripting functionalities even if it is tempting to do so.
- Limit the number of widgets used. This includes leveraging JavaScript methods such as `setStyle()`and `moveWidget()`.
- Use the "Load invisible widgets in background" setting to load invisible, inactive content in the background.
- Avoid executing a script in the `onInitialization` event, so as to not engage with widgets.

- Pause the refresh of data on charts and tables and leverage the pause refresh API to switch between refresh modes to reduce the number of backend calls for different scenarios.
- Split up content to distribute loading times and limit what is shown at startup by using multiple tabs or multiple analytics applications or leveraging filters to switch between content.
- Leverage built-in functionalities such as the flow layout panels and their break points to adapt a dashboard to different screen sizes, instead of only scripting everything.
- Avoid resizing a dashboard unnecessarily by preferring to resize in few intervals, by limiting the number of individual widgets being changed, and by avoiding resizing invisible content.
- Optimize the performance of scripting by measuring the performance of scripts using the analytics designer script performance popup tool and by using the follow scripting best practices among others:
  - Follow basic scripting best practices such as writing efficient loops, using the correct variables, and more.
  - Avoid changing the trigger of an `onResultChanged` event script in such a script.
  - Prefer using certain scripting methods, like using the `getResultSet()` instead of the `getMembers()` method and more.
  - Leverage scripting to improve performance by disabling planning on tables when not in use, reducing duplicate widgets by making use of the `moveWidget()` method, and more.

4.8 Summary

In this chapter, we talked about how the creator of a dashboard can improve the performance of an analytics application using the analytics designer for SAP Analytics Cloud. This includes general rules such as limiting the number of widgets, not overcomplicating things, and keeping in mind lessons learned from Chapter 3. When it comes to optimizing the analytics application structure, make sure to enable the loading of invisible widgets in the background, avoid using the `onInitialization` script, and split up content to distribute loading times and limit what is shown at startup. To adapt to varying screen sizes in an efficient manner, make sure you are leveraging built-in functionalities such as the flow layout panel and avoid resizing unnecessarily. Optimize the performance of scripting by following basic scripting best practices, carefully picking what to avoid, which methods to leverage, and more.

At the beginning of this chapter, we also briefly covered how to avoid poor performance when creating dashboards using the analytics designer by splitting up content into multiple files, leveraging the copy and paste functionality, and testing larger changes before implementing them. We also spent some time looking at how to use the script performance popup tool for the analytics designer for SAP Analytics Cloud in Section 4.6, which allows precise testing of scripting.

In the next few chapters, we will see how to further improve performance as the viewer of a dashboard, as the creator of the model, and when administrating the backend and tenant. Later on, in Chapter 10, we will see a specific use case of how to optimize a dashboard using the analytics designer for SAP Analytics Cloud, leveraging some of the performance improvements covered here.

Chapter 5
Modeler Performance

In this chapter, we'll talk about the choices you can make in the modeler and in your model in general to improve the performance of your SAP Analytics Cloud dashboard. We discuss how to optimize the performance of a planning model and how to properly set the right options for live connections.

This chapter deals with performance optimizations within the SAP Analytics Cloud modeler. We first discuss how general modeling settings can affect the overall performance of a story. Afterwards, we review different model types and how they impact the performance of a dashboard, such as models using acquired data or live connections. We conclude this section with a discussion on how to optimize the performance specifically for planning models.

5.1 General Modeler Settings to Improve Performance

In this section, we will cover general modeler settings that you can adjust in any situation to improve the performance of your SAP Analytics Cloud dashboards. This chapter is independent of the type of model or the type of data source you are using. This also includes the number of data sources, data preparation, unbooked data settings, and exception aggregation settings.

5.1.1 Number of Data Sources

A general rule is that, if you include less data in your model, the performance will be better compared to other identical settings. However, there are further choices to consider. Table 5.1 shows the time difference between one single, large data source versus multiple data sources. The total size of this dataset consists of 15,405 rows and, for this performance test, the single data source consists of all this data. The multiple data sources (three of them) add up to a total sum of 15,405 data rows and are in sum identical to the single data source. All models work with acquired data. The dashboard to conduct this performance test consists simply of a table with the full dataset, so as to keep it as simple as possible and focus only on the number of data sources.

Data Type	Loading Time
Single data source	5.02 sec
Multiple small data sources	6.13 sec

Table 5.1 Time Differences between One Large Data Source versus Multiple Smaller Data Sources

Important Note

For all tests that we perform in this chapter, we used the following computer: MacBook Pro (16-inch, 2019), macOS Ventura 13.3.1, Processor 2,6 GHz 6-Core Intel Core i7, 32 GB RAM.

General Modeling: Data Preparation

When talking about improving the model itself, improving the data preparation plays a major role. Thus, deleting unused dimensions and measures can already lead to an improved performance. Further details for the data preparation, especially for live connections, can be found in Chapter 6.

5.1.2 Show Unbooked Data in a Chart

Even though the **Unbooked Data** setting is done in the SAP Analytics Cloud story and not in the modeler, it interacts with the data structure in the model and the loading time of the data stores in the model. Unbooked data means that there is no data like a corresponding transaction for the belonging data point field. Thus, the unbooked data resides in the model and can't be deleted by the **Delete Facts** option, as unbooked data might be relevant for future planning scenarios.

But as these currently empty fields are not relevant in your dashboard, we can improve the performance without influence on the end user by the following steps. To improve performance, you should always enable the option to **Show Unbooked Data** in your charts. Due to showing the unbooked data, there is no calculation necessary to differentiate between unbooked and booked data in your dataset. To do so, select this option in the builder panel:

1. Open the **Builder Panel**.
2. Click on the **Action menu button** next to the dimension (see Figure 5.1).
3. Click on **Unbooked Data**.

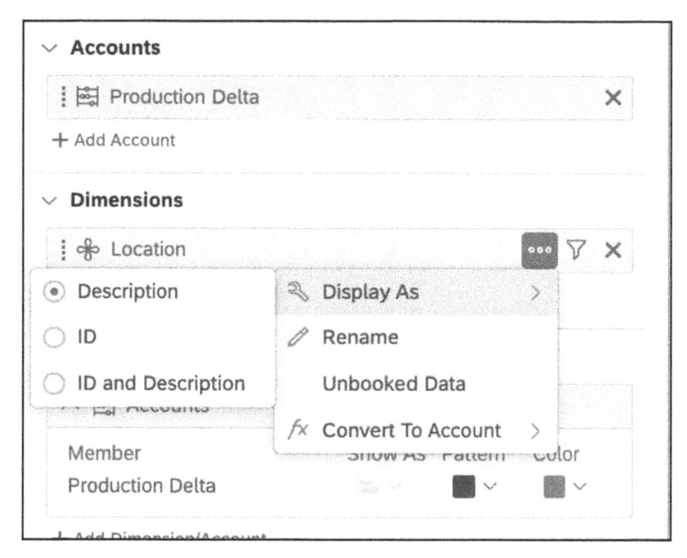

Figure 5.1 Show Unbooked Data in Your Chart to Save Calculation Power

> **Further Reading**
> Further performance best practices about the modeling process can be found at the following URL: *http://s-prs.co/v566949*.

5.1.3 Avoid Specifying Exception Aggregations

In the model, there is an option to specify an **Exception Aggregation Type** (see Figure 5.2). An exception aggregation means that the aggregation type deviates from the default or standard methods. A standard aggregation calculates a sum, whereas an exception aggregation defines different calculations to be performed while aggregating the corresponding measure. Examples of such exceptions are the calculation of an average, a minimum, maximum, a count, and so on. This additional calculation can affect performance for large data models.

To get to this view, follow these steps:

1. Open the relevant model.
2. Select the **Account** option in the left-hand panel.
3. Select the **Measure** that should be specified (**Latitude** in Figure 5.2).
4. Scroll down to **Aggregations** (see Figure 5.2).
5. Select the **Exception Aggregation Type** option.

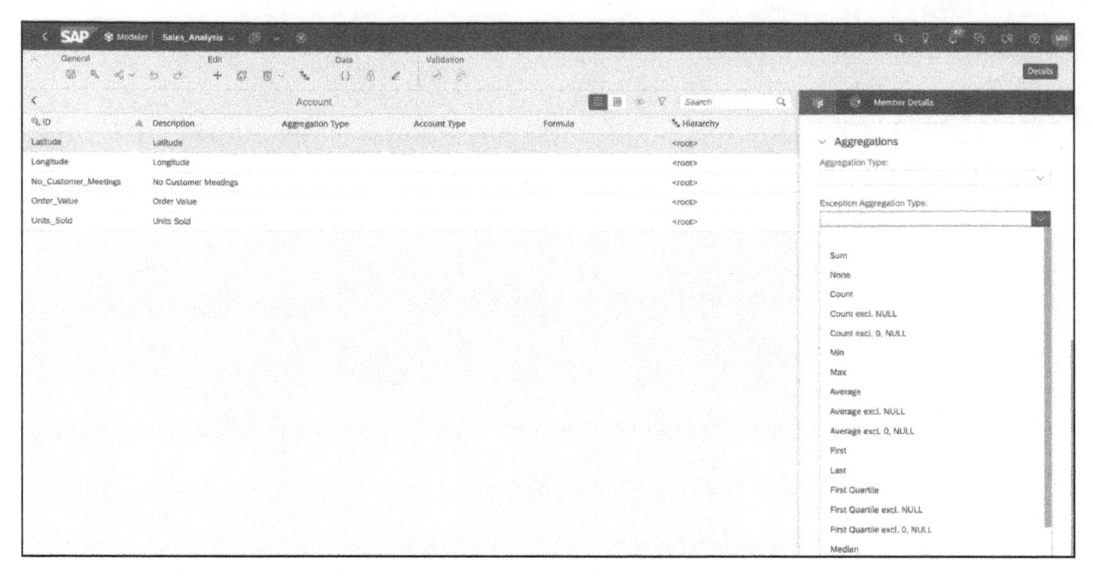

Figure 5.2 Avoid Specifying Exception Aggregations

However, if possible, including any specification there should be avoided. An alternative would be to use restricted measures or calculations in the backend or in the story itself. These can be chosen directly in the story in the builder panel, as shown in Figure 5.3.

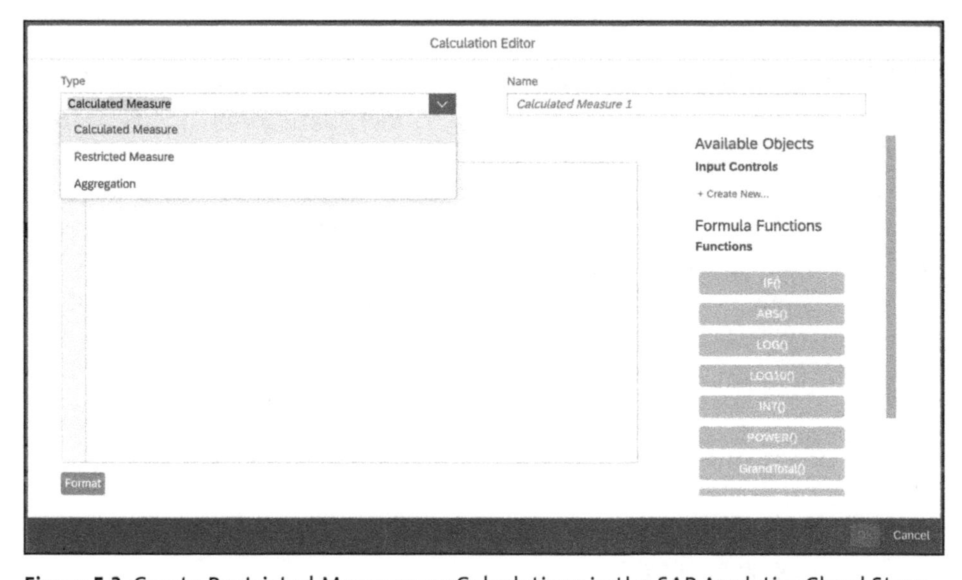

Figure 5.3 Create Restricted Measures or Calculations in the SAP Analytics Cloud Story

To create restricted or calculated measures, follow these steps:

1. Open the **Builder Panel** in the story.
2. Click **Add Measure**.

3. Click **Add Calculation**.
4. Select the **Restricted Measure** or **Calculated Measure** option (see Figure 5.3).

Further Resources

Further details and explanations about restricted measures or calculations can be found at the following URLs:

- Restricted measures: *http://s-prs.co/v566950*
- Calculations: *http://s-prs.co/v566951*

However, using restricted measures in an SAP Analytics Cloud story or in the application designer is slower than using the optimized calculation power of the backend. Thus, if possible, performing these types of calculations in the backend will lead to an even better performance. Further details can be found in Chapter 6.

Note

A new model feature was introduced in 2021. This model update can lead to performance improvements in terms of story opening, refreshing, filter selection, and data action run time, if you have a very large number of accounts and switch to using measures. Further information about the new model can be found online at the following URL: *http://s-prs.co/v566952*.

5.2 Choosing an Efficient Model

Before we take a deep dive into the different models and show how to optimize the performance for each of them, the first step of creating an efficient model is to choose the right model for the use case. A typical trade-off is performance versus functionality and complexity. Which model to use for which use case for optimal performance will be covered in this chapter in detail.

In general, there are two different high-level options in which the model must be chosen. The first one is the data source type, and the second one is the model type. We'll cover each of these model types in the following sections.

5.2.1 The Data Source Type

In terms of data sources, there are two high-level options available. An acquired SAP Analytics Cloud model, also called acquired data model, is a model where the data is imported into SAP Analytics Cloud. Here the data needs to be updated manually or via scheduled import jobs. The second high-level option is a live data connection to another data source like an SAP Business Warehouse (SAP BW) or SAP HANA Cloud system, where the most recent data from the database is used, whenever a story uses this model type.

The general guidance for the best possible performance is to use an acquired SAP Analytics Cloud model instead of a live connection. Table 5.2 shows a comparison between acquired data and an SAP BW data source, and Table 5.3 shows the comparison between acquired data and an SAP HANA Cloud data source. In both tables, we used the same data for both the live connection and the acquired model. The same holds for the dashboard that was created based on this data model (see Figure 5.4 for the SAP BW and Figure 5.5 for the SAP HANA model).

Data Type	Loading Time
Acquired SAP Analytics Cloud model	9.3 sec
Live connection (SAP BW)	13 sec

Table 5.2 Time Differences between Acquired SAP Analytics Cloud Model and SAP BW Live Data Connection

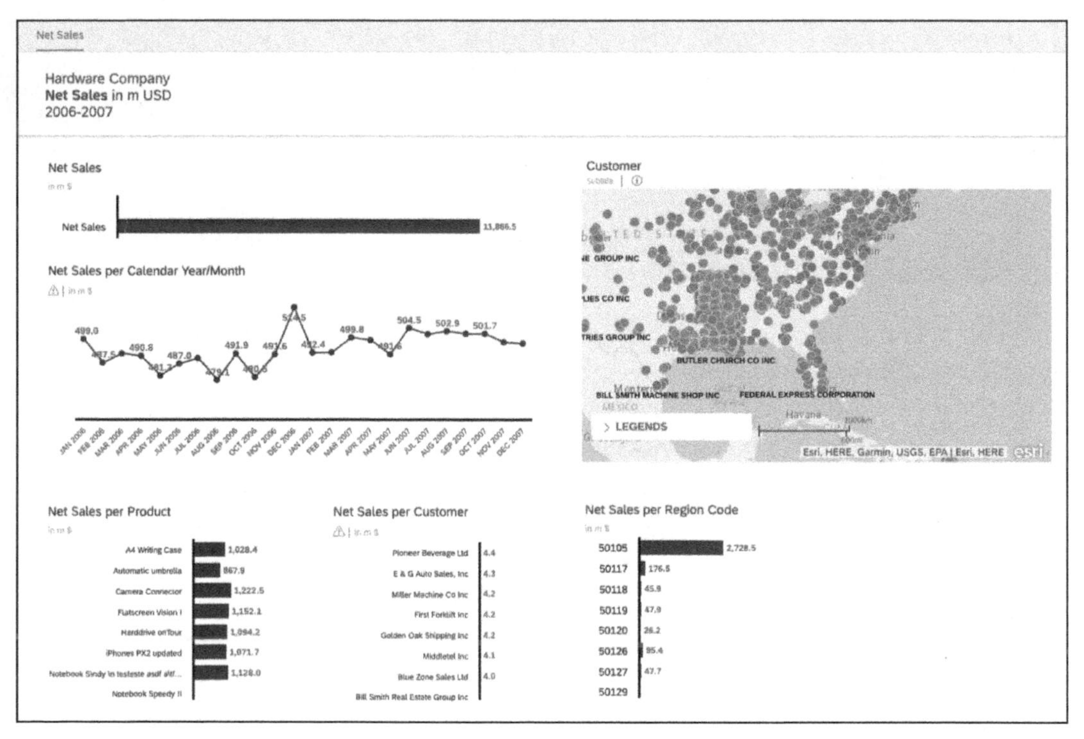

Figure 5.4 Comparing Timings between an Acquired SAP Analytics Cloud Model and an SAP BW Live Data Connection

Data Type	Loading Time
Acquired SAP Analytics Cloud model	6.2 sec
Live connection (SAP HANA Cloud)	8.7 sec

Table 5.3 Time Differences between an Acquired SAP Analytics Cloud Model and an SAP HANA Cloud Live Data Connection

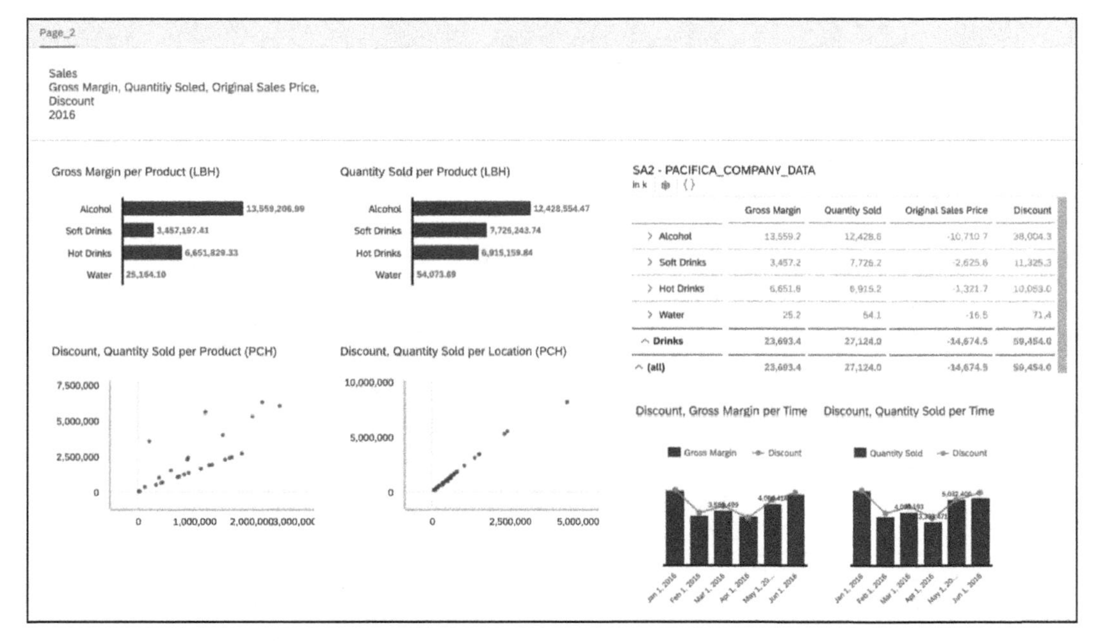

Figure 5.5 Comparing Timings between an Acquired SAP Analytics Cloud Model and an SAP HANA Cloud Live Data Connection

However, there are situations in which the general functionality of a live connection is required. For example, if you are dependent on a frequent data update or don't have the capacity to transfer the data from the database into the SAP Analytics Cloud model regularly, there are further options to improve the performance of this live model, which can be found in Section 5.3. In addition, Chapter 9 shows a practical use case of an optimized dashboard using a live connection.

5.2.2 The Model Type

The second general decision required to choose the right model is the model type. There are two model types available: planning models and analytic models. The general recommendation is to use planning models only when they are necessary, as analytic models are generally faster. This can be seen in Table 5.4, where the same data was used in the analytic model as well as in the planning model. Similarly, as before, the same dashboard was created based on the data model shown Figure 5.6.

Model Type	Loading Time
Analytic model	6.7 sec
Planning model	7.9 sec

Table 5.4 Time Differences between Analytic and Planning Models in SAP Analytics Cloud

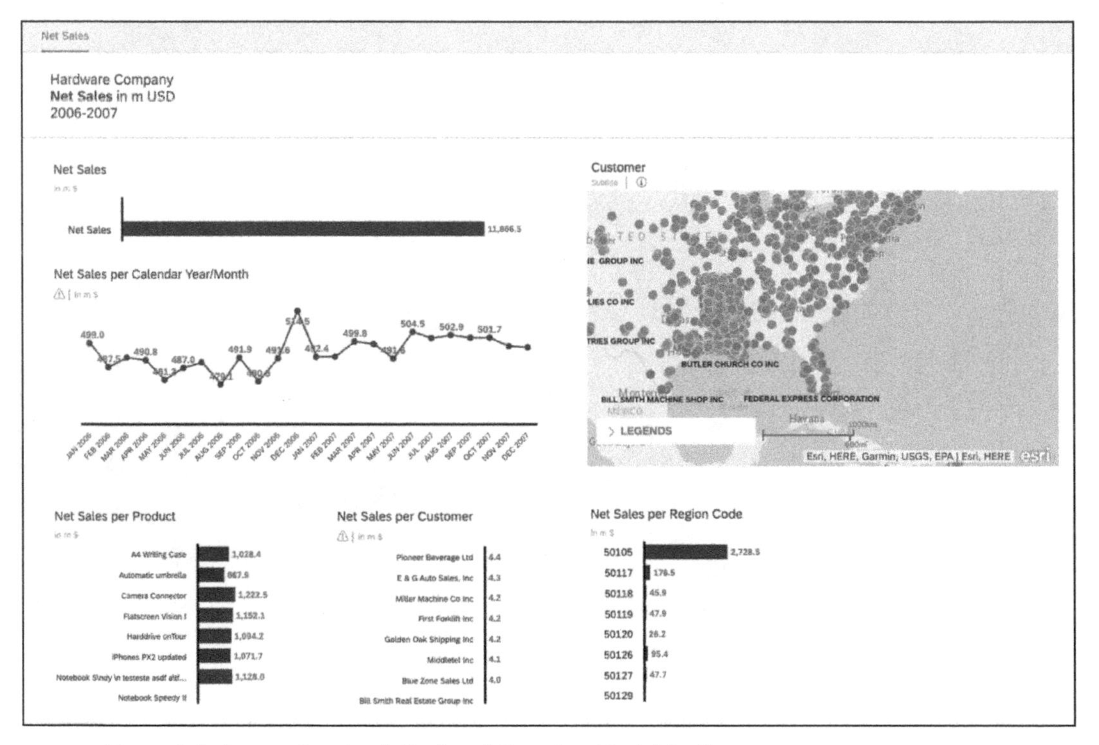

Figure 5.6 Comparing Analytical and Planning Model Performances

As in the data source section, there are some functionalities and requirements that make planning models necessary. This includes, for example, when companies not only want to analyze and report but also to plan and predict in the same application and based on the same data model. In Section 5.4, we explain further steps for optimizing the performance of a planning model.

5.2.3 Datasphere Model

Data modeling is still facing challenges in SAP Analytics Cloud. One of them is the elegant combination of multiple data sources, which can be challenging by itself. But additionally, it often leads to a bad performance of the SAP Analytics Cloud dashboard if one of the data sources contains a lot of data. One possible solution to these issues can be the SAP Datasphere, where all these data preparation and data wrangling steps are performed and one single, final view is then fed into the dashboard.

> **Further Resources**
>
> Further details and explanations about the connection between SAP Analytics Cloud and SAP Datasphere can be found at the following URL: *http://s-prs.co/v566953*.

5.3 Performance of Acquired Models and Live Connection Models

Follow these tips to optimize acquired and live connection models in SAP Analytics Cloud:

- **Acquired models**
  Section 5.1 covered the general recommendations that apply to all different types of data models. Furthermore, the necessary data preparation and backend settings will be covered in Chapter 6. This includes guidance like reducing the amount of data as early as possible and how to achieve this. For the acquired SAP Analytics Cloud model, no acquired data and analytical model specific performance improvements are required other than what is covered in the previous chapters.
- **Live connection models**
  The settings for live connection models are strongly tied together with the settings in the database used for the live connection. The database optimizations will be covered in Chapter 6. However, here are some examples of what will be explained in more detail in Chapter 6:
  - For SAP BW live connections:
    - Hide unused measures and dimensions.
    - Enable query batching and query merge.
    - Switch on the option for two-structure queries.
  - For SAP HANA live connections:
    - Hide unused measures and dimensions.
    - Enable query batching.
    - Don't blend with Excel files but in the main story model.

5.4 Optimizing Performance for Planning Models

In general, avoiding planning models if they're not necessary is recommended. However, if you need the planning capabilities, we will cover planning model optimization in this chapter. As in all SAP Analytics Cloud models, we aim to perform data preparation and reduction as early as possible and as close to the data sources as possible in the backend rather than in the model or even in the story.

5.4.1 Delete Private Versions

The planning functionalities in SAP Analytics Cloud allow version management of your company data. This includes the organization, comparison, and maintenance of different versions of this data. In the planning process, you sometimes want to keep your old version while already actively working on the new data version, which is possible with the version management options in SAP Analytics Cloud. Additionally, you can start working on a private version before you publish your final version as a public version or share it with another person.

However, collecting and using too many private versions might kill the performance of the planning model. Thus, use only public versions, if possible, and limit the number of private versions. They should be deleted or reverted into public versions, if possible. If you are an administrator or a user who has permission to delete versions for the model, you can delete all private versions, even from other users. This can be done in the model preferences (see Figure 5.7).

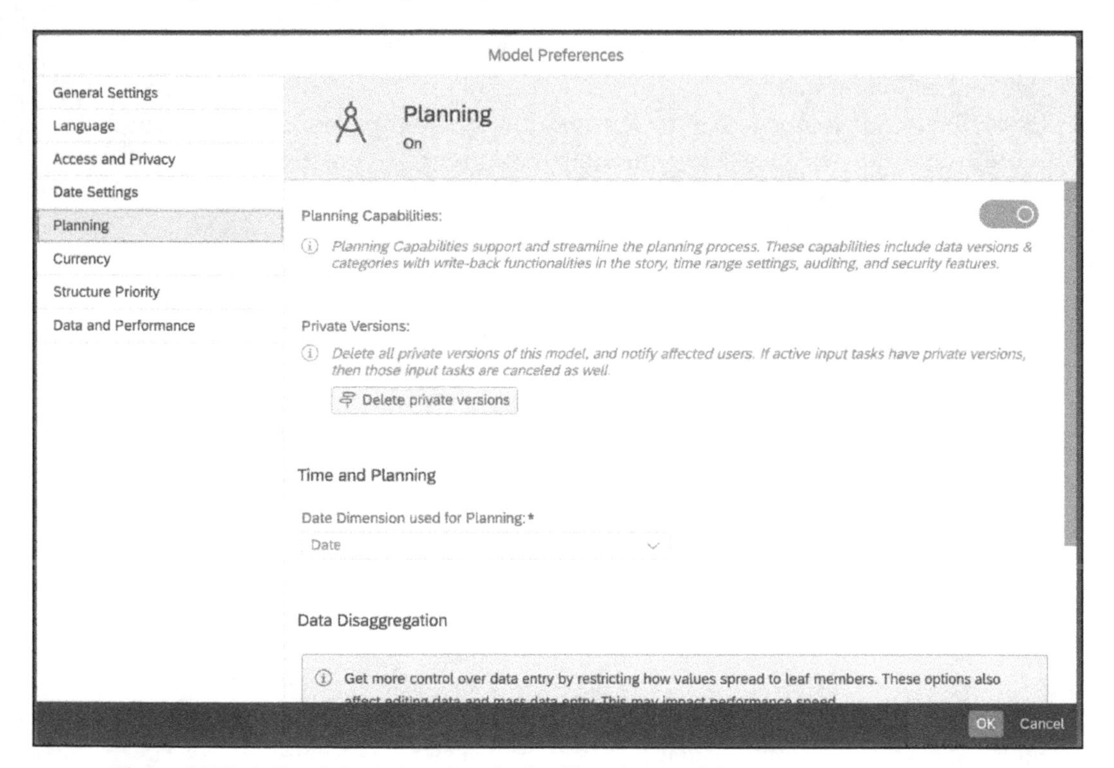

Figure 5.7 Deleting Private Versions in the Planning Model

Furthermore, it is recommended for optimal performance to limit the public version data used in the model.

To delete private versions, follow these steps:

1. Open the relevant model.
2. Open the model preferences via the wrench symbol .
3. Click on the **Planning** section in the left navigation panel (see Figure 5.7).
4. Click **Delete private versions.**
5. Complete the deletion via clicking **OK**.

Note

Only users with delete permission for the model have access to the button and will be able to delete private versions from a model.

5.4.2 Limit Public Version Data in Edit Mode

If your model enabled planning functionalities, everyone with the required permissions can edit the data of your model. To edit a public version, simply click into a cell and edit the corresponding value. After this, a temporary private version is created that only the editor can see until they publish those changes to the public version. This change can be seen when you look at the upper part of the table header where next to the name of the public version a small star shows up, as indicated in Figure 5.8 (next to the **Actual** string).

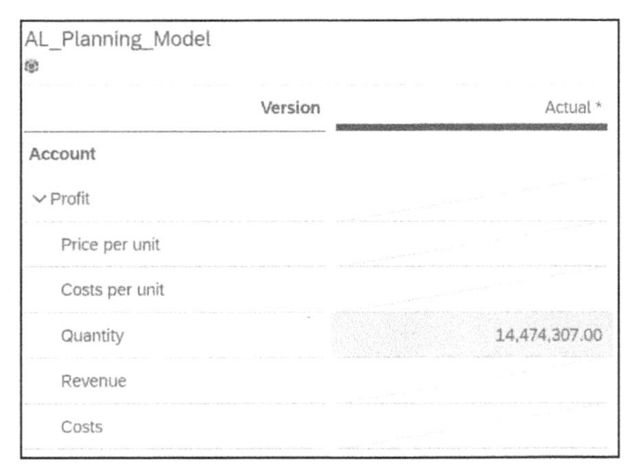

AL_Planning_Model
Version
Actual *
Account
Profit
Price per unit
Costs per unit
Quantity
14,474,307.00
Revenue
Costs

Figure 5.8 The Public Version Edit Created a Private Version in the Background

To increase the performance of your dashboard, avoid putting all data of a public version into edit mode, and limit it to the data required for the corresponding use case.

You can also specify in the modeler that only the recommended planning area can be put into edit mode.

5.4.3 Filtering during the Modeling Process

In the modeling process for planning models, there are multiple recommendations for filtering if you want to optimize the performance of your dashboard and in your planning process:

- Before copying data to a private version, filter it as much as possible.
- Before running data action, multi action, or an allocation, filter your data again as much as possible to perform the action on a minimalistic data slice.
- Before running allocations, filter by reference dimension.

5.4.4 Data Entry

One special capability of a planning model is the possibility to insert data directly within your story into the model. During this data entry process, you can add data to one single data point (see Figure 5.9) or to multiple data points at the same time. For an improved performance, avoid pasting too much data at the same time to multiple different measures and dimensions in your table.

Planning_Map

		Actual * (all)	2022	Q1 (2022)	Jan (2022)	Feb (2022)	Mar (2022)	Q2 (2022)	Q3 (2022)	Q4 (2022)
	India	2,044.94	1,022.47	255.62	85.21	85.21	85.21	255.62	255.62	255.62
	China	25,561.80	10,844.76	2,691.44	775.91	793.92	1,121.61	2,751.37	2,729.55	2,672.39
	USA	8,179.78	4,089.89	1,022.47	340.82	340.82	340.82	1,022.47	1,022.47	1,022.47
	Italy	3,333.26	1,666.63	416.66	138.89	138.89	138.89	416.66	416.66	416.66
	France	2,290.34	1,145.17	286.29	95.43	95.43	95.43	286.29	286.29	286.29
Production Delta	Germany	4,089.89	2,044.94	511.24	170.41	170.41	170.41	511.24	511.24	511.24

Figure 5.9 Data Entry for One Data Point

5.5 Best Practices

A general best practice tip is the minimal principle. Always select and choose the minimal scope that is required, and don't add further data and functionalities "just in case" if performance is your priority. Furthermore, choosing a native model within SAP Analytics Cloud will most likely be more efficient than any live connection model that uses an SAP BW or SAP HANA live connection. For further guidance on how to optimize your backend, we refer the reader to the corresponding literature.

Summarizing the chapter, this leads to the following best practice tips:

- **Choose the right model**
  - Prefer analytic models over planning models if the planning capabilities are not required
- **Choose the right data source**
  - Prefer an acquired data model over a live data connection if the live data connection capabilities are not required. Furthermore, only load the data you require in your model
  - Prefer a single data source instead of multiple smaller data sources
  - Consider modeling in SAP Datasphere if you need to combine multiple data sources
- **Reduce the amount of data**
  - Delete unnecessary private versions
  - Limit the amount of data that is in edit mode in a planning model
  - Filter during modeling as early as possible
- **General settings**
  - Choose general settings like **Optimized Story Building Performance**
  - Prefer to show unbooked data in your charts to reduce calculations to differentiate between unbooked and booked data
  - Avoid specifying exception aggregations
  - Avoid pasting too much data simultaneously to multiple different measure and dimensions in your table

5.6 Summary

In this chapter, we covered how to optimize the performance of SAP Analytics Cloud dashboards during the modeling process. First, general modeling settings were discussed, which is strongly tied to the data itself. In general, less data leads to better performance. However, there are further principles like showing unbooked data and avoiding specific aggregations that lead to an improved performance.

Afterwards, the different model types were discussed. This led to the general recommendation to use analytic and acquired models wherever possible. As this isn't always feasible, performance improvements of planning models were discussed lastly. The next chapter will give more insights into optimizing live data connections.

Chapter 6

Optimizing Backend and Tenant Settings

In this chapter, we'll talk about the choices that can be made in the backend and in the tenant settings to improve performance. These optimizations are typically but not exclusively performed by the administrator.

In this chapter, we discuss performance optimization in both backend and tenant settings. This includes data connection specific settings for SAP Business Warehouse (SAP BW) live connections and SAP HANA live connections. Furthermore, we will discuss data preparation steps like filter settings, calculations, and data blending, which happen before data is fed into the SAP Analytics Cloud model. Finally, the system configuration settings cover different settings as a tenant administrator. Typically, these changes are made by the administrator or similar roles.

6.1 Optimizing Backend Data Storage Connection

You may want to have a live connection to your data. This means that, when a user opens a story in SAP Analytics Cloud, the data is retrieved from the backend and any changes in the data in the backend data storage will be seen immediately.

Whenever new data is needed in the story, the story will request data from the model, and the model will request data from the backend. Once the model receives the data, it will need to perform any calculations in the model. These extra steps can increase the time required to update the story. There are several things you can do to minimize the performance impact.

We will focus on live data connections to SAP HANA and live data connections to SAP BW. Similar principles, however, apply also to other scenarios.

In general, for the best performance, you need to reduce the amount of data that is transferred from the backend to SAP Analytics Cloud and to leverage the power of the backend by doing as much data processing as possible in the backend. If you cannot reduce enough of the data in the data transfer, then you can delete or hide dimensions in the SAP Analytics Cloud model.

6.1.1 Reduce Data as Early as Possible

The more data that is transferred from the backend to the model and then to the front-end widgets, the more time it will require. There are several points where you can filter data. Data can be filtered in the frontend using widget filters, page filters, and story filters. Data can be filtered in the SAP Analytics Model by setting filters on the columns. Data can be filtered or processed in the backend. The earlier you can filter the data the better the performance will be.

You should consider what data will be required in the dashboard. When data is not required at all, you should filter it out in the backend. For this, consider both the data columns and rows. For instance, create a view that will provide only the required columns and rows. This may mean filtering out columns or rows and aggregating column and row data. For example, consider a table that tracks customer satisfaction gathered from a kiosk as customers leave an event facility and another table that tracks customer satisfaction from an email sent after the event.

If your dashboard just needs to track weekly satisfaction for a specific facility, then you could filter out all data that you don't need. In general, try to limit the granularity of the time dimension only to the necessary level.

Table 6.1 shows a simplified table of satisfaction scores that is gathered from multiple kiosks at multiple locations for multiple events. This table would contain many thousands of rows.

Response Date	Event Date	Facility	Kiosk ID	Satisfaction Score
2023-07-17	2023-07-17	WAT	21	4
2023-07-17	2023-07-17	WAT	21	5
2023-07-17	2023-07-17	CAM	13	3
2023-07-10	2023-07-10	WAT	18	2
2023-07-10	2023-07-10	KIT	17	3

Table 6.1 Table Data for Satisfaction Scores Gathered from Kiosks at the Event Location

Table 6.2 shows a simplified table of satisfaction scores that is gathered from email feedback request following multiple events at multiple locations. This table would contain many thousands of rows.

Response Date	Event Data	Facility	Campaign ID	Satisfaction Score
2023-07-18	2023-07-17	WAT	15498	5
2023-07-18	2023-07-17	WAT	15498	3
2023-07-10	2023-07-10	KIT	15467	1

Table 6.2 Table Data for Satisfaction Scores Gathered from Email Sent after the Event

Response Date	Event Data	Facility	Campaign ID	Satisfaction Score
2023-07-16	2023-07-10	WAT	15462	4
2023-07-12	2023-07-10	WAT	15462	5

Table 6.2 Table Data for Satisfaction Scores Gathered from Email Sent after the Event (Cont.)

There are different ways to reduce data when filtering and aggregating, such as the following:

- The table view could filter out rows by selecting only for WAT facilities.
- The table view could filter out columns by not including kiosk IDs or email campaign IDs.
- The table view could aggregate by row by averaging the satisfaction scores weekly—that is, only provide one row per week.
- The table view could aggregate by column by including the satisfaction responses from both the kiosk and email before averaging the weekly satisfaction scores.

Note

By aggregating rows, you'll naturally filter out columns that have smaller granularity than weeks, for instance, if there were multiple kiosks per week.

The resulting view would have much less data, particularly when there were many individual responses per week and many facilities.

Table 6.3 shows how, by aggregating and filtering the data, there will be much less data that needs to be sent to SAP Analytics Cloud. In this case, it sends just one record with few columns per event at the single location.

Event Date	Satisfaction Score
2023-07-17	4.25
2023-07-10	3.67

Table 6.3 Aggregated and Filtered Data for the WAT Facility

6.1.2 Delete Dimensions in the Model

If you are unable to create a view without the minimal amount of data, you can delete dimensions in the model that you don't need in the story.

To delete dimensions, follow these steps:

1. Open the live data model (see Figure 6.1).
2. Select the **Model Structure Workspace**.

3. Select the dimension to delete.
4. Click the delete icon.
5. Repeat this step for each dimension to delete.

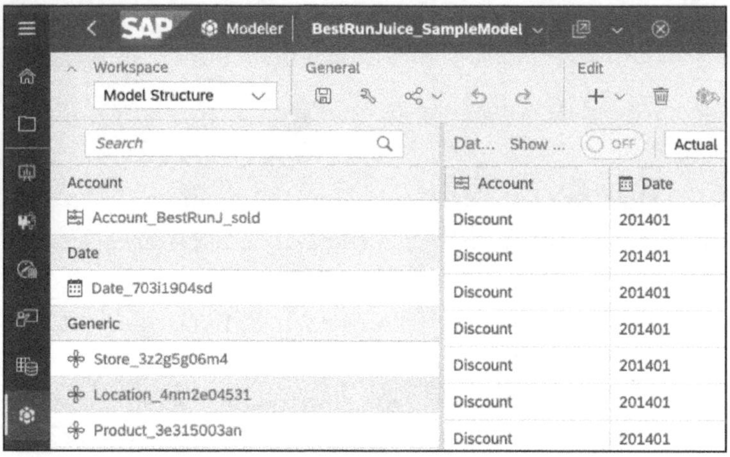

Figure 6.1 Delete Unnecessary Dimensions in the Model

If you delete a dimension that has already been used in calculations and story elements, you need to fix the elements that refer to it. This includes account formulas, variables, currency conversion, data locking, validation rules, value driver trees, data actions, charts, input controls, story filters, hyperlinks, tables, and cross calculations. SAP Analytics Cloud will let you know about any issues that need to be fixed. The dimension will automatically be removed from the data audit table, and comments on that dimension will also be removed. Any import job with a mapping based on the dimensions will no longer be valid. Make sure to redesign the import job manually.

6.1.3 Hide Dimensions in the Model Design

Live data models can have many dimensions. It can be challenging to find the desired dimension when configuring the widgets. This isn't necessarily a loading performance problem, but a usability problem that will affect your ability to efficiently build the story. You can hide unneeded dimensions in the model. The hidden dimensions in the model will not be retrieved as part of the metadata load while opening a story, and they will not be displayed in the list of dimensions to select from when modifying a widget.

To hide dimensions, follow these steps:

1. Open the live data model.
2. Select the **All Dimensions** tab. All dimensions in the model are shown in the list. (See Figure 6.2).
3. Select the **Hide** check boxes for the dimensions that aren't relevant.

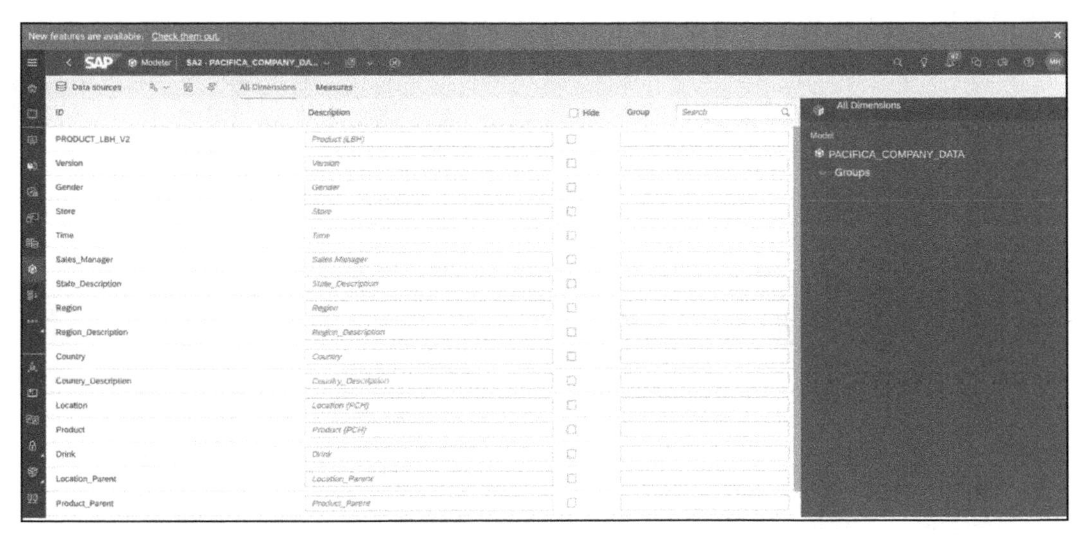

Figure 6.2 View of an SAP Analytics Cloud Model Based on SAP HANA Live Data

Note

Hiding dimensions isn't available for SAP BW live data models.

6.1.4 Do Calculations After Aggregation

The more calculations and the more complex the calculations that need to be executed, the more time it will require. As mentioned earlier, you want to retrieve as little data as required. Similarly, you want to do as few calculations as possible.

Consider the example in the previous section about customer satisfaction scores. Let's say that there were 10,000 records to consider over four weeks. The satisfaction scores were collected as values from 1 to 5, but you wanted to convert it to a scale of 0 to 100. If you did the conversion calculation first, then you would do 10,000 calculations (one for each row) then aggregate to four weekly records. If you did the aggregation first, you need to do the conversion calculations only on the four aggregated weekly records. You can see how this could improve performance, particularly if your aggregations eliminate many rows or if the calculations are complex and time-consuming.

6.1.5 Perform Calculations in the Backend

The backend database is faster than SAP Analytics Cloud and its modeling components. Therefore, wherever possible, use the power of the backend to do calculations. The more calculations and the more complex calculations that can be done faster in the backend will improve performance.

This includes restricted key figures and calculated key figures in live models, which should be created in the SAP BW modeling tools, not in SAP Analytics Cloud.

6.1.6 Write Scripts in a Way that Avoids Extra Calls Against the Backend

There are scripting functions in SAP Analytics Designer that were mentioned in Chapter 4 that are worth emphasizing here again.

If you need to set several variable values of the backend data, you can improve performance by writing the `setVariableValue()` commands in sequence without any other script API methods in between. This sequence is converted internally into a single backend call instead of submitting multiple ones.

Also, filtering does not require a roundtrip to the backend. Therefore, use `setDimensionFilter()` instead of `setVariableValue()` when filtering against data from a live connection to avoid the roundtrip to the backend server.

6.2 Optimizations in the Backend Data

When using live connections, such as to SAP HANA or SAP BW backend servers, you should consider what you can do to optimize the backend data sources themselves. In general, you should follow best practices for creating efficient data access, such as creating JOINS on key or indexed columns, not on calculated columns, although we will not discuss the details in this book. However, there are a few settings and considerations that we would like to point out:

- **Deactivate the 0CALDAY hierarchy in SAP BW**
  Both SAP BW and SAP Analytics Cloud can handle time hierarchies. The SAP BW 0CALDAY hierarchy can lead to slower load times because, initially, all the 0CAL hierarchies are set up, for instance, 0CALYEAR, 0CALWEEK, etc. If you need time and range for the 0CAL dimensions, performance will improve if you deactivate the 0CALDay hierarchy in SAP BW and use the time dimensions within the SAP Analytic Cloud model.
- **Set a memory limit for SAP BW queries**
  If there is high data volume in SAP BW queries, this can result in memory issues, and memory issues lead to performance issues. To improve performance, you can reduce the data volume of an SAP BW query by setting a maximum value for the online analytical processing (OLAP) effort in the SAP BW server.

  For more information, see SAP Note 2572550.
- **Enable HTTP/2 on SAP BW**
  HTTP/2 is an internet protocol that has faster web page loading. If you find that your queries are slow, longer than three seconds, then you can take advantage of the

HTTP/2 protocol for your dashboards with SAP BW live connections by activating HTTP/2 in the SAP BW backend server.

You need to enable two parameters in SAP BW to enable it for use with SAP Analytics Cloud:

- **Set parameter `icm/HTTP/support_http2 = TRUE`**
  This activates HTTP/2 on the SAP BW server.
- **Set parameter `wdisp/support_http2_to_backend = TRUE`**
  This activates HTTP/2 as a communication protocol between the SAP BW backend system and the frontend system, in this case SAP Analytics Cloud.

To ensure that the SAP BW server can process these requests in parallel and won't become a bottleneck, increase the setting in SAP Analytics Cloud that specifies the number of parallel sessions that can be sent to the SAP BW data source (Section 6.3.4). By increasing the number of parallel sessions allowed, you should ensure that the SAP BW server is configured to handle this load. It might be necessary to increase `icm/max_conn`, discussed in the next section.

Note

The internet protocol HTTP/2 was introduced by Google in 2015 and achieves faster web page loading by compressing HTTP headers, prioritizing requests, and multiplexing multiple requests over a single TCP connection. When using a single persistent TCP connection, there is less overhead overall since the memory and processing effort to create the connections is reduced by reducing the number of required connections.

- **Increase `icm/max_conn`**
  When the SAP BW servers are under load, if the number of simultaneous open connections allowed is too low, then the number of connections and requests that can be executed are limited. You may consider increasing the maximum number of open connections allowed in the Internet Communication Manager or in the SAP web dispatcher.

  Set parameter `icm/max_conn =` your desired value. The default value is 500.

  You should consider increasing the `icm/max_conn` setting, if you have increased the number of parallel sessions for SAP BW data sources in SAP Analytics Cloud (Section 6.3.4). You can consider increasing the `icm/max_conn` value to the maximum allowable value, as specified in the SAP Notes.

  For more information, see SAP Note 2007212.

- **Use Execute in: SQL Engine option**
  There are many optimizations that SAP HANA can perform against a graphical calculation view. This will provide the best patterns regarding performance, as well as the least maintenance efforts going forward. To explicitly enable these optimizations,

use the advanced view property **Execute In: SQL Engine**. For more information, see SAP Note 2223597.

- **Bring .xls data into the main story model, rather than blending**
  There may be cases where you have an SAP HANA live data model, and you want to augment it with other data. If you blend the live data model with an imported xls file, then create a chart with a filter on a specific dimension, the chart could take a long time to load. In this case, if possible, convert all data into an .xls file and load it into your main story model to avoid blending for better performance.
- **Set read mode in SAP HANA**
  In SAP HANA, the read mode determines how the OLAP processor acquires data during navigation. If read mode **Only Values in InfoProvider** (read mode D) has a long runtime, you can usually achieve a significant runtime gain by using **Values in Master Data Table** (read mode M). For more information, see SAP Note 2245483.

6.3 System Configuration Settings to Improve Performance

There are a few system configuration settings where you can get some quick wins in terms of performance. With these settings enabled, SAP Analytics Cloud will prevent ill-timed refreshes, batch queries together to reduce round-trip requests to the backend, increase the number of SAP BW queries that can be executed in parallel, and reduce the amount of metadata from SAP BW loading in your widget.

6.3.1 Optimize Story Building Performance

When building your story, the charts and tables will retrieve the data from the model and from the live data source. Every time you modify the chart or table, it must get the data and re-render the chart, even if it's only a minor change. To prevent this data from refreshing while you're building your dashboard, turn on optimize story build performance. This is described further in Chapter 3, Section 3.1.3.

Note

To take advantage of optimized view mode for SAP BW live connection, you may need to update the SAP BW InA interface.

6.3.2 Progressive Chart Rendering

When navigating between pages of your story, the charts must be refreshed and rendered every time you open a page, even if you recently viewed the page. By turning on progressive chart rendering, SAP Analytics Cloud will be able to display the charts more quickly if they have been visited recently.

When this feature is enabled, a version of the chart is cached for an hour. When the user visits the page again within that hour, the cached version of the chart is displayed. In the meantime, in the background, the story will retrieve the data and refresh the chart if necessary. This can be particularly helpful if you plan to review your dashboard in a meeting where these types of ill-timed refreshes can slow your meeting down. The cache is retained for only one hour. You'll need to refresh the chart if you'd like to re-cache the data for another hour. For instance, you may want to explicitly refresh immediately before your meeting starts.

When you interact with a cached chart, the data will be retrieved, and the chart will be refreshed, and you may see the loading icon during this refresh. All other charts on the page will remain cached if they are not modified.

Chart caching is available only for consumers and for chart widgets. There is no chart caching when editing a story. Geo visualizations, tables, input controls, and so on will refresh as usual. Chart caching works for data from any source, whether acquired (imported) or remote.

In some cases, a cached version is rendered first, then the chart is re-rendered based on other conditions. For instance, if there are multiple charts that are scaled similarly, the unscaled (cached) versions will be displayed first. After all the scaled charts are fully loaded, then they will be updated to the scaled version. This does not require a refresh, so it should not be disruptive. Another case is when a calculation input control is used. Initially a non-calculation input control (cached) version will be displayed, then the calculations and formulas are processed, which will trigger a re-render. Similarly, charts with forecasts will initially display a non-forecasted (cached) version, and then the forecast will be performed and will trigger a re-render.

To enable progressive chart rendering, follow these steps:

1. Go to the **Info** icon • **Administration** • **System Configuration** tab (see Figure 6.3).
2. Select the edit icon .
3. Set the **Enable Progressive Chart Rendering** switch to **ON**. It may help to find the setting by searching for "prog." By default, this is set to **OFF**.

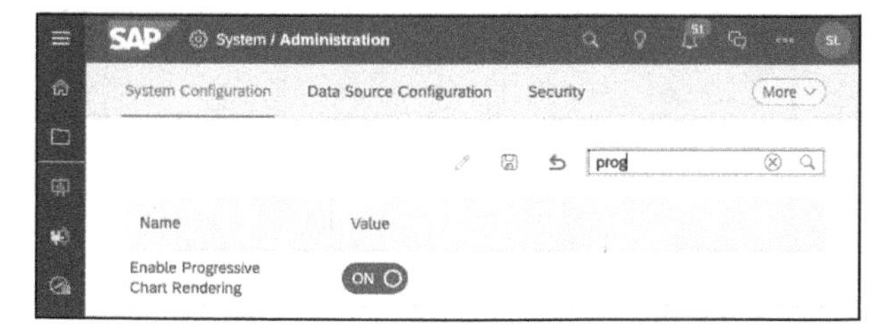

Figure 6.3 Enable Chart Caching in View Mode

4. Save the changes by clicking the save icon .

6.3.3 Query Batching

You may have multiple charts that require the same data. By enabling query batching, SAP Analytics Cloud will send the queries to the backend together. This will improve performance by requiring fewer round trips to the backend.

The following chart types support the query batching option:

- (Stacked) bar/column
- Combination (stacked) column and line
- Stacked area
- Line
- Bullet
- Numeric point

Note

Query batching is available in Google Chrome only in non-incognito mode.

In the following sections, we'll walk through enabling query batching for different scenarios.

Enabling Query Batching/Merging in an SAP Analytics Cloud Story

To enable query batching/merging in an SAP Analytics Cloud story, follow these steps:

1. Enter edit mode for your story by clicking the **Edit** button.
2. Select **More ... • Edit Story • Query Settings.**
3. For an SAP HANA live connection, turn on the **Enable Query Batching** switch (see Figure 6.4).

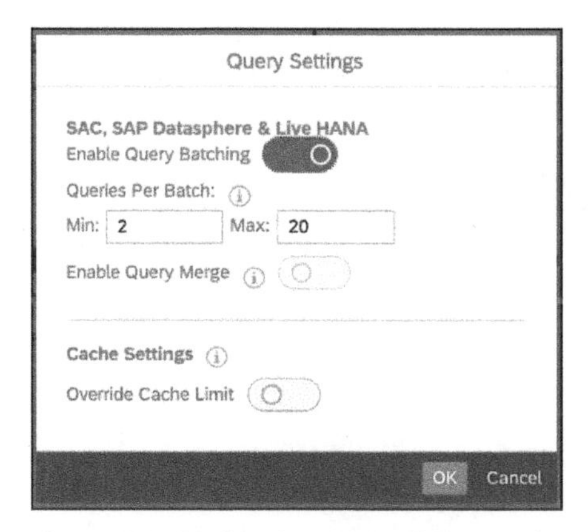

Figure 6.4 Enable Query Batching on the Story for the SAP HANA Live Backend

You can specify the number of queries to include in the batch. If there are fewer batch-able queries than the specified minimum, then the queries will be fired independently. If there are more queries than the specified maximum, then the queries will be split into the fewest number of batches.

4. For an SAP BW connection when using **Design Time & Class View Mode**, turn on the **Enable Query Merge** switch (see Figure 6.5).

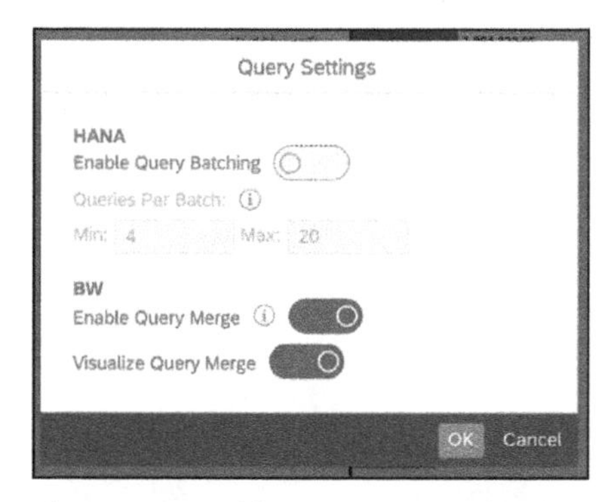

Figure 6.5 Enable Query Merge for the SAP BW Live Backend

> **Note**
>
> Once you change your story from **Classic Design Experience** to **Optimized Design Experience**, you can't switch it back again, and some features might not be available anymore. One example is the **Visualize Query Merge** for the time this book was written.

We recommend also turning on **Visualize Query Merge** so that you can see which charts have their queries merged during story edit mode. This will be illustrated later in this section.

Enable Query Batching in an Analytics Application

To enable query batching in an analytics application, follow these steps:

1. Enter edit mode for your analytic application by clicking the **Edit Analytic Application** button.
2. Select **Edit Analytic Application** (wrench) • **Query Settings**.
3. For an SAP HANA connection, turn on the **Enable Query Batching** switch (see Figure 6.6). Like the **Query Settings** for a story, you can set the minimum and maximum number of queries per batch.
4. For an SAP BW connection, turn on the **Enable Query Merge** switch (see Figure 6.7). Note that **Visualize Query Merge** is not an option.

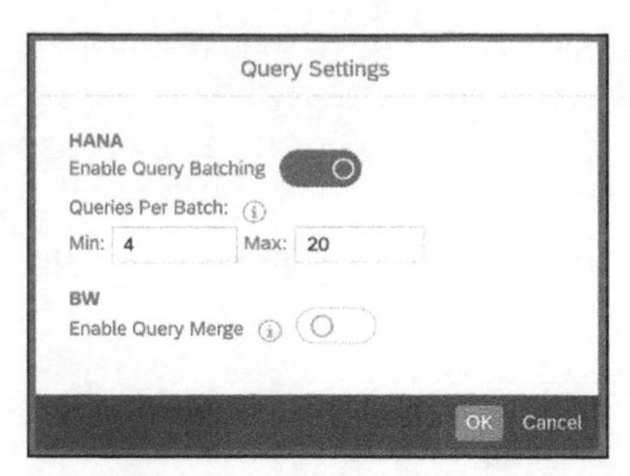

Figure 6.6 Enable Query Batching on the SAP Analytics Designer App for the SAP HANA Live Backend

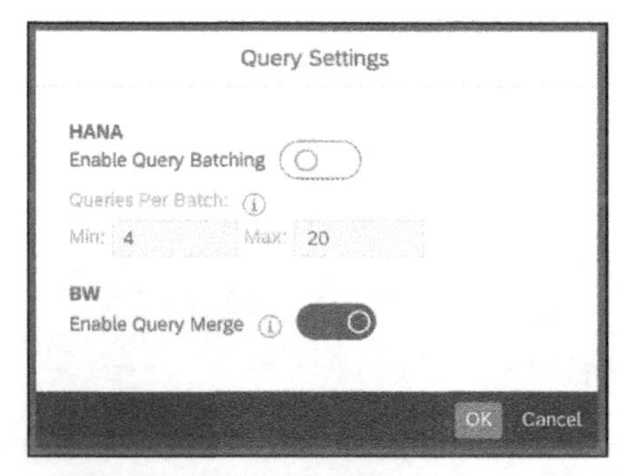

Figure 6.7 Enable Query Merge on the SAP Analytics Designer App for the SAP BW Live Backend

The charts within a story need to have the same query and the same variables to combine the queries. However, there are some prerequisites for merging queries, such as that the queries must contain the same dimensions with the same hierarchies and drill levels.

Scenario: Queries Contain the Same Dimensions with the Same Hierarchies and Drill Levels

Consider six charts using the same dimensions with different measures. Figure 6.8 shows all the charts merged as a single request in the same color as the same merged group ID.

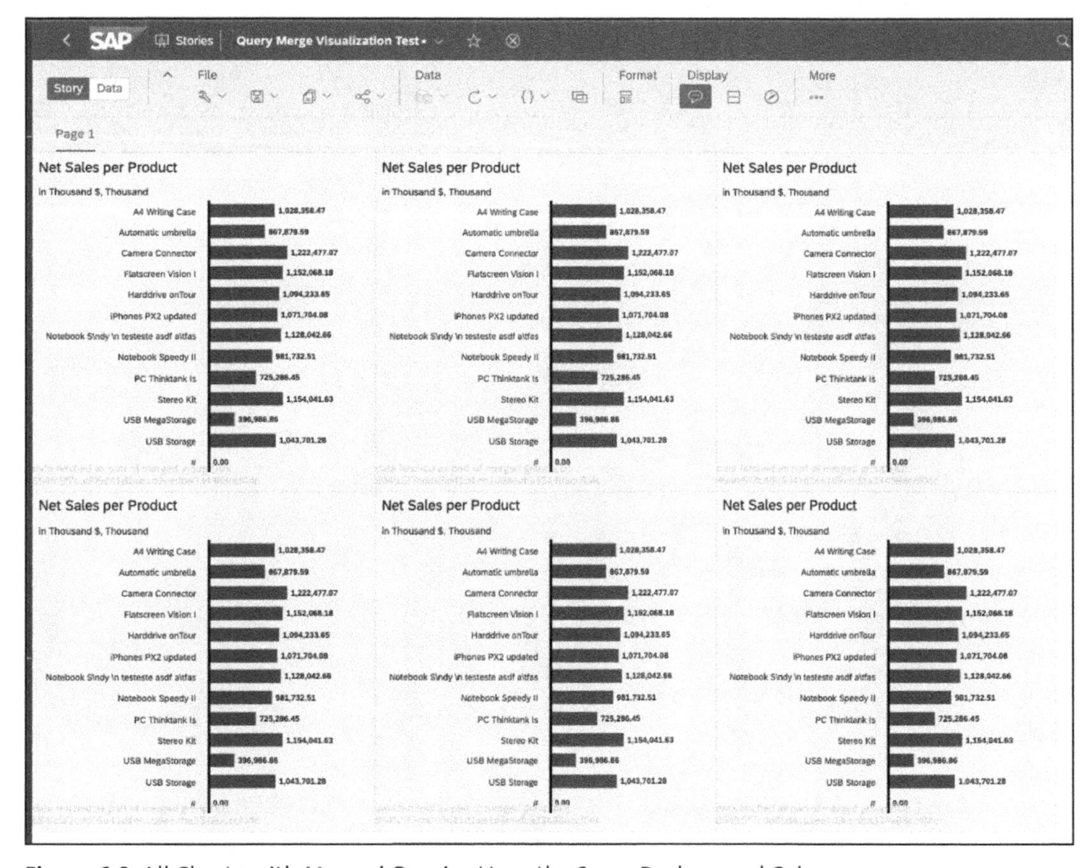

Figure 6.8 All Charts with Merged Queries Have the Same Background Color

Scenario: Queries Are Part of the Same Receiver Group If They Use Linked Analysis

Consider a story with a page filter based on dimension and six charts. The charts that are linked to the filter will have their queries merged. The charts that are not linked will have separate queries.

You can control which widgets are linked to the filter using these steps:

1. In the story, select the page filter.
2. Click on **Linked Analysis** in the action button of the page filter.
3. Select the **Only Selected Widgets** radio button option.
4. Select the checkboxes of the widgets that you want to be controlled by the filter (see Figure 6.9).

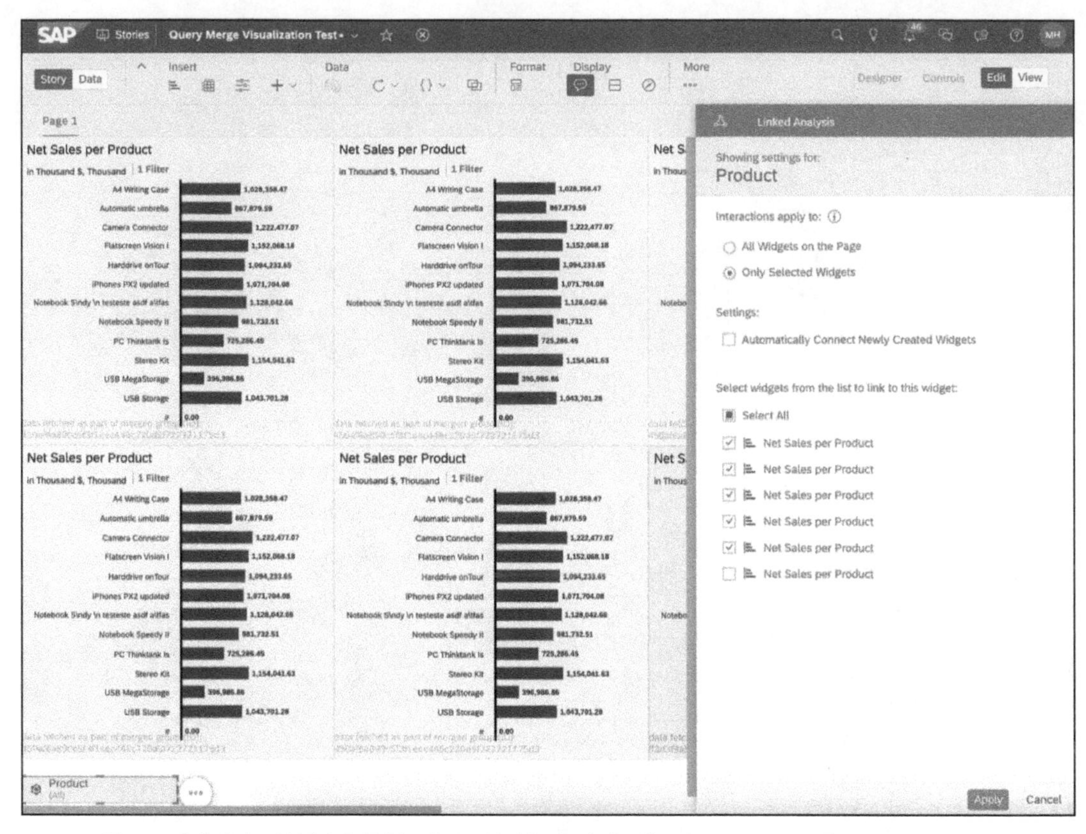

Figure 6.9 Select Which Widgets to Not Include in the Query Merge Group

The charts that are linked to the filter are part of a single query group, whereas the other charts not linked to the filter will be considered a different group, as shown in Figure 6.10.

There are additional scenarios in which the queries will be merged:

- Queries use the same sorting and ranking and don't have any filters.
- The story does not have filters defined inside the threshold panel.
- The widget does not have a local filter on a dimension that is also used in a restriction in SAP BW.
- The widget does not have a local filter on a member of the secondary structure of a query.
- The widget filter is not defined as a complex tuple or range filter.
- The presentation types are the same.

- Dimension is not selected in a chart in combination with a hierarchical widget filter or hierarchical drilldown filter on the same dimension.
- Zero suppression for the query is not active when any dimension is selected in the chart.

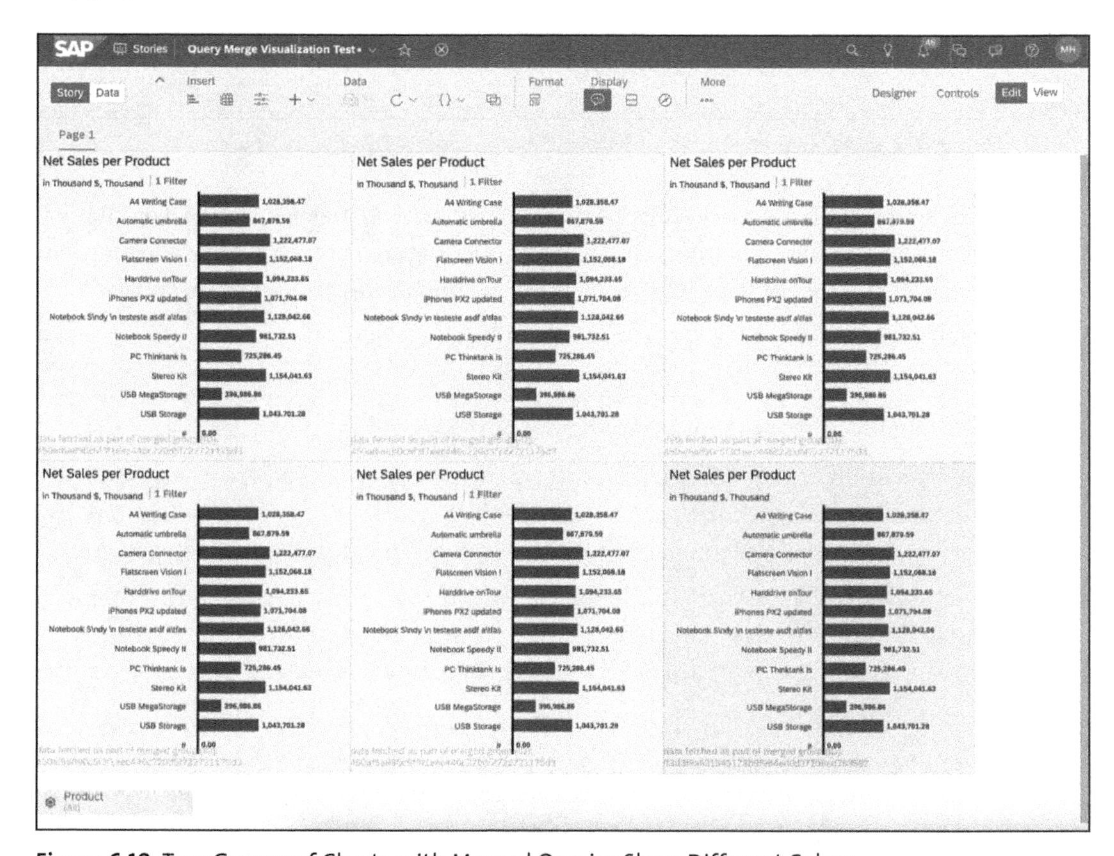

Figure 6.10 Two Groups of Charts with Merged Queries Show Different Colors

6.3.4 Increase the Number of SAP Business Warehouse Parallel Queries

By default, all SAP BW queries are executed in sequence, in a single session. You can improve performance by executing the queries in parallel by setting the number of additional parallel HTTP sessions used for executing SAP BW queries.

To increase the number of parallel sessions for SAP BW data sources, follow these steps:

1. Go to the info icon • **Administration** • **System Configuration** tab.
2. Select the edit icon.
3. Set the **Number of parallel sessions for SAP BW data sources** to your desired value (see Figure 6.11). It may help to find the setting by searching for "parallel." By default, this setting is set to 0. The maximum number of allowable parallel sessions is 12.

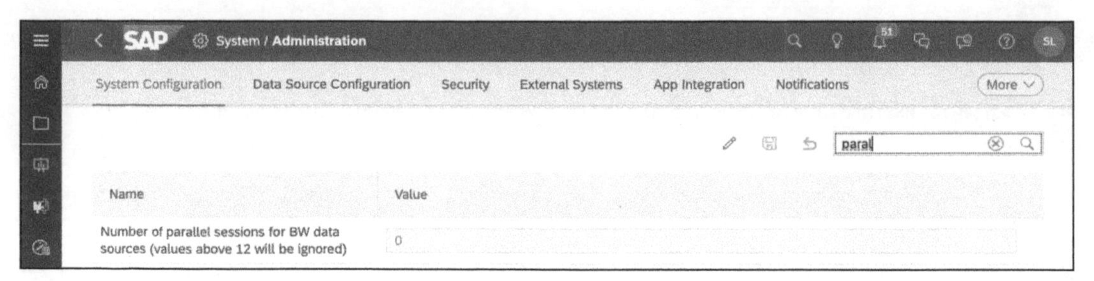

Figure 6.11 Increase the Number of Parallel Sessions for SAP BW Data Sources

Be aware that a higher number of parallel sessions will increase the load on the SAP BW server. Ensure that the SAP BW server is configured to handle this load. It might be necessary to increase `icm/max_conn`. See section Section 6.2 for more details.

4. Save the changes by clicking the save icon .

6.3.5 Reduce the Metadata Loading in Your Widget

When you are working with many structure members, you may notice decreased performance. You can optimize performance for two-structure queries or reduce SAP BW query metadata. Both methods reduce the amount of metadata that is being loaded.

Structures are objects that you define in the SAP BW query design environment. A structure forms the basic framework of the axes in a table (rows or columns). The structure can be key figures (basic key figures, restricted key figures, and calculated key figures) or characteristics.

Note

Keep the following points in mind:

- SAP BW key figures are a measurable object, such as quantity, revenue, weight, etc., which is like measures in SAP Analytics Cloud.
- SAP BW characteristics are informational attributes, for example, customer name, product, location, etc., which are like dimensions in SAP Analytics Cloud.
- SAP BW basic key figures are already in the InfoCube and can be used directly with no additional processing.
- SAP BW restricted key figures are defined by restricting basic key figures using a set of characteristics or by applying a filter on the data.
- SAP BW calculated key figures are defined by performing calculations on basic key figures.

A two-structure query in SAP BW has both key figures and characteristics. See an example of a two-structure dataset in Figure 6.12. There can also be specific formulas for each cell in the SAP BW query and rules for how to handle a formula collision. SAP Analytics

Cloud can connect to two-structure queries of SAP BW live connections where there are calculations in both rows and columns.

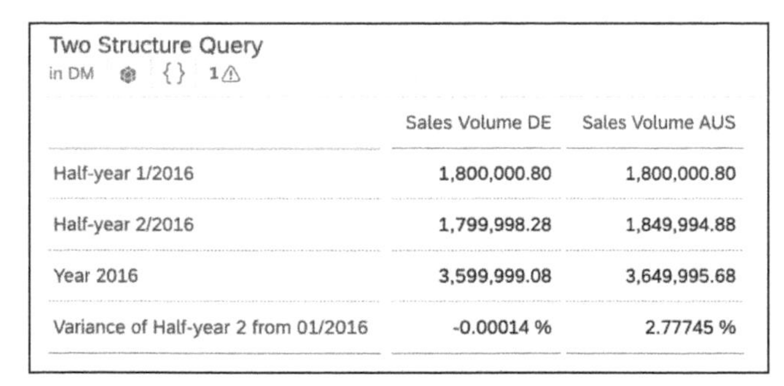

Two Structure Query
in DM {} 1

	Sales Volume DE	Sales Volume AUS
Half-year 1/2016	1,800,000.80	1,800,000.80
Half-year 2/2016	1,799,998.28	1,849,994.88
Year 2016	3,599,999.08	3,649,995.68
Variance of Half-year 2 from 01/2016	-0.00014 %	2.77745 %

Figure 6.12 Example of a Two-Structure Dataset

To optimize performance for two-structure queries, follow these steps:

1. Open your model and open **Model Preferences** by clicking the wrench icon.
2. Select the **Data and Performance** tab.
3. Select the option **Optimize Performance for Two-Structure Queries** (see Figure 6.13).

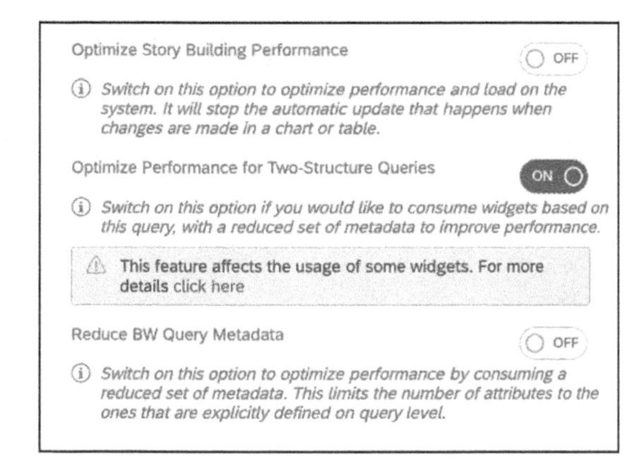

Figure 6.13 Enable Optimize Performance for Two-Structure Queries

Beware of the following impacts:

- User-defined formatting that is set up in the model is not applied. Instead, scale or decimal place settings from the SAP BW backend are adopted.
- Variance charts show reversed values in measures with sign reversal.
- Sign reversal for restricted measures is not supported.
- Error bars cannot build a percentage-specific formula for SAP BW percentage measures.
- The styling panel does not show correct values for scale and decimal places.
- In the geo tooltips, the scaling factor is not displayed according to the settings.

- Date and time measures cannot be used for charts or geo maps, even though they are displayed in the dropdown menu of the builder panel.

To reduce SAP BW query metadata, follow these steps:

1. Open your model and open **Model Preferences** by clicking the wrench icon.
2. Select the **Data and Performance** tab.
3. Select the option **Reduce SAP BW Query Metadata** (see Figure 6.14).

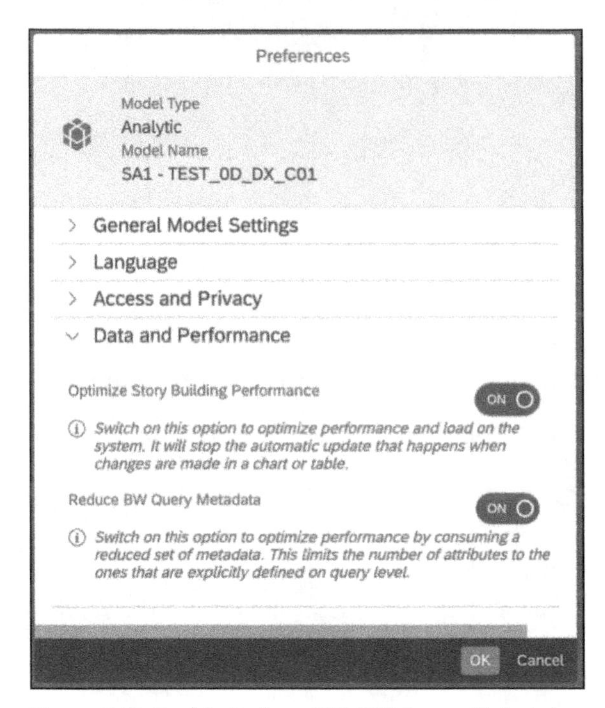

Figure 6.14 Enable Reduce SAP BW Query Metadata

6.4 Best Practices

As discussed in Chapter 5, there are pros and cons to using live data connections. Once you have decided to use live data connections, you should ensure you're following these best practices to get the best performance in your dashboard:

- Reduce data as early as possible in the backend
- Perform calculations in the backend, if possible, and do these calculations after aggregations
- Delete unnecessary dimensions in the model
- Otherwise, hide unnecessary dimensions in the model
- Deactivate the 0CALDAY hierarchy in SAP BW and instead use SAP Analytics Cloud for processing time dimension

- If possible, bring .xls data into the main story model rather than blending it with your live data model
- Use scripting API calls in the most efficient manner possible
- Use query batching or query merging to reduce roundtrip calls to the backend
- Optimize story building performance
- Use progressive chart rendering
- Increase the number of SAP BW parallel queries

Further Reading

Additional information for performance optimizations for tenant and live data settings can be found at the following online resources:

- SAP Help, "Data and Performance," available at: *http://s-prs.co/v566946*
- SAP Help, "Performance Optimization (Specifics for SAP BW)," available at *http://s-prs.co/v566947*
- SAP Knowledge Base Article #2591655, available at *http://s-prs.co/v566948*

6.5 Summary

In this chapter, we talked about choices you can make to improve dashboard performance when using SAP live data connections. This includes general approaches like reducing the amount of data that needs to be processed and transferred between systems. Do as much filtering, aggregation, and calculation in the backend as possible to harness the power of your backend and reduce the amount of data that is transferred between the backend and the SAP Analytics Cloud model.

If dimensions must be transferred to the SAP Analytics Cloud model but are not necessary, then you can delete or hide those dimensions in the model for some performance improvements.

We also talked about a variety of ways to reduce the number of roundtrip requests to the backend, including grouping several `setVariableValue()` API calls, which will batch these calls together. Where possible, use `setDimensionFilter()` instead of `setVariableValue()` to prevent any roundtrip call when filtering. Query batching and merging will also reduce roundtrip requests by sending several requests simultaneously.

Optimizing story building performance will prevent refreshes while building the dashboard, until you are ready to see your changes. Progressive chart rendering will show you cached charts while the data is being retrieved.

In the next chapter, we will talk about the choices that the consumer or the viewer of the dashboard can make to improve performance.

Chapter 7
Viewer Choices

In this chapter, we look at the choices that viewers or users of the dashboard can make to improve performance. This includes understanding the impact of network and computer characteristics, which usage interactions can be slow, and what you can do to reduce delays when presenting your dashboard to others.

All the optimizations discussed earlier are for improving the performance experienced by the viewer. Those optimizations are in the hands of the people who create the dashboard, that is, the dashboard creator, the data modeler, the administrator, the controller or business analyst, and the app designer. In addition to those optimizations, there are some things that the viewer can do to ensure good performance. In this chapter, we will start with general choices you can make when viewing and interacting with dashboards. Then we will talk specifically about choices you can make when you are presenting the dashboard to others in on-site meetings and in online settings.

7.1 Optimizations When Viewing Dashboards

When you are viewing and interacting with a dashboard, you arc trying to undcrstand the data for a greater purpose. You don't want to wait for the dashboard to load or reload the data in the charts as you are interacting with it. If performance is exceptionally slow, you may lose your train of thought about what you are trying to learn from the data, or you may get distracted by other tasks that you need to get done. Or you can be so frustrated that you don't want to use the dashboard at all, and you find workarounds by working with an Excel spreadsheet, which will take more time because now you need to design your own "dashboard" in Excel. Slow performance can get in the way of getting things done.

Performance choices that viewers can make fall into the following categories—choices that affect network speed, choices that affect rendering speed in the browser, and choices to avoid unnecessary user interactions when using the dashboard. In the following sections, we will discuss which browser to use, what to consider to ensure adequate network bandwidth, including the impact of using VPN, how rendering of your dashboard may be affected if your computer is very busy or very old, which specific user interactions may be unnecessary, and choices you can make when presenting your dashboard to a group of people.

7.1.1 Which Browser to Use

For earlier versions of SAP Analytics Cloud, it was recommended to use Google Chrome because the development team actively ensured that primarily Chrome was fully supported. However, as of publishing this book, both Google Chrome (latest version) and Microsoft Edge (latest version and Microsoft Edge browser based on the Chromium engine) are fully supported. Both Google and Microsoft release continuous updates to their browsers. The SAP Analytics Cloud development team tries to fully test and support the latest versions as they are released. Safari (latest version) is supported for stories in embed mode only.

It is important to know that all three browsers have a limit of six concurrent connections per host name. This means that it can handle only six requests for the widget calls at the same time. As soon as one of the six widget calls returns, it can launch another call. If your SAP Analytics Cloud dashboard has many more widgets than six, then you will see your widgets loading serially, with a maximum of six loading at one time.

Further Reading

To read more on concurrent connections limitations, visit the following URLs:

- Google Chrome: *http://s-prs.co/v566954*
- Microsoft Edge: *http://s-prs.co/v566955*
- Safari: *http://s-prs.co/v566956*

It is also recommended to use a minimum of 250 MB for your browser cache. SAP Analytics Cloud uses browser caching for static content such as image files. If you clear your cache, your dashboard will be slower as it needs to download the previously cached items. Once these items are downloaded to the browser again and cached, loading your dashboard the next time will be faster.

To compare the performance of Google Chrome and Microsoft Edge, we created a poorly performing dashboard that violates our best practices. It is a dashboard with 29 scatterplots with 2,000 points per scatterplot (see Figure 7.1). This dashboard will be used in other tests in later sections of this chapter. Then we tested the loading time when using Chrome and Edge.

Based on our timing tests, shown in Table 7.1, it appears that Google Chrome has a very slight advantage over Microsoft Edge. So, you may want to use Google Chrome when viewing your SAP Analytics Cloud dashboard.

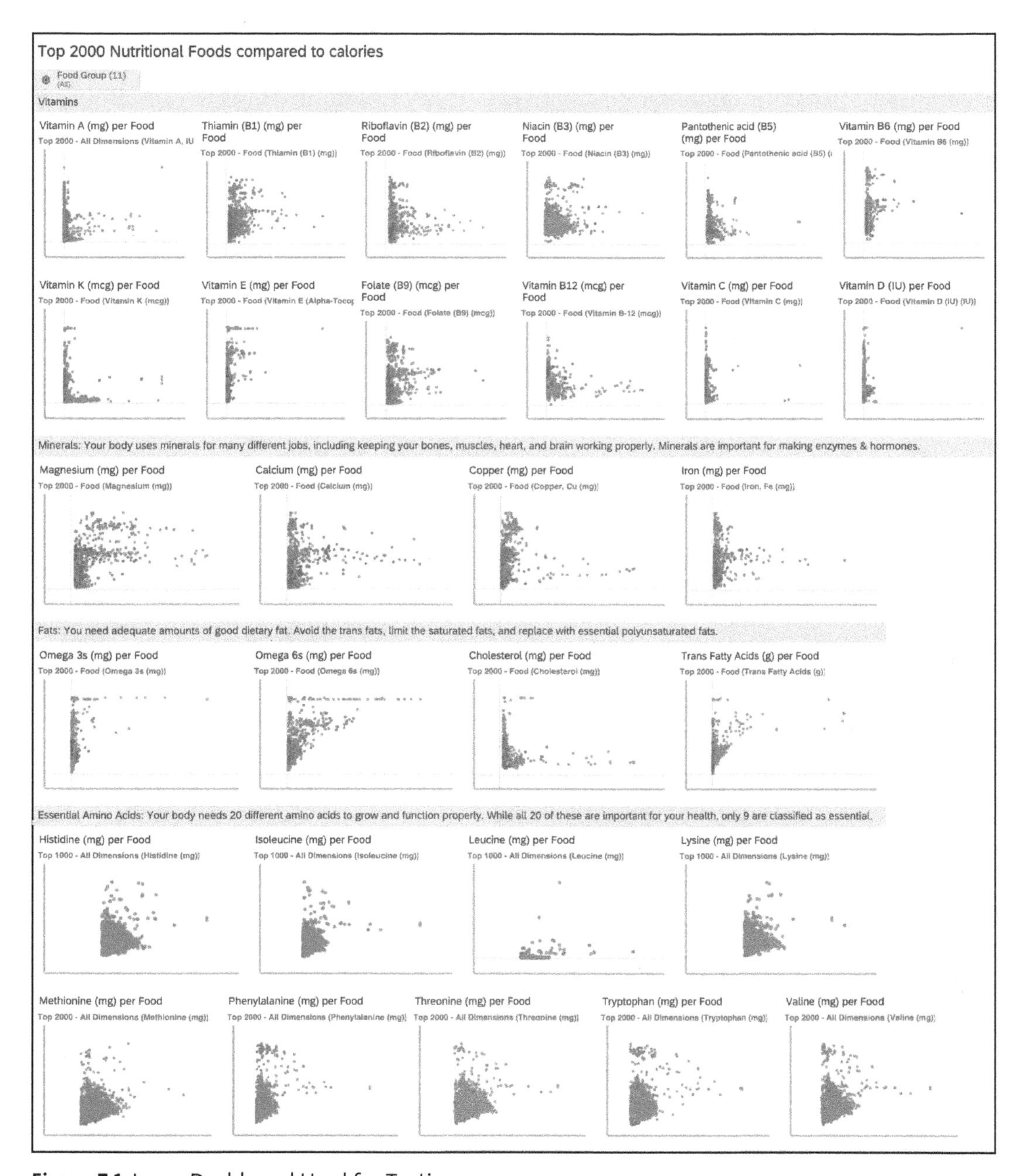

Figure 7.1 Large Dashboard Used for Testing

Browser	Dashboard Loading Time
Google Chrome (on Windows)	22.9 seconds
Microsoft Edge (on Windows)	24.1 seconds

Table 7.1 Loading Times of a Large Dashboard for Google Chrome and Microsoft Edge

Important Note

For testing, we used the following computers:

- MacBook Pro (16-inch, 2021), macOS Monterey Version 12.5.1, Apple M1 Pro (chip), 10 cores (8 performance and 2 efficiency), 16 GB RAM
- Lenovo Yoga 9i, 12th Generation Intel Core i7, 512 GB-SSD, 12 cores, 16 GB RAM

Further Reading

To read more about client software requirements, visit the following URL: *http://s-prs.co/v566957*.

7.1.2 Network Issues

Since you are connecting to your SAP Analytics Cloud tenant over the internet, there is a minimum bandwidth required to access the data. The SAP Analytics Cloud help portal states that the minimum bandwidth required is 500 to 800 kilobits per second per user, adding, "In general, SAP Analytics Cloud requires no more bandwidth than is required to browse the internet. All application modules are designed for speed and responsiveness with minimal use of large graphic files."

If you have good bandwidth through your internet provider and Wi-Fi access point, then you shouldn't have an issue. Typically, in a corporate setting, bandwidth is not an issue. A company typically builds out the Wi-Fi and intranet to support their expected number of users. Yet Wi-Fi access of a very busy office may still appear slower than that of an office with fewer users. However, if you are working from home or from a coffee shop, your effective bandwidth may not be ideal. Note that your maximum effective bandwidth is the lowest bandwidth capabilities of all the components in the path. That is, it is the lowest of the bandwidth capabilities of your wireless device, the Wi-Fi router, your internet access point, and your internet provider. The effective bandwidth available for SAP Analytics Cloud is also affected by the bandwidth used by other applications, but that will be discussed later.

The speed that your computer is capable of will depend on the Wi-Fi standard that your computer supports. Most modern computers support the 802.11ac wireless standard, which corresponds to 200 Mbps bandwidth. Wi-Fi routers typically support 200 Mbps (megabits per second) to 2 Gbps over Wi-Fi. Internet speeds are variable around the world; however, many countries have adequate speeds. Your maximum bandwidth is the lowest of the speeds in your data path.

Further Reading

To learn more about internet speeds around the world, visit the following URL: *www.speedtest.net/global-index*. For instance, speedtest.net reports that United Arab Emirates has the highest mean internet speed at 249.96 Mbps. The top 25 countries report >110 Mbps, with half the reported countries reporting >45 Mbps.

Your effective speed may be less than this maximum. There are a few reasons why your effective bandwidth could be less than necessary:

- **Inadequate bandwidth from your internet provider**
  You may not have adequate bandwidth from your internet provider. Some internet providers don't guarantee a particular speed and if there are many users in your neighborhood, your effective bandwidth may be reduced.
- **Too many internet-heavy activities at once**
  When there are multiple people using the same internet access point and each person is using a lot of the bandwidth, such as when streaming videos or downloading materials from the web, then the effective bandwidth available to you may be inadequate.
- **Improperly sized Wi-Fi access point**
  Your Wi-Fi access point is likely supporting multiple wireless devices, and if it has not been sized properly, then there may not be enough bandwidth to satisfy all devices.
- **Use of a Wi-Fi repeater**
  When your Wi-Fi range is not adequate, you can use a Wi-Fi repeater to boost the Wi-Fi signal. However, the Wi-Fi repeater connects to your router and wireless devices on the same frequency. This means that your wireless devices will get only half of the bandwidth available. If you don't have excess bandwidth from your service provider and you use a Wi-Fi repeater, then you may not have enough bandwidth for all your internet activities.

Inadequate bandwidth will have a serious impact on the loading time of your dashboard. Fortunately, most will have adequate bandwidth unless you have other applications that share your bandwidth, leaving you with too little for your dashboard.

To see the impact of inadequate bandwidth, we tested the loading time of the large dashboard described in Figure 7.1 with various states of adequate and inadequate bandwidth. The bandwidth was controlled by throttling the network available using the Chrome developer tools.

Based on our timing tests, shown in Table 7.2, it appears the download speed will need to be quite slow, less than 20 Mbps, before it impacts the performance of your dashboard. Keep in mind that this needs to be the bandwidth available to you. That is, your internet provider may provide adequate bandwidth, but if other devices or applications are hogging the bandwidth, it will effectively limit the bandwidth available to you.

Activity	Download Speed	Dashboard Loading Time
Satisfactory loading time	507 Mbps	19 seconds
Satisfactory loading time	20 Mbps	20 seconds
Unsatisfactory loading time	10 Mbps	31 seconds
Unsatisfactory loading time	5 Mbps	38 seconds
Unsatisfactory loading time	2 Mbps	75 seconds

Table 7.2 The Effect of Inadequate Bandwidth/Download Speed on the Loading Time of an SAP Analytics Dashboard

If your bandwidth issues are due to an improperly sized Wi-Fi access point or use of a Wi-Fi repeater, then you should consider using ethernet to connect to the internet rather than Wi-Fi. Note that modern computers don't have an ethernet port, so you would need to purchase an ethernet adapter.

Using ethernet means that you have a dedicated path from your computer to your wired intranet. Typically, your ethernet will be 1 Gbps (gigabits per second). As stated earlier, Wi-Fi routers typically support 200 Mbps to 2 Gbps over Wi-Fi. However, the Wi-Fi router is used by multiple wireless devices.

The most effective way to determine available bandwidth is to test your network speed using one of the many internet speed testing sites. For instance, go to speedtest.net and click the Go button. This will check your download speed in Mbps. You can also determine if Wi-Fi is affecting your available bandwidth by doing a speed test over Wi-Fi and again over ethernet and comparing the speeds.

7.1.3 The Impact of Using a Virtual Private Network

Your data throughput can be affected by using a virtual private network (VPN). A VPN encrypts your connection and sends it through a specific secure VPN server. This extends your protected corporate network to your computer over a public network. Using a VPN may affect performance as you encrypt and decrypt your connection and tunnel to your SAP Analytics Cloud server. Additionally, it's likely that your VPN server may not be near your location or the SAP Analytics Cloud server. This extra hop on the internet may also affect performance. To test if a VPN is affecting the performance of your dashboard, you can do a speed test (using a site like speedtest.net) both with and without the VPN and compare speeds. It is likely that using a VPN will have a significant performance impact on your SAP Analytics dashboard only if your internet speed is already very slow without the VPN. If this is the case, avoid using a VPN if possible.

7.1.4 Computer Resources

When your computer is very busy with other activities, there may not be enough computer processing power left for your browser to render the DOM of your SAP Analytics Cloud dashboard in a timely fashion. Modern computers have multiple cores and have much processing power. However, some applications can consume much of your central processing unit (CPU). You should ensure that no CPU-intensive apps are running that you don't need if you are having performance problems with your SAP Analytics Cloud dashboard.

To test the impact of inadequate CPU resources, we tested the loading time of the large dashboard shown in Figure 7.1 while running a benchmarking tool (Cinebench) that stresses the system, including using much of the CPU. The reported CPU percentage is normalized to 100 percent of the entire machine—not the sum of the CPU percentage of each core.

Based on our timing test, shown in Table 7.3, the loading time of the dashboard slows very much when your CPU is busy with other activities.

Activity	CPU Usage	Dashboard Loading Time
Satisfactory loading time	~1%	21.63 seconds
Unsatisfactory loading time	~85%	35.38 seconds

Table 7.3 The Effect of Inadequate CPU on the Loading Time of an SAP Analytics Dashboard

You should ensure that no processes on your computer are using too many of the computer processing resources. On a Mac, you can look at the Activity Monitor, shown later in Figure 7.3, to see if there are any processes that use much of the CPU. Search for "Activity Monitor" in Spotlight, shown in Figure 7.2.

Figure 7.2 Spotlight to Launch the Activity Monitor on a Mac

Select the **CPU** tab. Ensure that it is sorted by % CPU. Look for processes that are using much of the CPU. Note that it is reporting the cumulative CPU usage across all cores. That is, if you have ten cores, the maximum CPU usage will be 1000%. Notice in Figure 7.3 that Cinebench is using much of the Mac's resources—specifically, 917 percent of a

10-core machine, which is equivalent to 91.7 percent of the overall CPU resources. The CPU load chart also shows that the CPU usage started to spike. This corresponds to when the Cinebench app was launched.

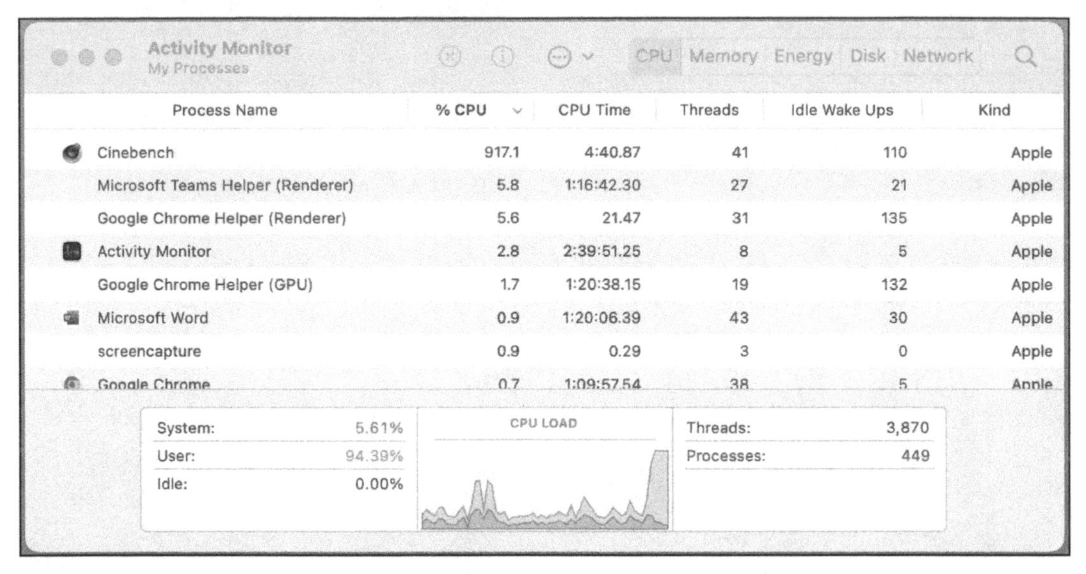

Figure 7.3 Activity Monitor on a Mac (CPU Tab)

Further Reading

To learn more about the Activity Monitor on a Mac, visit the following URL: *http://s-prs.co/v566958*.

On a Windows machine, you can look at the Task Manager to see if there are any processes that use much of the CPU. Search for "Task Manager" in the Windows search box, as shown in Figure 7.4.

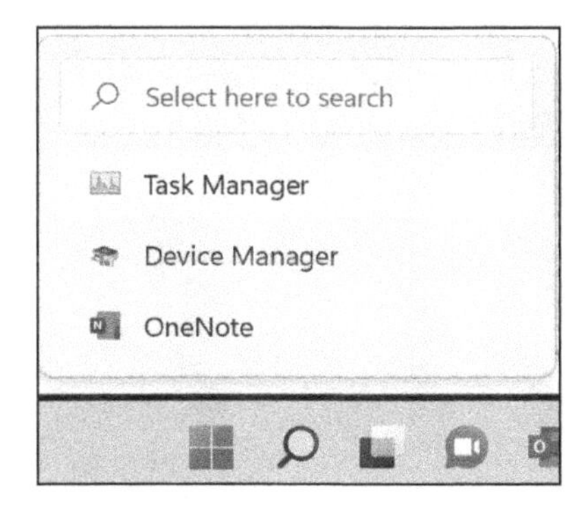

Figure 7.4 Windows Search Box to Launch the Task Manager on a Windows Machine

Select the **Processes** tab. Ensure that it is sorted by CPU. Look for processes that are using much of the CPU. Notice in Figure 7.5 that Cinebench is using much of Windows' resources, that is, 84.4 percent of the CPU resources.

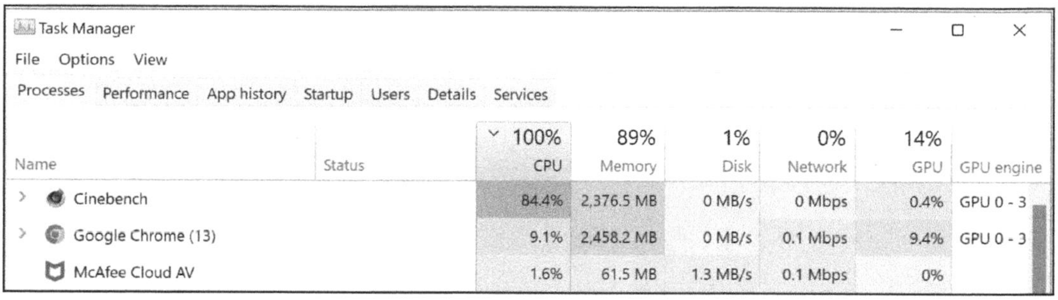

Task Manager

File Options View

Processes Performance App history Startup Users Details Services

Name	Status	100% CPU	89% Memory	1% Disk	0% Network	14% GPU	GPU engine
Cinebench		84.4%	2,376.5 MB	0 MB/s	0 Mbps	0.4%	GPU 0 - 3
Google Chrome (13)		9.1%	2,458.2 MB	0 MB/s	0.1 Mbps	9.4%	GPU 0 - 3
McAfee Cloud AV		1.6%	61.5 MB	1.3 MB/s	0.1 Mbps	0%	

Figure 7.5 Task Manager on a Windows Machine (Processes Tab)

Further Reading

To learn more about the Task Manager on Windows, visit the following URL: *http://s-prs.co/v566959*.

7.1.5 Older Computers

If you have an older computer, it may be slower due to a few factors. Your older computer may have less computing power, less RAM, and it may be using an older, lower-bandwidth network standard.

If your older computer doesn't have adequate RAM, then it will constantly swap memory as necessary, which will drastically negatively affect the performance. A 2013 MacBook was configurable to 8 GB or 16 GB. Given the current memory requirements for Chrome and the memory requirements for the OS, there would not be enough memory if the computer was configured to only 8 GB. There would be enough memory if configured to 16 GB if you don't have many other applications running, consuming the remaining approximately 5 GB. The specific RAM configuration and OS memory requirements would be different on other machines.

To analyze the memory usage in old and new machines, we looked at the amount of memory that the OS required for each machine. We assumed that Chrome would require equivalent memory since Chrome is updated frequently and the SAP Analytics Cloud dashboard would require equivalent memory since it is a cloud application. In Table 7.4, notice how the total memory usage for the 2013 Mac exceeds 8 GB. If your older computer is configured only for 8 GB, then you will run into extreme performance issues.

Software	Memory Usage on 2021 Mac	Memory Usage on 2013 Mac
OS on 2021 Mac	8.32 GB	6.87 GB
Chrome on Mac	3.83 GB	3.83 GB
SAP Analytics Cloud	0.10 GB	0.10 GB
Total	12.25 GB	10.9 GB

Table 7.4 Memory Usage of the OS, Chrome, and SAP Analytics Cloud on New and Old Machines

7.1.6 Interacting with the Dashboard

There are some interactions you can do (or avoid doing) when using your dashboard to increase performance or to avoid unnecessary loading of a page:

- **Skip unnecessary levels when drilling down**
  If your dashboard shows hierarchical data, you can avoid unnecessary loading time by skipping levels when drilling down. This way, you can avoid loading levels that you are not interested in. For more details, see Chapter 3, Section 3.3.1.
- **In the planning tool, avoid pasting data to many different members and dimensions in a table**
  When you are entering data in the planning tool, you can paste multiple table cells at once. When there are multiple dimensions on the table, you can paste to different sets of members for each dimension. To avoid slow performance, you'll be notified when you try to paste to an area that includes many different sets. For more details, see Chapter 3, Section 3.6.2.
- **In the planning tool, don't update too many cells at the same time**
  When updating multiple cells, the planning tool runs dependency checks and verifies potential restrictions pairwise. This leads to quadratic growth of checks with the number of changed cells. It is faster to split the update into multiple smaller updates, rather than running a single large update at once.

  A technical limit restricts the number of low-level data changes to avoid runtimes growing too long. When that limit is exceeded, the application produces an error message and data entries are rejected.

  Note these dependency checks are not necessary when all visible dimensions are restricted to leaves or when there are no visible cells using one of the following features: formulas, lookup, dynamic time navigation, or calculated dimensions. For more details, see Chapter 3, Section 3.6.2.
- **In the planning tool, don't include all data when you copy to a private version**
  When using the planning tool, you may want to copy an existing version to a private version and then edit this private version. Later, you can publish your version for

others to see. The amount of data in multiple private versions, including versions from other users, affects performance. You can help maintain the performance by not copying all the data. Some options are copying visible data by using the current table filters and manually choosing which data to copy. For more details, see Chapter 3, section 3.6.1.

7.2 Optimizations When Presenting to Others

You may have experienced the situation of something not going quite right during a presentation. Perhaps your computer is not connecting to the projector properly, your internet connection is choppy, or the application that you are demonstrating is misbehaving. Even though these types of things happen to all of us, they can bring on unneeded stress to you as the presenter and can waste the time of your audience.

When performance issues happen when showing your SAP Analytics Cloud dashboard, you may feel that same stress and awkward silence that happens as you wait for the page to load. Knowing how to control performance issues or to anticipate and explain them will make them easier to deal with.

7.2.1 Preloading Dashboards

For any presentation, it is good practice to open your presentation slide deck and open your SAP Analytics Cloud dashboard before the meeting to ensure that everything looks as expected. Additionally, by opening the dashboard before the meeting, you will preload the dashboard, so any wait required during loading does not happen during the meeting in front of your audience.

Since some of the charts can have delayed loading, it is best to visit all the pages that you expect to demo to ensure everything is preloaded, then go back to the page where you plan to start your demo.

Keep in mind that SAP Analytics Cloud has a session timeout. If you don't interact with the system for that amount of time, then you will be logged out of the system. Then, when it is your turn to show the dashboard during the meeting, you'll have to load the dashboard, possibly resulting in awkward waiting time as your dashboard loads. The default session timeout duration is one hour. However, your administrators may have changed this duration to more or less time. If you are approaching the time when you will be automatically logged out, then you should quickly interact with the dashboard to stay logged in. "Interact with the system" means requiring access to the SAP Analytics Cloud model. For instance, the following interactions are not considered interactions by SAP Analytics Cloud: changing the browser window size so that the charts move around, hovering over tooltips to read some helpful information, and hovering over data points to see the hover-over. To interact, you must request data from the model by refreshing, going to another page, filtering a page or chart, or drilling-in on a chart.

7.2.2 Screen Sharing

If you are presenting the SAP Analytics Cloud dashboard over video conferencing software, such as Zoom or Microsoft Teams, you should be aware that this may slow loading of the dashboard as well. When attendees of the call have their cameras on, the video conferencing software requires some of your available bandwidth and some of your computer's processing time.

Table 7.5 lists the download bandwidth requirements of the main video conferencing software, as stated in their respective documentation.

Number of Participants with Camera On	Recommended Bandwidth	Bandwidth for Best Quality
Zoom		
0	0.15 Mbps	
2	1.2 Mbps	3.0 Mbps
2+	1.8 Mbps	3.0 Mbps
MS Teams		
2	1.5 Mbps	4.0 Mbps
2+	2.5 Mbps	4.0 Mbps
Skype		
2	0.5 Mbps	1.5 Mbps
3	2.0 Mbps	
5	4.0 Mbps	
7+	8.0 Mbps	
Slack		
2	0.6 Mbps	
3	1.2 Mbps	
5	2.0 Mbps	

Table 7.5 Screen Sharing Download Bandwidth Requirements for Various Video Conferencing Software

Number of Participants with Camera On	Recommended Bandwidth	Bandwidth for Best Quality
Google Meet		
2	1.0 Mbps	2.6 Mbps
5	1.5 Mbps	3.2 Mbps
10	2.0 Mbps	4.0 Mbps

Table 7.5 Screen Sharing Download Bandwidth Requirements for Various Video Conferencing Software (Cont.)

Notice that Zoom explicitly states the bandwidth requirements for just screen sharing with no cameras on. The bandwidth requirement is very low compared to the bandwidth requirement for video (cameras on). We would expect the other software companies to have similarly low requirements if the cameras are off. Note that turning your camera off will have very little effect because your video is measured by the upload bandwidth. Your download bandwidth will accommodate your SAP Analytics Cloud dashboard and all the camera videos of the other participants in the meeting.

Some of the video conferencing software companies, such as Zoom and Microsoft, state that they dynamically adjust the quality of the video to best accommodate the available bandwidth.

Further Reading

To learn about all the bandwidth requirements of these video conferencing software, you can read their documentation:

- Zoom: *http://s-prs.co/v566960*
- Microsoft Teams: *http://s-prs.co/v566961*
- Skype: *http://s-prs.co/v566962*
- Slack: *http://s-prs.co/v566963*
- Google Meet: *http://s-prs.co/v56694*

You can ask others to temporarily turn off their cameras. However, this may go against your company culture. If someone comments on the poor performance, you can explain that it is faster when not using screen or video sharing. If you time how long it takes to load without video conferencing software running, then you can say how long it would take to load if you aren't on a video conference call.

7.2.3 Use of a Wireless Projector in a Hybrid Meeting

Using a wireless projector is like a special case of Wi-Fi access. If you are in a meeting room where you are using video conferencing software and sharing your screen with remote participants and you want to connect to a wireless projector to share with meeting participants in the room, you may have performance problems if there are many people in the room who are also using their computers to access the Wi-Fi.

Because Wi-Fi is over the air, it does not have a dedicated up and down channel. Your computer will be given a slice of time to access the Wi-Fi router to handle both up (to send information to the projector and to send information to the video-conferencing app) and down (to receive the SAP Analytics Cloud content). If many other wireless devices are also getting time slices to access the Wi-Fi router, you may not get enough of the bandwidth to perform all the data transfer that you need to.

In this case, you may get better performance if your machine only sends information to the video-conferencing app (i.e., you do the screen sharing) and receives the SAP Analytics Cloud content (i.e., you show your dashboard), but you have another computer access the video conferencing app and project the meeting to the wireless projector. This will reduce the bandwidth burden on your machine.

7.3 Best Practices

If you find you're having performance problems with SAP Analytics Cloud, it's important to know if there is anything you can do to improve the performance. One thing that we haven't discussed is that you could ask a colleague to load the dashboard into their environment to compare performance. If you both have slow performance, not much has been learned. However, if their performance is better, it may provide clues as to what may be in your environment that is different.

To find out what specific things in your environment may be causing performance issues, you should:

- Use Google Chrome for a slight advantage over Microsoft Edge
- Run speedtest.net to see if you have adequate bandwidth
- If you don't have adequate bandwidth, try using an ethernet cable to see if you can get more available bandwidth
- Test if your VPN is affecting your performance by testing with and without a VPN
- Look at the CPU on your machine to ensure that you have adequate computer processing power to render the SAP Analytics Cloud dashboard DOM
- Preload your dashboard if you will be showing it to others
- Be prepared to explain potential slow performance if you are using video conferencing software or ask everyone to turn off their cameras
- Have another computer connect to the wireless projector in a meeting room to project your video conference screen sharing

You can also proactively interact with your dashboard in ways that help the performance:

- Skip unnecessary levels when drilling down
- In the planning tool, avoid pasting data to many different members and dimensions in a table
- In the planning tool, don't update too many cells at the same time
- In the planning tool, don't include all data when you copy to a private version

7.4 Summary

In this chapter, we talked about choices that viewers of the dashboard can make to improve performance. This includes ensuring that you have adequate bandwidth. This may require doing speed tests to see if Wi-Fi, VPN, or other network applications are limiting your available bandwidth and then taking appropriate corrective actions.

This also includes ensuring that your computer has adequate computer processing power to render the SAP Analytics Cloud dashboard DOM. This may require viewing the CPU usage of processes on your machine to see if there are any heavy processes running. You can view the CPU usage percentage by viewing the Activity Monitor on a Mac or the Task Manager on Windows. If so, you could take corrective actions by stopping the other processes or waiting until they are complete.

If you are presenting to others, you can save time by preloading your dashboard or, if you have bandwidth issues due to limited Wi-Fi bandwidth, you can have another computer project your video conference screen sharing to the wireless projector.

You can also save time by interacting with the dashboard in efficient ways, such as skipping unnecessary levels when drilling down. Also in the planning tool, avoid pasting data to many different members and dimensions and avoiding updating too many cells at the same time. Also, you can limit the amount of data included when you copy your planning dashboard to a private version.

In the next chapters, we will apply the tips discussed in Chapter 3 to Chapter 7 to dashboard design to see how these tips can add up to significant performance improvements.

Chapter 8
Optimized Dashboard Using Acquired Data

In this chapter, we'll take what was discussed in the earlier chapters and apply it to dashboard design. The dashboard will use a spreadsheet as its data source.

This chapter is for business analysts and power consumers who want to build a dashboard for their specific scenario. The data is imported from a file into an SAP Analytics Cloud model. The dashboard is then created based on the model.

For this and the following two chapters, we'll follow the personas in a fictitious live theater company who are responsible for managing multiple theaters in a local region. The theater company has multiple short-run theater performances that travel and are performed at various theaters over the year.

For the dashboard described in this chapter using acquired data, our analyst persona is Julia, the assistant to the artistic director, Alex. We'll be using a case study that acquires data from a Microsoft Excel spreadsheet into a model for play planning for the next year.

The structure of this and the next chapters is as follows: First, in Section 8.1, we'll describe the use case of the dashboard. Then in Section 8.2, we look at where the data is coming from, and how to manipulate the data into the desired format. In Section 8.3, we discuss what specific questions the dashboard will address and describe the dashboard's structure. Finally, in Section 8.4, you can follow a step-by-step guide on how the dashboard was built.

8.1 Scenario

When designing and building any tool, you need to start with the scenario. The scenario includes who will be using it, when and where they will use it, and why they are using it—that is, what they are trying to achieve. When building a dashboard, the scenario should also include what data they need to see and what type of analysis needs to be supported.

In this scenario, as the artistic director of a theater company, Alex is responsible for selecting which plays will be performed in the next performance season. The theater company has several theater locations across the region. The plays are short-run performances, typically four weeks, which then travel to another theater location. Alex has professional insights regarding which plays do well. However, he wants to augment his knowledge with data when making his decisions. Julia is designing the dashboard for Alex so that Alex can see which plays were most successful, which helps when planning which plays to perform next year. Alex will also want to present his findings to the board of directors. The dashboard needs to be readable and understandable and allow for thorough analysis of multiple factors of the play's success.

Alex is interested in which plays were most successful from multiple perspectives—audience satisfaction, tickets sales, secondary sales such as drinks and snack sales, staging expense, and actor expense. This theater company also includes student performers with non-speaking roles if a play provides that opportunity. The theater company also tracks the time of day of the performance (morning, matinee, evening) as well as if the performance had students as part of a school trip in the audience. He will also analyze whether theaters have regional differences, such as preferring dramas or musicals.

Julia will build the dashboard into three dashboard pages. Figure 8.1 shows the first page, where the metrics are shown individually. Figure 8.2 shows the second page, where the metrics are presented so that Alex can look for correlations between the metrics. Figure 8.3 shows the third, where the data is shown by theater so that Alex can look for regional differences. Julia will design the dashboard to be International Business Communication Standards (IBCS)-compliant.

We'll follow Julia through all the building stages—from getting the data from multiple sources and importing it into SAP Analytics Cloud to building the model, defining the scenario for the dashboard, and using SAP Analytics Cloud to create the dashboard, all while ensuring that the dashboard will be efficient.

Figure 8.1 Individual Metrics

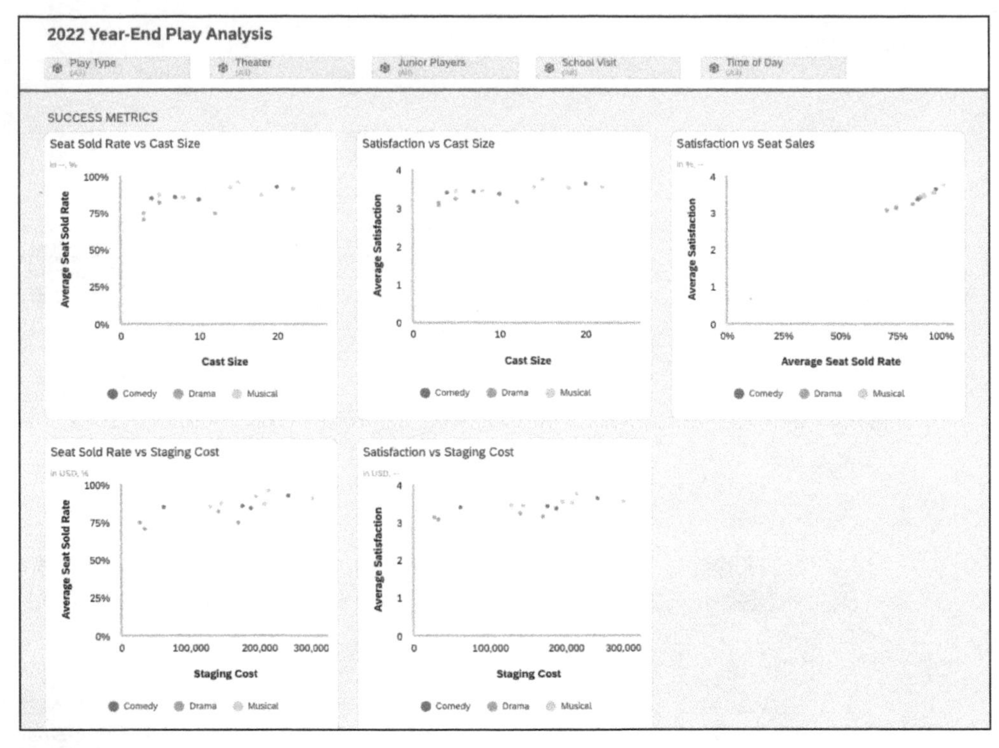

Figure 8.2 Scatter Plots to Show Interactions between Metrics

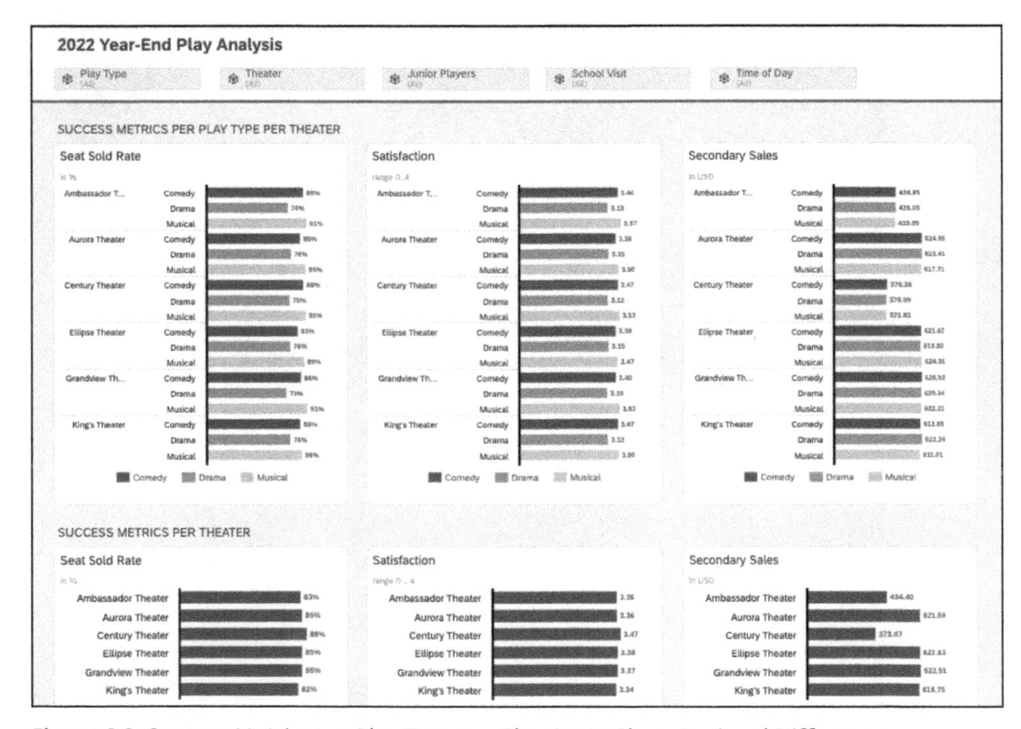

Figure 8.3 Success Metrics per Play Type per Theater to Show Regional Differences

8.2 Data Structure

In this section, first we will discuss where Julia's data comes from and why she is using an acquired data model. Then we'll jump into building the model for the dashboard.

8.2.1 Data Source

Much of the data that Julia loads into the dashboard comes from the backend system, like ticket sales, merchandise and drink sales, staging expense, and actor expense. She could get data from a live connection; however, an important component of Alex's play analysis will be the audience satisfaction scores. There is a survey that audience members can complete via a kiosk in the theater lobbies or via email sent to the person who purchased the tickets. This data is not available in the backend system and has much more volume than the other data that she needs.

In Chapter 6, it was suggested that you pull all your data together in a spreadsheet rather than blending a spreadsheet with your live connection. Since this dashboard needs to import the data only once as we are looking at data from last year, it is easy for Julia to export the necessary data from her backend system and then merge it with the survey data in Excel.

She exports the following data from the backend system for each performance date per play and per theater:

- Sold ticket percentage, that is, number of tickets sold as a percentage of the available seats
- Merchandise/drinks/snacks sales
- Time of day of the performance (morning, matinee, evening)
- School visit, that is, are there students in the audience as part of a school trip

She exports the following data from the backend system per play:

- Staging expense, that is, the cost to build the set and costumes
- Actor expense, as measured by cast size
- Junior players, that is, are student performers involved; student performers are not counted as part of the cast size because they are not paid for their involvement

She also exports the survey data from the third-party survey tool, Qualtrics, which has multiple responses for each performance date per play and per theater:

- Satisfaction score
- Time of day (morning, matinee, evening)

She joins all this data together using the theater, play, and performance data as the keys for the join. She could use all the individual responses from the survey responses to join with the other data, but we learned in Chapter 6 to perform aggregations as early as possible. So, she decides to aggregate the survey responses in Excel before joining with the other data.

Aggregating the Survey Data in Excel

Julia aggregates and reduces the survey data to only what she needs in Excel by deleting unneeded columns, grouping and calculating subtotals, then manipulating the data so that only the summary rows are included, and each summary row has no empty values and no Excel formulas. The result can be saved as a .CSV file.

Julia takes the following steps to aggregate the survey data:

1. **Delete unnecessary columns.**
   It will simplify the process and improve performance to delete the columns that are not needed in the survey data. Qualtrics data has many columns that are not needed. Julia deletes all columns except **End Date, Satisfaction, Theater, Play,** and **Time of Day**. She renames **End Date** to **Date.**
2. **Create a column that acts as a primary key column.**
   Julia wants a summary row for each unique combination of **Theater** (column A), **Play** (column B), **Date** (column C), and **Time of Day** (column D). To do this, there needs to be a single column that will act as the composite primary key that can be sorted and grouped to make the subtotals. First, she creates a new column called **Primary Key** and catenates the columns that are members of the composite primary key.

   In the first row of the newly created primary key column, she enters the concatenate formula:

   ```
   =CONCAT(A2, " ", B2, " ", C2, " ", D2)
   ```
3. **Sort by this new Primary Key column.**
   The following step will create summary data whenever the data in the primary key column changes. She sorts the rows by the **Primary Key** column so that all the primary key values will be grouped together.
4. **Create subtotals based on this new primary key column.**
   In Excel, there is a subtotal function. Julia selects the entire table. On the **Data** tab, she presses the **Subtotal** button. On the **Subtotal** dialog (see Figure 8.4), she specifies **At each change in** to be the **Primary Key** column, the **Use function** to be **Average,** and **Add subtotal to** to be **Satisfaction**. Now each unique combination of **Theater, Play, Date,** and **Time of Day** has a summary row with the average audience satisfaction value for that specific performance at that theater.

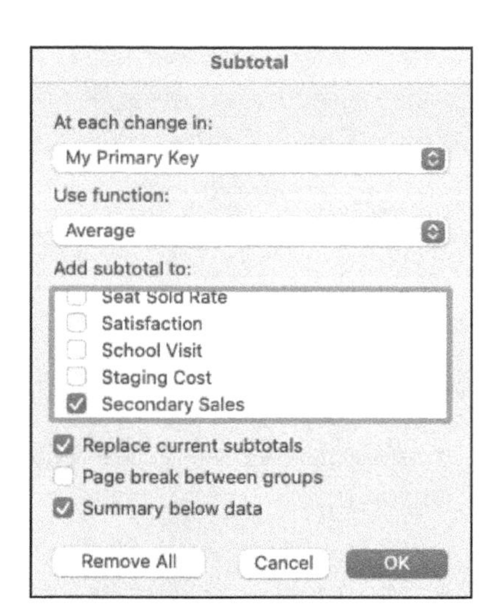

Figure 8.4 Subtotal Dialog (from the Data Tab) to Create Subtotal Rows in Excel

5. **Create duplicate columns of the other columns and fill cells with an Excel formula.**
   When creating the subtotal summary rows, the columns that were not involved in the subtotal operation are empty. Only the **Satisfaction** and **Primary Key** columns will have data. The **Satisfaction** column has the average satisfaction and the **Primary Key** column has the primary key with the function used in the subtotal operation appended (e.g., Aurora Theater Art 44573 Average). In the summary rows, we need to populate the other columns with the appropriate data and then delete the individual rows, leaving only the summary rows.

   To ensure that the columns that should be included in the summary row are filled appropriately (**Date, Theater, Play, Time of Day**), Julia creates duplicate columns for these and uses the Excel = formula, where she selects the cell in the row above for the associated original column, that is, for row 2, she selects the row 1 in the original column. Then she fills down for all rows. In Figure 8.5, you can see that columns D, E, and F are duplicates of columns A, B, and C, where cell D113 is set to =A112.

	A	B	C	D	E
1	My Primary Key	Response ID	Response ID	Theater	Theater
208	Aurora Theater Art 2022-01-12 Morning	207		Aurora Theater	
209	**Aurora Theater Art 2022-01-12 Morning Average**		207		=D208

Figure 8.5 Duplicate Columns That Have Empty Cells in the Summary Row

6. **Copy the entire table and paste into new spreadsheet as values to remove formulas.**
   Julia selects the entire table and pastes it into a new spreadsheet by using the **Paste Special • Values** menu item. This removes all formulas.
7. **Hide all non-summary rows.**
   The summary rows will have blank fields in the original **Date, Theater, Play,** and **Time of Day** columns (i.e., columns A, B, C). To select just the summary rows, she wants to

select the rows with these blank fields. Julia clicks on the header for one of these columns, then in the **Home** ribbon, she selects **Sort & Filter • Filter**. She deselects all columns except **(Blanks)**. This results in only the summary rows being shown.

8. **Select all the columns that you need and paste them in a new spreadsheet.**
   Julia selects the new columns for the **Date, Theater, Play**, and **Satisfaction** columns and pastes these into a new spreadsheet. She now has a spreadsheet with summary values and no blank cells.

Joining the Data in the Three Spreadsheets

Julia now has all the data that she needs in three separate spreadsheets—two directly from the backend system, and this newly manipulated survey data spreadsheet. She needs to join these into a single flat spreadsheet.

To join the spreadsheets, she can use either the Excel `LOOKUP` function or the Relationship functionality (which is only available on the Windows version of Excel).

For either of these methods, there need to be unique columns of data that will act as the composite primary key that you use in one spreadsheet to identify which data you're looking for in the other spreadsheet. You can use the `CONCAT` Excel function to create the unique column (similar to step 2 above).

Recall that Julia has three spreadsheets with the following data:

- *Survey_Satisfaction.xlsx*: **Theater, Play, Date, Time of Day, Satisfaction**
- *Performance_Info.xlsx*: **THEATER, Play, Date, Time of Day, Percentage Tickets Sold, Secondary Sales**
- *Play_Costs.xlsx*: **Play, Staging Expense, Cast Size**

Julia plans to add the performance information and play costs to the existing **Survey_ Satisfaction** file.

Julia creates a column in both the *Survey_Satifaction.xlsx* spreadsheet and the *Performance_Info.xlsx* spreadsheet that concatenates the **Theater**, **Play**, and **Date** columns. She doesn't need to do this for the *Play_Costs.xlsx* spreadsheet because using the Play column is sufficient. Then she takes the following steps:

1. **Create a column that acts as a primary key column in the Survey_Satisfaction spreadsheet.**
   She creates a new column called **Primary Key**. In the first row of the newly created column, she enters the concatenate formula:

   ```
   =CONCAT(A2, " ", B2, " ", C2)
   ```

2. **Create a column that acts as a primary key column in Performance_Info spreadsheet.**
   She repeats the previous step in the *Performance_Info* spreadsheet.

3. **Add the Percentage Tickets Sold column to the Survey_Satisfaction spreadsheet.**
   She uses the Excel LOOKUP function to join these spreadsheets. She adds a column, called **Percentage Tickets Sold**, to the *Survey_Satisfaction.xlsx* spreadsheet and enters the function to the first data cell:

   ```
   =LOOKUP(E2,'[Performance_Info.xlsx]Sheet1'!A2:A3201,'[Performance_
   Info.xlsx]Sheet1':E3201)
   ```

   The equation elements are defined as the following:
   - E2 is the first row of the Primary Key column in the *Survey_Satisfaction* file
   - '[Performance_Info.xlsx]Sheet1'!A2:A3201 is the column corresponding to the primary key column in the *Performance_Info* file. These two columns should have similar values in them.
   - '[Performance_Info.xlsx]Sheet1':E3201 is the column that you want to appear in the *Survey_Satisfaction* file (i.e., **Percentage Tickets Sold**)
4. **Add the Secondary Sales column to the Survey_Satisfaction spreadsheet.**
   She repeats the previous step to add the **Secondary Sales** column.
5. **Add the Staging Expense column to the Survey_Satisfaction file.**
   She repeats this step to add the **Staging Expense** column. However, she uses the **Play** column in both files as the primary key.
6. **Add the Number of Performers column to the Survey_Satisfaction file.**
   She repeats this step to add the number of performers, again, using the **Play** column in both files as the primary key.

Julia now has one spreadsheet with all the necessary columns that she can import into the SAP Analytics Cloud model.

Golden Rule #2 – Data Manipulation

Julia made a choice to improve the performance of the dashboard that correspond to golden rule #2:

- *Perform aggregations early*: She performed aggregations as early as possible. She aggregated the data in the survey spreadsheet reducing it from 566,666 records to 3,200 records. She also performed aggregations in the backed before exporting the data. For instance, she exported the seat sold rate as an average number of seats sold per performance rather than exporting the individual tickets sales. She also exported the secondary sales as a total per performance rather than the individual sales transactions.

Golden Rule #3 – Data Model

Julia also made choices to improve the performance of the dashboard that correspond to golden rule #3:

- *Remove unnecessary dimensions*: She deleted data (columns) that was not necessary. There were a lot of extra columns in the survey data from the Qualtrics export that were not needed for her dashboard.
- *Avoid too much blending*: She pulled all the data together in a spreadsheet rather than blending the spreadsheet data with a live connection backend source.

8.2.2 Building a Model in SAP Analytics Cloud

As the dashboard builds on an acquired model based on the Excel spreadsheet that we created, this section will describe importing the data from Excel and preparing the data in the data modeler.

Importing the Data from an Excel Spreadsheet

To import the data from the spreadsheet into its model, Julia does the following steps:

1. In the side navigation, select **Modeler** and then choose **From a CSV or Excel File** in the **Create New** area.
2. Click the **Select Source File** button and browse to the Excel file that we created earlier.
3. Select the checkbox to **Use the first row as column headers.**
4. Click **Import.**

The spreadsheet data loads into the modeler. The **Details** side panel contains settings for the model, as shown in Figure 8.6.

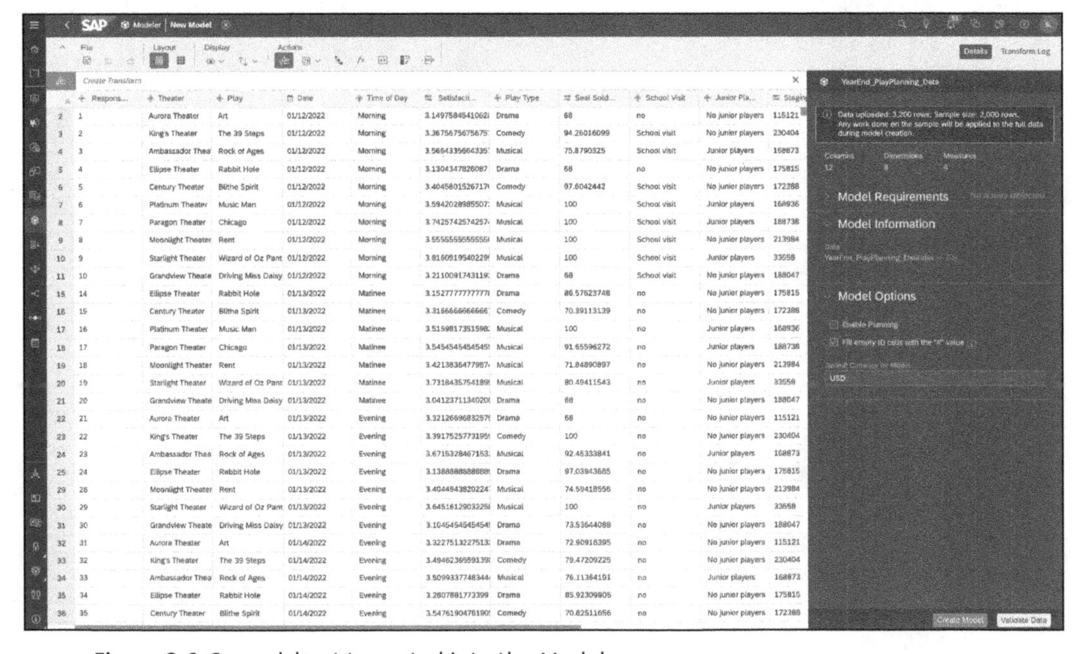

Figure 8.6 Spreadsheet Imported into the Modeler

At the top of the **Details** panel, you'll see general information about the data, such as an information box that states that only a sample size of 2,000 row was uploaded and during model creation the settings will be applied to the full dataset. It also shows the number of columns, dimensions, and measures. It will also indicate if there are any issues with the data.

Preparing the Data

SAP Analytics Cloud automatically designates columns as dimensions, accounts, or dates. Julia needs to check each column to see that they are correct. She uses these steps:

1. For each column, check that the data looks as expected. Specifically, look at the column type (dimension, account, date) and look at the data distribution.
2. If the column type is incorrect, reassign the column type. In the modeler table view, when a measure column is presented as a dimension, reassign the column type.
   - Click the column header.
   - In the **Modeling** section of the **Details** panel, click in the **Type** dropdown list and select the correct type (see Figure 8.7).

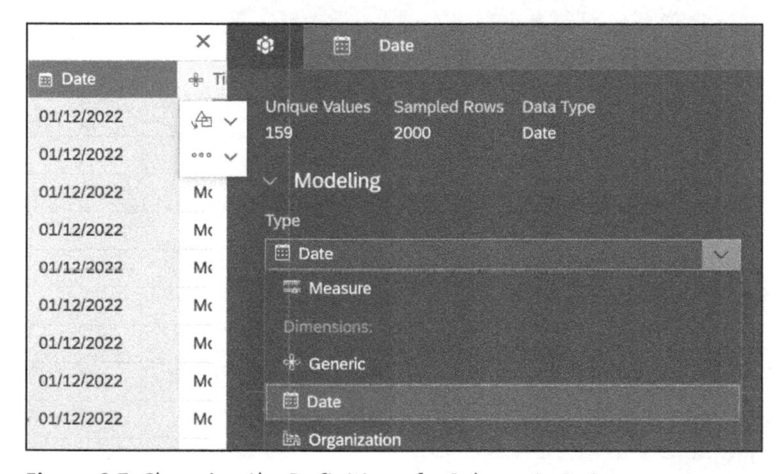

Figure 8.7 Changing the Definition of a Column to Date

3. If the distribution reveals issues, modify the data in the columns by using the **Create a Transform** or **Convert Case** menu items in the column's action menu. However, since Julia is importing from a spreadsheet, it may be easier to fix the data in the spreadsheet and import the spreadsheet again.
4. If required, delete, hide, or duplicate columns to modify your data before creating the model. Since Julia cleaned the data in the spreadsheet, this step is not required.
5. Create any desired hierarchies. Make a hierarchy with **Play Type** and **Play** by clicking the **Hierarchy** button. Add the **Play** dimension in the control at the bottom, then add the **Play Type** dimension in the node above (see Figure 8.8).

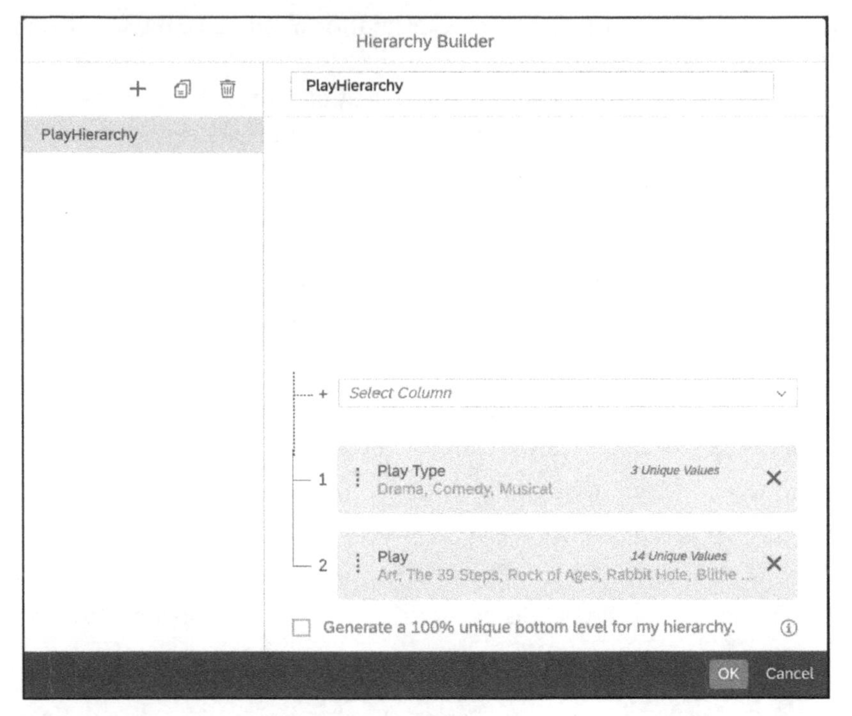

Figure 8.8 Build the Play Type to Play Hierarchy

6. Now, click **Validate Data** so SAP Analytics Cloud can run a check on the changes made.
7. Click **Create Model** and give it a name and browse to where the model will be stored.

This completes the data preparation. The model is now saved, which will be the data source for Alex's play analysis dashboard that Julia is creating.

Note

You can check out the SAP Analytics Cloud official documentation for complete information on model options at the SAP Help Portal: *http://s-prs.co/v523501*.

In the next sections, we'll follow Julia's process for designing the dashboard and determining which features to include. After the design phase, we'll start building the dashboard.

8.3 Dashboard Features

We now have the data required to build the dashboard, but first we need to determine what specific questions Alex would like answered in this dashboard so that the dashboard is designed and structured well.

The plays have variable costs based on the number of actors in the plays and on the staging expense. Alex wants to select the type of plays that resonate with the audience to ensure as much income as possible to cover the costs. At the same time, he wants to offer a variety of plays to satisfy most audience preferences.

He will be looking for which types of play and which plays specifically were most successful, as measured by seat sales and customer satisfaction. He will want to compare this with the costs involved in producing the plays. Once he figures out the mix of type of play (drama, comedy, musical) that he'd like to offer, he may want to focus on each play type to understand the success of the plays within the genre.

Julia created a three-page dashboard. On the first page, Alex can explore the metrics. On the second page, he will be able to compare the metrics to find optimal plays, that is, the plays with the lowest cost and the highest success metrics. On the third page, he will also see the metrics compared by theater location. His theater company has several regional theater locations, and so he will also be looking for regional differences. On each of these pages, he will be able to filter for any of the metrics that he finds interesting.

Normally, Alex's company likes everything to be designed with their branding, including their logo and photo-banner. But since this is an internal tool only, it will not be needed.

See the three dashboard pages shown previously in Figure 8.1, Figure 8.2, and Figure 8.3.

8.4 Building an Efficient Dashboard

Now that we have the data, and we know what we want the dashboard to look like and how the user can interact with it, we can start building the dashboard. We'll discuss the steps to build each dashboard page in the following sections.

8.4.1 Building the Dashboard Page 1 (Metrics)

To create the dashboard canvas with a page title, Julia does the following steps:

1. In the side navigation, select **Stories** and then choose **Canvas** from the **Create New** area.
2. Select **Optimized Design Experience** when prompted.
3. In the **Assets** panel (on the left), under **Containers**, drag and drop **Panel** to the canvas and move it to the top left and resize it to be wide and not very tall.
4. Drag and drop a **Text** widget from the **Widgets** section in the **Assets** panel into the panel created in the previous step. Move it near the upper left.
5. Click in the text widget and add the title, "2022 Year-End Play Analysis."

6. Select the title text and in the **Styling** panel (on the right), set the **Text type** to **Header 1** in the **Font** section.
7. Select the panel that was added to the canvas and in the **Styling** panel, in the **Widget** section, click the **Background Color** color picker and select white.
8. In the **Widget** section, set the **Border** to **Bottom Border. Style, Color**, and **Line Width** controls will appear.
9. Set the border **Color** to the desired color. She chose a blue.
10. Set the **Line Width** to **4**.
11. Deselect the panel so that no widget should be selected. In the **Canvas** section of the **Styling** panel, and set the **Background Color** to the desired color. She chose a very pale gray (hex F3F5F7).
12. To change the page tab name, click on the down icon next to the **Page_1** page name and select **Edit Title** (see Figure 8.9). The **Page_1** name is replaced with an edit control. Type "Metrics."

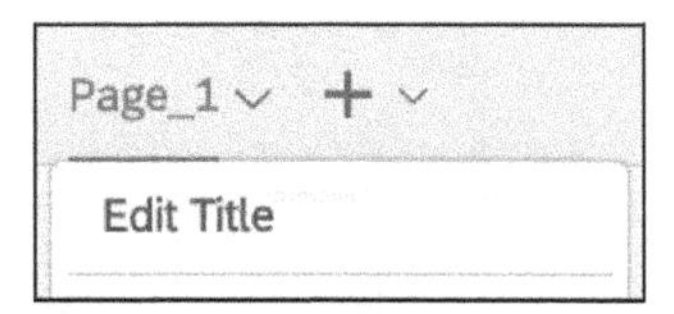

Figure 8.9 Change Name of the Page by Clicking the Down Icon next to "Page_1"

Julia is now ready to add charts to the canvas area. She will add headers to each set of charts:

1. To add a heading above the charts showing success metrics, in the **Assets** panel under **Widgets**, drag and drop **Text** to the canvas.
2. Set the title to "Success Metrics" and position it below the header panel.

To add a bar chart to the dashboard to show **Seat Sold Rate per Play**, she follows these steps:

1. In the **Assets** panel under **Widgets**, drag and drop **Chart** to the canvas and place it under the **Success Metrics** title. It will ask which model to use. Select the model that we created earlier.
2. Select the chart and in the **Styling** panel in the **Widget** section, set the **Background Color** to white.
3. In the **Widget** section, set the **Border** to **All Borders**.
4. Set the border **Color** to a gray that is only slightly darker than the background color. She chose hex E5E8EA.
5. Set the **Corner Radius** to **10px** by dragging the slider.
6. In the **Builder** panel, click **+ At least 1 Account required**.

7. To show the average satisfaction, click **+ Add Calculation**. As shown in Figure 8.10, specify the following fields:
   - **Type: Aggregation**
   - **Name: Average Seat Sold Rate**
   - **Operation: AVERAGE excl. NULL**
   - **Account: Seat Sold Rate**
   - **Aggregation Dimensions: Response ID**

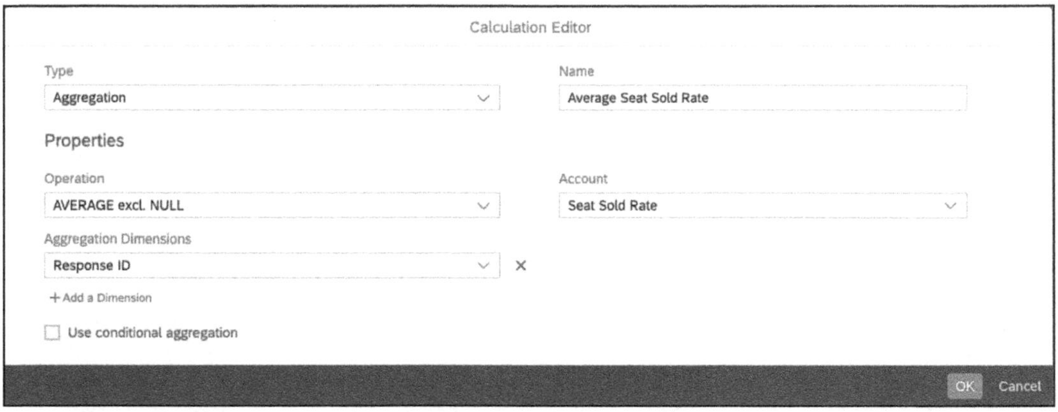

Figure 8.10 Create the Average Seat Sold Rate Aggregated Account

8. Click **+ Add Dimension** and select **Play**.
9. To show the play level of the **PlayHierarchy**, select the hierarchy button on the **Play** dimension in the **Builder** panel and select **Level 3** (see Figure 8.11).

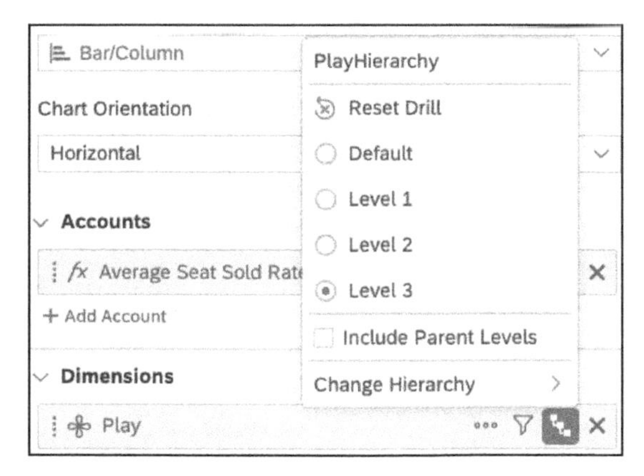

Figure 8.11 Set the Play Dimension to Show Level 3 of the Hierarchy So That It Shows the Play Names

10. To color by play type, under the **Color** section, click **+ Add Dimension/Account** and select **Play Type**.

11. She changes the colors by selecting an existing color palette from the color palette dropdown by clicking **+ Create New Palette** in the color dropdown. She wants to use IBCS coloring, so she created a new palette.

    She needs only the first three colors that will correspond to the play type—comedy, drama, and musical. For each, select the colored circle and set its color. She used neutral colors: hex 354A5F, hex 8494A8, and hex C5CED8 (see Figure 8.12).

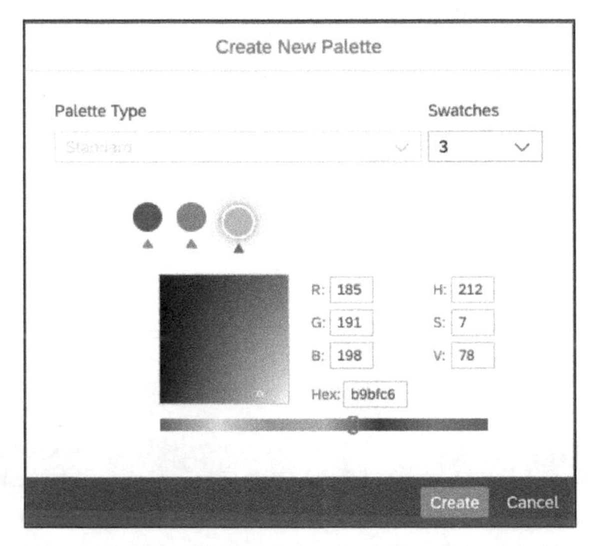

Figure 8.12 Modify the Colors in a New Color Palette

12. Scale the bars so that they can range from 0% to 100% values. When this is applied to all charts showing the seat sold rate, they will all be scaled the same so that the bar lengths will have the same scale across the various bar charts. From the **Action Menu** (ellipsis button), select **Edit Axis** and enter a **Minimum Value** of 0 and a **Maximum Value** of 1, which represents 100%.
13. Move the legend to the bottom. With the chart selected, open the **Styling** panel, and in the **Legend** section, select the placement option **Below Chart**.
14. She wants the whole percentages reported. In the **Styling** panel in the **Number Format** section, set **Decimal Places** to 0.
15. To be IBCS compliant, change the axis labels to be darker. In the **Styling** panel in the **Font** section, change the color to black.
16. Change the title of the chart slightly by removing "Play Type" by simply editing the title in place. The title is now "Seat Sold Rate per Play."

The chart now shows the average seat sold rate for each of the play and is colored by play type (see Figure 8.13).

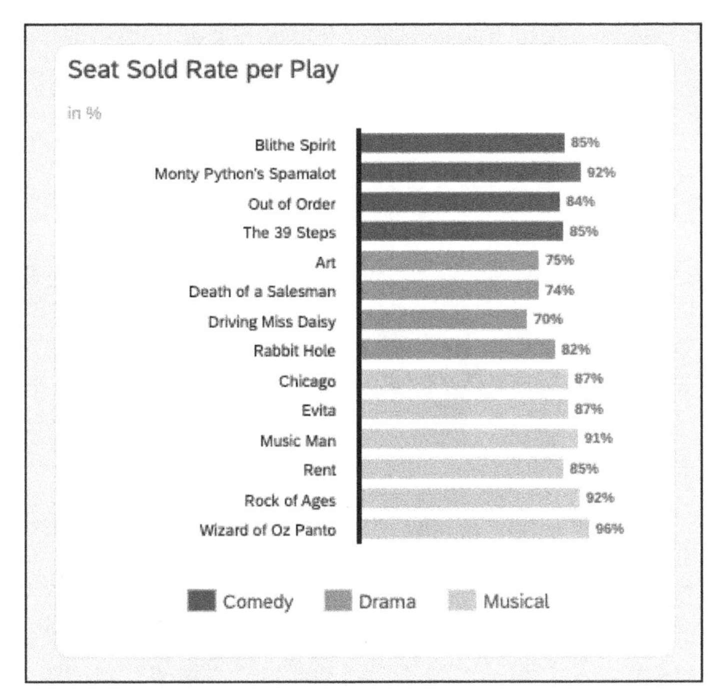

Figure 8.13 Seat Sold Rate per Play Bar Chart

Next, Julia will add a bar chart to show the **Patron Satisfaction per Play.** This chart is very similar to the **Seat Sold Rate** chart. She can either follow similar steps, or she can copy the chart and modify the account that is used to show the satisfaction scores. By copying, the tile styling will already be set.

To copy and modify the chart, Julia does the following steps:

1. Select the **Seat Sold Rate** chart and click the **Action Menu** button.
2. Select **Copy • Duplicate.** SAP Analytics Cloud will create a copy of the chart. She moves it where she likes it, to the right of the previous chart.
3. Select the new chart and, in the **Builder** panel, remove the existing account and click the **+ At least 1 Account required** button.
4. Repeat the steps in the first chart to create an **Average Satisfaction** account.
5. In the **Styling** panel, set **Decimal Places** to 1.
6. From the **Action Menu** (ellipsis button), select **Edit Axis** and enter a **Minimum Value** of 0 and a **Maximum Value** of 4.
7. Change the title to "Satisfaction per Play."
8. Resize the chart to ensure all the play bars are shown without scrolling.

She'll now add a bar chart to show the **Secondary Sales per Play.** This chart is very similar to the previous two charts, although she doesn't need an average for secondary sales:

1. Duplicate one of the previous charts and move it to the right of the previous chart.
2. When adding the account, simply select **Secondary Sales**. This will total the secondary sales.
3. To show the numbers as currency, select the chart, open the **Styling** panel, and in the **Number Format** section, set **Decimal Places** to 0. She could have also decided to leave the **Scale** unformatted or as **Thousand**.
4. From the **Action Menu** (ellipsis button), select **Edit Axis** and enter a **Minimum Value** of 0 and a **Maximum Value** of a value that seems reasonable given the data that you are seeing. In this case, she chose 700. Note that, after the other charts based on the same metric are added, she re-evaluated to see if the chosen maximum is appropriate for all charts.
5. Change the title to "Secondary Sale per Play."

Some plays have junior cast members who are typically aged 9 to 14 and don't have speaking roles. They come on and as a group dance across the stage or become part of the staging. Julia expects that they may have more seats sold or greater satisfaction as their family members or classmates come to see them in the show. To add a bar chart to show the seat sold rate for junior player involvement, Julia will follow these steps:

1. Duplicate the **Seat Sold Rate per Play** chart and move it below the chart that was copied.
2. Change **Dimensions** to **Junior Players**.
3. Remove the **Color** by **Play Type** setting.
4. Set the **Decimal Places** to 0 in the **Styling** panel **Number Format** section.
5. Select the color palette that we created earlier so that the bars use a darker gray color.
6. Modifying the axis scaling is not required as it was inherited from the copied chart.
7. Change the title to "Seat Sold Rate by inclusion of Junior Players."
8. Size the chart to be shorter as there are only two bars in the bar chart.

Next, she'll add a bar chart to show the seat sold rate for the time of day using these steps:

1. Duplicate the **Seat Sold Rate with Junior Players** chart and move it below the chart that was copied.
2. Change the **Dimensions** to **Time of Day**.
3. Modifying the axis scaling is not required as it was inherited from the copied chart.
4. Change the title to "Seat Sold Rate by Time of Day."

She'll now add a bar chart to show the seat sold rate for school visits using these steps:

1. Duplicate the **Seat Sold Rate with Junior Players** chart and move it below the chart that was copied.
2. Change the **Dimensions** to **School Visits**.

3. Modifying the axis scaling is not required as it was inherited from the copied chart.
4. Change the title to "Seat Sold Rate for School Visits."

Next, she'll add a bar chart to show satisfaction for junior player involvement:

1. Duplicate the **Seat Sold Rate with Junior Players** chart and move it to the right of the chart that was copied.
2. Change the **Accounts** to **Average Satisfaction**.
3. Scale the chart by selecting the action button, then select **Edit Axis** and enter a **Minimum Value** of 0 and a **Maximum Value** of 4.
4. Change the title to "Satisfaction by inclusion of Junior Players."

She'll also add a bar chart to show satisfaction for time of day:

1. Duplicate the **Satisfaction by inclusion of Junior Players** chart and move it to the below the chart that was copied.
2. Change the **Dimensions** to **Time of Day**.
3. Modifying the axis scaling is not required as it was inherited from the copied chart.
4. Change the title to "Satisfaction by Time of Day."

Then, she'll add a bar chart to show satisfaction for school visits:

1. Duplicate the **Satisfaction by inclusion of Junior Players** chart and move it below the chart that was copied.
2. Change the **Dimensions** to **School Visits**.
3. Modifying the axis scaling is not required as it was inherited from the copied chart.
4. Change the title to "Satisfaction by School Visits."

To add a bar chart to show secondary sales for junior player involvement, she'll follow these steps:

1. Duplicate the **Satisfaction by inclusion of Junior Players** chart and move it to the right of the chart that was copied.
2. Change the **Accounts** to **Average Secondary Sales**.
3. Scale the chart by selecting **Action Button • Edit Axis** and enter a **Minimum Value** of 0 and a **Maximum Value** of the value used in the **Secondary Sales per Play** chart.
4. Change the title to "Secondary Sales by inclusion of Junior Players."

To add a bar chart to show **Secondary Sales by Time of Day**, she'll follow these steps:

1. Duplicate the **Secondary Sales by inclusion of Junior Players** chart and move it below the chart that was copied.
2. Change the **Accounts** to **Average Secondary Sales**.
3. Modifying the axis scaling is not required as it was inherited from the copied chart.
4. Change the title to "Secondary Sales by Time of Day."

To add a bar chart to show secondary sales for school visits, she'll follow these steps:

1. Duplicate the **Secondary Sales by Time of Day** chart and move it below the chart that was copied.
2. Change the **Accounts** to **Average Secondary Sales**.
3. Modifying the axis scaling is not required as it was inherited from the copied chart.
4. Change the title to "Secondary Sales for School Visits."

To add a heading below the previous charts and above the charts showing expenses, she'll follow these steps:

1. In the **Assets** panel under **Widgets**, drag and drop **Text** to the canvas below the charts that have been created so far.
2. Set the title to "Expenses per Play" and position it below the charts that are on canvas already. This will allow us to not specify "per Play" on each chart to be added below.

Next, she'll add a bar chart to show the cast size per play. This chart is very similar to the **Seat Sold Rate per Play** chart, which was the first chart we created. She will need to calculate the average cast size per play since there are multiple records for each play:

1. Duplicate the **Seat Sold Rate per Play** chart and move it below the first column of charts.
2. Repeat the steps described for the first chart to create an average cast size account, but name it "Cast Size" and set it as the chart **Account**.

   There is only a single cast size count per play. We must calculate the average because we imported the data in a denormalized form that repeated the cast size for every record.
3. Since there are no fractional cast members, set **Decimal Places** to 0 in the **Styling** panel.
4. Change the title to "Cast Size."

As with the cast size chart, Julia will need to calculate the staging cost per play using these steps:

1. Duplicate the previous cast size chart and move it to the right.
2. Repeat the steps in the first chart to create an average staging cost account, although name it "Staging Cost." Like cast size, there is only a single staging cost per play.
3. To show only whole dollars, set **Decimal Places** to 0 in the **Styling** panel.
4. Change the title to "Staging Cost."

Finally, she'll add filters in the header panel using these steps:

1. From the **Assets** panel in the **Widgets** section, drag an **Input Control** widget to the header panel until the title text.
2. Click on the down button in the **Input Control** and select **Dimensions • Play • Play Type** (see Figure 8.14).

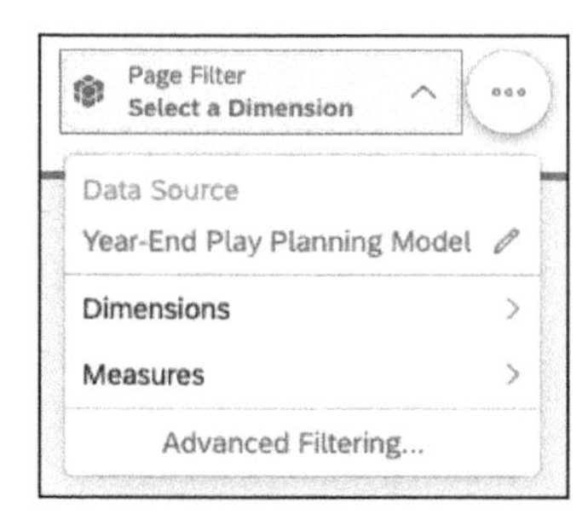

Figure 8.14 Add Input Control Filter

3. Upon adding the filter, SAP Analytics Cloud shows a tip warning beside the tab name. Hover over the warning icon to see the details. It states that you are using process-heavy widgets and should consider using less widgets or less process-heavy widgets (See Figure 8.15).

   Since Julia followed golden rules #2 and #3 when aggregating and modeling the data, it may not be too much of an issue. She saves the dashboard and tries to view it. She also asks a colleague to do the same from a different computer. Loading the dashboard is still fast enough, so she ignores this tip.

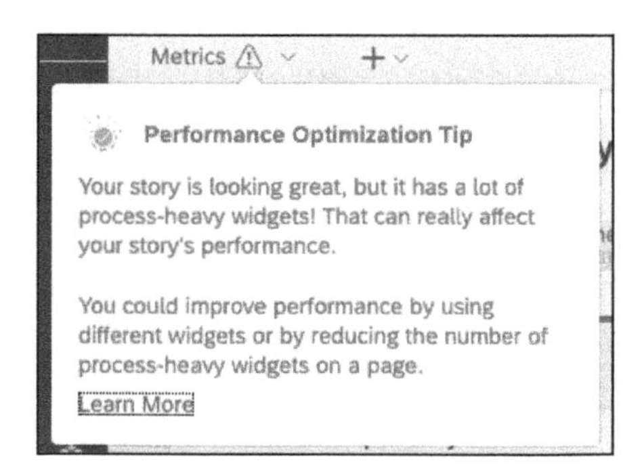

Figure 8.15 Performance Optimization Tip Popup

4. Repeat these steps to create an input control for each of the following: **Theater, Junior Players, School Visits,** and **Time of Day.**

This completes the creation of the first page (refer back to Figure 8.1).

8.4.2 Building the Dashboard Page 2 (Comparison)

The charts on the first **Metrics** page will allow Alex to look at individual metrics per play. Now Julia wants to add charts to allow Alex to see how these metrics relate. She will add a new page in the same visual style and will add multiple scatter plots.

Julia starts by adding a second page and preparing it with the header and background color:

1. Click the new page button and select **Add Canvas Page**. See Figure 8.16.

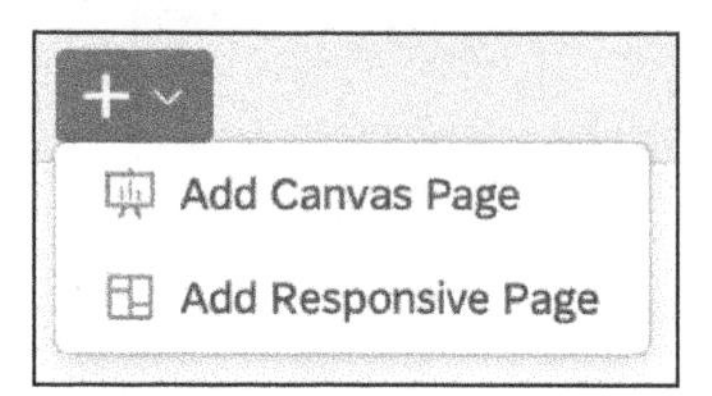

Figure 8.16 Add a New Page by Clicking the + Button and Selecting Add Canvas Page

2. On the new page, set the canvas **Background Color** to the very pale gray used in the previous page.

To add the title header panel and a heading above the charts, Julia does the following steps:

1. On the **Metrics** page, select the title header panel and click the **Action Menu** and select **Copy • Copy To • Page_2**. See Figure 8.17. It will copy all the elements that are in the panel with it.

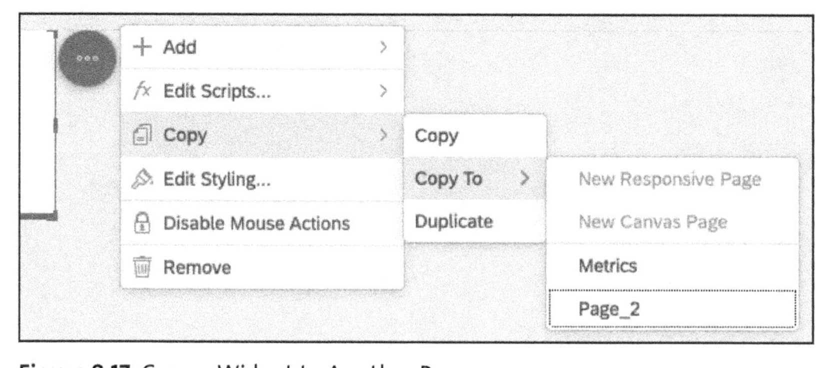

Figure 8.17 Copy a Widget to Another Page

2. In the **Assets** panel under **Widgets**, drag and drop **Text** to the canvas.
3. Set the title to "Success Metrics" and position it below the title header panel.

Julia is now ready to add charts to the canvas area. To add a scatter plot chart to show **Seat Sold Rate versus Cast Size**, she follows these steps:

1. To use the same size, color, and rounded corners as the charts on the **Metrics** page, copy the **Seat Sold Rate per Play** bar chart to **Page_2** in the same way the title header panel was copied.
2. In the **Builder** panel, change the **Currently Selected Chart** to **Scatterplot**.
3. Set **X-Axis** to the calculation **Cast Size**.
4. Set **Y-Axis** to **Average Seat Sold Rate**.
5. Change the title to "Seat Sold Rate vs Cast Size."

To add a similar scatter plot to show **Satisfaction versus Cast Size**, Julia follows these steps to duplicate and modify the previous chart by following these steps:

1. Duplicate the **Seat Sold Rate vs Cast Size** scatter plot and move it to the right.
2. In the **Builder** panel, change the **Y-Axis** to **Average Satisfaction**.
3. Change the title to "Satisfaction vs Cast Size."

To add a scatter plot to show satisfaction versus seat sales, she again duplicates and modifies the previous chart by following these steps:

1. Duplicate the **Satisfaction vs Cast Size** scatter plot chart and move it to the right.
2. In the **Builder** panel, change the **X-Axis** to **Average Seat Sold Rate**.
3. Change the title to "Satisfaction vs Seat Sales."

To add a scatter plot to show **Seat Sold Rate vs Staging Cost**, she duplicates and modifies a previous chart by following these steps:

1. Duplicate the **Seat Sold Rate vs Cast Size** scatter plot chart and move it below.
2. Change the **X-Axis** to the calculation **Staging Cost**.
3. Change the title to "Seat Sold Rate vs Staging Cost."

To add a scatter plot to show **Satisfaction versus Staging Cost**, she again duplicates and modifies the previous chart by following these steps:

1. Duplicate the **Seat Sold Rate vs Staging Cost** scatter plot chart and move it to the right.
2. Change the **Y-Axis** to the calculation **Average Satisfaction**.
3. Change the title to "Satisfaction vs Staging Cost."

Finally, Julia changes the tab name for this page to "Comparisons" by clicking on the down icon next to the **Page_2** name and select **Edit Title**. The **Page_1** name is replaced with an edit control. Type "Comparisons."

This completes the creation of the second page (refer back to Figure 8.2).

8.4.3 Building the Dashboard Page 3 (Theaters)

Now Julia wants to add charts to allow Alex to look for theater (regional) differences. She will add a new page in the same visual style and will add multiple bar charts that show metrics per theater.

Julia adds a third page and prepares it will the header and background color by following these steps:

1. Follow the steps described for the second page to create a new page and to set the page tab name to "Theaters."
2. Set the canvas background color and copy the title header panel.
3. Add a **Text** widget to the canvas below the title header and set the name to "Success Metrics Per Play Type Per Theater."

She is now ready to add the charts. She adds the bar charts by copying other charts and modifying the details. She adds a bar chart to show **Seat Sold Rate per Play Type per Theater** by following these steps:

1. To use the same styling for other bar chart tiles, copy the first bar chart from the **Metrics** page to this page.
2. In the **Build** panel, add **Theater** as a second **Dimension**. And reorder the dimensions by dragging and dropping so that **Theater** is above **Play**.
3. To show **Play Type** in the bar chart instead of **Play**, change the hierarchy level of **Play** to **Level 2**. See Figure 8.11, but choose **Level 2**.
4. Resize the chart widget so it is tall enough to show all the bars without a scrollbar.
5. Modifying the axis scaling is not required as it was inherited from the copied chart.
6. Change the title to "Seat Sold Rate."

To add a bar chart to show **Satisfaction per Play Type per Theater**, Julia follows these steps:

1. Copy the bar chart for **Seat Sold Rate per Play Type per Theater** and move it to the right.
2. Change the **Account** to **Average Satisfaction**.
3. Scale the chart by selecting action button • **Edit Axis** and enter a **Minimum Value** of 0 and a **Maximum Value** of 4.
4. Change the title to "Satisfaction."

To add a bar chart to show **Secondary Sales per Play Type per Theater**, she follows these steps:

1. Copy the bar chart for **Seat Sold Rate per Play Type per Theater** and move it to the right.

2. Change the **Account** to **Average Secondary Sales**.
3. Scale the chart by selecting the action button and then select **Edit Axis** and enter a **Minimum Value** of 0 and a **Maximum Value** of the value used in the **Secondary Sales per Play** chart.
4. Change the title to "Secondary Sales."

She wants to add more bar charts that simply show the metrics per theater without a breakdown by play type. She wants to create a title separator, so she adds a text header by adding a **Text** widget to the canvas below bar charts and set the name to "Success Metrics Per Theater."

To add a bar chart to show **Seat Sold Rate per Theater**, she follows these steps:

1. Copy the bar chart for **Seat Sold Rate per Play Type per Theater** and move it below the text header.
2. Remove **Play** from the **Dimensions** setting.
3. Remove **Play Type** from the **Color** setting.
4. Modifying the axis scaling is not required as it was inherited from the copied chart.
5. Change the title to "Seat Sold Rate."
6. Resize the chart to be shorter as there are less bars shown.

To add a bar chart to show **Satisfaction per Theater**, she follows these steps:

1. Copy the bar chart for **Satisfaction per Play Type per Theater**.
2. Remove **Play** from the **Dimensions** setting.
3. Remove **Play Type** from the **Color** setting.
4. Modifying the axis scaling is not required as it was inherited from the copied chart.
5. Change the title to "Satisfaction."
6. Resize the chart to be shorter.

To add a bar chart to show **Average Secondary Sale per Theater**, she follows these steps:

1. Copy the bar chart for **Average Secondary Sales per Play Type per Theater**.
2. Remove **Play** from the **Dimensions** setting.
3. Remove **Play Type** from the **Color** setting.
4. Modifying the axis scaling is not required as it was inherited from the copied chart.
5. Change the title to "Satisfaction."
6. Resize the chart to be shorter.

This completes the creation of the last page (refer back to Figure 8.3).

Steps to be IBCS Compliant

Although IBCS compliance is not the focus of this book, it is recommended to design your dashboards to be IBCS compliant for better readability. To learn more about IBCS, visit *www.ibcs.com*.

The following steps were taken for the dashboard in this chapter to be IBCS compliant:

- **Use bar charts where possible.**
  Don't use different chart types just for visual interest.
- **Use horizontal bar charts for non-time-based dimensions.**
  Bars should be vertical along the x-axis to represent time. Otherwise, the bars should be horizontal along the y-axis.
- **Use the same axis scaling for all chart with the same measure.**
  The length of the bars should be consistent for a given measure across bar charts.
- **Try to make the bar widths similar.**
  Bar widths should be roughly similar; however, this is not always possible with SAP Analytics Cloud. You can control the bar width only by changing the entire chart's height. For the charts with only two bars, we can't make the chart small enough to make the bar widths like the bar charts with many bars.
- **Choose neutral colors.**
  Primarily use a dark gray or dark blue if only one color is required. Use shades of gray if multiple colors are required.
- **Choose a darker color for axis labels.**
  By default, the axis labels are a light gray. IBCS requires a dark gray or black for axis and legend labels.
- **Choose titles that describe the measure with dimension breakdowns.**
  E.g., Satisfaction (as the measure) per Play Type (as a dimension) per Theater (as a dimension).
- **Move some of the title details to a headers area.**
  E.g., Success Metrics per Play Type per Theater as a header. This allows you to remove the "per Play Type per Theater" text from each of the following charts.

Golden Rule #5 – Information Architecture

Julia also made choices to improve the performance of the dashboard that correspond to golden rule #5:

- **Use optimized design experience.**
  When she created the dashboard, SAP Analytics Cloud prompted her to use the optimized design experience. She selected this option.
- **Avoided too much blending.**
  She pulled all the data together in a spreadsheet rather than blending the spreadsheet data with a live connection backend source.

- **Avoid fancy charts or heavy images.**
  During the initial design concept (Section 8.3 Section 8.3), she decided not to use their photo banner as branding.
- **Reduce number of charts per page.**
  She spread the charts across three pages. This speeds the loading time of each page.
- **Use story and page filters instead of widget filters.**
  She used page filters in the title header area that apply to all the charts in the canvas area below.

To compare performance improvements afforded by applying the golden rules, Julia created a separate model and dashboard that did not apply the golden rules. That is, the spreadsheet data was not aggregated and contained 1.4 million records, and the dashboard was a single page dashboard with all the charts on the one page. Table 8.1 shows that by applying the golden rules there are significant performance improvements.

Dashboard	Time to load
Dashboard applying golden rules	8.8 seconds
Dashboard without applying golden rules	15.3 seconds

Table 8.1 Time to Load the Dashboard That Applied Golden Rules versus the Dashboard That Did Not Apply Golden Rules

Important Note

For testing, we used the following computer: MacBook Pro (16-inch, 2021), macOS Monterey Version 12.5.1, Apple M1 Pro (chip), 10 cores (8 performance and 2 efficiency), 16 GB RAM.

When Alex uses the dashboard, he looks at each page in turn and then filters by specific metrics when he sees something interesting. He bookmarks interesting pages as he wants to share what he found with his board of directors. When he presents to the board, he wants to ensure good performance, so he ensures that he has access to a Chrome browser at the board meeting. The meeting was held when there were few staff at the theater. Also, he knows that he has high bandwidth when on-site at the theater. Just to be sure everything will go smoothly, he preloads the dashboard just before the meeting begins.

Golden Rule #10 – Viewer Choices

Alex made choices to improve the performance of the dashboard that correspond to golden rule #10:

- *Use Chrome* – He normally uses Chrome, but he ensured that the computer that he would be presenting with at the Board meeting had a Chrome browser.
- *Ensure high enough bandwidth* – The theater has a high-bandwidth internet connection and high-bandwidth WiFi router.
- *Avoid other network-heavy operations* – The board meeting was held in off-hours when there were few other staff. So, it is unlikely that there will be network-heavy traffic during the meeting.
- *Preload the dashboard* – He preloads the dashboard just before the meeting starts.

8.5 Summary

We've finished creating Julia's and Alex's dashboard. We've followed the dashboard design lifecycle from defining what analysis features the dashboard should support to building the dashboard and presenting the play analysis findings at a board meeting. Along the way, Julia and Alex made decisions to ensure a performing dashboard.

Chapter 8 was the first chapter in the book on the design of an actual efficient dashboard. We compared the well-designed dashboard with a similar dashboard that did not follow the performance recommendations, which helped to illustrate how helpful the golden rules for efficient SAP Analytics Cloud dashboards can be.

The next two chapters will explore different aspects of building efficient dashboards. Chapter 9 will explain how to design an efficient dashboard based on live data connections.

Chapter 9
Optimized Dashboard Using Live Data Connection

In this chapter, we'll create two dashboards using an SAP BW and an SAP HANA live data connection. The performance of these dashboards is optimized using the tips and tricks from the previous chapters.

In this chapter, we provide two end-to-end examples for creating an efficient dashboard using live data connections—one SAP BW and one SAP HANA live connection. When using live data connections, changes made to the data in the source system are reflected immediately, while data and the queries are processed in the backend system. We will build efficient dashboards on these live connections, thereby combining optimization methods covered earlier in the book.

9.1 Live Data Connection Scenarios

As covered in Chapter 5, for the optimal performance of a dashboard, we prefer using an acquired data model over the live data connection model. However, there are scenarios where it is crucial to use a live data connection or where the advantages of a live data connection outweigh the disadvantages. In this chapter, we go into more depth about these advantages and disadvantages and discuss scenarios in which live data connections would be chosen. These two scenarios cover different aspects of our theater. One of them covers net sales and the dependencies of net sales, and the second one covers the gross margin and further information like the influence of discounts.

Some criteria to consider for the data model decision are the following:

- Functional needs
- Data privacy constraints
- Data volume constraints

Further Resources

Further details and considerations about choosing a live connection and importing data can be found in this SAP Help section: *http://s-prs.co/v566938*.

9.1.1 Advantages and Disadvantages of a Live Data Connection

As described in Chapter 5, frequent data updates or lacking the capacity for regular database uploads are both reasons to use a live data connection. The frequent data update is a strong advantage, as live data connections make instant updates in real time possible. Thus, if the use case requires real-time data, live data connections should be chosen. Furthermore, the capacity for database uploads means that scheduling jobs for data input is not necessary anymore.

Additionally, there are advantages specific to data connections. For example, SAP BW components can be easily reused in the SAP Analytics Cloud live connection model. This covers hierarchies and variables, amongst others. Also, SAP BW query changes will be reflected immediately and directly in SAP Analytics Cloud, if they are embedded via a live data connection.

The two main disadvantages of a live data connection are linked to the performance and to the available SAP Analytics Cloud features:

- As discussed in Chapter 5, for the optimal performance of an SAP Analytics Cloud dashboard, acquired models will achieve better results compared to live data connections. Additionally, it is important to build the data queries for the live connection tuned to the requirements of the dashboard. But even with this improvement the overall performance will be worse compared to an acquired data model.
- The second main disadvantage of live data connections is that not all SAP Analytics Cloud features are fully supported (yet) in dashboards using live data models. Some examples are smart features like Search to Insight and prediction features. More details on this topic are described in Section 9.3.

Tip

Keep the following tip in mind if you are using live data connections: Every wave or every quarter, a list of new SAP Analytics Cloud features is released. We recommend to always check if those features are supported for live data connections before you try to test them or include them in your dashboards.

9.1.2 Scenario 1

In our first scenario, we are covering the net sales of our snacks and beverages of a theater. The data comes from a live connection data model built upon an SAP BW database. In our use case, this saves us capacity for manual or scheduled data upload. Furthermore, we can track the snack and beverage inventory of our theater locations in real time. Thus, if there are major events like a theater premiere in some of the locations, short notice updates and steering of the inventory can be done. For such use cases, real-time data is necessary.

Additionally, the **Net Sales** dashboard can also be used for a broader analysis like the development over time where there is a positive trend in net sales visible in 2022 compared to 2021. However, in the year 2021, there was a huge peak in December, which wasn't the case in the year 2022. This could now be further analyzed in the dashboard (drilling into the locations, special offers, number of plays, etc.) and externally (coming out of Covid restrictions, special guests, etc.).

The geo map shows clearly that there are locations that mainly drive the net sales of our beverages. To reduce the number of variables for a more detailed analysis, you could also filter on those main driving locations as a first step.

Further details of the functionalities (like custom-made hierarchies on SAP BW live connections) and further performance optimizations will be covered in the following chapters. Figure 9.1 shows the overview page of the **Net Sales** dashboard of our theater.

9

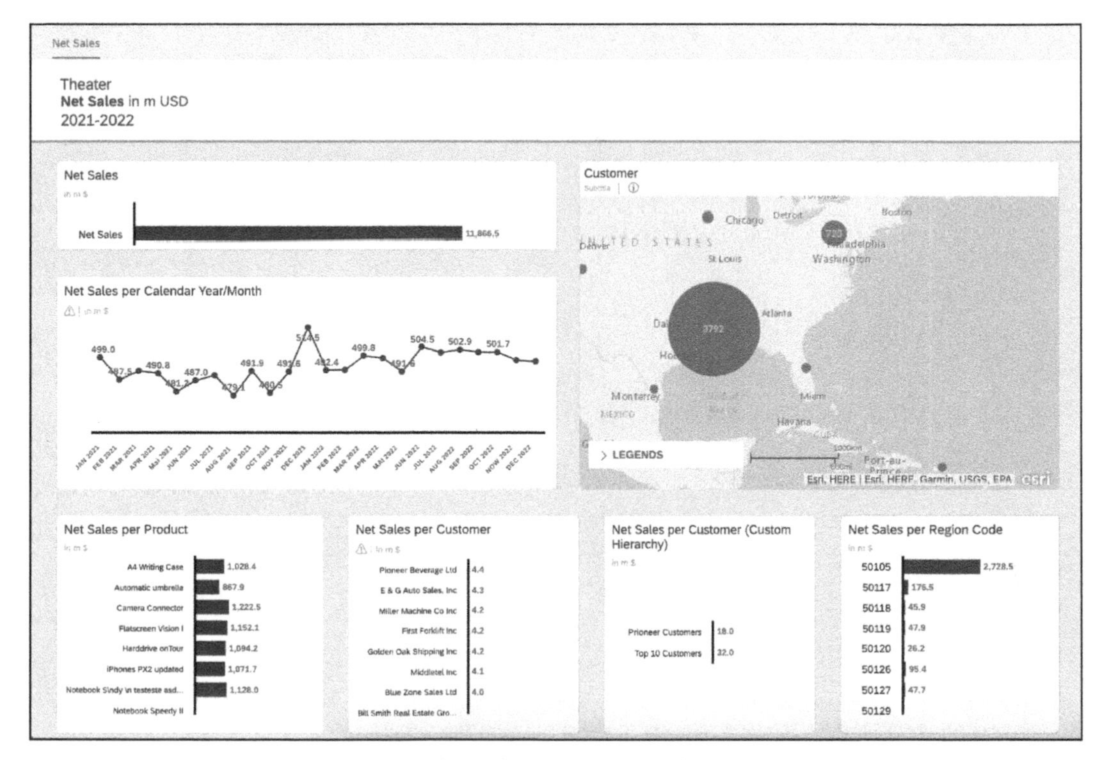

Figure 9.1 Scenario 1: Net Sales of Snacks and Beverages in a Theater

9.1.3 Scenario 2

This scenario covers another live data connection, this time set up with an SAP HANA live connection. The business content still covers our theater business steering. In this view, we do cover the gross margin and thus sales of beverages in the theater. The dashboard covers the gross margin, quantity sold as well as the influence of discounts on beverages sold.

As a general analysis, this overview would be totally fine as an acquired data dashboard for a review of the sold beverages after each month. However, such a dashboard could also be used to make real-time decisions during an evening or during the day.

If we compare the **Quantity Sold per Product** with our current stock amount, we will see if some beverages are running low or are getting close to being sold out. Thus, the theater manager can start steering immediately or inform the cashiers that some beverages are sold out. Additionally, this steering could include some real live discount options. If the market allows this, beverages that did not sell well during the day could be discounted during the next presentation in the evening, for example —not during the same play. For better discount decisions, the influence of the discount is directly shown in the same dashboard. You can view this dashboard in Figure 9.2.

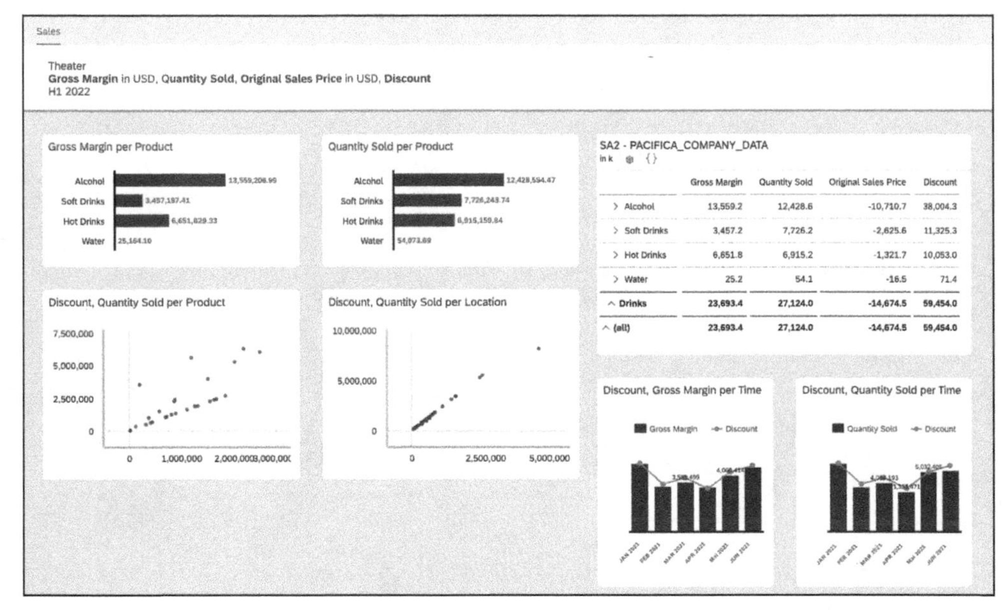

Figure 9.2 Scenario 2: Gross Margin, Quantity Sold, Original Sales, Price, and Discounts of Our Products

9.2 Data Structure

To understand the data structure, we will have a look at the SAP Analytics Cloud model based on these live connections. But first, we will have a look at how these live connections were set up in the following sections.

9.2.1 Creation of an SAP Business Warehouse Connection

Let us start with the SAP BW Live Connection that was used for Scenario 1 in Section 9.1.2. First, create a connection to your database using these steps:

1. Go to the **Connections** area in SAP Analytics Cloud (see Figure 9.3).
2. Click on the **+** sign to add a new connection.

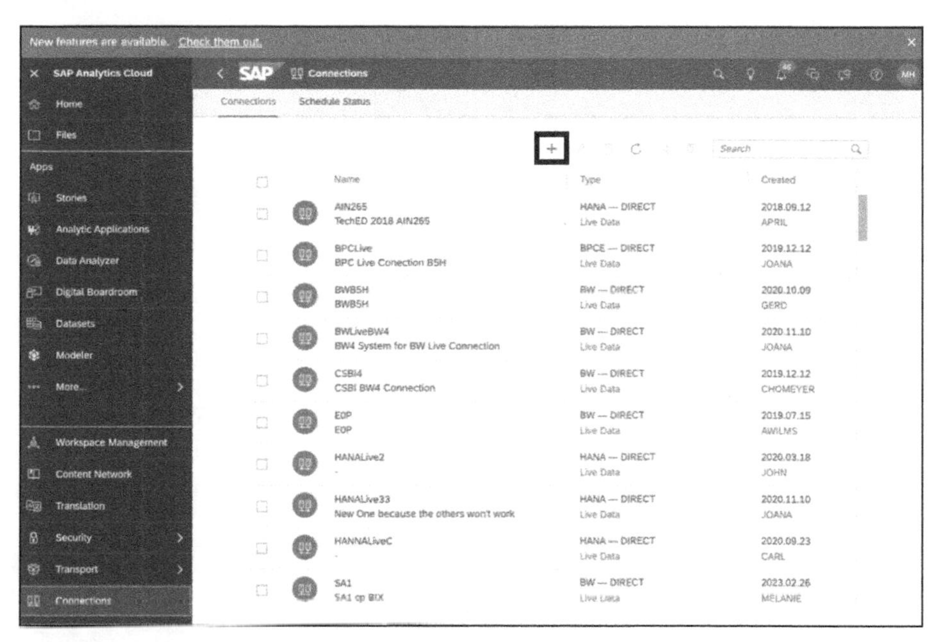

Figure 9.3 First Two Steps of Creating a Live Data Connection in SAP Analytics Cloud to an SAP BW Database

3. Expand **Connection to Live Data** (see Figure 9.4).
4. Click on **SAP BW**.

Figure 9.4 Step 3 and 4 of Creating a Live Data Connection in SAP Analytics Cloud to an SAP BW Database

5. Enter the **Connection Details** to your SAP BW live connection (see Figure 9.5).
6. Click **OK.**

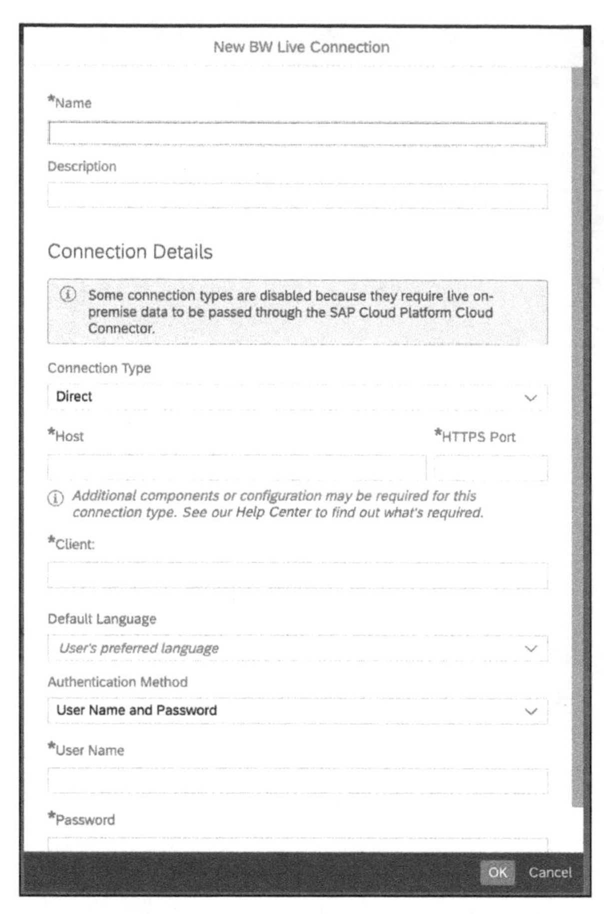

Figure 9.5 Final Step of Creating a Live Data Connection in SAP Analytics Cloud to Your SAP BW Database

> **Tip**
> Depending on the privacy settings of your live connection, you might need to enable your VPN client.

9.2.2 Creation of an SAP HANA Connection

The creation of an SAP HANA live connection is done in the same way as the creation of the SAP BW live connection. The only difference is to choose the SAP HANA connection instead of the SAP BW connection in Figure 9.4 in the **Connect to Live Data** area, and then insert your connection details in the window that opens for the SAP HANA live connection, as shown in Figure 9.6.

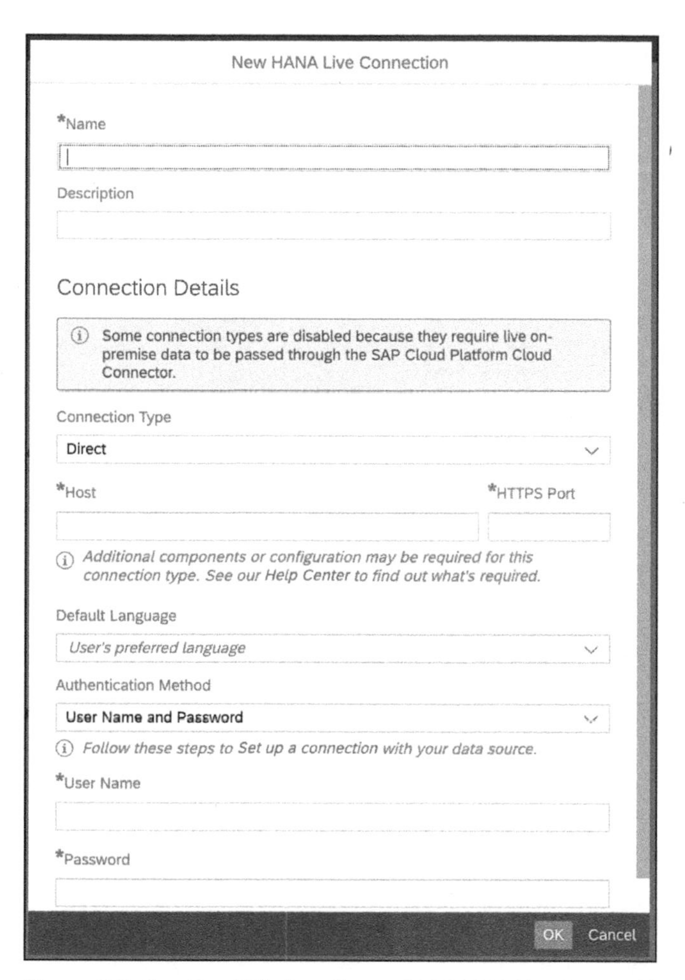

Figure 9.6 Creation Window for an SAP HANA Live Connection in SAP Analytics Cloud

9.2.3 Creation of a Model

Once the connection is created, we can continue with the creation of the model. This step is identical for both SAP BW and SAP HANA live connections and thus inserted once in this chapter only with the example of our created SAP BW live connection. You can create an SAP Analytics Cloud model based on this connection using these steps:

1. Go to the **Modeler** area in SAP Analytics Cloud (see Figure 9.7).
2. Click on **Live Data Model** to add a new model based on your live data connection.
3. Enter your **System Type** (**SAP BW**) and the name of the **Connection** you just created. (We named this connection **SA1**, as shown in Figure 9.8.)
4. Select the **Data Source** of your connection that you would like to use (these are the existing queries in your database). In our case, we used the data source **TEST_OD_DX_C01**.

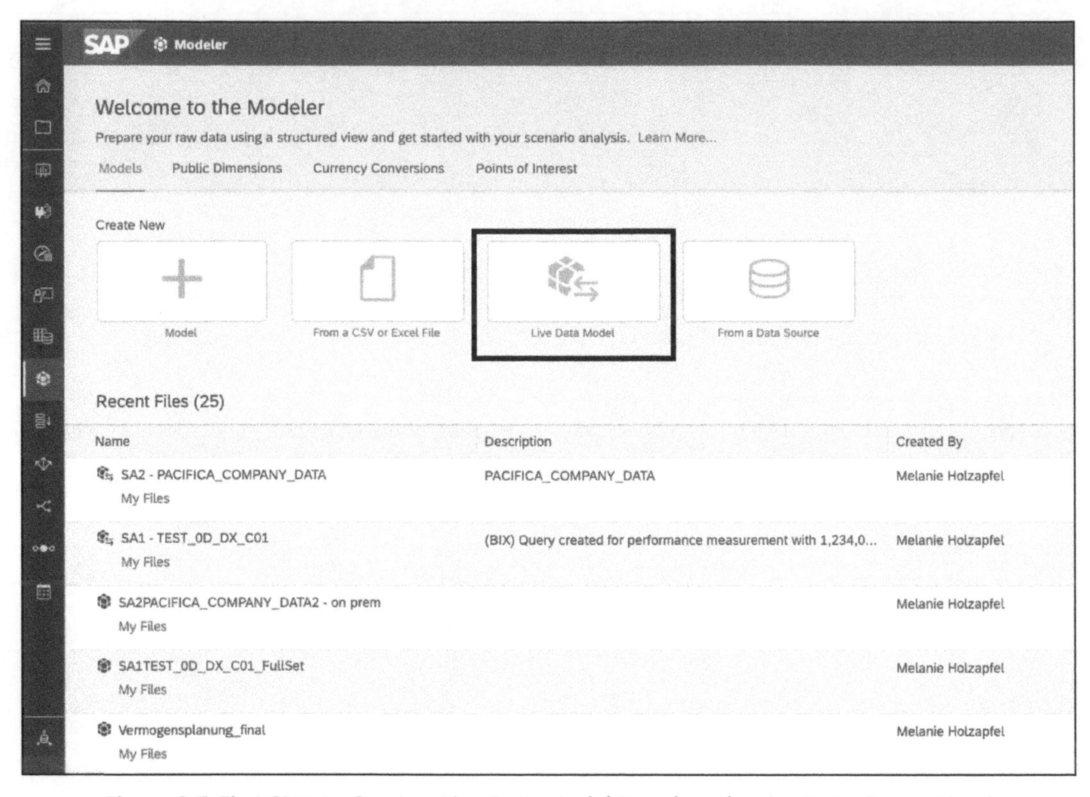

Figure 9.7 First Step to Create a Live Data Model Based on the Live Data Connection in SAP Analytics Cloud

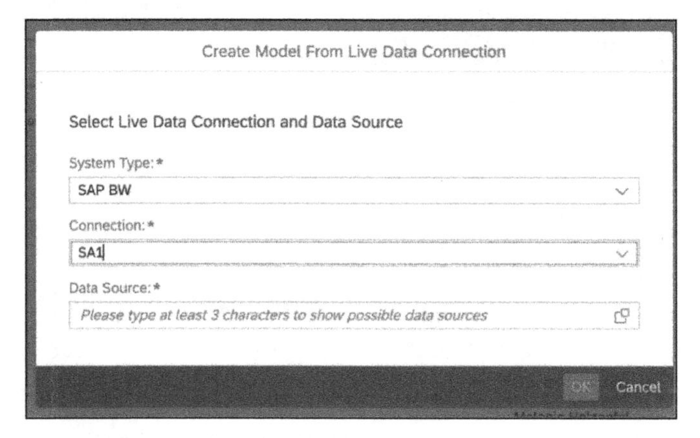

Figure 9.8 Insert Your System Type and Your Connection to Create an SAP Analytics Cloud Model Based on Your Live Data Connection

5. Now save your model by clicking **Save** (see Figure 9.9).
6. Based on this model, create your SAP Analytics Cloud dashboard as usual.

In our case, the selected query **TEST_0D_DX_C01** consists of 1,234,045 records and thus is perfect for performance testing.

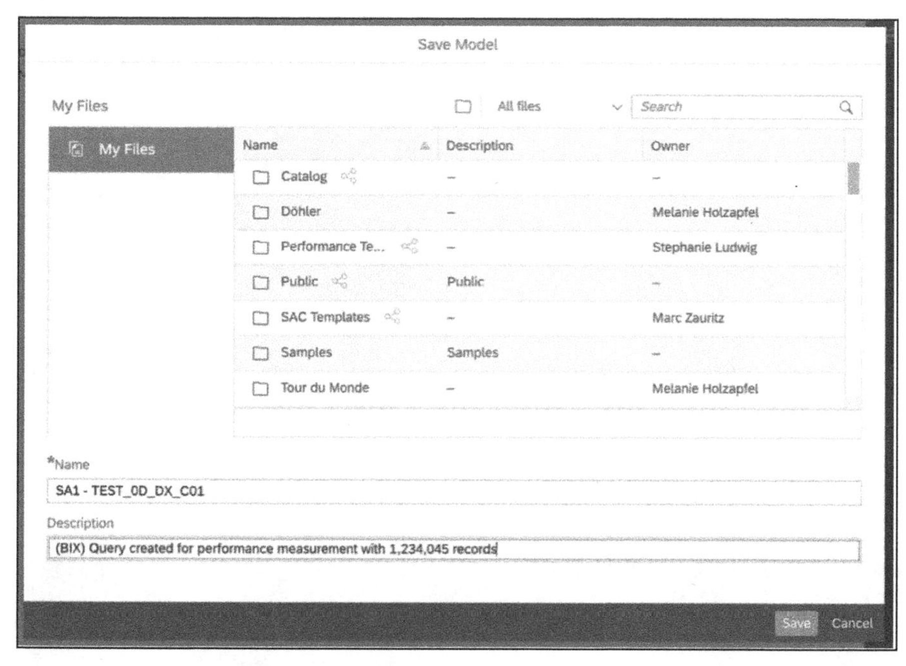

Figure 9.9 Save Your Final Model Based on Your Live Data Connection

9.2.4 Scenario 1: Data Structure of an SAP Business Warehouse Connection

Starting with the SAP BW model that we used for our net sales scenario in Section 9.1.2, we assume that the builder of the dashboard has full access to SAP Analytics Cloud and thus to the creation process of the model as described in Section 9.2.3. However, we don't assume that the builder of the dashboard also has full access to the database or to the creation of the queries. If they now want to understand the data and the data structure of this query, there are two options. Either there is great documentation of the existing queries and underlying data, or they have a look at the model they created based on this query.

In our case, we will follow the second scenario from the viewpoint of the modeler. To do so, we need to navigate in our folders to the model we have just created. Once this model is opened, the view is shown in Figure 9.10, where all the measures from this model are listed. In our case, as shown in Figure 9.10 and Figure 9.11, our model is kept as simple as possible, containing only the data that is required to build the dashboard. For this use case, this means it contains one measure, **Net Sales**. To switch to the dimensions, choose the tab **All Dimensions** in the modeler, as shown in Figure 9.11. This example model contains multiple dimensions, such as the **Sales unit**, **Request ID**, **Calendar Year/Month**, **Region Code**, **Customer**, and **Product**.

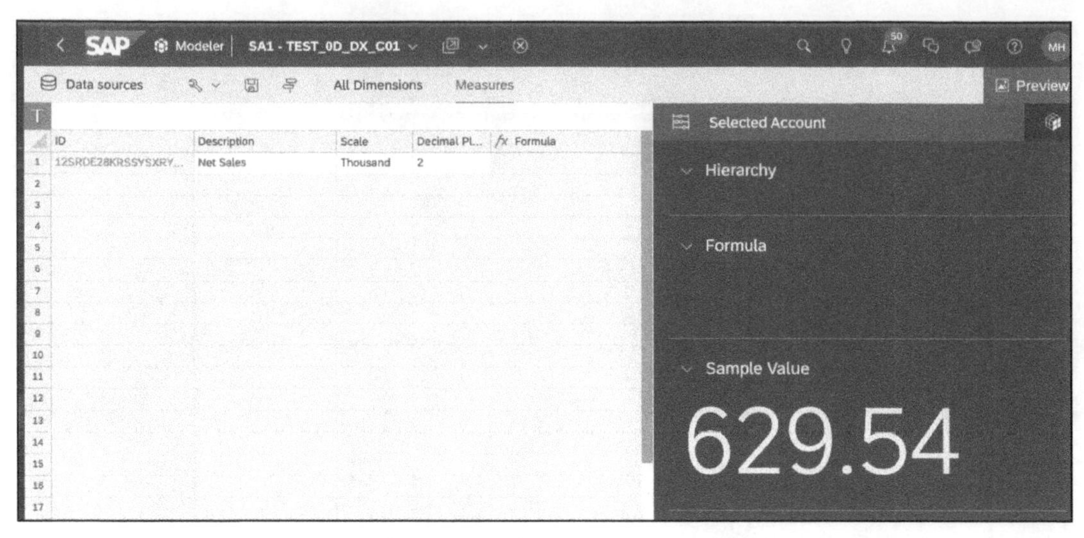

Figure 9.10 SAP Analytics Cloud Model "TEST_0D_DX_C01" Based on SAP BW Live Connection, View of the Model Showing All Measures

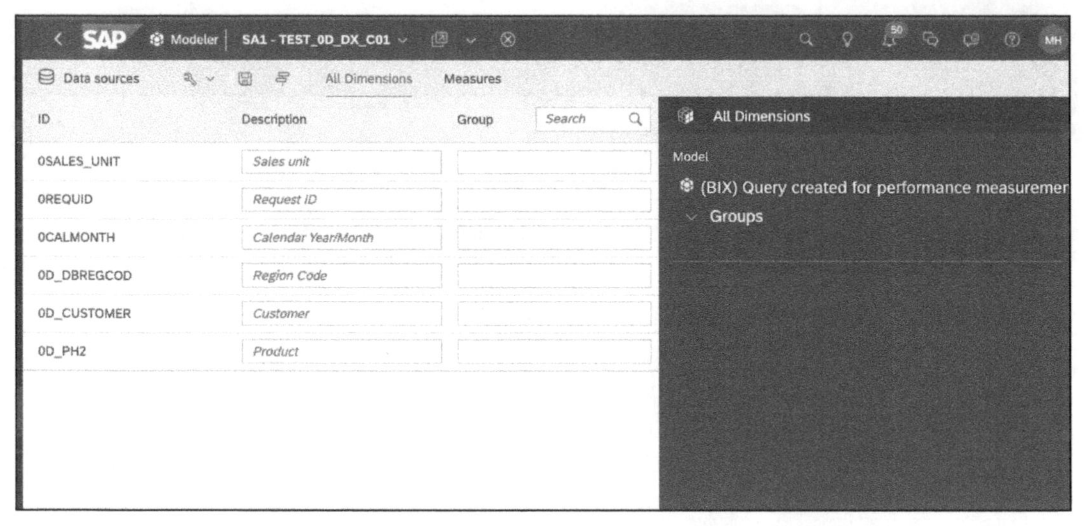

Figure 9.11 SAP Analytics Cloud Model "TEST_0D_DX_C01" Based on SAP BW Live Connection, View of the Model Showing All Dimensions

9.2.5 Scenario 2: Data Structure of an SAP HANA Connection

For our second scenario, based on an SAP HANA live connection, we can repeat the same steps as in Section 9.2.4 to get to the view of the modeler. In this model, we have multiple measures, as shown in Figure 9.12, including **Discount**, **Gross Margin**, **Original Sales Price**, and **Quantity Sold**.

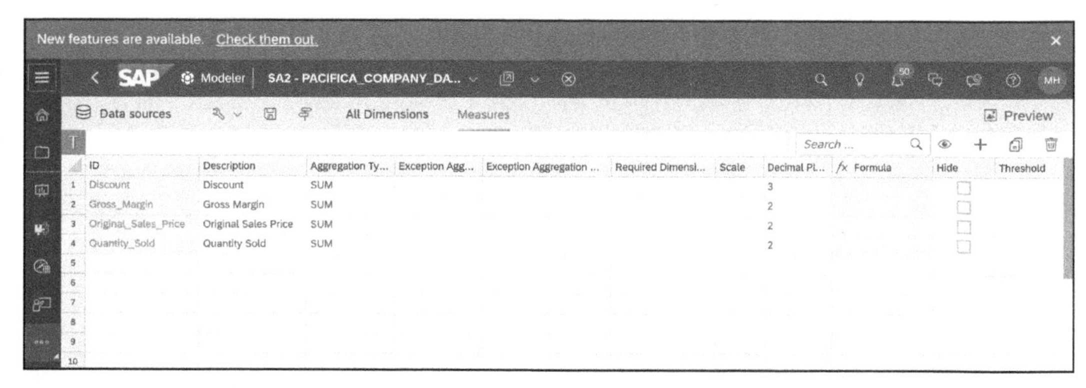

Figure 9.12 SAP Analytics Cloud Model "SA2 – PACIFIC_COMPANY_DATA" Based on SAP HANA Live Connection, View of the Model Showing Measures

> **Tip**
>
> In Figure 9.12, the column **Hide** indicates the option to hide measures that are not needed in the SAP Analytics Cloud model based on the SAP HANA view. This is another great option to improve the performance of your dashboard.

Switching again to the **All Dimensions** tab in the model, Figure 9.13 shows all dimensions of this model. Again, we do have the option to hide dimensions that are in the query but not needed in the SAP Analytics Cloud model.

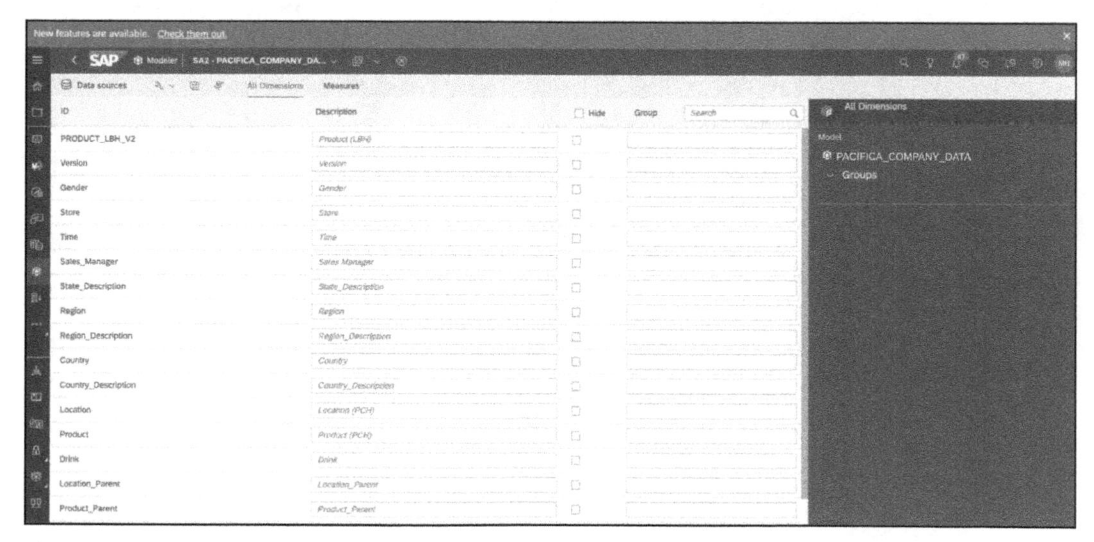

Figure 9.13 SAP Analytics Cloud Model "SA2 – PACIFIC_COMPANY_DATA" Based on SAP HANA Live Connection, View of the Model Showing Dimensions

Table 9.1 shows a comparison between hidden and not hidden measures and dimensions. For this experiment, the performance is measured first with all visible measures and dimensions. Secondly, we included the loading time for only the dimensions hidden and only the measures hidden, both times except one. Finally, adding all measures and dimensions to the experiment, each except one, hidden. Note that this is a small dataset, and the advantages of hiding measures and dimensions increase the bigger the dataset is. The timing was done for a refresh of the story to avoid inserting the credentials for the live data connection every time to reduce the amount of external influence on the timing.

Data Type	Loading Time
All data visible	10.5 sec
All measures hidden except one	9.8 sec
All dimensions hidden except one	9.0 sec
All measures and dimensions hidden, each except one	8.3 sec

Table 9.1 Time Differences between Visible and Hidden Measures and Dimensions

Golden Rule #1 – Tenant and Backend

We made a choice to improve the performance of the dashboard that corresponds to golden rule #1:

- *Parallel queries and model settings* – In both the model and the story, you have options to update your settings to an optimized performance. This includes query merges (in the story), query batching (in the story), and the optimized story building performance (in the model).

Golden Rule #3 – Data Model

We made a choice to improve the performance of the dashboard that correspond to golden rule #3:

- *Removing unnecessary measures and dimensions* – As shown earlier in this section, removing unnecessary measures and dimensions improves the performance of your dashboard even for smaller datasets. Thus, this is a valuable way of saving loading time. But remember to hide only the measures and dimensions you don't need in your dashboard, as these won't be displayed in the story anymore!

9.3 Dashboard Features

In this section, we will have a look at the dashboard features of our two scenarios. We will cover the general functionality of the dashboards we have created and how to optimize them for the best possible performance, live data connection specific features like custom build hierarchies in SAP BW live connections, the limitations of features for live data connections, as well as general dashboard building recommendations like the International Business Communication Standards (IBCS).

But before we dive deep into the two scenarios and the two dashboards, here is another additional performance tip. If you are creating your own dashboard, you can open the **Performance Optimization** option via the tools panel, as shown in Figure 9.14.

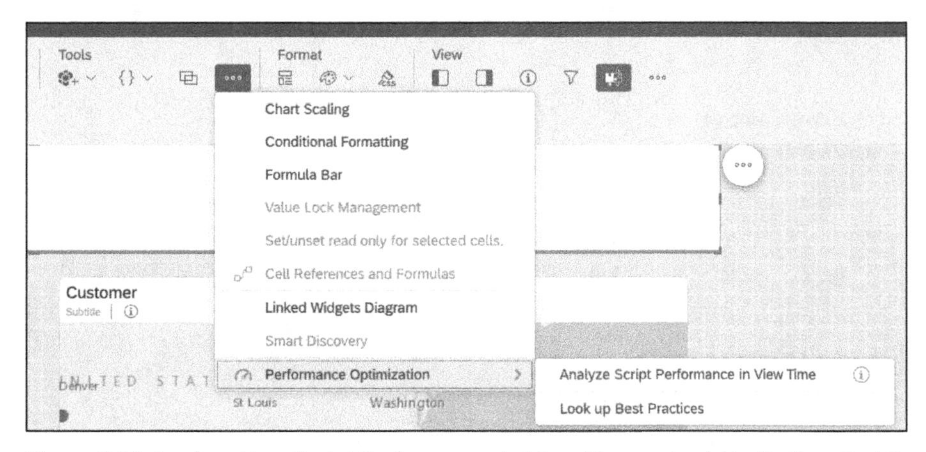

Figure 9.14 Analyze Your Script Performance in View Time or Look Up Further Best Practices

From here you can choose to **Analyze Script Performance in View Time** or to **Look up Best Practices**. For the latter, see Figure 9.15. Here you can find an extensive overview of **Best Practices for Performance Optimization in Your Story Design**, which is complementary to this book.

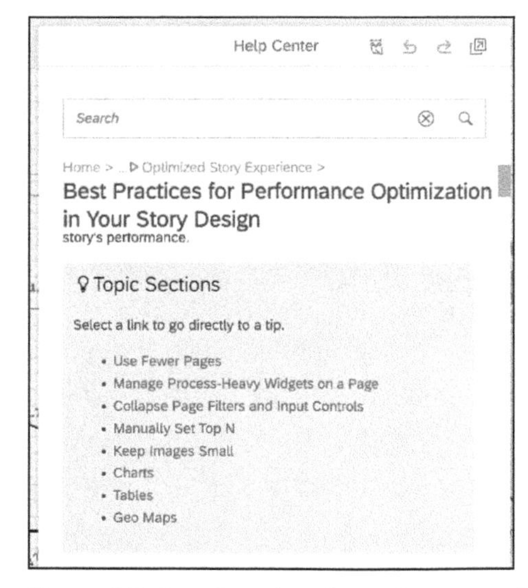

Figure 9.15 Best Practices for Performance Optimization in Your Story Design Overview

9.3.1 Scenario 1: SAP Business Warehouse Connection

Figure 9.16 shows the dashboard of our first scenario with the SAP BW live connection and the features that we will discuss in this section. These features cover an SAP BW custom hierarchy, the rank and sort feature, geo maps, as well as chart scaling.

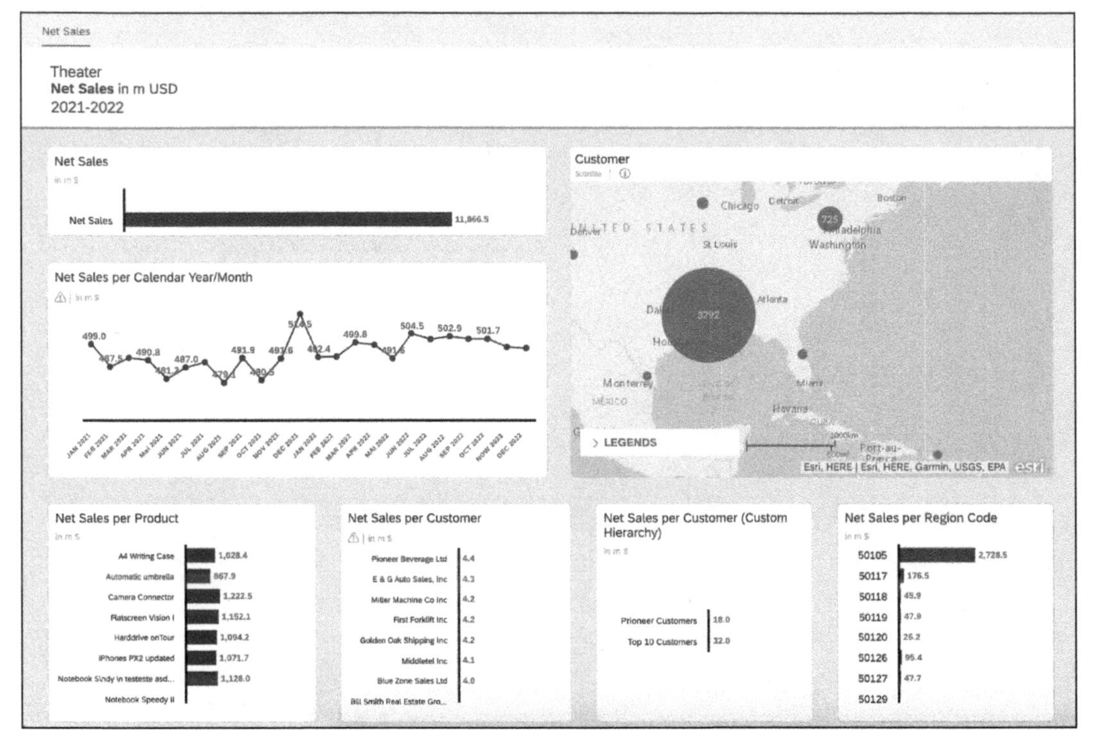

Figure 9.16 Scenario 1: Net Sales of Our Snacks and Beverages of our Theaters

Custom Hierarchy

You are probably already familiar with the hierarchies in SAP Analytics Cloud dimensions, which reflect the data structure in a nested way, using subgroups. This allows us to drill down and to drill up in this hierarchy for a better understanding of dependencies between values and general data exploration.

If hierarchies are set up in your SAP BW system, they will typically also be available in your SAP Analytics Cloud model and dashboard. Usually, these hierarchies are set up in the model and are fixed. However, using SAP BW live connections you have the option to customize your dimension hierarchy or the grouping directly in your story. This is limited to SAP BW dimensions in a live connection.

You can create a custom hierarchy using an SAP BW live connection using the following steps:

1. Go to the **Builder** area in SAP Analytics Cloud and select the widget where the custom hierarchy should be displayed (see Figure 9.17).

2. Click on the **Action Menu** button next to the dimension on which you want to create your custom hierarchy.
3. Click on the **Manage Custom Groups** setting.
4. Click on **+ Create Custom Groups** to open the **Custom Group** panel.

Figure 9.17 First Four Steps in the Creation of a Custom Group in a Dashboard Using an SAP BW Live Data Connection

5. Create your custom hierarchy via drag and drop (see Figure 9.18).

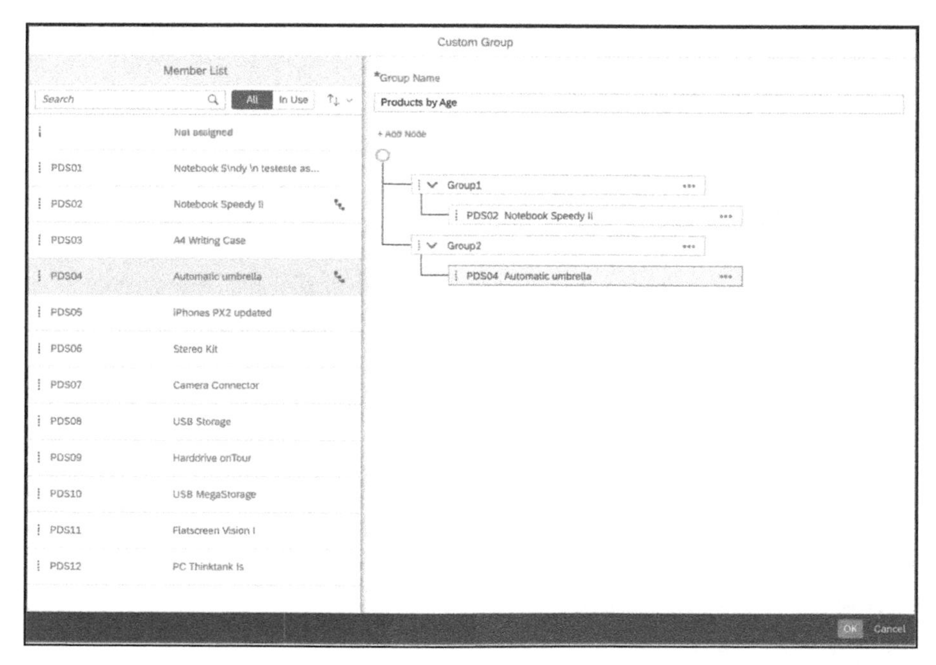

Figure 9.18 Builder Panel of the Creation of Your Custom Group or Custom Hierarchy in a Model Based on an SAP BW Live Connection

An example of a custom hierarchy was shown earlier in Figure 9.16, where the **Net Sales per Customer** were summarized in two groups, **Pioneer Customers** and **Top 10 Customers**, which makes a comparison between the pioneer customers and the top ten customers much easier. Optimally, an **Others** category would be included as well.

Rank/Sort

The dashboard automatically uses Top N if there are too many dimensions otherwise, as shown in Figure 9.19. The general advantages were also described in Chapter 3, Section 3.2.2. This is a useful feature for both performance optimization and the optimization of the user experience of your end-user of your SAP Analytics Cloud dashboard. As the human brain can't process too many data points at the same time, it is valuable to draw attention to the most important points in a dashboard, which are often achieved by showing the Top N or Bottom N entries of a certain dimension.

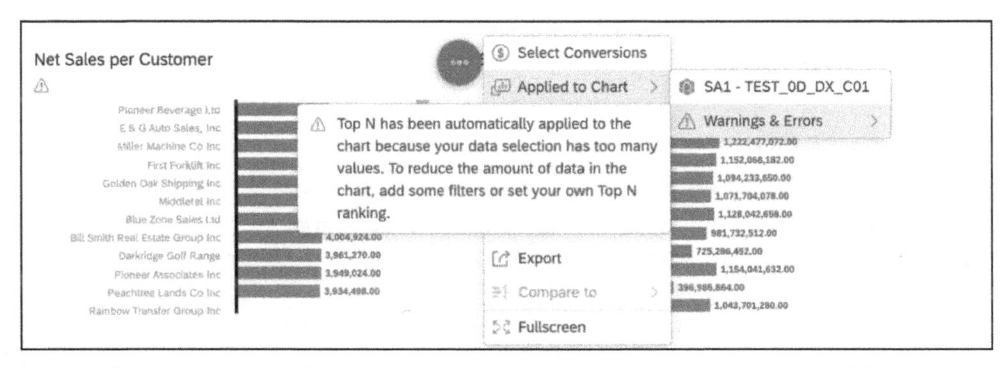

Figure 9.19 Automatic Application of Top N, If the Number of Data Points Would Be Too Big in a Bar Chart Widget in SAP Analytics Cloud

> **Golden Rule #6 – Filtering**
>
> We made a choice to improve the performance of the dashboard that correspond to golden rule #6:
>
> - *Use Top N ranking* – Using the automatic application of Top N, or even reducing the amount even further to a custom chosen number of Top N data points, can improve the performance of your dashboard.

Geo Map

Geo maps are a great way to visualize geo-dimensional or location data and were already covered shortly in Chapter 3. In general, you have the option to use the geo-dimension in a map to highlight the connection between the location and up to two measures using bubble charts. One measure is represented by the size of the bubbles in the map, and the second measure can be highlighted either by the color of the bubbles or as a pie chart in the bubbles.

If you are using the area of the map colored according to one measure, you should consider only measures that are proportional to the area, like the amount of rain per square meter. Otherwise, the chart could send the wrong signals and contradict the actual data. As in Figure 9.20, this is not a recommended visualization for this type of data. On the other hand, rain per square meter would be a perfectly valid measure for such a visualization.

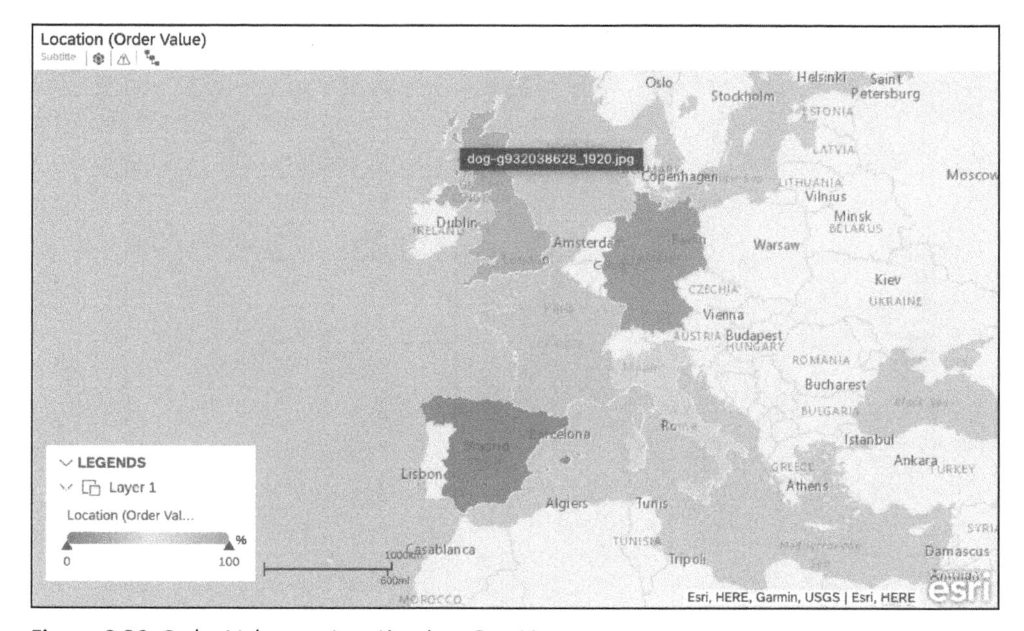

Figure 9.20 Order Value per Location in a Geo Map

> **Note**
>
> If you want to create geo maps, your model must include geo-dimensional information. For the area of the map, a normal dimension with country name, for example, would be sufficient to map with the geo location. But for the bubble chart, the model must not only contain the dimensional data of the cities, countries, etc., but also their coordinate information added as geo-dimensional data in the model directly.

For the geo map widget, these are some recommendations to optimize the performance of the geo map in the **Builder** panel from Figure 9.21:

- Reduce the number of data points that are displayed in the geo map.
- Enable location clustering and decrease the clustering to 1,000+ points instead of the default setting of 5,000+ cluster points.
- Construct your geo map in a way that limits the zoom abilities and panning if you enabled location clustering, as each change will trigger a query to the backend.

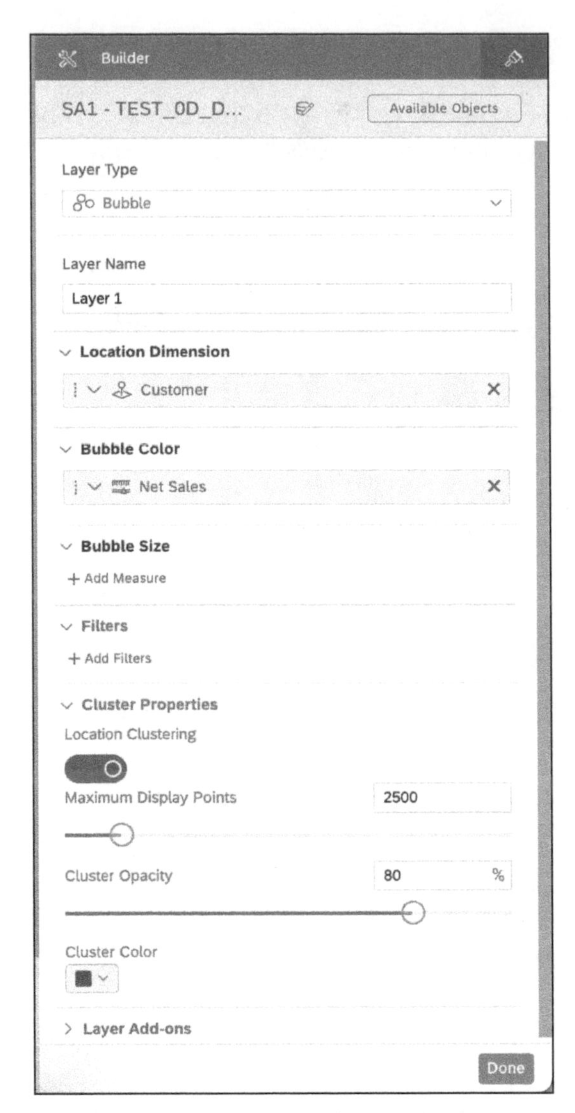

Figure 9.21 Builder Panel with the Selection Options for the Geo Map Widget

Golden Rule #6 – Filtering

We made choices to improve the performance of the dashboard that correspond to golden rule #6:

- *Leverage drilling capabilities* – Geo maps are not the first thought when talking about filters and drilling capabilities. But reducing the amount of the maximum display points from the default of over 5,000 data points to the chosen 2,500 data points improves both the performance and the usability and readability of the dashboard.

Chart Scaling

Chart scaling means that at least the same measures are using the same scale in a dashboard. Thus, if you compare two widgets visually, the numbers should also match. In the optimal case, even all measures with the same unit would be scaled together, which makes the visual comparison even easier and more intuitive.

However, as this requires an update of all linked widgets every time a filter is set, for example, in one of the charts, performance suffers heavily under this functionality. But it delivers a huge advantage for the end user analyzing the dashboard.

> **Note**
>
> Especially if you want to follow the IBCS guidelines, you should always enable common chart scaling between all measures that carry the same unit.

9.3.2 Scenario 2: SAP HANA Connection

Figure 9.22 shows the dashboard of our second scenario with the SAP HANA live connection.

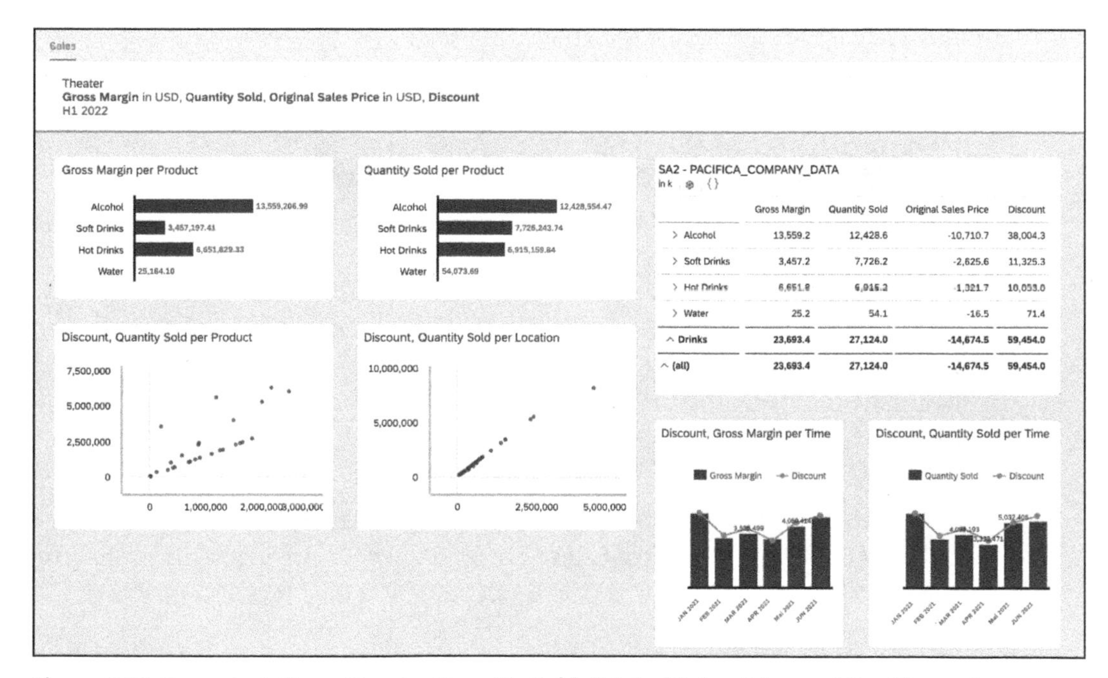

Figure 9.22 Scenario 2: Gross Margin, Quantity Sold, Original Sales, Price, and the Discounts of Our Products

We'll discuss its features in the following list:

- **Filtering and prompting**
  In Chapter 3, the performance effects of filters were already explained. Prompting, variables, and variants are another way to reduce the loaded amount of data further.

  Among other uses, variables can restrict users from accessing certain data and are a parameter of the SAP BW query. Furthermore, these variables are the input the user needs to set in the prompt window before accessing the story. This leads us to variants, as these can be understood like bookmarks for these prompts. This also reduces the possibility of errors in inserting invalid prompt entries. Figure 9.23 shows the default prompt settings (variables) of our SAP HANA live connection of scenario 2.

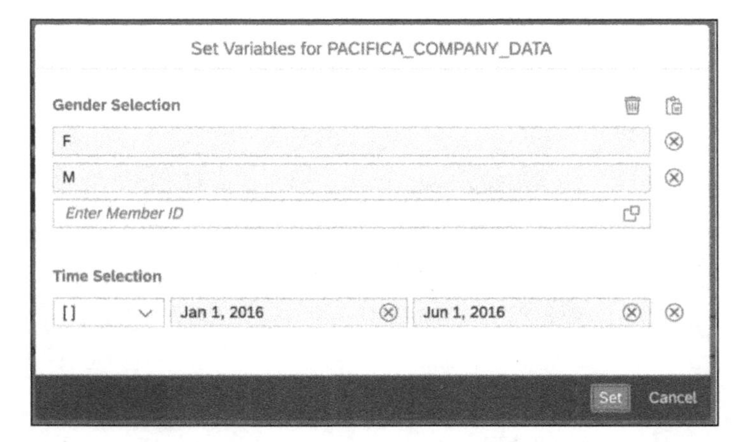

Figure 9.23 Prompt Settings of Our SAP HANA Live Connection

- **IBCS or reporting table**
  The table is created based on the guidelines from IBCS. This includes (among others) the semantics of the hierarchy and the expansion of the hierarchy to the top and not to the bottom, as it is a mathematically natural way to display the sum of subgroups below and not above the single entries.

- **Rank/sort**
  As the dimensions in this dashboard consist of fewer entries, we don't need to use the Top N or Bottom N feature. Instead, we used only the ranking or sorting feature to display the most important sold products directly at the top, where they draw the most attention.

- **Scatter plot**
  The scatter plot is used to investigate a possible correlation between two measures, where a correlation would appear as linear extrapolation between the single scatter points.

9.3.3 Other Live Connection-specific Features

As already covered in Chapter 5, using a live connection over an acquired data connection leads to worse performance. However, there are further advantages other than the instant data update in real time for your dashboard when you are using a live connection.

Some of these live connection specific features were already covered in Section 9.3.1 and Section 9.3.2, such as the custom hierarchy based on SAP BW live connections. Another advantage of using a live data connection to your SAP BW or SAP HANA database is the easy access to the data analyzer and search to insight tools. If you are using acquired data, you must set up a data model in SAP Analytics Cloud before you can use the data analyzer. However, if you are using live connections, you can directly use the data analyzer based on these queries (see Figure 9.24 and Figure 9.25) and don't need to create an extra live data model.

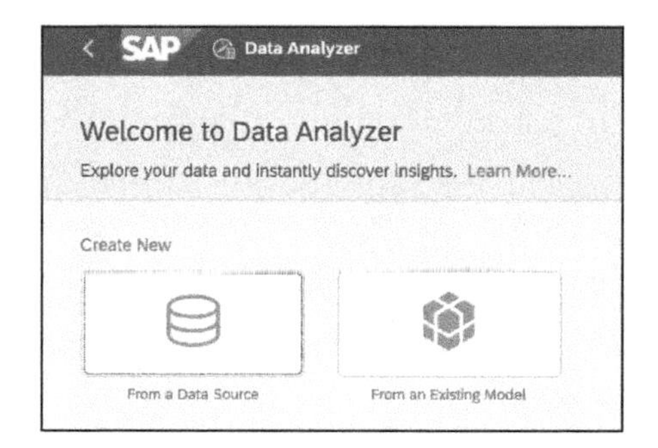

Figure 9.24 Data Analyzer Can Be Used from an Existing Model or Directly from a Data Source

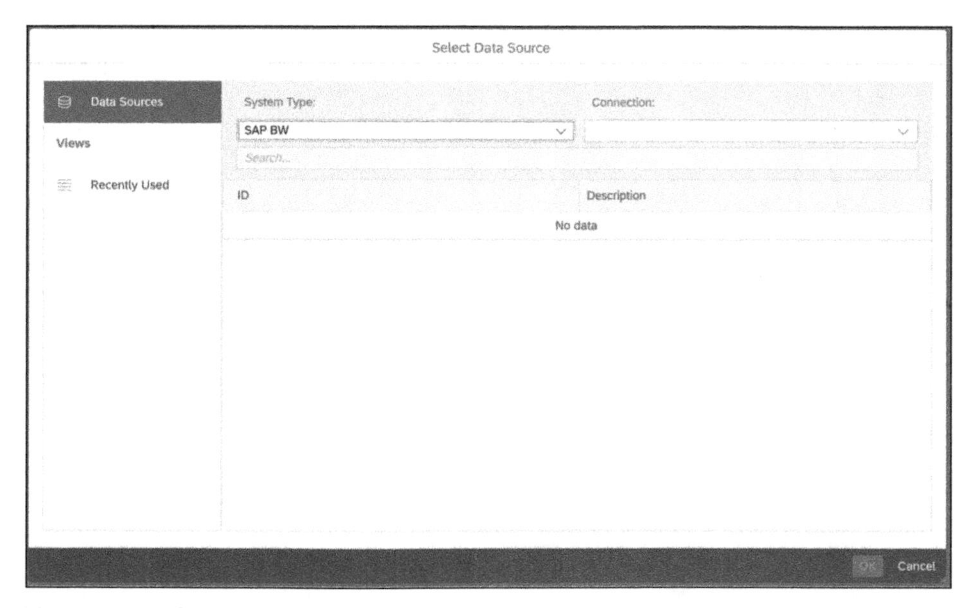

Figure 9.25 Selecting Data Source in the Data Analyzer

Just Ask (previous known as Search to Insight) is a feature using natural language, where you can ask a question related to your business data in your normal, natural language, and Just Ask delivers your response based on your available data directly in your interaction field, as shown in Figure 9.26.

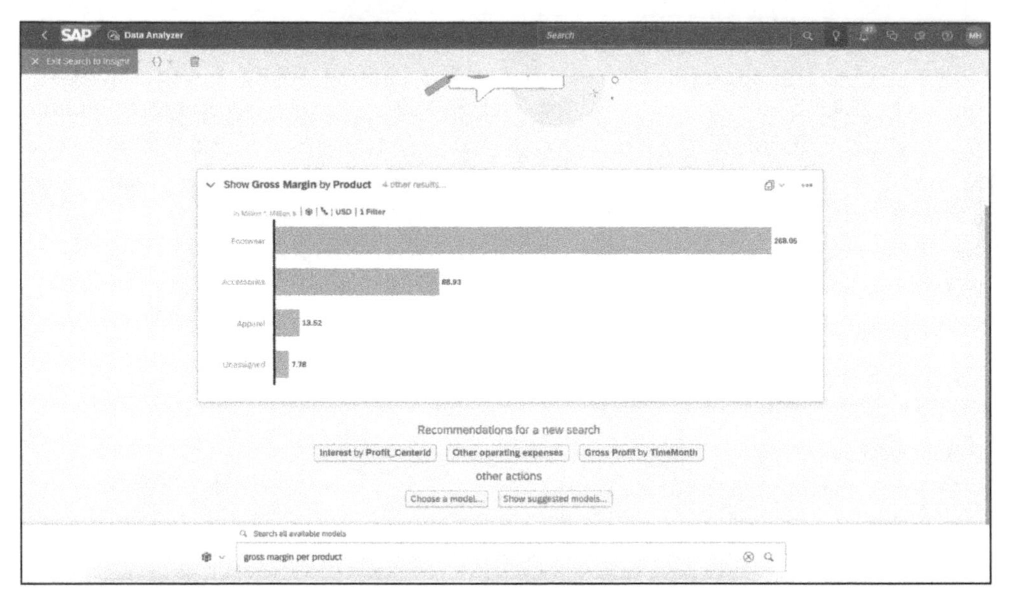

Figure 9.26 Just Ask Feature Working on Existing SAP Analytics Cloud Models, or Directly on Live Data Connections

9.3.4 Live Connection Limitations

While there are advantages of a live connection, there are also some disadvantages and limitations of using an SAP live connection.

> **Tip**
>
> If you are using live connections in your dashboards: when going through the list of new features in SAP Analytics Cloud, always check for those new features if they are supported in your respective live connections type.

The following list gives some examples of these limitations; however, keep in mind that this is not a complete list of all current limitations, and limitations may change with each release:

- **Predictive features**
  Predictive features like smart predict are an easy way to create predictions based on your data that could be used as a basis for your business planning. But there are also some limitations if you want to use these predictive features with live data connections:

- Smart Discovery is not supported.
- Time Series forecasting in line charts is not supported.
- Cloud deployments of SAP HANA systems are currently not supported.
- Limit of 1,000 columns when using live datasets with predictive models.

Further Reading

For a more extensive overview of these restrictions of smart predict using live connections, visit the following URL: *http://s-prs.co/v566939.*

- **Smart insights**
  Smart insights is a feature that helps you get quick and ad-hoc background information on your datapoints that you are currently investigating. This includes adding context and driving factors of your data, making data exploration easier and more automatic, with less manual labor. Smart Insights is accessible on models based on live SAP HANA connections. However, there are some restrictions like the SAP HANA version or the maximal number of rows in your model.

Further Reading

For a more extensive overview of these restrictions of smart insights and live SAP HANA connections, visit the following URL: *http://s-prs.co/v566940.*

Tip

For the full overview of all supported or not supported features in combination with live connections, you can check the following help pages:

- SAP Analytics Cloud Support Matrix for Live Connectivity to SAP NetWeaver BW and SAP BW/4HANA: *http://s-prs.co/v566941.*
- Restrictions to SAP HANA and BTP Live Data Connections: *http://s-prs.co/v566942.*

9.4 Guidelines for Building an Efficient Dashboard

To build an efficient dashboard with SAP Analytics Cloud, there are three guiding principles you should follow that cover the best practices for dashboard design, SAP Analytics Cloud, and optimized performance in it. These three guidelines are the following:

- Golden rules of this book from Chapter 2
- Golden rules of the book *Designing Dashboards with SAP Analytics Cloud*
- SUCCESS formula of the IBCS

If you follow these rules, there is little room for personal decisions about the design itself, and all freedom is based on the content, which should be the most important part of each dashboard.

Further Reading

For general guidelines on how to design dashboards, we recommend the book *Designing Dashboards with SAP Analytics Cloud* (SAP PRESS, 2021, *www.sap-press.com/5235*).

One of the recommendations of IBCS is the usage of a notations handbook that covers the general styling decisions for your dashboard to ensure consistency between your dashboards. The IBCS notation handbook can be found on their website.

In our case, we applied the same notation handbook as in the book *Designing Dashboards with SAP Analytics Cloud*, which is a slightly adapted version of the IBCS notations handbook.

Further Reading

Check out the IBCS website/institute and its open-source content at *www.ibcs.com*.

9.5 Summary

In this chapter, we discussed how to optimize the performance in a real example scenario, using a live data connection. For this we created two live connections, one SAP HANA live connection and one SAP BW live connection to highlight the similarities and differences between these two data type connections.

In the following chapter, we discussed the scenario of our two examples as well as their data. Then we talked about the specific dashboard features we used in these examples, like further tips on improving a geo map and special features of live connections, such as the custom hierarchy for SAP BW live connections. Additionally, feature limitations as well as further resources were provided.

In the last part, we covered the general creation of the dashboard using dashboard design guidelines such as, for example, the IBCS guidelines. This led to an overall performance of 18 seconds for the SAP BW dashboard from scenario 1, and 12 seconds for the SAP HANA dashboard from scenario 2. Please note that the size of both datasets is different, and thus these two timings can't be compared to each other. The timing in general covers the time from clicking on the story to when the full story is loaded. However, the time for including the credentials for both connections was not included, which was around four to five seconds.

Chapter 10
Optimized Dashboard Using the Analytics Designer

The analytics designer expands on the standard story builder tool by adding features that enable the creation of more complex and customizable applications. As a result of this freedom, creating a dashboard using the analytics designer comes with a unique set of performance challenges, alongside many of the story builder. This chapter takes a holistic view of creating a high-performing dashboard with the analytics designer.

In Chapter 3 through Chapter 7, we covered in detail the different variables of the performance equation, seeing what individual changes can impact performance. As part of this, in Chapter 4 we looked at the analytics designer for SAP Analytics Cloud with its unique performance topics. To get better insight into what using the performance improvements talked about in Chapter 3 through Chapter 7 looks like, Chapter 8 through Chapter 10 take a holistic look at creating an efficient dashboard from beginning to end, where the focus scenario of this chapter is building a well-performing dashboard using the analytics designer for SAP Analytics Cloud. This means focusing mainly on the differing challenges compared to the previous two scenarios, which used the story designer for SAP Analytics Cloud, although some steps will sound familiar.

In the following sections, we'll first go over the scenario used throughout this chapter to give vitally important context for the creation of the efficient dashboard. We'll then cover the data structure, meaning what data is available and how to import and structure it so it is ready as an optimally efficient SAP Analytics Cloud model for building the dashboard. Also included is a section on the dashboard features, followed by how to build the dashboard with optimal performance in mind, thus creating a step-by-step guide.

As with the previous two chapters, as a scenario we follow a fictional live theater company and the individual employees responsible for managing several theaters in a local region. The theater company has several short theatrical shows that are performed in different theaters throughout the year. The dashboard described in this chapter is based on acquired data. The analyst persona building the dashboard is Julia, the assistant to Alex, the artistic director. The data will be taken from a Microsoft Excel spreadsheet and put into an SAP Analytics Cloud model, after which a dashboard using the analytics designer for SAP Analytics Cloud will be built mainly for understanding the sales of food and drinks.

10.1 Scenario

As in Chapter 8 and Chapter 9, the scenario used in this chapter entails creating an SAP Analytics Cloud dashboard for managing a regional live theater company with several locations.

The theater company manages theaters in ten different locations, all within the same region of Canada, and is led by Alex. Theaters can typically hold a capacity of several hundred people per play, with plays being put on daily. The plays and theater locations switch roughly monthly, depending on various factors such as, for example, the success of the play. Other sources of income next to the primary income from ticket sales include the sale of food and drinks before the play begins and at intermissions, as well as some souvenirs and merchandise. Next to the actors, the play staff includes the artistic director and set builders, with further staff often including ticket agents, ushers, food and merchandise sales, bartenders, as well as managerial and administrative staff to run the theater company, such as Alex's assistant Julia, who will be building the dashboard.

On top of the dashboards shown in Chapter 8 and Chapter 9, which focus on more general operational numbers such as percentage of seats sold, viewer satisfaction rating, number of actors, expenses, and sales on a monthly and per location basis, Alex needs another dashboard to focus on food and drink sales. It should be updated once a month. As previous dashboards have already been built using SAP Analytics Cloud, Julia has some experience with the tool, and it thus makes sense to leverage the potential of SAP Analytics Cloud once again.

The main goal for creating this dashboard is to leverage the already existing data to its fullest extent by:

- Making the data easy to interpret and compare for Alex. He is trying to increase secondary sales, and thus wants to make it possible to see what works and what doesn't for different locations, weather situations, and more. A concrete question could be: For the Aurora theater we used all medium drink sizes; how do our sales compare after switching to three different drink sizes?
- Making the data easily accessible on different devices. As Alex is quite mobile, there is an inherent need to be able to work on the road from small devices such as a small laptop, a tablet, or even the phone.

The scope of this project is defined by the goals and circumstances listed above. It is limited to the data available in the backend system but not restricted in time or otherwise. With new data coming once a month, it will be necessary to continuously update at least the data model, but potentially also the displayed charts.

Julia builds the dashboard in two pages:

1. The first page in Figure 10.1 gives an overview of the sales numbers, looking at how ticket and merchandise sales compare to food and drink sales, how food and drink sales are split up, and the sales for different locations, weather stations, and seasons.
2. The second page in Figure 10.2 shows in more detail the gross margin for different food and drink items, enabling comparisons for different drink sizes and more.

Julia creates the dashboard in February 2023, meaning only data for January is fully available. Over time, more data will get filled in, such as additional theater locations. We will follow her throughout the building process, ensuring that the dashboard will be efficient.

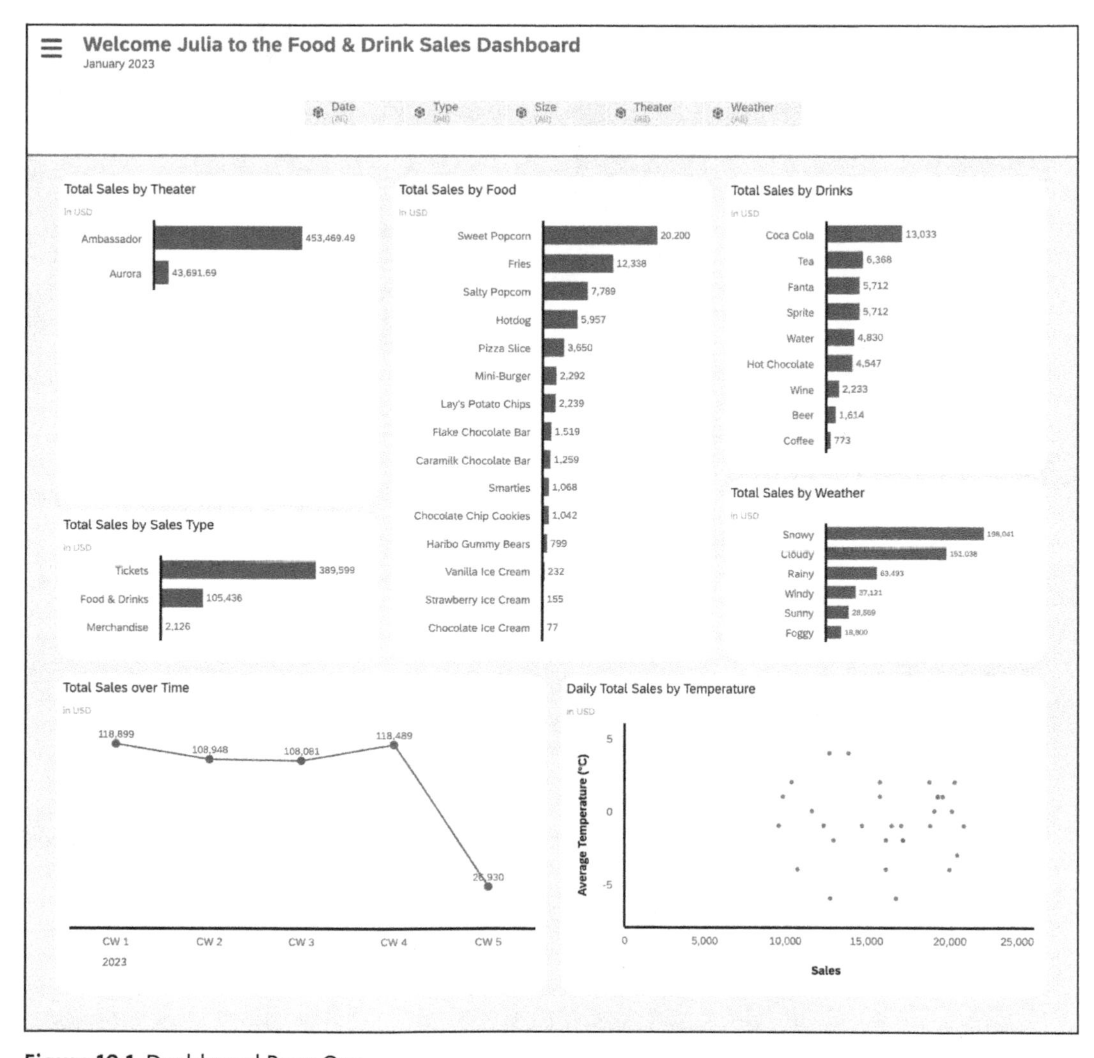

Figure 10.1 Dashboard Page One

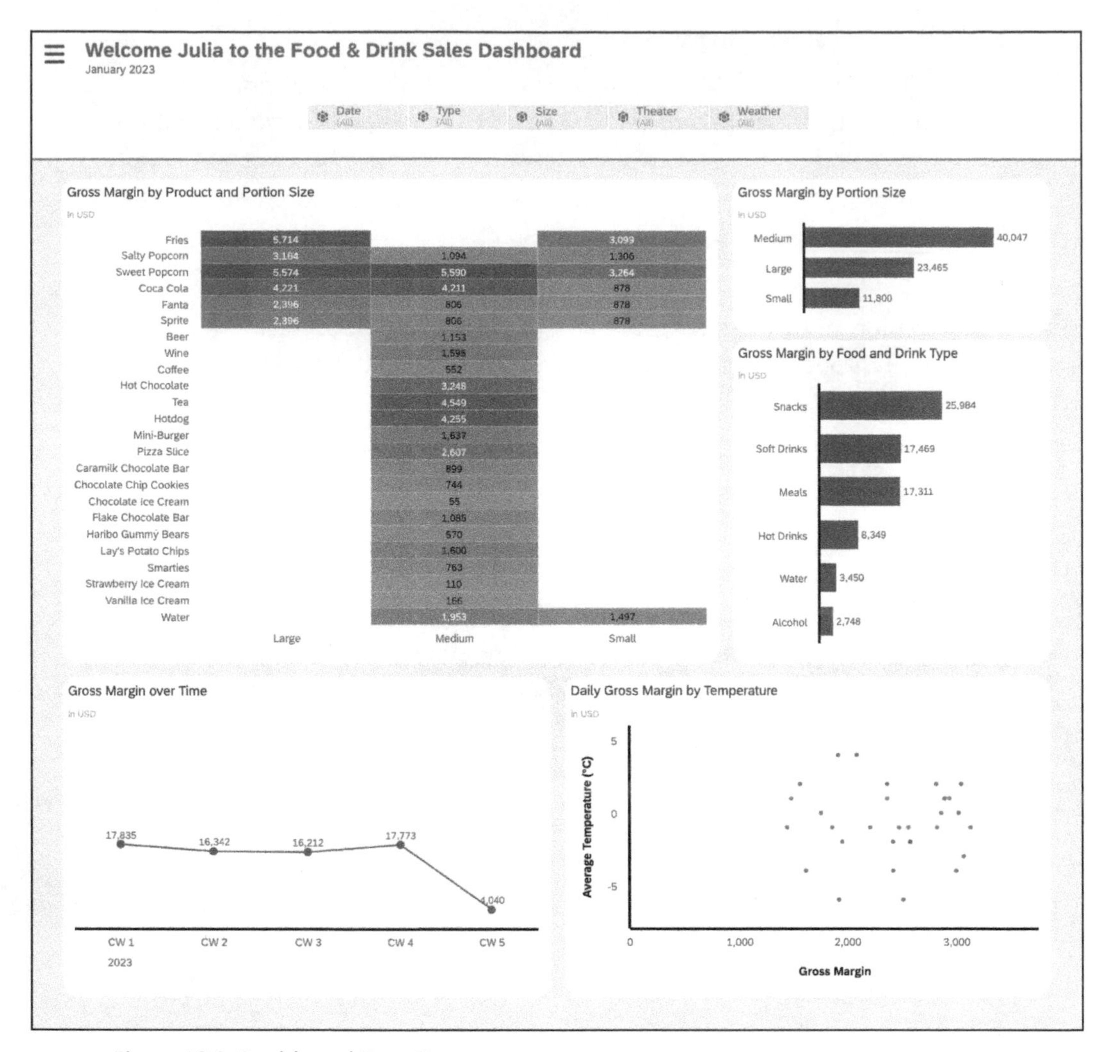

Figure 10.2 Dashboard Page Two

10.2 Data Structure

This section covers everything that has to do with data. Where the data Julia uses comes from, how it is transformed, and how and why the data is used to build an acquired model in SAP Analytics Cloud.

10.2.1 Data Source

The data needed for this dashboard consists of multiple data sources. It includes most of the required data coming from their backend system, such as tickets, merchandise, food and drink sales, portion size, number of units sold, and more. This data needs to be supplemented manually with information not available in the backend system but still important for this dashboard, including data on temperature and weather.

One reason Julia chose to create an acquired model instead of using a live connection to import the data into SAP Analytics Cloud is the need to add the weather report data, which she gets online. Including multiple data sources would require blending a live data model with an imported Microsoft Excel file in SAP Analytics Cloud. Since this is not as efficient as a single data source, this would not be a good choice here.

In addition, depending on the type and speed of the connection, using a live connection on its own would not be as efficient as a well set-up acquired model. Since a live connection is not needed as data only needs to be updated monthly, Julia correctly chooses to create an acquired model.

Since data needs to be updated monthly, Julia will have to take the following steps to export the data, supplement it in Microsoft Excel, and append it into the SAP Analytics Cloud model. This shouldn't put too much of a strain on Julia's overall workload, as it is a straightforward process.

She exports the following data from the backend system per **Date, Portion Size**, and **Sales Type** dimension (which makes a three-level hierarchy split among the three columns: **Sales Type lvl1, Sales Type lvl2**, and **Sales Type lvl3**):

- **Gross Margin**
- **Sales**
- **Theater Location**

She then manually adds supplementary information not available in the backend to the exported Microsoft Excel spreadsheet by creating a new column for each point listed below and filling them with daily values:

- **Average Temperature (°C)**
- **Weather**, with the dimension members **Rainy, Sunny, Cloudy, Windy, Foggy**, and **Snowy**

Julia keeps the number of measures to a minimum for optimal performance. However, if changes in the scope and visualizations are expected over time, it could make sense to include some additional columns that are likely to be needed in the future, if the drain on performance is not significant, to avoid the potential need for time-consuming redesigns later.

Reducing the number of data rows by aggregating on the basis of **per Portion Size, Sales Type, Theater Location, Average Temperature**, and **Weather** would theoretically be possible but not feasible in this case, as having the data on a day-by-day basis is useful for some insights.

Julia doesn't have to perform any calculations, as all necessary measures are already available. She makes sure that there are no errors in the data that must be cleaned up.

Figure 10.3 shows what the Microsoft Excel spreadsheet now looks like, ready to be imported into SAP Analytics Cloud. It shows the data from January 2023, consisting of 10 columns and 1,178 data rows.

	A	B	C	D	E	F	G	H	I	J
1	Date	Theater Location	Weather	Average Temperature (°C)	Sales Type lvl1	Sales Type lvl2	Sales Type lvl3	Portion Size	Gross Margin	Sales
2	01. Jan 23	Ambassador	Snowy	2	Tickets	Tickets	Tickets			8016,82
3	01. Jan 23	Ambassador	Snowy	2	Merchandise	Merchandise	Merchandise			62,21
4	01. Jan 23	Ambassador	Snowy	2	Food & Drinks	Meals	Pizza Slice	Medium	84,1	117,74
5	01. Jan 23	Ambassador	Snowy	2	Food & Drinks	Meals	Hotdog	Medium	137,25	192,15
6	01. Jan 23	Ambassador	Snowy	2	Food & Drinks	Meals	Mini-Burger	Medium	52,8	73,92
7	01. Jan 23	Ambassador	Snowy	2	Food & Drinks	Meals	Fries	Small	99,96	139,94
8	01. Jan 23	Ambassador	Snowy	2	Food & Drinks	Meals	Fries	Large	184,32	258,05
9	01. Jan 23	Ambassador	Snowy	2	Food & Drinks	Snacks	Sweet Popcorn	Small	105,3	147,42
10	01. Jan 23	Ambassador	Snowy	2	Food & Drinks	Snacks	Sweet Popcorn	Medium	180,32	252,45
11	01. Jan 23	Ambassador	Snowy	2	Food & Drinks	Snacks	Sweet Popcorn	Large	179,82	251,75
12	01. Jan 23	Ambassador	Snowy	2	Food & Drinks	Snacks	Salty Popcorn	Small	42,12	58,97
13	01. Jan 23	Ambassador	Snowy	2	Food & Drinks	Snacks	Salty Popcorn	Medium	35,28	49,39
14	01. Jan 23	Ambassador	Snowy	2	Food & Drinks	Snacks	Salty Popcorn	Large	102,06	142,88
15	01. Jan 23	Ambassador	Snowy	2	Food & Drinks	Snacks	Lay's Potato Chips	Medium	51,6	72,24
16	01. Jan 23	Ambassador	Snowy	2	Food & Drinks	Snacks	Chocolate Chip Cookies	Medium	24	33,6
17	01. Jan 23	Ambassador	Snowy	2	Food & Drinks	Snacks	Haribo Gummy Bears	Medium	18,4	25,76
18	01. Jan 23	Ambassador	Snowy	2	Food & Drinks	Snacks	Caramilk Chocolate Bar	Medium	29	40,6
19	01. Jan 23	Ambassador	Snowy	2	Food & Drinks	Snacks	Flake Chocolate Bar	Medium	35	49
20	01. Jan 23	Ambassador	Snowy	2	Food & Drinks	Snacks	Smarties	Medium	24,6	34,44
21	01. Jan 23	Ambassador	Snowy	2	Food & Drinks	Snacks	Chocolate Ice Cream	Medium	1,78	2,49
22	01. Jan 23	Ambassador	Snowy	2	Food & Drinks	Snacks	Vanilla Ice Cream	Medium	5,34	7,48
23	01. Jan 23	Ambassador	Snowy	2	Food & Drinks	Snacks	Strawberry Ice Cream	Medium	3,56	4,98
24	01. Jan 23	Ambassador	Snowy	2	Food & Drinks	Hot Drinks	Tea	Medium	146,73	205,42
25	01. Jan 23	Ambassador	Snowy	2	Food & Drinks	Hot Drinks	Hot Chocolate	Medium	104,78	146,69
26	01. Jan 23	Ambassador	Snowy	2	Food & Drinks	Hot Drinks	Coffee	Medium	17,81	24,93
27	01. Jan 23	Ambassador	Snowy	2	Food & Drinks	Soft Drinks	Coca Cola	Small	28,32	39,65
28	01. Jan 23	Ambassador	Snowy	2	Food & Drinks	Soft Drinks	Coca Cola	Medium	135,83	190,16
29	01. Jan 23	Ambassador	Snowy	2	Food & Drinks	Soft Drinks	Coca Cola	Large	136,16	190,62
30	01. Jan 23	Ambassador	Snowy	2	Food & Drinks	Soft Drinks	Sprite	Small	28,32	39,65
31	01. Jan 23	Ambassador	Snowy	2	Food & Drinks	Soft Drinks	Sprite	Medium	26,01	36,41
32	01. Jan 23	Ambassador	Snowy	2	Food & Drinks	Soft Drinks	Sprite	Large	77,28	108,19
33	01. Jan 23	Ambassador	Snowy	2	Food & Drinks	Soft Drinks	Fanta	Small	28,32	39,65
34	01. Jan 23	Ambassador	Snowy	2	Food & Drinks	Soft Drinks	Fanta	Medium	26,01	36,41
35	01. Jan 23	Ambassador	Snowy	2	Food & Drinks	Soft Drinks	Fanta	Large	77,28	108,19
36	01. Jan 23	Ambassador	Snowy	2	Food & Drinks	Alcohol	Beer	Medium	37,2	52,08
37	01. Jan 23	Ambassador	Snowy	2	Food & Drinks	Alcohol	Wine	Medium	51,45	72,03
38	01. Jan 23	Ambassador	Snowy	2	Food & Drinks	Water	Water	Small	48,3	67,62
39	01. Jan 23	Ambassador	Snowy	2	Food & Drinks	Water	Water	Medium	63	88,2

Figure 10.3 The Microsoft Excel Spreadsheet to Be Imported

10.2.2 Building a Model in SAP Analytics Cloud

Now that the spreadsheet is finished, Julia can continue by importing the first month's data spreadsheet into SAP Analytics Cloud, by creating an acquired model.

Importing the Data from a Microsoft Excel Spreadsheet

To create an acquired model in SAP Analytics Cloud based on an Excel Spreadsheet, Julia takes the following steps:

1. Access the **Modeler** section in SAP Analytics Cloud using the icon in the collapsed side navigation bar or by selecting **Modeler** in the expanded side navigation bar.
2. Start creating a new model by selecting **From a CSV or Excel File** in the **Create New** section.
3. Click **Select Source File**, then navigate to and select the correct Microsoft Excel spreadsheet.

4. Make sure the **Use first row as column header** checkbox is checked.
5. Click **Import**.

The data is now being loaded into the **Modeler**. However, some more steps are necessary before the model itself is fully created. Figure 10.4 shows the screen that is automatically opened. If you leave this view before clicking the **Create Model** button, the same screen can be accessed again via the **Draft Data** dropdown in the **Files** section toolbar.

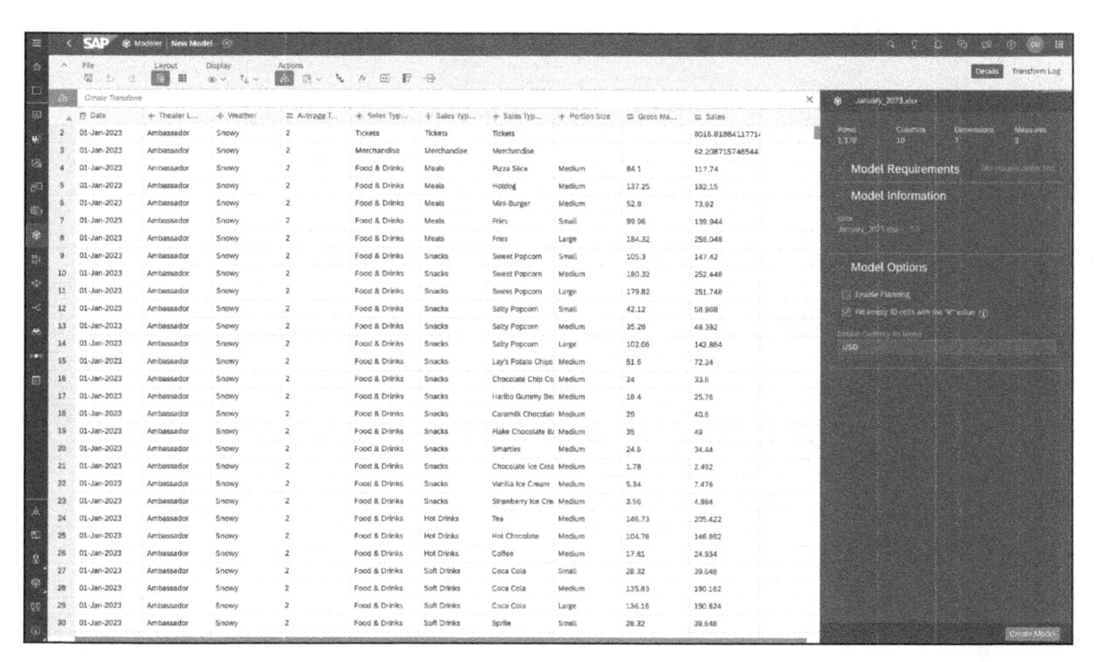

Figure 10.4 Creating an Acquired Model

The **Details** panel on the right side is automatically opened. It allows Julia to validate that everything was uploaded correctly by seeing general information about the imported data, such as that no issue was detected, which file was uploaded, and the number of data rows and columns that were uploaded. She can also check that **USD** was selected as the **Default Currency for Model** and that planning is disabled, as it is not needed and enabling it generally affects performance.

When selecting a column, the **Details** panel will show more detailed information about the selected data, such as the quality and distribution, thus allowing for further validation.

Preparing the Data

Upon importing the spreadsheet into SAP Analytics Cloud, each column is classified as a dimension or a measure. Julia does the following steps before she clicks the **Create Model** button at the bottom right of the screen:

1. She checks the assignment of dimensions and measures for each column and adapts it by selecting a column and then changing the **Type** under **Modeling** in the **Details** panel on the right by choosing between one of the options. She makes sure that the **Date** column is a **Date** dimension, that all columns containing numbers are **Measures**, and that all other columns are **Generic** dimensions.
2. She double checks that there are no errors in the data that need to be cleaned up. As this was already done in the spreadsheet, no effort is needed here. In most cases, it is simpler to do such fixes in the spreadsheet before importing into SAP Analytics Cloud.
3. She creates a hierarchy for the three sales type columns. This can be done by clicking the **Hierarchy** button and then adding dimensions to it in the **Hierarchy Builder** popup, as is done in Chapter 8. Alternatively, Julia can select the three dimensions **Sales Type lvl1**, **Sales Type lvl2**, and **Sales Type lvl3** in that order and then click the **Hierarchy** button, thus automatically adding the dimensions correctly to the hierarchy. Finish by clicking **OK**. See Figure 10.5.

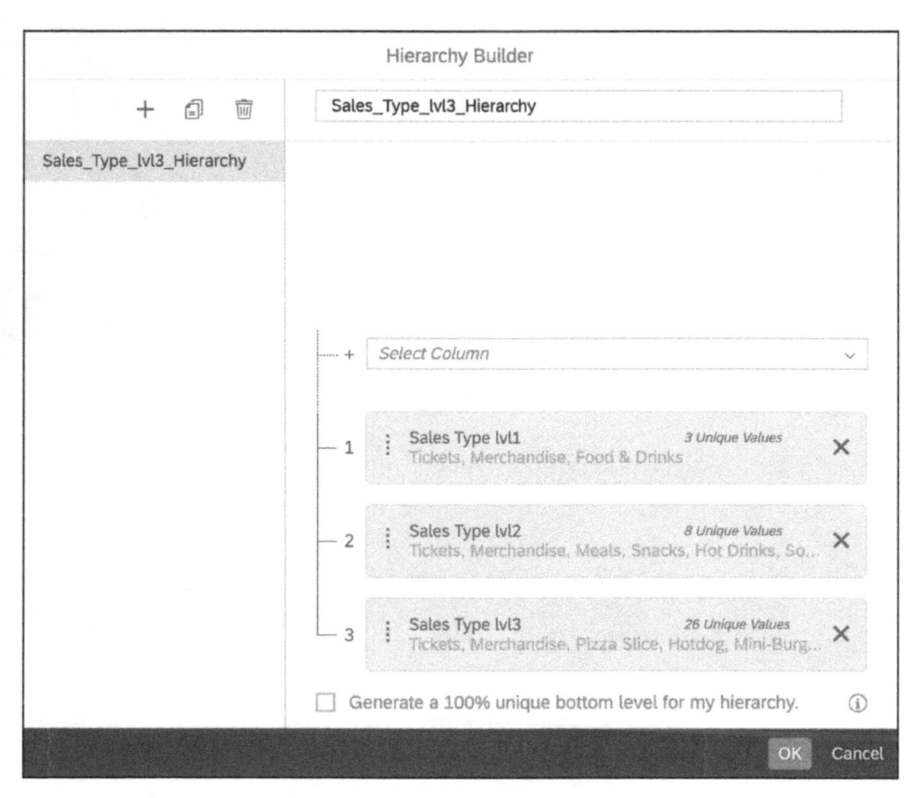

Figure 10.5 Building a Hierarchy in the Hierarchy Builder

Click the **Create Model** button and enter an appropriate name and target location for the model to be stored to finish preparing the data. The data source needed for creating the food and drink sales dashboard is now available.

The created model will automatically open in the same tab and can be seen in Figure 10.6. All the measures are folded into the account column. This is why the image of the model doesn't include as many columns as the spreadsheet.

Although all the necessary data was already calculated in the backend, we will add an **Exception Aggregation Type** for the **Average Temperature (°C) Measure**, as SAP Analytics Cloud performs a sum operation by default, when we want it to perform an average. One way of doing this is to go into **Account**, select **Average** as **Exception Aggregation Type** and all dimensions as **Exception Aggregation Dimensions.** It is important to note that exception aggregations are not optimal for performance and should be avoided wherever possible.

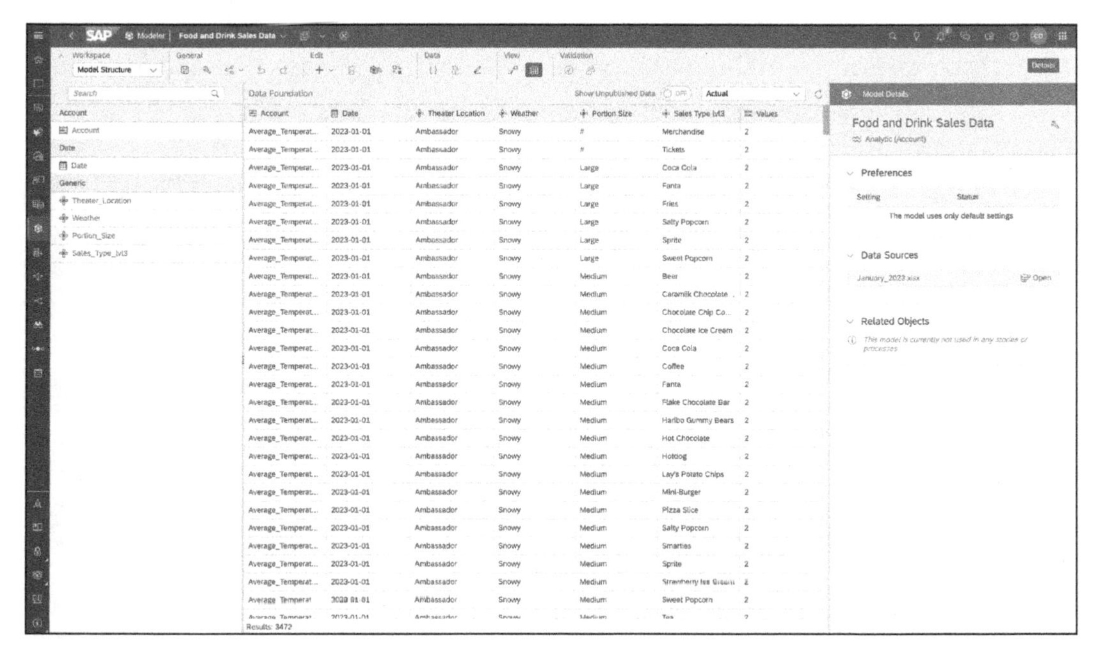

Figure 10.6 The Acquired Data Model

Appending the Data with a New Microsoft Excel Spreadsheet

With new data available to be added monthly, Julia needs to upload a spreadsheet with the new data once a month. As discussed in Section 10.2.1, this includes downloading the data from the backend system, supplementing it in Microsoft Excel with weather data, validating the correctness of the data, and then appending the existing data in the **Modeler** with the new data.

To be able to append the existing model instead of creating a new one and reconnecting all data-related widgets, the new spreadsheets must have the same format as the original. Julia then must take the following steps:

1. Go into the already created SAP Analytics Cloud Model visible in Figure 10.6 and access the **Data Management** section under **Workspace** in the top navigation bar.

2. Click [icon] **Import Data** and select **File**.
3. Click **Select Source File**, then navigate to and select the correct Microsoft Excel spreadsheet.
4. Make sure the **Use first row as column header** checkbox is checked.
5. Click **Import**.

The data should now be imported. Once this is done, take the following steps to complete adding the data to the model:

1. Click on the newly created **Query** under **Draft Sources**.
2. Make sure **Append** is selected as the **Import Method** in the **Details** section and that **Existing Version** is selected as the **Version** in the right-side bar.
3. Make sure the all the dimensions and measures are mapped like in Figure 10.7.
4. Click **Finish Mapping**.

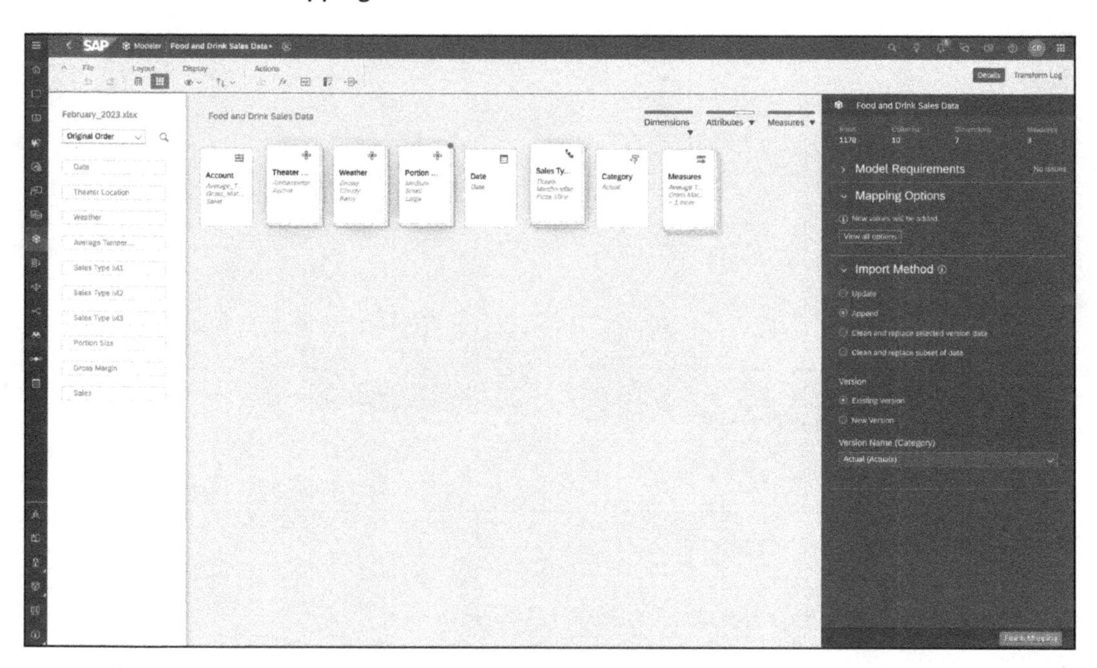

Figure 10.7 Importing Data into an Existing Model

10.3 Dashboard Features

Based on the scope, target audience, and general goals covered in the scenario section, as well as having covered the data required in the data structure section, we can now discuss the features required for this dashboard as determined mainly by the questions Alex would like to answer with this dashboard. So, when building the dashboard in the analytics designer for SAP Analytics Cloud, Julia should include the following:

- Alex wants to be able to have a closer look at food and drink data. Questions the dashboard should answer include but are not limited to: How are food and drink sales impacted by seasonality, temperature, and weather? How does portion sizing impact the generated value per drink or snack type? How do different theater locations compare to each other?

  To answer these questions, Julia needs to split the dashboard into two pages, so as to not overload a single page with widgets. One page will give an overview of the general sales figures, and one page will dive deeper into the numbers for food and drink. To help with dynamic comparisons, the dashboard should include a filter section at the top, as filters allow for further investigation of the data shown, thus offering more insights than what is shown upfront per chart.
- Alex wants to be able to use the dashboard with different devices, including his laptop, tablet, and mobile phone. Hence, the design should be adaptive to different screen sizes and easily usable regardless of whether a touchscreen, mouse, or keyboard is used.
- The dashboard should include a collapsible navigation menu on the top-left corner of the dashboard for switching between different pages, as it will not take up much space when collapsed and will still be easy to use when expanded on a smaller device.

The two dashboard pages can be seen in Figure 10.1 and Figure 10.2.

10.4 Building an Efficient Dashboard

With the data already available in SAP Analytics Cloud and knowing what the dashboard should include, Julia can start building the dashboard itself. She has decided to use the analytics designer for SAP Analytics Cloud, as it will offer more flexibility, with possibilities including a custom navigation menu and more.

This section will cover the building process for creating an efficient dashboard using the analytics designer for SAP Analytics Cloud based on the scenario, data structure, and features covered in the previous sections. Since the previous sections are relevant to creating an efficient dashboard and a good dashboard in general, we will first explain what should be prepared before starting the building process in SAP Analytics Cloud, then we will detail the different steps of the creation process, and finally we will talk about what to consider when and after releasing the dashboard to users.

10.4.1 Building the Dashboard Foundation

Before starting to build individual charts, we start with structuring the dashboard, enabling some basic settings, and creating the dashboard header and navigation.

Creating an Analytics Application in SAP Analytics Cloud

The first question Julia asks herself is if she should create multiple analytics applications to split up content, or if one is enough. As the dashboard isn't intended to contain too many charts, she decides it will be sufficient to use a single analytics application file. In addition, it is likely that Alex will frequently navigate between different tabs when using the dashboard, so having the pages as separate files would likely be less efficient performance-wise. She believes the benefits outweigh the downsides, even if this means a slightly longer initial loading time.

To create an analytics application, Julia takes the following steps:

1. Access the Analytics Application section in SAP Analytics Cloud using the icon in the collapsed side navigation bar or by selecting **Analytics Application** in the expanded side navigation bar.
2. Once the scene in Figure 10.8 is visible, start creating a new analytics application by selecting **Application** in the **Create New** section.
3. Select **Classic Design Experience** and then click **OK**.

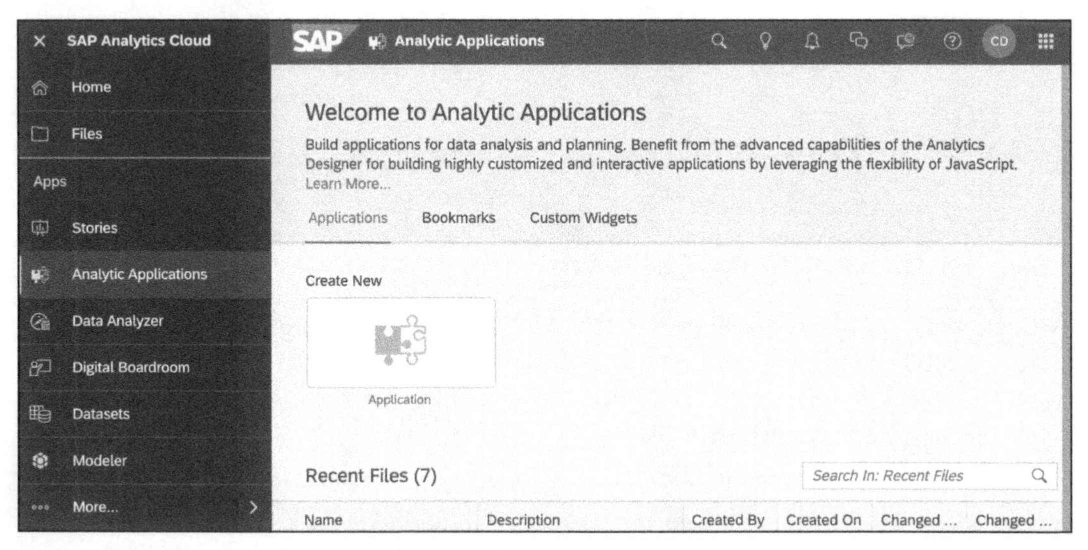

Figure 10.8 Creating an Analytics Application

We opted not to select the **Optimized Design Experience**, as it redirects to the story designer. Additionally, although this mode improves the experience for dashboard creators and adds some new functionalities, it is still in development and thus currently also removes some features.

Once the analytics application file is created and while no widget is selected, click on **Designer** (on the top right) to open the **Styling** panel. Here, set the **Background Color**, which is the first setting, to a pale gray: hex F3F5F7.

To make sure no progress is lost and the folder in which the file should be located is defined, we immediately save the analytics application by:

1. Clicking the **Save** icon in the top navigation bar and selecting **Save**.
2. Entering a fitting name, navigating to the intended save location, and clicking **OK**.

We regularly save the analytics application to make sure we are not losing any progress, as autosave is not available in SAP Analytics Cloud.

Enabling the Load Invisible Widgets in Background Setting

As it almost always makes sense to enable the load invisible widgets in background setting, enabling the setting becomes a sensible first step to do when starting with a new analytics application. By activating **Load invisible widgets in background**, we can reduce the perceived loading time by making the startup screen load faster, as only visible widgets are initialized at first and only when this is done are the invisible widgets initialized. This means the user will see and be able to interact with an already loaded application, while the rest of the widgets are being loaded in the background. This setting can be turned on as follows:

1. In the toolbar under **File** select **Edit Analytics Application**.
2. Select **Analytics Application Settings**.
3. Within the now open dialog window (displayed in Figure 10.9) select **Load invisible widgets in the background**, and then click **OK**.

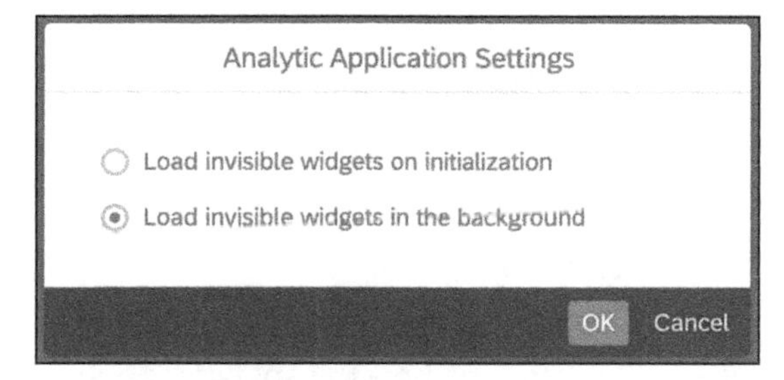

Figure 10.9 Load Invisible Widgets in Background Setting

Golden Rule #8 – Lazy Loading

Julia made a choice to improve the performance of the dashboard that correspond to golden rule #8:

- *Load invisible widgets in the background* – She made sure invisible widgets are being loaded in the background by enabling the **Load invisible widgets in background** setting. Only the widgets of the first page will be loaded on application startup, with the loading of the remaining invisible widgets being delayed.

Enabling Mobile Support

As the dashboard is intended to be used also on smaller devices such as mobile phones, Julia enables the mobile support setting, which can be seen in Figure 10.10. She goes to **Edit Analytics Application** in the toolbar under **File**, selects **Analytics Application Details**, and activates the switch next to **Enable mobile support**.

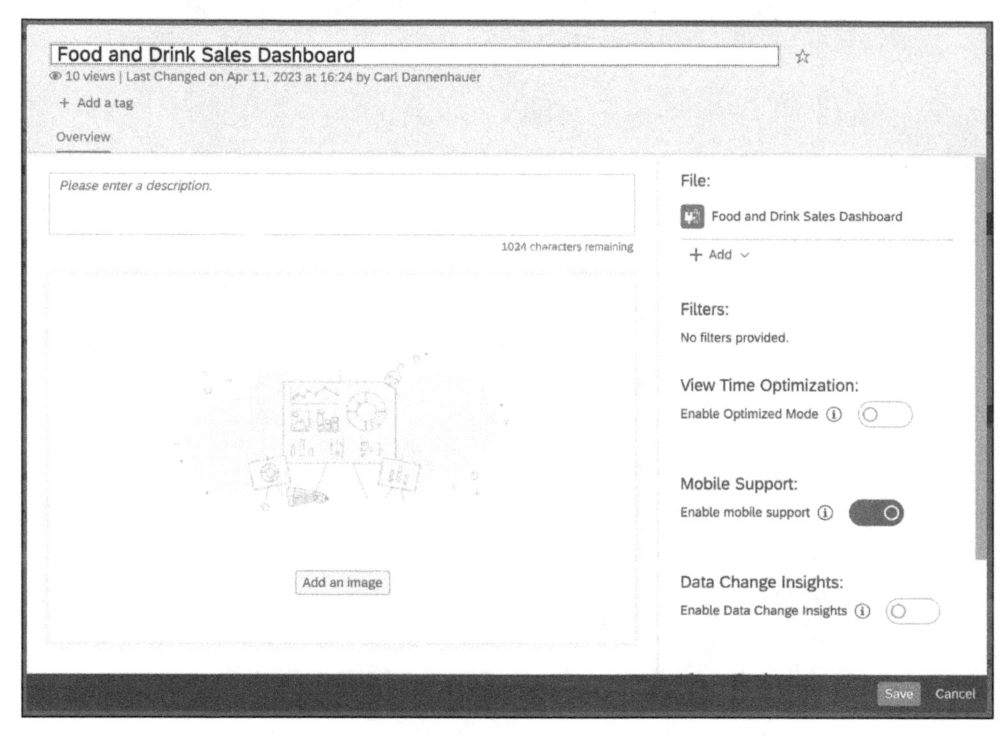

Figure 10.10 Enabling the Mobile Support Setting

Create a Dashboard Structure Adaptable to Several Devices

We start creating the dashboard by adding the main panels and flow layout panels. This is a sensible first step, as we can start testing and improving how the analytics application will behave on different devices, without having the burden of many data-related and data-unrelated widgets slowing us down.

We start by creating a flow layout panel for the header:

1. Add the header flow layout panel by going to **Insert**, **Add** [+ ∨], **Flow Layout Panel**.
2. Set the **Background Color** in the **Styling** panel to white and set the **Border** to **Bottom Border**, with a **Line Width** of four and a blue border **Color**: hex 377bab.
3. Set the **Width** to 100% and **Height** to 160px, while **Left (X)** and **Top (Y)** should remain at 0 px.

Then we create one flow layout panel with included panels and flow layout panels for each content page, so later only charts must be added into the respective panels. First, we create the overview page structure, the widget outline of which is shown in Figure 10.11 and the finished structure of which is visible in Figure 10.12.

We'll only go over creating the widgets visible in the widget outline of the overview page show in Figure 10.11 step by step. This doesn't mean the remaining panels don't have to be filled in, but covering all of it in detail here would bring little benefit:

1. Add a flow layout panel by going to **Insert**, **Add** , **Flow Layout Panel**. We named it *Overview_Tab*.
2. For the *Overview_Tab* panel, remove the **Background Color** in the **Styling** panel, set the **Width** and **Height** to auto, **Left (X)** and **Right** to 16 px, **Top (Y)** to 176 px to be below the header flow layout panel, and **Bottom** to 0 px.
3. Add two more flow layout panels to the *Overview_Tab* panel by going to **Insert**, **Add** , **Flow Layout Panel**. We named them *First_Row* and *Second _Row*.
4. For both, remove the **Background Color** in the **Styling** panel, set the **Width** to 100%, and set the **Height** for *First_Row* to 600 px and for *Second_Row* to 400 px.
5. Add three panels to the *First_Row* panel by going to **Insert**, **Add** , **Panel**. We named them *First_Tile, Second_Tile*, and *Third_Tile*.
6. For all, remove the **Background Color** in the **Styling** panel. For all three, set the **Width** to 33% and the **Height** to 100%.
7. Add another panel to the *Second_ Tile* panel by going to **Insert**, **Add** , **Panel**. We named it *Second_Tile_inner*.
8. For the *Second_Tile_inner* panel, set the **Background Color** in the **Styling** panel to white, set the **Border** to **All Borders**, set the **Corner Radius** to 20 px, remove the border **Color**, set the **Width** and **Height** to Auto, and set **Left (X)**, **Right**, **Top (Y)** and **Bottom** to 8 px.

Note that Julia has set up the panel sizes to be dynamic to the screen size. She is not expecting Alex to be using the dashboard on a large monitor where having the tiles in a fixed size would be useful for readability.

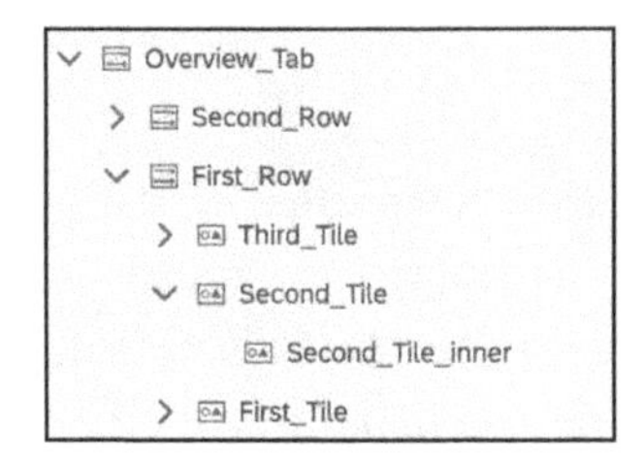

Figure 10.11 Widget Outline, Showing the Panel Structure

We can see what the dashboard now looks like in Figure 10.12, with the panel structure in place but no content filled in yet. To create the structure for the second by **Food/ Drink** page, we can now duplicate the first page and adapt the sizes of individual panels as well as remove or add panels to fit to how we want this page to look.

In Chapter 4, Section 4.4, we said that having widgets in fixed sections that are then moved around as a single unit is optimal. Since we are planning to include only a single widget per tile, that being the chart, we can ignore this tip here and not lose significant performance but gain a better design.

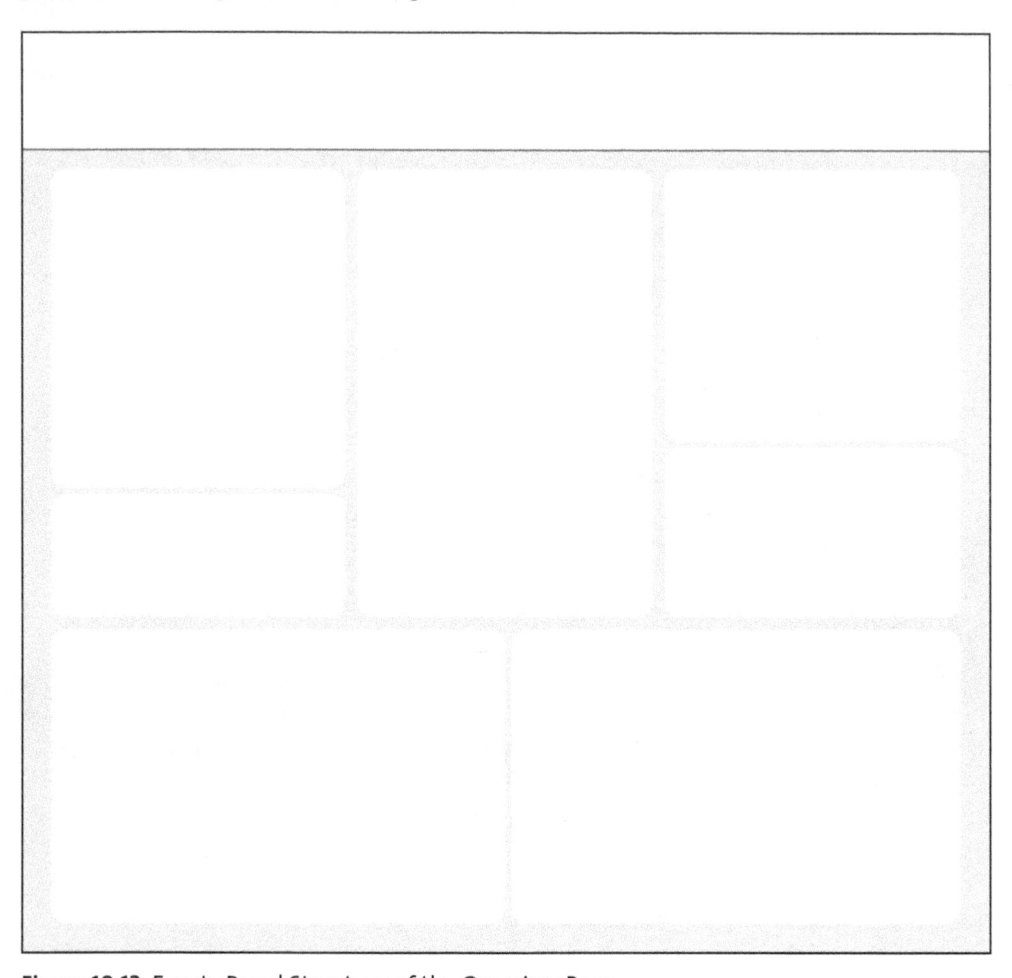

Figure 10.12 Empty Panel Structure of the Overview Page

Next, we can start adding break points into the flow layout panels. They determine the screen width at which widgets within the flow layout panel should be hidden, resized to a percentage width, or resized to a pixel height. Julia leverages this instead of using scripting, as it is more efficient. Figure 10.13 shows a break point that can be set up by going to the **Builder** panel when any flow layout panel is selected and clicking **Add Breakpoint**.

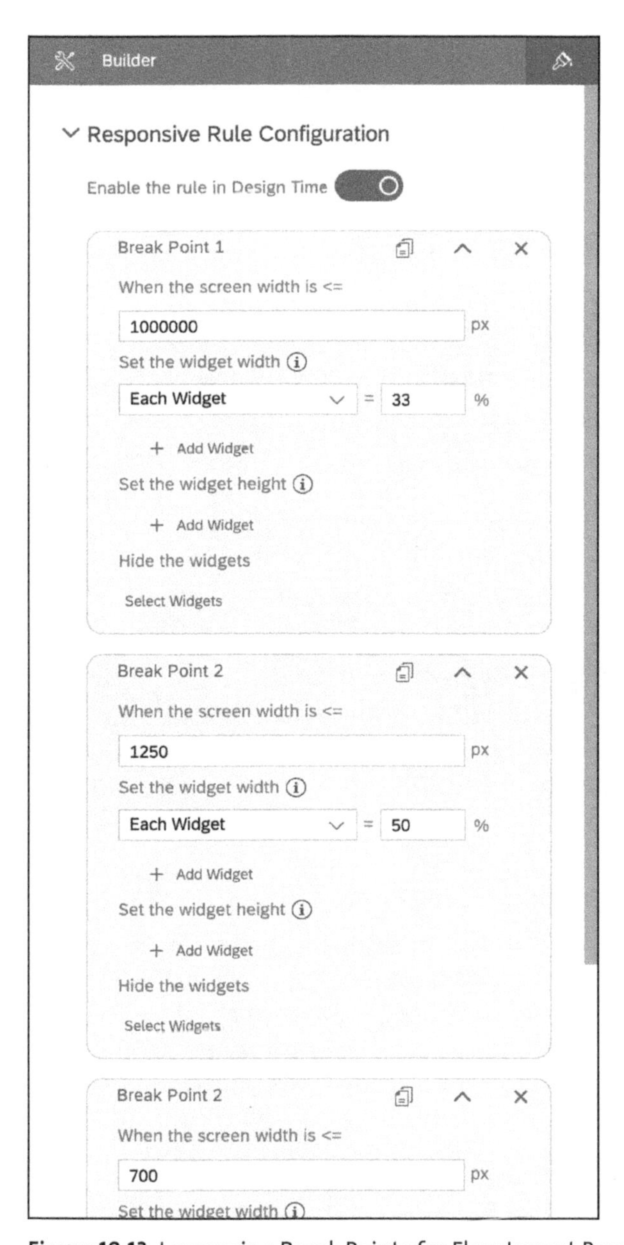

Figure 10.13 Leveraging Break Points for Flow Layout Panels

Again using the flow layout panels shown in Figure 10.13, we can go over where to add break points step by step without taking up too much space by going over every widget. For the *First_Row* panel, as the screen gets too small to comfortably fit all charts at a width of around 1250 px and again at around 700 px, we need three break points:

1. At under 100,000 px, the width of **Each Widget** should be set to 33%. This breakpoint is not strictly necessary as we have already set each tile to a width of 33%. Note that

if the tiles have a fixed px width meant for large screens, as previously mentioned, this breakpoint should be removed.

2. At under 1250 px, the width of **Each Widget** should be set to 50%.
3. At under 700 px, the width of **Each Widget** should be set to 100%

For the *Overview_Tab* panel, we will be using the same breakpoints to make sure no scrollbars appear by having the *First_Tile, Second_Tile*, and *Third_Tile* widgets under each other instead of next to each other:

1. At under 100,000 px, the height of **First_Row** should be set to 600 px. This breakpoint is not strictly necessary, as we have already set each tile to a height of 600 px.
2. At under 1250 px, the height of **First_Row** should be set to 1200 px.
3. At under 700px, the height of **First_Row** should be set to 1800 px.

Golden Rule #7 – Functional Complexity

Julia made choices to improve the performance of the dashboard that correspond to golden rule #7:

- *Avoid resizing widgets* – She avoided resizing widgets via script.
- *Don't overcomplicate things* – She avoids adding additional functionalities that are not strictly necessary, such as a more dynamic responsive design with changing graphics more suitable to different devices or users.

Creating the Dashboard Header, Including Title and Filters

After having created the content structure using panels and flow layout panels, the first content is added to the dashboard in the form of the header. This includes the title, subtitle, custom navigation, and dashboard filters. When creating the header, Julia needs to keep in mind that the dashboard header should look good on the different devices Alex uses. Figure 10.14 shows what the header looks like when opened on a mobile phone.

Figure 10.14 Dashboard Header Opened on a Mobile Device

We first create a panel that will contain the title and navigation button:

1. Add the header flow layout panel by going to **Insert**, **Add**, **Panel**.
2. We remove the **Background Color** in the **Styling** panel and set the **Width** to 100% and **Height** to 92 px, so there will be enough space to contain the title and navigation button even on smaller screens.

To create the navigation button, we follow these steps:

1. Into the created panel we add the navigation button by going to **Insert**, **Add**, **Button**.
2. Select **Lite Button** as the **Type** under **Button Style**. We change the displayed text to a burger menu text icon and adapt the **Font**. We select a custom **Font** that will allow the icon to show, a **Size** of 32, and a black **Color**: hex 000000.
3. Set the **Width** and **Height** to 48px, **Left (X)** and **Top (Y)** to 8 px.

Julia chose to avoid including company branding such as a logo to avoid additional non-functional widgets. To still personalize the viewing experience, the title should include the name of the person viewing the dashboard. To achieve this, the user's name can dynamically be included in the title text through scripting or by using dynamic text. While scripting allows more customization, such as first name only, Julia chooses to use dynamic text as it avoids having to execute a script in the `onInitialization` event:

1. Into the created panel, we add a text widget by going to **Insert**, **Add**, **Text**.
2. Add the text the title should have to the widget. We start by adding the dynamic by clicking the **More Actions** meatball menu next to the widget, then **Add**, then **Dynamic Text**, and then select **Current User**. With the current user's name dynamically displayed, we can add the rest of the title text around it: "Welcome <username> to the Food and Drink Sales Dashboard".
3. Also add the subtitle into the next line, consisting of this month's date, January 2023.
4. Ensure that the font styling is correct. We select the 72 web **Font**, a **Size** of 24 for the title and 14 for the subtitle, the bold **Style** for the title, and a dark gray **Color**: hex 4b4850.

Then we create a flow layout panel that will contain the filters:

1. Add a flow layout panel widget by going to **Insert**, **Add**, **Flow Layout Panel** and then resizing it to fit 100% of the width of the surrounding panel and 32 px high.
2. We remove the **Background Color** in the **Styling** panel and set the **Width** to 100% and **Height** to 64 px, so there will be enough space to contain the filters even on smaller screens.
3. Set the **Widget Alignment** to **Center**.

And finally, we will add the filters into the just-created flow layout panel:

1. Add a filter by going to **Insert**, **Add** [+ ⌄], **Input Control**.
2. As this is the first data-related widget of the analytics application, a popup will open where we select the model created in Section 10.2.
3. Set the filters dimension by clicking on the input control widget, **Dimensions**, and selecting the one that is needed. Then in the popup, select **All Members** so all members of the dimension are included in the filter for users to use.
4. Set the **Width** to 120 px and the **Height** to 32 px.
5. Repeat the process of adding an input control, so each filter is added. We repeat it four times.

Setup the Dashboard Navigation

With the rest of the header complete, we now focus on setting up the dashboard's navigation. We have already created a button that will open the navigation menu, but before we can write the script to link them, we need to create the navigation menu itself (Figure 10.15 shows what this will look like):

1. Add the navigation menu panel by going to **Insert**, **Add** [+ ⌄], **Panel**.
2. Disable **Show this item at view time** in the **Styling** panel.
3. Set the **Background Color** in the **Styling** panel to white and set the **Border** to **All Borders**, with a **Line Width** of 2, a **Corner Radius** of 10 px, and a light gray border **Color**: hex ededed.
4. Set the **Width** to 200 px, **Height** to 120 px, **Left (X)** to 8 px, and **Top (Y)** to 56 px.
5. Add a button by going to **Insert**, **Add** [+ ⌄], **Button**.
6. Select **Lite Button** as the **Type** under **Button Style**, change the displayed text to *Overview*, and adapt the **Font**. We select the 72 web **Font**, a **Size** of 18, the bold **Style**, and a black **Color** – hex: 000000.
7. Set the **Width** to auto, **Left (X)** and **Right** to 8 px, **Top (Y)** to 16 px, and **Height** to 32 px.

Figure 10.15 Extended Navigation Menu Opened on a Mobile Device

Then add the correct event script by selecting **Edit Scripts** [fx] when hovering over the button in the **Outline** and then choosing **onClick**. The script will set the navigation menu and unwanted content panels invisible, while setting the panel to be opened visible:

```
Navigation_Menu.setVisible(false);
Content_ByFoodDrink.setVisible(false);
Content_Overview.setVisible(true);
```

We now duplicate the created button, while changing the displayed text to "by Food/ Drink," positioning it below the first button and changing the script to set correct panels visible and invisible.

The following script is now added to the **onClick** event of the button, which will open the navigation menu:

```
if (Navigation_Menu.isVisible() === false){
    Navigation_Menu.setVisible(true);
} else {
    Navigation_Menu.setVisible(false);
}
```


Golden Rule #4 – Scripting

Julia made choices to improve the performance of the dashboard that correspond to golden rule #4:

- *Use scripting API calls in the most efficient manner* – She introduced scripting related to navigating the dashboard in an efficient manner. By limiting the number of widgets that are interacted with via the script, more widgets are loaded in the background.
- *Avoid installing an onInitialization script* – She didn't include an `onInitialization` event script, thus reducing the number of widgets that must be loaded or reloaded on application startup due to being interacted with via the script.
- *Use built-in functionalities instead of complicated scripting* – She used more efficient built-in functionalities instead of introducing scripting, which would increase the loading time. This includes creating break points for flow layout panels to setup a responsive design and using dynamic text instead of scripting to include the dashboard viewer's name.

10.4.2 Building the Dashboard Page 1 (Overview Page)

This page will allow Alex to get an overview of the selected metrics.

To add the first bar chart of the dashboard to the first tile to show the sales by theater location, Julia takes the following steps:

1. Add a chart by selecting **Chart** in the **Assets** panel under **Widgets** while being in the correct panel.

2. Set the **Width** and the **Height** to 100%.
3. In the **Builder** panel, under **Measures** click **+ Add Measure**.
4. We want to show the sales, so select the **Sales** measure.
5. Change the measures color under **Color** to a dark blue – hex: 354a5f.
6. In the **Builder** panel, under **Dimensions** click **+ Add Dimension**.
7. We want to show sales by location, so add the **Theater Location** dimension.
8. We don't need the legend. Similarly, we don't need any chart details. So, we go to the meatball menu of the chart, select **Show/Hide**, and make sure **Legend** is not selected. For **Chart Details**, make sure nothing is selected here. Also make sure **Chart Subtitle** is selected.
9. We do not want numbers reported with a decimal place. So, in the **Styling** panel in the **Number Format** section, set **Decimal Places** to 0.
10. To sort the chart bars, click the Action Menu button, select **Sort • Sales • Highest to Lowest**.
11. We want to change the title and subtitle of the chart slightly, so simply edit them in place. The title should now be "Total Sales by Theater" and the subtitle should now be "in USD." This is more efficient than creating a separate text widget to include this information.

With data for only two locations currently available and the chart being quite tall, the bars will be very wide. To get around this, we can either decrease the height of the chart to, for example, 160 px or set a fixed bar width by adding chart scaling as follows:

1. Go to **Chart Scaling** under **Tools** in the toolbar and click **Add Scaling**.
2. Select the appropriate measure(s) from the correct model.
3. Then click **Edit Scaling • Fix Bar Width** on the now-created chart scaling and insert the desired pixel amount.

Note that, from a design perspective and to be IBCS compliant, having chart scaling enabled is recommended so as not to give the dashboard viewer any false impressions. Add chart scaling to make sure that there is a coherent scaling of the measure(s) across the dashboard, so that, for example, two bar charts showing the same numbers don't display the bars with a different length simply because there is more space available for one of the charts.

Julia now adds another bar chart to the second tile to show the sales by sales type. This chart is very similar to the previous chart. You can either follow similar steps, or you can copy the chart and modify the account that is used to show the cost. By copying the chart, the tile styling will already be set.

To copy and modify the chart, we do the following steps:

1. Select the previous chart and click the **Action Menu** button.
2. Select **Copy • Duplicate**.

   SAP Analytics Cloud will create a copy of the chart. You may need to move it where you would like it. We moved it into the second tile.
3. Set the **Width** and the **Height** to 100%.
4. Change the **Dimension** to **Sales Type lvl3** and, when hovering over the dimension, select the hierarchy icon and set the drill level to **Level 2**.
5. To sort the chart bars, click the **Action Menu** button, select **Sort • Sales • Highest to Lowest**.
6. Change the title to "Total Sales by Sales Type."

To add the next bar chart to the third tile to show sales by food, Julia follows these steps:

1. Duplicate the previous chart and move it into the third tile.
2. Set the **Width** and the **Height** to 100%.
3. Add a **Dimensions Filter** to **Sales Type lvl3** by hovering over the dimension, selecting the filter icon , and selecting only food items.
4. Change the title to "Total Sales by Food."

To add a bar chart to the fourth tile to show sales by drinks, she follows these steps:

1. Duplicate the previous chart and move it into the fourth tile.
2. Set the **Width** and the **Height** to 100%.
3. Change the **Filters** to select only drink items.
4. Change the title to "Total Sales by Drink."

To add the first line chart to the fifth tile to show sales by weather, Julia follows these steps:

1. Duplicate the previous chart and move it to the fifth tile.
2. In the **Styling** panel, set the **Width** and the **Height** to 100%.
3. Change the **Dimension** to Weather.
4. Change the measures color under **Color** to a dark blue: hex 354a5f.
5. To sort the chart bars, click the Action Menu button, select **Sort • Sales • Highest to Lowest**.
6. Change the title to "Total Sales by Weather."

To add another line chart to the sixth tile to show sales over time, Julia follows these steps:

1. Duplicate a chart from tiles one to four and move it to the sixth tile.
2. In the **Styling** panel, set the **Width** and the **Height** to 100%.
3. Change the chart type in the **Builder** panel by selecting **Line** under **Chart Structure, Trend**.
4. Change the **Dimension** to Date. We also change the dimension hierarchy under the hierarchy icon by going to **Set Hierarchy** and selecting **Year**, **Week**, and **Day** to better show the currently only limited data available.
5. Change the title to "Total Sales over Time."

To add a scatter plot chart to the seventh tile to show daily sales by temperature, she follows these steps:

1. Duplicate a chart from tiles one to four and move it to the sixth tile.
2. In the **Styling** panel, set the **Width** and the **Height** to 100%.
3. Change the chart type in the **Builder** panel by selecting **Scatterplot** under **Chart Structure, Correlation**.
4. Change the **Y-Axis** measure to **Average Temperature (°C)**.
5. Change the **Dimension** to Date and select **Level 5** as drill level to show each day as an individual dot.
6. Change the **Color**, so click on the color bar and select **Create New Palette**. Make sure 1 is selected under **Swatches** and then change the colors to a dark blue: hex 354a5f.
7. Change the title to "Daily Total Sales by Temperature."

10.4.3 Building the Dashboard Page 2 (by Food/Drink Page)

After having finished the overview page, Julia can now start working on the second "by Food/Drink" page, visible in Figure 1.2.

She first adds a heat map chart to the first tile of the second page to show the profit margin by product and portion size:

1. Add a chart by selecting **Chart** in the **Assets** panel under **Widgets** while being in the correct panel.
2. Select the chart and change the chart type in the **Builder** panel by selecting **Heat Map** under **Chart Structure, Distribution**.
3. In the **Styling** panel, set the **Width** and the **Height** to 100%.
4. In the **Builder** panel, under **Color** click **+ Add Measure**.
5. We want to show the profit margin, so select the **Gross Margin** measure.
6. We want to change the assigned colors, so click on the color bar and select **Create New Palette**. Then change the colors to a dark blue: hex 354a5f and lighter blue gray: hex 8396ab.

7. In the **Builder** panel, under **Dimensions**, under **X-Axis** and **Y-Axis** click **+ Add Dimension.**
8. We want to show profit margin by product and portion size, so add the **Product Size** dimension to the **Y-Axis** and the **Sales Type lvl3** dimension to the **X-Axis**.
9. When hovering over the **Sales Type lvl3** dimension, select the hierarchy icon and set the drill level to **Level 4** to show individual products.
10. We don't need the legend. Similarly, we don't need any chart details. So, we go to the meatball menu of the chart, select **Show/Hide**, and make sure **Legend** is not selected. For **Chart Details**, make sure nothing is selected here. Also make sure **Chart Subtitle** is selected.
11. We do not want numbers reported with a decimal place. So, in the **Styling** panel in the **Number Format** section, set **Decimal Places** to 0.
12. We change the title and subtitle of the chart slightly, so simply edit them in place. The title should now be "Profit Margin by Product and Portion Size" and the subtitle should now be "in USD."

To add a bar chart to the second tile to show gross margin by portion size, Julia follows these steps:

1. Duplicate one of the previous bar charts from page one and move it to the second tile.
2. In the **Styling** panel, set the **Width** and the **Height** to 100%.
3. Change the **Measure** to **Gross Margin.**
4. Change the measures color under **Color** to a dark blue: hex 354a5f.
5. Change the **Dimension** to **Portion Size.**
6. To sort the chart bars, click the **Action Menu** button, select **Sort • Gross Margin • Highest to Lowest.**
7. Change the title to "Gross Margin by Portion Size."

To add a bar chart to the third tile to show gross margin by food and drink type, Julia follows these steps:

1. Duplicate the previous bar chart and move it to the third tile.
2. In the **Styling** panel, set the **Width** and the **Height** to 100%.
3. Change the **Dimension** to **Sales Type lvl3** and when hovering over the dimension, select the hierarchy icon and set the drill level to **Level 2.**
4. Add a **Dimensions Filter** to **Sales Type lvl3** by hovering over the dimension, selecting the filter icon and making sure merchandise and tickets are not included in the chart.

5. To sort the chart bars, click the **Action Menu** button, select **Sort • Gross Margin • Highest to Lowest**.
6. Change the title to "Gross Margin by Food and Drink Type."

To add a line chart to the fourth tile to show gross margin over time, Julia follows these steps:

1. Duplicate the previous chart and move it to the fourth tile.
2. In the **Styling** panel, set the **Width** and the **Height** to 100%.
3. Change the chart type in the **Builder** panel by selecting **Line** under **Chart Structure, Trend**.
4. Change the **Dimension** to **Date**. We also change the dimension hierarchy under the hierarchy icon, by going to **Set Hierarchy** and selecting **Year, Week, Day**, to better show the currently only limited data available. Also set the drill level to **Level 3**.
5. Change the title to "Gross Margin over Time."

To add a scatter plot chart to the fifth tile to show daily gross margin by temperature, Julia follows these steps:

1. Duplicate the previous chart and move it to the fifth tile.
2. In the **Styling** panel, set the **Width** and the **Height** to 100%.
3. Change the chart type in the **Builder** panel by selecting **Scatterplot** under **Chart Structure, Correlation**.
4. Change the **Y-Axis** measure to **Average Temperature (°C)**.
5. Change the **Dimension** to Date and select **Level 5** as drill level to show each day as an individual dot.
6. Change the **Color** to the previously for page one created color palette, which uses a dark blue color: hex 354a5f.
7. Change the title to "Daily Gross Margin by Temperature."

Golden Rule #5 – Information Architecture

Julia made choices to improve the performance of the dashboard that correspond to golden rule #5:

- *Avoid fancy charts or heavy images* – During the initial design concept, she decided not to use their photo banner as branding.
- *Increase information density* – She also decided during the initial design concept to limit the number of total charts and instead increase the information density per chart, also by making it possible for the user to leverage filter widgets connected to all charts.

- *Reduce the number of charts per page* – She spread the charts across two pages. This speeds the loading time of each page.
- *Use story and page filters instead of widget filters* – She used page filters in the title header area that apply to all the charts in the area below.

To compare performance improvements afforded by applying the golden rules, we created a separate dashboard that did not apply the golden rules. That is, the dashboard doesn't split up content into two pages, doesn't use lazy loading, uses an inefficient design to fit to all devices, doesn't follow scripting best practices, doesn't reduce the number of widgets to a minimum by, for example, leveraging filters and increasing information density per chart, generally doesn't simplify enough, and more. Table 10.1 shows that, by applying the golden rules, we have significant performance improvements.

Setting	Time to load
Dashboard applying golden rules	10.6 seconds
Dashboard without applying golden rules	16.3 seconds

Table 10.1 Time It Took Us to Load the Dashboard that Applied Golden Rules versus the Dashboard That Did Not Apply Golden Rules

10.5 Summary

This concludes Julia's task of creating Alex's dashboard. We followed her through the dashboard design process, including defining what features the dashboard should support, setting up an acquired data model, building the dashboard structure, and filling the dashboard with charts. Every step taken by Julia was considered from a performance perspective to ensure an efficient dashboard. The effectiveness of this approach was confirmed by comparing this well-designed dashboard to a similar poorly made dashboard.

While Julia took many steps to ensure a good performance, she specifically followed and focused on these golden rules:

- Golden rule #4 – Scripting: Write your own code in an efficient manner.
- Golden rule #5 – Information architecture: Reduce the number of charts, pages, and images.
- Golden rule #7 – Functional complexity: Keep the dashboard as simple as possible.
- Golden rule #8 – Lazy loading: Load information only when needed.

Appendix A
Further Reading

This appendix contains additional resources to help you expand upon the knowledge you gained throughout the book.

A.1 Chapter 1: Introduction

Few, Stephen. *Information Dashboard Design. Displaying Data for At-a-glance Monitoring*. Analytics Press, 2013.

Henoekl, Clemens. *Influence of Usability and User Experience on User Performance*. University of Nebraska at Omaha, 2015.

Hogan, Lara Callender. *Designing for Performance*. O'Reilly Media, 2014.

Sidiq, Abassin. *SAP Analytics Cloud*. SAP PRESS, 2022.

A.2 Chapter 2: Measuring, Testing, and Monitoring Performance

Fitzpatrick, Harry. *Master Functional Programming Techniques With This Comprehensive Guide For Writing Cleaner, Safer, And Performant JavaScript Code*. Independently published, 2022.

Gladen, Werner. *Performance Measurement*. Springer, 2005.

Killelea, Patrick. *Web Performance Tuning*. O'Reilly Media, 2002.

Shivakumar, Shailesh Kumar. *Modern Web Performance Optimization*. Apress, 2020.

Wagner, Jeremy, *Web Performance in Action*. Manning, 2016.

Sedgewick, Robert and Kevin Wayne, *Algorithms*. Addison Wesley, 2011.

Cormen, Thomas, and Carl Leiserson, Ronald Rives, and Clifford Stein, *Introduction to Algorithms*. MIT Press, 2022.

Schneider, Thomas, *SAP Performance Optimization Guide*. SAP PRESS, 2018.

A.3 Chapter 3: Story Builder Performance

Bertram, Erik, James Charlton, Nina Hollender, Melanie Holzapfel, Nico Licht, and Carmen Paduraru. *Designing Dashboards with SAP Analytics Cloud*. SAP PRESS, 2021.

Das, Satwik, Marius Berner, Suvir Shahani, and Ankit Harish. *SAP Analytics Cloud: Financial Planning and Analysis*. SAP PRESS, 2022.

A.4 Chapter 4: Analytics Designer Performance

Hampp, Josef, and Jan Lang. *Applikationsdesign mit SAP Analytics Cloud*. SAP PRESS, 2022.

SAP Analytics Cloud, Analytics Designer Developer Handbook, 2022, available at *http://s-prs.co/v566965*.

A.5 Chapter 5: Modeler Performance

Datar, Pravin. *Introducing the New Model in SAP Analytics Cloud*. SAP PRESS, 2021.

SAP Help Online Resources, SAP Analytics Cloud Connection Guide, available at *http://s-prs.co/v566966*.

Sidiq, Abassin. *SAP Analytics Cloud*. SAP PRESS, 2022.

A.6 Chapter 6: Optimizing Backend and Tenant Settings

Knigge, Marlene, and Ruth Heselhaus. *SAP BW/4HANA: Das umfassende Handbuch*. SAP PRESS, 2021.

Lüdtke, Thorsten, and Marina Lüdtke. *SAP BW/4HANA 2.0: The Comprehensive Guide*. SAP PRESS, 2021.

Zaleski, Konrad. *Data Modeling with SAP BW/4HANA 2.0*. Springer, 2021.

A.7 Chapter 7: Viewer Choices

Abdulezer, Loren, Susan Abdulezer, Howard Dammond, and Niklas Zennstrom. *Skype for Dummies*. For Dummies, 2011.

Lewis, Barry, and Peter Davis. *Wireless Networks for Dummies*. For Dummies, 2004.

McFedries, Paul. *G Suite for Dummies*. For Dummies, 2020.

Merkow, Mark. *Virtual Private Networks for Dummies*. For Dummies, 1999.

Simon, Phil. *Slack for Dummies*. For Dummies, 2020.

Simon, Phil. *Zoom for Dummies*. For Dummies, 2020.

Withee, Rosemarie. *Microsoft Teams for Dummies*. For Dummies, 2021.

Appendix B
The Authors

Erik Bertram started his professional career at SAP in 2016, where he worked as a JavaScript developer in the planning department of SAP Analytics Cloud. Today, he leads the Operations and User Insights team of the SAP Business Technology Platform Experience organization. Before joining SAP, Erik received his PhD in theoretical astrophysics from Heidelberg University. Since 2020, he has been a professor of digital business management at Fresenius University in Heidelberg.

Carl Dannenhauer joined SAP in 2020, where he works as a data scientist in the SAP Business Technology Platform Experience organization. He has spent his entire professional career fostering data-driven decisions by building advanced dashboards and generating actionable insights by analyzing user feedback. As an SAP Analytics Cloud expert, his focus lies in developing effective and easy-to-use dashboards. Carl has an academic background in business informatics.

Melanie Holzapfel is a certified IBCS consultant and joined SAP in 2019 as a data scientist, where she was responsible for analyzing customer feedback to increase adoption and to continuously improve the products. Since 2022, she works as Executive Assistant in the SAP Business Technology Platform Experience organization. She is an expert in building dashboards that increase efficiency and enable data-driven, confident decision-making. Before her professional career at SAP, she studied physics at the Heidelberg University and at the University of York.

Stephanie Range joined SAP in 2021, working as a data scientist in the SAP Business Technology Platform Experience organization. Before joining SAP, Stephanie worked as a data scientist in a pharma company, where she developed and automated statistical methods, configured databases, and validated business processes. Today, her expertise lies in optimizing and building SAP Analytics Cloud dashboards. She holds a master's degree in physics.

Sandra Loop joined SAP in 2016 and is a user researcher in the SAP Business Technology Platform Experience organization. She has been a user experience designer and user researcher for over 25 years. Prior to joining SAP, she was a developer and UX designer for a data visualization company, and she was also a product manager where dashboards were a major component of the product's user interface. Sandra believes that a good user experience is crucial for product success and that good performance is an important factor of the user experience.

Index

D

E

F

N

O

P